Antigone's Daughters?

Antigone's Daughters?

Gender, Genealogy,
and the Politics of Authorship
in 20th-Century
Portuguese Women's Writing

Hilary Owen
and
Cláudia Pazos Alonso

Lewisburg
Bucknell University Press

The cover illustration is a drawing for 'The Dance' by Paula Rego © Tate, London 2010.

Copyright permission for the two poems by Natália Correia that appear on page 157 was given by the Sociedade Portuguesa de Autores.

Published by Bucknell University Press
Co-published with The Rowman & Littlefield Publishing Group, Inc.
4501 Forbes Boulevard, Suite 200, Lanham, Maryland 20706
www.rlpgbooks.com

Estover Road, Plymouth PL6 7PY, United Kingdom

British Library Cataloguing in Publication Information Available

Library of Congress Cataloging-in-Publication Data

Library of Congress Cataloguing-in-Publication Data on file under LC#2010019597
ISBN: 978-1-61148-002-3 (cl. : alk. paper)
eISBN: 978-1-61148-003-0

∞ ™ The paper used in this publication meets the minimum requirements of American National Standard for Information Sciences—Permanence of Paper for Printed Library Materials, ANSI/NISO Z39.48-1992.

Printed in the United States of America

Dedication

To Till, as always
To my mum and dad, Frances and Bill

Para a Clara e a Luzia, minhas irmãs
E para os meus pais e os meus filhos também

Quanto mais funda e lúgubre a descida,
Mais alta é a ladeira que não cansa!

—Florbela Espanca, Soneto X, *Charneca em Flor*

Contents

Acknowledgments

Hilary and Cláudia: First of all we would both like to thank very warmly Lídia Jorge and Hélia Correia, who figure in this study and who have always been helpful and supportive of our work in our dialogues with them over the years. We are deeply grateful to Richard Zenith for his magnificent English translations of poetry by Florbela Espanca, Irene Lisboa, and Natália Correia in the appendices. We also express sincere thanks to Paula Rego and Tate Images for permission to reproduce the image on the front cover, and to Michael Johnson, for helpful work on the bibliography. We thank the Sociedade Portuguesa de Autores for permission to translate the poetry by Natália Correia. We would both like to thank our friends in the profession who have been a wonderful source of ongoing intellectual stimulus and help in our work: Ana Paula Ferreira, Ellen Sapega, Paulo de Medeiros, Phillip Rothwell, Anna Klobucka, Ana Luísa Amaral, Graça Abranches, Maria Irene Ramalho de Sousa Santos, Manucha Lisboa, Pat Odber de Baubeta, and Mark Sabine. Anna Klobucka, in particular, has been a huge source of inspiration, positive feedback, and encouragement in respect of this book. Last but not least, we sincerely thank each other. It has been an extraordinary journey of discovery that certainly *valeu a pena!*

Cláudia: I would like to thank my colleagues in the subfaculty of Portuguese at the University of Oxford. Tom Earle and Stephen Parkinson have generously offered me wise advice, expert knowledge, and meaningful support over many years, as has Claire Williams since her arrival in 2009. Their examples are a source of professional and personal inspiration. I am also grateful to the current *leitoras,* Ana Teresa Marques dos Santos and Catarina Fouto, for their invaluable and cheerful presence. The Modern Languages Faculty and Wadham College kindly granted me three terms of sabbatical leave between 2004 and 2008, and I am indebted to Mariana Gray de Castro and Inês Alves Mendes who took on some of my lecturing and tutorial teaching during those absences. It is also a privilege to work with so many congenial colleagues at Wadham. Robin Fiddian, Christina Howells and Carolin Duttlinger deserve particular thanks, but many others have freely given me their help in various guises over the years.

Last but not least, I wish to express my profound gratitude to both my immediate family and my "extended family" network: to the former, I dedicate this book; and to the latter, especially Filipa Varanda Pires, Lia Correia Raitt, Elizabeth Challinor and Júlio dos Santos, Susana Barreto and Jorge Menezes, as well as many old friends, including the "Auntie Natal" group, *obrigada e bem haja.*

Hilary: I would like to thank Catherine Davies who was a source of support and good advice in the early phases of this project. I also thank my Manchester colleagues in Spanish, Portuguese and Latin American Studies, Núria Triana Toribio, Chris Perriam, Lúcia Sá and Patience Schell, and in German, Margaret Littler, who have been a tremendous source of friendship, wisdom, and encouragement at different stages. I have also benefited much from the feedback and insight of Adriana Bebiano and the Estudos Feministas team at Coimbra University. I thank Manchester University and the Arts and Humanities Research Council for valuable research leaves in 2004 and 2006, and also Carmen Ramos Villar for covering my research leave so ably and well. I am very grateful to Ana Mafalda Leite and Bem Vinda, and to Ellen Sapega for generous practical support and Lisbon accommodation at crucial stages in this project. I also thank my Manchester MA and PhD students working on women's writing in Portuguese, Ana Margarida Dias Martins, Maria Tavares, and Vanessa Pereira, for their valuable debate and dialogue, and for letting me "try things out" with them in my teaching. I warmly thank my family, the Owens, particularly my mother, Frances and father Bill, who did not live to see the conclusion of this project but inspired long ago an understanding of why women's writing matters. Finally, I thank my husband Till Geiger (and Mustard and Tigerlily), whose academic, practical, intellectual, and culinary support on this book has been constant and cannot be bettered.

Antigone's Daughters?

Introduction

The search for descent is not the erecting of foundations: on the contrary, it disturbs what was previously considered immobile; it fragments what was thought unified; it shows the heterogeneity of what was imagined consistent with itself.

— Michel Foucault, *Language, Counter-Memory, Practice*

I who have always been a Lego set therefore leave you as my legacy my (our) passing and this game as an end (or not?)

— Maria Isabel Barreno, Maria Teresa Horta, and Maria Velho da Costa, *New Portuguese Letters* (our translation)

[Vos lego, pois, sempre, eu sempre Lego, o passamento meu (nosso) e este jogo (como não) final?]

— Maria Isabel Barreno, Maria Teresa Horta, and Maria Velho da Costa, *Novas Cartas Portuguesas*

"New memory [is] a powerful impulse toward political action."

— Jane Flax, "Re-Membering the Selves"

CULTURAL MEMORY, GENDER, AND GENIUS

As a result of the 1974 Carnation Revolution and its aftermath, Portugal has often been quoted as exemplifying a particularly sharp about-turn in women's official political status, with the incorporation of women's equality into the Constitution of 1976, and a notable rise in women's publishing output after 1974.[1] Nonetheless, the formal position of women writers in relation to the national cultural memory that is inscribed in literary histories, canons, and institutional critical practices has remained largely that of an isolated minority. Few major initiatives have been undertaken to reconnect women's literary works of the present with the lost or suppressed generations of women writers in the early decades of the twentieth century or before.[2] This inevitably raises significant questions regarding a gendered politics of cultural memory loss, inflecting women's writing, subjectivity, and reception as women writers in Portugal.

13

The concern of the current volume is to explore these issues, as we seek to uncover what the gendering of Portuguese literary genius and the masculinization of the national literary canon have meant for specific Portuguese women writers of the twentieth century. It should be emphasized that this is not a project devoted to archaeological retrieval of lost women's work, although we fully acknowledge the political urgency of such projects in the wider field of feminist literary studies in Portugal. Rather, we engage with women who have either achieved recognition from the outset, or who have, in the late twentieth and early twenty-first centuries, gone beyond the need for an overt politics of retrieval. This reflects our view that the process of achieving female canonicity is also, in itself, deserving of study within a feminist political framework.

Our study focuses on six well-known women writers, who have, to varying degrees, become "consagradas" or canonized: Florbela Espanca (1894–1930), Irene Lisboa (1892–1958), Agustina Bessa Luís (1923–), Natália Correia (1923–93), Hélia Correia (1949–) and Lídia Jorge (1946–), in order to ascertain how they have engaged with the gendering of Portuguese cultural memory, both in their negotiations of female writing subjectivity, and in their dialogues with male- and female-authored influence from Portugal and abroad. The feminist critical methodology that we develop for this analysis takes us back to the second citation given above, from *Novas Cartas Portuguesas,* invoking as it does the flexible nature of a child's construction "lego set." In this study, the question of legacy and continuity will be central to our considerations of how the writer's critical self-recognition and cultural memory come to be gendered constructs, and what this has meant, at different points in the twentieth century, for the works of the women writers above.[3]

UNLAYING THE FOUNDATIONS

In the three and a half decades since it was published, no Portuguese literary or critical text has yet superceded [*Novas Cartas Portuguesas*] *New Portuguese Letters*, by Maria Isabel Barreno, Maria Teresa Horta, and Maria Velho da Costa (The Three Marias), in its iconic role as the "founding text" of Portuguese second-wave feminism.[4] Despite fading into obscurity, and being out of print in Portugal for much of the 1980s and 1990s, *Novas Cartas* has proven a peculiarly resilient milestone of national cultural memory for Portuguese feminist politics and literary culture, well into the twenty-first century, with a new edition appearing in 1998. At the same time, it is difficult to imagine a more challenging and problematic "point of origin" for studying twentieth-century women's writing in Portugal. Produced collectively as an epistolary text by its three coauthors, it was famously banned for offending public morality during the closing years of the Estado Novo regime under Caetano in 1972.

Its deceptively straightforward, scholarly starting point was a revision of the seventeenth-century text *Lettres Portugaises,* a series of five letters written in French from the perspective of a Portuguese nun, Mariana Alcoforado, to her cavalier lover, the Chevalier de Chamilly, at the time of Portugal's struggle for independence against Spain.[5] At first thought to be the work of a real historical nun, and an indication of women's capacity for genius, the letters were later proven more or less conclusively to be the work of a French male writer, Gabriel-Joseph de Lavergne de Guilleragues, who had claimed that he had found and "translated" them.[6] In the hands of the Three Marias, this slippery "original" was transmuted into *Novas Cartas Portuguesas* and written in Portuguese, with key embedded passages in French. Exposing, but also going far beyond, the feminist discontents of their generation, *Novas Cartas* gained national and international notoriety by challenging the Caetano dictatorship with a critique of empire during the Colonial Wars in Africa and with a strong assertion of women's sexual embodiment and political rights.

Despite the impact of *Novas Cartas* and the Three Marias' prosecution, both nationally and internationally in 1972, actual feminist influence on Portuguese literary history, institutional pedagogy, and critical tradition post-1974, has been rather circumscribed, not only in comparison with Northern Europe and North America, but also in relation to Spain and Italy.[7] In 1993 Ana Paula Ferreira asks, "why is it that in the country of the 'Three Marias', literary criticism, with the notable exception of Isabel Allegro de Magalhães, has still had such difficulty forging a discursive space for feminist literary studies?"[8] Seven years later in 2000, in the introduction to her volume recuperating women writers of the 1930s and 1940s, little had changed as she asserts "studies of Portuguese literature have been practically impermeable to perspectives that are centered either on the category 'women writers', or on issues relating to sexual politics."[9] While the growing impact of feminism and gender studies in history, social sciences, and women's studies in Portugal has certainly been observable over the last decade, the feminist critique of Portuguese literary canons as such has remained confined to a small but important group of Portuguese scholars, many of whom were trained in Anglo-American studies and/or Comparative Literature, and to feminist academics working in Portuguese studies abroad, usually in the United States and United Kingdom.[10] The result is a notable emphasis on Anglo-American liberal gynocritical theory, and a tendency to introduce feminist critique of Portuguese texts in comparatist frames.[11] Indeed it is arguable that Portuguese women writers have, numerically at least, achieved more extensive coverage in "world" literary and cultural encyclopedias published abroad than in Portugal itself, particularly as regards diachronic representation connecting different historical periods. Examples of this would be Darlene Sadlier's Portuguese entries in Claire Buck's *Bloomsbury Guide to Women's Literature* in 1992 and the French *Dictionnaire des Femmes Créatrices,* published with Éditions des Femmes, edited by Antoinette Fouque, Mireille Calle-Gruber, and Béatrice Didier.[12] Conversely, the move to disseminate Anglo-American, and to a lesser extent, French poststructuralist, feminist theory in Portugal constitutes a very significant step undertaken by Ana Gabriela Macedo and Ana Luísa Amaral in their *Dicionário da crítica feminista,* and by the former in her collection of key Anglo-American and French feminist essays translated into Portuguese in *Género, Identidade e Desejo: Antologia Crítica do Feminismo Contemporâneo.*[13]

In relation to Portuguese literature specifically, the first really pioneering move of feminist criticism post-1974 took the form of two studies by Isabel Allegro de Magalhães, *O Tempo das Mulheres* and *O Sexo dos Textos,* both of which focus on prose fiction, in the first case by women only, in the second by women and men. The first of these explored the construction of temporality in novels by women. The second of these works argued that texts by women and men exhibit clear temporal, aesthetic, linguistic, and thematic characteristics that may be defined as "feminine writing" or "escrita feminina."[14] This line of argument, broadly derived from French *écriture féminine,* provoked an important response from Maria Irene Ramalho de Sousa Santos and Ana Luísa Amaral in a groundbreaking 1997 essay for the Coimbra Centro de Estudos Sociais workshop "On 'Escrita Feminina'" [Sobre a "Escrita Feminina"]. In this article, the two coauthors take as their starting point their decision to place their own quotation marks around the term "escrita feminina," insisting instead on the "chameleon-like pretence of the poetic mask" and working from the "Foucauldian notion of the 'subject' as a 'place' or 'position' within multiple possibilities."[15] Marking a clear poststructuralist turn away from Magalhães's largely thematic sexing of the "feminine text," this article effectively paved the way for Portuguese feminist criticism to go beyond both humanist sexual identity politics (the gynocritical sexing of the writer) and "escrita feminina" (the sexing of the text). Taking an incisive deconstructive position on metaphysical categories and essentialized identities, Sousa Santos and Amaral focus here on gender construction and performativity, drawing productively on Michel Foucault and Judith Butler. On one level this mirrors ongoing priorities, and divides, in international feminist debate, but it has also had a specific instrumental importance in Portugal. Given the extent to which popular press and media characterizations in Portugal have tended to foreclose literary feminism as nothing more than "sexing the text" as "escrita feminina," Sousa Santos and Amaral's poststructuralist refusal of essentialism, electing instead to empha-size the operations of discourse, locatedness and institutional power rela-tions, has done much to keep feminist debate open, particularly as regards the question of heterosexual normativity.[16]

This is a position that Sousa Santos develops further in her *Portuguese Studies* article in 1997, "Re-inventing Orpheus," which explores the Nietz-schean masking of the lyric subject in an "embodiment of strategies for the interrogation, if not the subversion, of poetic roles."[17] Here she analyzes closely some examples of appropriation, reversal, and revision undertaken by women poets in relation to the mythical subject/object positions canonized by men in the orphic tradition. By analyzing women's ironic debunking from within of masculine symbolization, Sousa Santos also opens up impor-tant considerations regarding the unacknowledged phantasmatic nature of the "neutral" position from which the male speaks as authoritative artist and critic.[18]

Strongly endorsing this pioneering turn away from "escrita feminina" es-sentialism, we would also draw out and emphasize two of its key implications for feminist critical politics. The first concerns the need to avoid falling into too ready a belief that women have historically enjoyed access on equal terms with men to strategies of gender masking, the fluidity of signature, and aes-thetic transgression of the sexual symbolic. Not all gender masquerades are equally liberating or universally transgressive.[19] Neither does the connection between gender transgression or "deviance" and genius work on equal terms for men and women, and it has, in any event, long been embedded in homo-sexual and homophobic histories of the construction of artistic genius, as Andrew Elfenbein has pointed out in his work on eighteenth-century genius in English literature. He details the longstanding discursive link between the "exceptional" nature of genius and the "exceptional" or socially "abnormal-ized" nature of homosexuality, showing how it plays out in various problem-atic ways for artistic men and women at different times. He argues that the traditional tendency to view exceptional, genius women as also having ab-normally masculine characteristics sends "the double message of female ge-nius: although masculine women are abnormal, only they can achieve anything valuable because merely feminine women are worthless."[20]

Our second, related point concerns the risk of disavowing misogynist his-tories of artistic creativity, arising from the conviction that material histories of the body, sexed or otherwise, are somehow dissolved or transcended under the sign of Great Art. This question as it pertains to the historical gendering of the idea of genius is at the heart of the British feminist philosopher Christine Battersby's classic work, *Gender and Genius*. She asks how women have managed to "manipulate aesthetic concepts taken from a mythology and biology that were profoundly anti-female"?[21] Battersby's historical discussion of the conceptualization of genius from the Greek and Roman classics, through eighteenth- and nineteenth-century enlightenment philosophy and Romantic literature to the modern era, demonstrates how the gendering of genius as male simultaneously relied on a misogynistic Othering of the female body. Her study shows how genius was historically grounded in the procreative energy of biological men, the *logos spermatikos* idea, a term which Battersby adopts from Carl Jung, but traces back to the Greek stoics. In demonstrating that the "vocabularies of aesthetic praise and those of sexual difference" have been profoundly intertwined in the history of western thought, Battersby shares important common ground with the feminist philosophy of Luce Irigaray.[22]

The crucial complication that Battersby identifies throughout her project concerns the male artist's appropriation of "feminine" characteristics, constructing genius as a quasidivine attribute. For Battersby, this displacement or sublimation of male procreativity effectively works as a cultural alibi masking the exclusion of the biologically female feminine body from genius. For example, eighteenth- and nineteenth-century discourses of genius "praised 'feminine' qualities in male creators . . . but claimed females could not—or should not—create", so that "a man with genius was *like a woman* . . . but was *not a woman*."[23] In this gendered hall of mirrors, the biologism and misogyny informing the *logos spermatikos* are conveniently glossed by an apparent validation of "femininity" which works, in effect, to license artistic genius only when this "femininity" is applied to men. Thus, as she goes on to point out, the gender crossover implied by the feminization of male genius could work in a positive sense for men but not the other way round, so "a woman who created was faced with a double bind: either to surrender her sexuality (becoming not *masculine*, but a surrogate *male*), or to be *feminine* and *female*, and hence to fail to count as a genius."[24]

Writing in the late 1990s, Andrew Elfenbein's work broadly concurs with Battersby's position that the cult of genius has historically blocked the path of women artists and that male genius appropriated "femininity" at the expense of real female geniuses.[25] However, working from a queer history perspective, he points to the blindspots in Battersby's binarized model of gender appropriation, leading her to elide sexuality issues, as he observes that "genius created a possible breakdown in the assumption of natural heterosexual desire."[26] In this respect Elfenbein leads the genius discussion usefully away from the potentially essentialist pitfalls of Battersby's concluding statement, that "a feminist aesthetics is one that exposes the prejudice that represents the female as lacking, seeks to show how we can escape it . . . and then goes on to trace matrilineal traditions of cultural achievement."[27]

While our current analysis underscores the imperative of exposing and resisting gender prejudice in literary history, we explore some alternatives to Battersby's injunction that this exposure must necessarily lead on to the tracing of matrilineal traditions of cultural achievement. Indeed, as we go on to show later in this introduction, matrilineal tradition in Portugal has its own historical problems and specificities, its own complex and conflicted place in the discourse of gender and radical politics expounded by second wave texts such as *Novas Cartas Portuguesas*. We therefore reorientate Battersby's political agenda of exposing the mechanisms of historical prejudice, so as to emphasize the historical construction of the embodied subject through discourse, meaning here the construction of the embodied writing subject through literary historical discourse. This move relies substantially on Michel Foucault's "Nietzsche, Genealogy and History" in which he argues that a Nietzschean genealogy of history should be "situated within the articulation of the body and history. Its task is to expose a body totally imprinted by history and the process of history's destruction of the body."[28]

Exposing the Gendered Canon—A Paragraph of One's Own?

Chatarina Edfeldt's study, *Uma história na História,* stands out in Portugal and beyond as the first comprehensive study to analyze the recurrent discursive mechanisms of literary tradition, which have caused women's exclusion from, or marginality in relation to, the male-authored national canon in Portugal.[29] Edfeldt's work is refreshingly overt in declaring its intentions to reopen the question of women writers' relationship to Portuguese literary history. She goes on to demonstrate in concrete terms the fact that women writers are still subject to gender discrimination in the Portuguese literary establishment as manifested in official, canon-building discourses. Edfeldt thus draws on social constructionism, Foucauldian discourse theory, and Laclau and Mouffe's concept of contingency to explore the workings of gender power and ideology in a corpus of Portuguese literary histories, encyclopedias, and dictionaries dating from the 1930s to the early twenty-first century. One of the most telling, and still relevant, points that she makes is the fact that canonical literary histories function as self-fulfilling prophesies of gender inequality, where the underlying textual structures that work against women's inclusion are never radically reexamined or recognized as being political in the first place.

The exclusion of women writing before the 1950s was found to be partic-

ularly extreme, but there was surprisingly little visible change in the hegemonic gendering of literary historiographical discourse even after this date,
even where "more women," in numerical terms, appeared to be included.
Edfeldt usefully identifies the following five discursive mechanisms as being
instrumental in the practice of "othering" women writers in Portuguese literary history: (1) treating women writers as a homogeneous and atemporal category apart; (2) failing to provide sociopolitical and literary contextualization
of their work; (3) not being able to connect women writers to important
taxonomical categories such as movements and generations which conventionally structure literary histories; (4) not tracing women's own literary histories and genealogies; and (5) downplaying the political content of work
dealing with gender inequality and feminist issues.[30] The alternative approaches that she proposes involve denaturalizing the supposed "imma-
nence" and "objectivity" of literary historical discourse, recognizing the
political and ideological nature of its exclusions, and combining the strategic
study of women writers on their own terms with a critique of normatively
masculine literary historiography.

The ongoing masculine predominance in the canon and literary historical
tradition of Portugal, even in the face of women's rising literary output, particularly post-1974, raises significant questions about female cultural memory loss and its impact on the sexual politics of women's authorship.
Edfeldt's study give evidence to suggest that the nontransformation of Portuguese literary historical and canon-making paradigms continues to sustain a
gendered glass ceiling that is also, to some degree, a mirror reflecting male
homosocial nationhood back to itself.[31] As Klobucka has pointed out, the
business of canon-making is historically bound up with the project of liberal
nation-building. Thus, she states, "it is precisely the concept of nationally
specific literary canon that has been given, from the early nineteenth century
onward, a central place in the articulations of nationness and a crucial function in the forging of a homogeneous consciousness."[32]

Carlos Reis' seminal work, *O Conhecimento da Literatura. Introdução aos
Estudos Literários,* describes particularly clearly how the conventional articulation of national literary history maps onto a discourse of "evolution" in
which each generation, movement, or —ismo displaces the previous one
through successive, and progressive, vanguard innovations and intergenerational struggle.[33] Reis performs the important task here of denaturalizing and
politicizing the process of literary history formation by noting the workings
of ideological discourse in the evolutionary process. At the same time, this
largely Darwinian, natural science model of evolutionary development
through struggle is, as Vítor Aguiar e Silva remarks, very much reliant on a
gendered metahistorical paradigm, the Freudian Oedipal drama of the son

battling the castrating father figure, as emblematized for literary historical studies by Harold Bloom's classic work *The Anxiety of Influence*.[34] Furthermore, this model of linear, developmental time is central to nineteenth-century conceptualizations of imperial and national space. As McClintock observes, "social evolutionism and anthropology thus gave to politics and economics a concept of natural time as *familial . . .* There is a problem here, however, for the family Tree represents evolutionary time as a *time without women*."[35] If the time of national literary canonicity is structured as a familial "time without women," what roles does this then leave for "the feminine" and for "feminine alterity" in relation to the patrilinear, evolutionary canon?

Aguiar e Silva has observed that, in the Oedipal struggle of the son seeking to dethrone and replace the father, even this apparent "discontinuity" reveals, in the negative, the workings of memory itself inside the semiotic system of textuality. This memory which the textual system has of and within itself, affords a "vertical context" as Aguiar e Silva calls it, made up of "homosystemic referents." The memory of the literary system has an important role to play, then, as the semiotic mechanism that permits the literary reading and decoding of texts.[36] But how then do women writers establish their images, ideas, and cultural codings in this "homosystemic" web of references built on the paternal evolutionary history of male "same relating to same," be it through emulation or displacement? The position that Aguiar e Silva tellingly allots to the "feminine" in this system is that of symbolizing memory itself, recalling the classical mythical disposition whereby "in Greek culture, from Hesiod on, the Muses are considered to be the daughters of Zeus and of Memory (Mnemosyne)."[37] Yet, this construction of the feminine, as has long been noted in feminist poststructuralist theory and elsewhere, has historically constrained women to serve merely as the *symbols* that enable (masculine) literature's systemic memory to plot its own vertical course.[38]

In Portuguese national historiography, we have identified two particular ways in which women function, apparently "within" the canon, but effectively only in order to symbolize the male literary community's systemic memory of itself. The first concerns an essentially static image of women, the exceptional women or "mulheres extraordinárias" who are admitted to the canon on the basis of one or two per generation.[39] Acting in a manner similar to the symbolic border guards or boundary markers of national culture, these women guarantee the unity of collective national consciousness and hegemonic cultural memory, precisely by marking its limits, as the solitary exceptions, the necessary reminders of the "others" that the system normally excludes.[40] An example of this would be Agustina Bessa Luís, at least as regards her accession to canonicity with *A Sibila* [The Sybil], still her most famous novel, more than half a century after it first appeared in 1954.

The second role to which women accede in the canon-building process allows them to be somewhat more numerous than one at a time. Here, they function not so much as boundary markers, reminding the system of its outside, but rather as milestones of the progress of evolutionary modernity, demonstrating how far the system has come, and proving that the integration of women is finally "complete" and gender inequality superseded. The workings of this process are visible in the oft-repeated mantrum of "female liberation that has finally arrived" to be found in both pre- and postrevolution literary histories of Portugal, at very different junctures over the last fifty years. The prevalence of this discourse has led to the curious phenomenon of literary historians attributing a wide range of different official "start dates" to the advent of women's literary breakthrough, in a process that Edfeldt has observed closely. By reading comparatively, but diachronically, across literary histories and encyclopedias, she reveals a constant "adiamento" or postponement of the fact of women's authorship, starting at ever later points in the twentieth century, depending on the broader ideological interests that structure the history in question at the time.[41]

Two major literary historical works produced in 2002 to mark the turn of the twenty-first century, one in Portugal and one in the United States, are particularly revealing for their treatment of the "woman question" in Portuguese literature. *100 Livros Portugueses do Século Vinte. Uma Selecção de Obras Literárias* was edited by Fernando Pinto do Amaral, published as a series of parallel bilingual volumes (Portuguese paired with English, Spanish, and French) and sponsored by the Camões Institute, specifically for the millennium.[42] Adopting the popular format of defining a "century in great books," it explores a series of separate works in relation to the year they appeared in the twentieth century (although some years are deliberately represented more than once, and some are omitted), and it provides a brief explication of the work's main qualities and significance. Explicitly distancing itself from the canonical function of a literary history, it aims at disseminating a selection of works based on a combination of "aesthetic merit and historical impact."[43] At one level, this volume promised much for women, laudably avoiding as it does the focus on exceptional individuals and homosocial literary movements that militate against female inclusion. The inclusion of *Novas Cartas Portuguesas* for 1972 is also certainly noteworthy, as is its recognition, given its long decades of oblivion in the 1980s and 1990s, as a feminist text symbolizing "the struggle for female emancipation."[44]

At the same time, the total number of women authors that this format achieves is still only nineteen out of one hundred and four, less than eighteen per cent, providing an ironic statement perhaps on the lack of historical repercussion that the Marias' much-vaunted female emancipation actually had on twentieth-century national canon-making. Furthermore, only one of the Three Marias has a book considered in its own right, Maria Velho da Costa's *Maina Mendes*. On the other hand, the classic but rather conservative reference work, the 1955 *História da Literatura Portuguesa* by António José Saraiva and Óscar Lopes, is the only nonliterary work included in the study, in a decidedly circular gesture that works to doubly ensure male canonicity by canonizing the canon-makers. Not only do men score better for literary "merit," but they are implicitly portrayed as more apt than women to reveal the national spirit of the age, that is, more apt to protagonize, rather than merely symbolize, history. Thus, the narrative of the "great men" tends even here to "leak out" from behind the cover of the "great books" genre.

The image of Portuguese national genius conceived from abroad, condensed for the "world literature" format, fares very markedly worse, judging from Harold Bloom's monumental work, *Genius. A Mosaic of One Hundred Exemplary Creative Minds.*[45] This singles out three Portuguese writers, Luís Vaz de Camões, Eça de Queiroz, and Fernando Pessoa. Bloom's definition of "genius" in terms of "the God within" is informed by longstanding classical and Romantic traditions of gendering individual genius in terms of masculine sexuality and male creative energies, as revealed in Battersby's analyses of gender and genius above.[46] In Portugal's Bloomian paternalist lineage, Camões becomes the legitimate presiding Father God, the "transcendental genius of his nation, true ancestor of Eça, Pessoa, Saramago."[47] Harking back to his seminal *Anxiety of Influence,* Bloom's vision of genius here remains resolutely genealogical, tied to the Oedipal drama of father and son.

OEDIPUS AND ANTIGONE

If Oedipus still reigns unchallenged over the patrilinear evolution of literary tradition as genealogy, a question remains as to the alternatives open to women for inscribing the fact of feminine literary creativity in terms which record women's historical connections and foster women's communal memory. In Anglo-American and Francophone Canadian liberal feminist criticism of the 1970s and 1980s, matrilinear genealogy certainly became a very common paradigm.[48] Furthermore, as various feminist critics have noted, there is ample material written by women in Portugal, in the twentieth century and earlier, that is ripe for this type of recuperation.[49] The issue is certainly not lack of material. In particular, much remains to be retrieved and republished from the Salazarist suppression of Portugal's Republican feminist past, which occurred when the New State set out to either eliminate or coopt the specific forms that women's communal cultural memory could take. Particularly instrumental in preventing the forging of female literary community on its own terms were acts such as the forced closure of the 1947 women's book exhibition and the disbanding of the Republican feminist organization, Conselho Nacional das Mulheres Portuguesas, which had organized the exhibition, headed by Maria Lamas.[50] But it is also worth asking, in this context, how far women's political dissidence in writing, particularly in the 1960s and 1970s, came to assume the form of cultural counter-memory emphasizing antifoundationalism and working against genealogical models, by way precisely of opposing the essentialist forms of maternal womanhood handed down by both Republican and New State patriotism.[51] How far did the need for a clear epistemic break with the matrilinear genealogy of the Republican Mothers feed into the ways that women writers of the New State period and after viewed women's cultural identity? How far did the material suppression of women's Republican political culture combine with women's own anxiety of influence about a gender-conservative matriarchal past? At the very least, we wish to acknowledge that the possibilities afforded by matrilinear genealogy in the struggle against paternal canons are often, in Portugal, greeted with ambivalence and resistance.

In order to discuss the theoretical implications of pitting genealogy against countergenealogy, in the fight against the Oedipal paternal canon, we turn now to the classic rebel figure of Oedipus's daughter/sister, Antigone, who permits a radically flexible reconfiguring of the concepts of family, genealogy, historical time, and mother/daughter relations.[52] With this in mind, we explore the possibilities offered by different feminist and queer theory reworkings of Antigone, asking what they enable us to do, for the women's cultural memory question, both inside and outside of the Oedipal metahistorical narrative of literary genealogy. In her book *The Antigone Complex. Ethics and the Invention of Feminine Desire,* Cecilia Sjöholm follows Judith Butler in picking up the rhetorical question first posed by George Steiner, "what would happen if psychoanalysis were to have taken Antigone rather than Oedipus as its point of departure?"[53] A highly contested and ambivalent figure for philosophy, psychoanalytical theory, and gender studies, Antigone serves as a particularly productive index for reading conflicting feminist views on the interrelationship of gender and genealogy. For Lacan, as Isabel Capeloa Gil observes in her readings of Hélia Correia's reworking of Sophocles, Antigone is the quintessentially silenced and "dead woman" who enables the production of western culture through the exclusion of Woman as its "Other."[54] Judith Butler has noted that Antigone's name, according to one interpretation of its etymology, means "anti/gone" or "anti-generation."[55] Yet Luce Irigaray, in most of her work on Antigone, rather demands precisely a rereading of mother/daughter relations and matrilinear connections.[56]

The name Antigone has thus served to conjure both a symbolic defense of genealogical connection through the bonds of kinship, the gods of the hearth and the household, and the discontinuity of her own physical genealogy through her choice of childless suicide. The differing critical perspectives on Antigone adopted by Luce Irigaray and Judith Butler have particularly focused on this issue of continuity versus noncontinuity of lineage, respectively enabling and foreclosing the use of matrilinear genealogy as literary historical paradigm for women. As Sjöholm points out, Irigaray has "evoked Antigone as a symbol of feminine desire, replacing Oedipus not as a symmetrical alternative but as a figure representing another lineage."[57] Seeking to create a feminine symbolic wholly outside the patriarchal order, Irigaray's writings on Antigone call for an ethics of sexual difference that would go beyond the Hegelian (masculine) dialectic of universality which necessarily excludes women from self-consciousness and reduces her difference to being merely the "other of the same." Thus Antigone is read in terms of her potential for enabling alternative spaces of feminine self-recognition, based on unlimited, rather than dialectical, differentiation, free-flowing feminine desire, and a reinstatement of historically suppressed mother-daughter relations.

As Irigaray writes, "the offence of Oedipus, of psychoanalysis, is to forget the importance of the mother-daughter relation, and of women's genealogy, especially in their relations to natural fruitfulness, but also in their necessary part in constituting a living and ethical gender identity."[58] Irigaray thus reads Antigone, among other things, in terms of the need to restore maternal relations and matrilinear tradition to women. Antigone and her brother Polynices are siblings born of the same womb to the same mother so that Antigone's defense of the brother is ultimately, for Irigaray, a sign of her loyalty to the mother that bore him.[59] As Sjöholm points out, this connects Antigone's defense of the dead brother to a maternal genealogy standing in opposition to Creon's patriarchal state, effectively allowing the tragedy to be read as the drama of a maternal lineage whose defeat by patriarchy prevented the emergence of a true ethics of sexual difference.[60] The emphasis on the empowerment afforded by matrilinear tradition and mother/daughter self-recognition in Irigaray's Antigone, partly explains her importance for feminist philosophers such as Christine Battersby, referred to above. Battersby's chapter on Antigone in *The Phenomenal Woman* rereads the interpretations of Antigone propounded by Hegel, Lacan, and Irigaray, with a view to positing "an other kind of identity politics" that would be a "not disreputable dream."[61]

One of the most significant counterpositions to feminist identity politics, and to Irigarayan philosophy, has been that evinced by Judith Butler who also takes up the Antigone theme in her work *Antigone's Claim. Kinship between Life and Death* (2000). Here Butler responds to Hegel, Irigaray, and Lacan, in a poststructuralist reworking of Levi-Straussian structuralist laws of kinship which focuses not only on Antigone's ambivalent position in relation to patriarchal and matriarchal kinship, but also on her challengingly blurred sexuality, as she stands, "like a man" in opposition to Creon.

As Butler points out, one central concern which Antigone's story raises for feminists is the very inflexibility and absolutism of her self-sacrificial rebellion against the state. Her defense of kinship is such that she cannot affirm its rights and yet still continue to live. Her story thus exposes particularly clearly the dilemmas inherent in politicizing the domestic spheres of household and kinship when this is done in the very terms laid down by the public sphere of the state.

Luce Irigaray may have argued, as Butler puts it, that Antigone represents a "feminine defiance of statism and an example of anti-authoritarianism" yet, if family and state coauthorize each other, Antigone's act of public resistance effectively reinvests in the very forms of power which the state represents.[62] In her act of rebelling then, Antigone merely assimilates "the terms of sovereignty she refuses" and appropriates her rhetoric of agency from Creon himself.[63] Rejecting any clear-cut dichotomizing of state versus family interests as the defining edge of a Lacanian symbolic order, Butler uses Antigone's story to demonstrate that the symbolic order should not be read as an absolute cut-off but rather as the result of social gestures and practices which sediment gradually over time and are therefore open to ironic variations, "dragging" strategies, and parodic disruption. This effectively prevents the symbolic order from reaching closure. In this context Butler seeks strategies to transmit the "curse [of kinship] in aberrant form, exposing its fragility and fracture in the repetition and reinstitution of its terms . . . [a] breaking from the law, that takes place in the reinstituting of the law."[64]

Battersby's work on Antigone has criticized Butlerian strategies of operating as the "enemy within" patriarchal tradition, for privileging epistemological over ontological concerns, and thus needlessly overemphasizing the importance of Lacanian symbolic Father Law, precisely by not positing alternatives to it.[65] Focusing on Butler's acts of caricature that become parodic by revealing themselves to be caricature, Battersby's critique of Butler summarizes her position as pertaining to a "non-necessary (but nevertheless useful) irony at the edge of the 'female community'—both inside and outside 'our' sex."[66] This is born out by Butler's closing statements on Antigone's sexuality. While she does not go so far as to claim her as a gay heroine representing a sexuality that is not heterosexual, Butler does indicate Antigone's refusal of heterosexual symbolic closure for the Oedipus tragedy, and thence her potential for destabilizing normative heterosexual kinship. As Butler puts it, "she does seem to deinstitute heterosexuality by refusing to do what is necessary to stay alive for Haemon, by refusing to become a mother and a wife."[67] In this respect, Butler's work performs the valuable task of revealing the Oedipal model to be a contingent one, and the origins of social kinship to be arbitrary, as Sjöholm points out.[68] With respect to our problem of responding to the Oedipal metahistory of canons, what Butler's Antigone importantly affords us is a position from which to critique essentialized sexual identity politics based on nostalgia for lost matriarchal origins and the pursuit of utopian matrilinearity, while also undermining the absolutism of Oedipal paternal kin relations and genealogies by exposing their contingency.

PORTUGUESE LETTERS—OLD AND NEW

The contingency of kin relations and of genealogy are central issues in the Portuguese feminist theory text with which we began, *Novas Cartas Portuguesas* [*New Portuguese Letters*]. This 1972 work about the Portuguese nun Mariana Alcoforado clearly takes a different mythical inspiration from that of the Antigone drama in any classical sense. There are areas of commonality, however, between the fate of Antigone, walled up alive and choosing to die childless as a protest against the paternal state, and that of the dowerless Portuguese nun similarly walled into her convent and dying, also childless, as a statement of female surplus outside the marriage economy that sustains the state. In this context, feminist and gender debates surrounding the "Antigone complex" afford a productive point of entry to *Novas Cartas'* central structuring device, the use of the rebellious nun, to deconstruct both paternal and maternal genealogical lineage. Furthermore, it can be argued that both Antigone and Mariana derive their voice from a position outside of conventional (maternal) heterosexual closure. As the foregoing will show, *Novas Cartas,* with its multiple and evolving feminist positions, effectively restages for us many of the tensions between Irigaray's and Butler's theorizations of Antigone, as statements about the value of feminine lineage and the approaches to literary historicism that they imply.

The position of the feminine, as mother and matrix, occupies an important position in *Novas Cartas* as Mariana Alcoforado's relationship with her mother, and those of other similarly named mothers and daughters, are traced down the ages, with crucial variants, from the seventeenth century to the present. At the same time, Mariana becomes the "Mother" that each of the Three Marias never had, and vice versa. They become textual "mothers" to each other, in a psychoanalytical process akin to transference, and they correspondingly rewrite the feminine in the Portuguese national symbolic, rehabilitating figures such as the tragic Inês de Castro and the treacherous medieval Queen Dona Tareja.[69] Their apparent backward gaze to the destruction of the mother/daughter relation under patrilinear systems begs a question, then, as to the conditions under which this relationship could be reestablished as a unique source of gynocentric cultural power. On one level, this pattern corresponds in historical terms to a radical feminist, and in a related guise Engelsian, quest to trace the history of women's oppression to its source, to identify the root cause and the precise "original" moment implying, in line with Engels and with anthropological "Mother Right" theorists at the turn of the last century, the world historical defeat of ancient matriarchal rule by patriarchy.[70] In their "turning of love back in the direction of history and politics" [reviragem do amor em direcção à história e à política] the Marias set out on a fundamental journey to "root out what terrifies us" (92) [desentulhamos o que de assustador temos para nós (93)]. Hence, one of the Marias declares in Third Letter IV, "we must trace our way back along the river-course of domination, unravel its historical circumstances and analyse them in order to destroy its roots" (88) [temos de remontar o curso da dominação, desmontar suas circunstâncias históricas, para destruir suas raízes (90)]. Yet, the quest for a historical origin becomes increasingly rhetorical in the later letters, as one of them remarks, "the destiny of the man and the woman irremediably branched off in two opposite directions—but when, O when, did this happen?" (219) [foram bifurcados, irremediavelmente, o destino do homem e da mulher, mas quando, mas quando? (219)].

In "Second Final Letter," close to the end of the book, one Maria concedes, "we failed to follow the trail to the end, to trace the total pattern of the characters and its roots, whether rotten or not, and its tentacles, its waves that fan out in every direction, into others, into things, into the past, into the future" (301) [lhe faltou seguirmos o traço até ao fim, o desenho todo das personagens, e as suas raízes, podres ou não e os seus tentáculos, as suas ondas que se espalham a toda a volta, nos outros, nas coisas, no passado, no futuro (301–2)]. In point of fact, the teleological quest for origins and sources has been progressively resisted, undermined, and rendered impossible. In her role as the rebellious female partner in passion, the nun's appropriation of subjectivity and writing voice implicates her in disrupting and displacing dynastic lineage. The Three Marias's reinvented "Marianas" reject women's role as the warrior's repose, the bearer of male heirs, the matrix of genealogical continuity which allows man to elude the finite nature of his own existence. Rather they indicate the unequal risk which a woman incurs through transgressive passion where "blood shed during abortion is not blood shed for the King, it is always blood shed against all of you" (135) [sangue de aborto não é sangue vertido pelo rei, é sangue vertido contra vós todos (137)] so that the blood of abortion is made to stand in rebellious opposition to the blood ties of the dynasty, king, and state.

In their subversive approach to blood ties, death, and the sacrificial order of war, the Three Marias mark their most significant departure from the Antigonean model, as posed by Irigaray. For Irigaray, "woman is the guardian of the blood. But as both she and it have had to use their substance to nourish the universal consciousness of self, it is in the form of *bloodless shadows*—of unconscious fantasies—that they maintain an underground subsistence."[71] In *Novas Cartas,* the Antigonean pact is broken by the Mariana who speaks of abortion as blood shed against the state. Confronting man with the blood of abortion, she marks her refusal to be cast as either the bloodless "other" underpinning a patriarchally-defined "universal consciousness," or the restoration of a feminine bloodline alternative. She will not enable man to overcome the limits of death through her body, either literally through motherhood or metonymically through the symbolic mediating function of burying man in the womb of the earth, that is traditionally the role of an Antigone (or of a nun). She will not reproduce the future, and nor will she "bury the brothers," be they the soldiers who have embarked on the war in Africa, or the revolutionary brother Marxists espousing antifascist revolt. Blood ties emerge as an unstable basis for asserting origins, essences, truths, or rights. The descendant of Mariana who is born around 1800 tellingly remarks, "if men create families and lineages in order to ensure that their names and property are passed along to their descendants, is it not logical for women to use their nameless, propertyless line of descent to perpetuate scandal, to pass along what is unacceptable" (150) [se os homens constituíssem famílias e linhagens para se garantirem descendência de nomes e de propriedades, não será lógico que as mulheres utilizem sua descendência sem nome nem propriedade para perpetuar o escândalo e o inaceitável (151)]. The Marias's recreation of the original nun, Mariana, turns out to be, through a series of progressive revelations in the letters, her mother's illegitimate daughter by a lover, and therefore not a true-blood Alcoforado after all (196).[72]

One alternative to patrilinearity that is outlined is not the mother-daughter line, but rather that of aunt and niece which the Three Marias term "a spontaneous, philosophically minded offshoot of the female line" [rebento extemporâneo e filosófico desta linhagem feminina] creating a "lineage opposed to the forgetting and the diluting, the rapid absorption of a scandal within the peace of a family circle" (150) [linhagem assim oposta ao esquecimento e à diluição, à absorção rápida de um escândalo na paz das famílias e das sociedades (151)]. In this gesture they associate female counterlineage with female acts of countermemory, establishing an alternative temporality. In this respect, they bring a diagonal dimension to the ethical order combining the vertical matrilinearity and horizontal sisterhood called for by Irigaray.[73] Thus, Mariana's nieces, grandnieces, and great-grandnieces become commentators on her historical legacy, as well as their own historical age, in a series of tangential, deconstructive statements about the "monumental moments" of enlightenment and revolution history. The Mariana born in 1800 remarks

> We are living in an age of civilization and enlightenment, men write scientific treatises and encyclopaedias, nations continually change and transform their political structure, the oppressed raise their voices, a king of France has been sent to the guillotine and his courtiers along with him, the United States of America has gained its independence . . . what else? What else is there in history that I find of interest to recount? What has changed in the life of women? (151)

> [Estamos em tempo de civilização e de luzes, os homens fazem livros científicos e enciclopédias, as nações mudam e mudam a sua política, os oprimidos levantam a voz, um rei de França é decapitado e com ele os seus cortesãos, os Estados Unidos da América do Norte tornam-se independentes . . . que mais? Que mais me interessa enunciar a história? O que mudou na vida das mulheres? (152)].

Maria Alzira Seixo has aptly noted that the text departs from "a creative paraphrasing of literary history [*Lettres Portugaises*] but ends up decisively founding its own temporality."[74] The paradigm shift from creative paraphrase of literary history to an entirely new temporality marks out the text's antifoundationalism.[75] Indeed, the priority of establishing alternative temporalities is prepared for at the beginning with the synchronic collapsing of monumental revolutionary dates, the October of Portugal's 1910 Revolution founding the Republic (and also that of the 1917 Bolshevik Revolution) and May '68, into a single lateral project of feminist uprising, as one Maria writes, "only out of vengeance will we make an October, a May, and a new month to cover the entire calendar" (13) [Só de vinganças, faremos um Outubro, um Maio, e novo mês para cobrir o calendário (11)].

The deconstruction of both maternal and paternal lineages extends by analogy to an interrogation and decentering of all Hegelian teleological discourses of historical progress. The "revolution," when it comes, will not be enough to liberate women. There can be no mapping of progress onto the "naturalized" development of genealogies or the dialectical unfolding of Marxist utopian advance. Rather *Novas Cartas* embodies the paradox of being a founding text that is antifoundationalist. Ana Luísa Amaral's reading of *Novas Cartas* through the insights of queer theory significantly focuses on "destabilizing the centers" marked by heteropatriarchal norms. Interestingly for our purpose here, Amaral goes on to connect the Marias' undoing of rigidly dichotomized sex roles with challenging "the very rigidity attributed to historical periodization."[76]

This antifoundationalism is nowhere more obvious than in the fact that the Three Marias do not look back, either, to any possible Portuguese foremothers in First Wave Republican feminism, to the "great individuals" of the feminist past.[77] On one level, it must be recalled, as noted above, that the Estado Novo made such intellectual connections pragmatically very difficult, as well as politically risky, by actively suppressing women's history from the Republic period (1910–26) and the early campaigns for suffrage. Nonetheless, writings by the exiled Maria Lamas, the most emblematic surviving feminist of that era, and a renowned opponent of the state, were in circulation in Portugal in the early 1970s.[78] Rather, the Marias seem to have chosen to initiate clear epistemic breaks with the recent past, both in their choice of aesthetic method and their selection of a seventeenth-century source. The ideology of compulsory, essentialist maternalism which the New State itself espoused as a major element of its family and state legal discourses weighed too heavily for the Marias to reinstate it under the guise of a genealogical discourse of female liberation. The mother-daughter bonding suggested by following Irigaray's female symbolic to the letter, always risked cohering back into an authoritarian matriliny tainted, in the Portuguese context, by association with the dictatorship.

The Marias's approach to female literary foremothers is similarly symptomatic in this regard. As Klobucka and others have noted, Florbela Espanca receives minimal, and overtly marginalizing, treatment in *Novas Cartas* evoked by a big photograph hanging in the hall, traditionally the type of tutelary public display afforded a vigilant, paternalist image of the dictator.[79] And indeed the Three Marias explicitly dissociate their project from the maternal authority of Agustina Bessa Luís, seeking to avoid the fate of her heroine in the short story "A mãe de um rio" [The Mother of a River] which allegorizes the sacrificial price of "castration" to be paid for the feminine creative gift (53). Luciana Stegagno Picchio presciently noted back in 1980 the problems that *Novas Cartas* presents as a "foremother" or "grandmother" text for Portuguese women's writing in any linear or genealogical sense.[80]

Novas Cartas, with its "new memory" of an "old dynasty" rather becomes the transitional space in which the critical usage of the term "genealogy" undergoes a paradigm shift in the direction of Foucault's coinage. Foucault refers to his "effective" practice of history that "seeks to establish the various systems of subjection."[81] This is to be pursued by exploring how regimes of truth are produced and consolidated over time, by the discursive operations of power.[82] Thus, despite *Novas Cartas'* periodic appeals to discover the single "origin" of woman's suppression by man, in the manner of some grand historical defeat of matriarchy by patriarchy, the recursive structuring of the text makes the search for an "origin," like its grounding in the illusory *Lettres Portugaises,* a web of fissures and fractures beset by multiple claims to truth. Rather the Marias' reinventions of Mariana recall Butler's guerrilla "enemies within" the patriarchal symbolic as they hold their invented male interlocutors, and male poetic intertextuality, always in play. Emphasizing contingency over essentialism and deinstituting heteropatriarchal identity norms, the Three Marias enact what Foucault terms "countermemory [as] a transformation of history into a totally different form of time."[83]

COUNTERREMEMBERING WOMEN AND CULTURE

As Marianne Hirsch and Valerie Smith have indicated in their considerations on the gendering of cultural memory, the "present" of an act of remembering may at the same time be composed of "numerous layered temporalities."[84] It is this layering of temporality in the structure of *Novas Cartas* that allows for feminine identity to be asserted as contingent and nonabsolute. For example, each of the letters or fragments, poems, essays, and word games points in at least two temporal directions at once, often more. The different sections and contributions to *Novas Cartas* were produced through a very particular, preordained group practice of cultural production, as the Three Marias agreed to meet twice a week, once in public and once in private, to exchange pieces of writing on their agreed theme.[85] One result of this practice is that each piece bears its date of composition at the bottom. Thus the only linearity that is permitted to the text, and that does structure the organization of the pieces, is that of their composition, on dates running throughout 1971. In addition to this, many of the letters have a fictitious date at the top or in the text itself, relating either to the original seventeenth-century letters or to later periods that afford points of comparison. And the close rewritings of the original five *Lettres Portugaises* refer back intertextually to the seventeenth century, as do other even earlier intertextual allusions, such as those to Camões.

Multiple temporalities, and their different political and historical logic, may thus inhabit and traverse any one piece, so that writer and addressee also simultaneously speak and respond as subjects of discourse who are differently constructed at one and the same time, acting as countermemories of them-selves. The "Letter from Mariana, Niece of Mariana Alcoforado, Left Be-tween the Pages of Her Diary, for Publication after Her Death, as a Reply for Monsieur Antoine de Chamilly" provides a particularly good case in point (130–35). As the letter written by Mariana's descendant and niece, it points back intertextually to *Lettres Portugaises,* and also within the *Novas Cartas* context, back to the aunt, Mariana Alcoforado. Furthermore, this niece writes a reply to de Chamilly's last letter, in which she adopts the name and voice of her now dead aunt speaking, as it were, from beyond the grave, while also pointing forward beyond the date of this already double act of composition toward her own death as the letter's sender, since the letter is to be published only posthumously. Its content additionally evokes both the Portuguese War of Independence from Spain in the seventeenth century and also, with its coded military references, the twentieth-century Portuguese Colonial Wars in Africa, as well as framing the entire letter within its own actual date of composition by one of the Three Marias collective, April 20, 1971. The result is a form of contingent feminist positioning that brings other forms of political identification simultaneously into play, not least those relating to antifascist resistance, colonial war, and class politics.

These multiple and distinct temporalities inhabiting the "present" of each text mark the presence of different discourses inscribing their speakers and listeners in diverse political subjectivities. In this sense, then, the text remains at any given point politically locatable but nonessentialist. The interrelated forms of feminine subjectivity that emerge in *Novas Cartas* approximate to the political theorist Chantal Mouffe's definition of "articulation" as part of her move to describe nonessentialist political citizenship in the context of a quest for radical democracy. For Mouffe, moving away from Foucault's separation and dispersal of subject positions, the principle of articulation "es-tablishes between various positions a contingent, unpredetermined relation. . . . Even though there is no necessary link between different subject positions, in the field of politics there are always discourses that try to pro-vide an articulation from different standpoints."[86]

CONCLUSION

Graça Abranches has tellingly commented that in the absence (or suppres-sion) of a strong female literary tradition in Portuguese, women's need to find or invent other genealogies or traditions of writing has translated either into a closer form of "intersextuality . . . with more marked re-accentuations, revaluings or underground interpellations of the alien, masculine word, or into a more intimate dialogue with other [foreign] literary traditions."[87] Where then does this leave us regarding *Novas Cartas?* The text began its life in the early 1970s Caetano period as a counternational memory, undoing the coordinates of New State nation and empire. In the present, it has arguably moved much closer to being a national countermemory, a defining moment for Portugal's collective history of antifascism and the April 1974 Revolution. The positioning we have proposed for it here is a third option that takes us beyond previous tendencies to dichotomize the work as feminist abroad but antifascist in Portugal.[88] Paying attention to important scholarship in Portugal, by Abranches, Amaral, and Seixo that clearly reenvisions *Novas Cartas'* feminist relevance in a Portuguese context, our focus on the text draws out the tensions inherent in its status as the antifoundationalist founding work of modern feminist criticism in Portugal.[89] In this respect, we draw together insights from both Irigaray's and Butler's Antigonean readings. In line with Irigarayan feminist politics, broadly conceived, the text centers on the gender prejudices and exclusions of the canon and their effects on women's narrative aesthetics in the history of western culture. The choice of Mariana Alcoforado as the Marias' theme evidently evokes the absence of women's place in Portugal's national literary symbolic. Yet from a Butlerian perspective, the text permits guerrilla attacks on patriarchy from within the national literary symbolic, refusing the dangerous nostalgia of a singular influence or maternal genealogy marked as a monolithic "alternative." The result is a different form of "genealogical" reading, following Foucault, as he writes that genealogy, "must record the singularity of events outside of any monotonous finality; it must seek them in the most unpromising places, in what we tend to feel is without history—in sentiments, love, conscience, instincts; it must be sensitive to their recurrence, not in order to trace the gradual curve of their evolution, but to isolate the different scenes where they engaged in different roles."[90]

Our foregoing analysis enables the consideration within a common political frame of six Portuguese women writers, working across all genres, and spanning a period from 1919 to 1998. In this process, however, we allow for Chantal Mouffe's politically contingent, but nonessentialized, articulation between subject positions so that, our chronological ordering of writers notwithstanding, we do not seek to chart a women's literary evolution. Rather our "paired" selection of writers, Florbela Espanca and Irene Lisboa, Agustina Bessa Luís and Natália Correia, Hélia Correia and Lídia Jorge emphasizes the status of each pair as contemporaries and invites synchronic readings. Nor, as must be self-evident, do we make any pretence to provide a full or comprehensive analysis of twentieth-century women's letters in Portugal, a project that is far beyond the scope of this work, while remaining an important feminist objective. We are, however, sensitive to the recurrence of two particularly insistent feminist questions that emerge from our readings of *Novas Cartas* and find themselves repeated, with important variations, across our six different literary scenes.

Firstly we ask how our six women have thematized the question of female authorship itself in their works. How have they related to questions of creativity under conditions of male canonicity, installing itself as the "law" governing the "body" of female writing? How do they see and recognize "woman (as) writer" in their texts? To this end, we focus on what Susan Wolstenholme calls "reflexive gestures in texts, coded moments that suggest the texts' preoccupation with their own production, instances where these texts teach us to read them as rewritings that are re-readings."[91] Secondly, drawing on the self-reflexive nature of Foucault's genealogical histories, we ask how women writers have engaged in Abranches's intertextual dialogues with both male and female literary forebears, and with the perceived lack, suppression, or refusal, of a female cultural memory. Our theoretical inspiration for this exercise derives from placing *Novas Cartas* in dialogue with contemporary feminist debate on Antigone. Through this creative mapping of women's disrupted cultural memory as countermemory, we ask how key Portuguese women writers of the twentieth century have gone about disclosing the figure of "woman," as reader, as writer, and as critic, working simultaneously both inside and outside the conditioning of sexuality, as well as inside and outside, of their national literary tradition.

1

Florbela Espanca and Female Genius:
Alone of All Her Sex?

No poet, no artist of any art, has complete meaning alone. His significance, his appreciation, is the appreciation of his relation to the dead
poets and artists.

—T. S. Eliot, "Tradition and the Individual Talent"

> Dying
> Is an art, like everything else.
> I do it exceptionally well.
>
> —Sylvia Plath, *Ariel*

WHEN IN 1924 TERESA LEITÃO DE BARROS PUBLISHED THE FIRST VOLUME OF
her monumental *Escritoras de Portugal* [Women Writers of Portugal] she perhaps provocatively subtitled it *Génio feminino revelado na literatura portuguesa* [Female Genius Unveiled in Portuguese Literature]. Unavoidably, in
the introduction, she feels she has to explain her choice and does so over the
course of a lengthy but revealing statement, which we cite here.

> In justifying the subtitle of this work, I am not saying that some of the female
> figures of our Literature can be considered 'geniuses' in the full sense of the word.
> I think, on the contrary, that none of them warrants the epithet *excep-
> tional* . . .
> But if we bear in mind the intellectual obscurantism, the restrictive atmo-
> sphere of prejudice, and the shortcomings of education that have, for centuries,
> beset generations of women who only *exceptionally*, and through the fortunate
> intervention of chance, were able to leave representatives of their collective ideals
> and their spiritual yearnings, can we not in those circumstances look at the eru-
> dite Infanta and her humanist ladies, Sister Mariana and her blazing torch of
> passion, the aristocratic Alcipe and her frosty odes, and other scattered female
> smiles that illuminated the face of our literary past, as diverse sparks from the
> same flash of genius, as a great and gracious chain of select souls who did manage
> to fly higher than their peers, and who, considered from a distance, with a gener-

ous and egalitarian glance, could indeed be grouped under that vague, honorific classification called "Female Genius"? (our italics)

[Justificar a sub-epígrafe deste trabalho, não é afirmar que algumas figuras femininas da nossa Literatura possam considerar-se "génios", no sentido completo do termo.

Penso, pelo contrário, que nenhuma merece o epíteto *excepcional . . .*

Mas, se levarmos em linha de conta o obscurantismo intelectual, a cerrada atmosfera de preconceitos e as deficiências de instrução que rodearam, durante séculos, gerações de mulheres que só *excepcionalmente*, e por intervenção feliz do acaso, deixaram representantes do seu ideal colectivo e dos seus anseios de espiritualidade,—não será possível olhar a Infanta erudita e as suas damas humanistas, Soror Mariana e o seu grande facho de amor, a aristocrática Alcipe com as suas odes gélidas, e um ou outro sorriso feminino que iluminou o nosso passado literário, como diversas centelhas do mesmo clarão de génio, como graciosa e extensa cadeia de almas eleitas que conseguiram voar mais alto que as suas iguais e que, consideradas de longe, num relance generoso e igualitário, se agrupariam bem sob essa vaga e honorífica designação de "Génio Feminino"?][1]

Leitão de Barros's work provided a pioneering overview of women's literary production from the sixteenth century right up to her own day.[2] Her reluctance to grant the title of genius in the full meaning of the word to a single woman writer, while simultaneously detailing the constraints under which they operated, begs the question of the criteria required to qualify as exceptional. On a theoretical level, it problematizes, retrospectively at least, the category of genius as man-made rather than as universally applicable.

In fact, at the time of her impressive overview, several female poets were already beginning to engage on a practical level with the struggle to fit into man-made categories of genius, but none more extensively than Florbela Espanca (1894–1930). Such battle permeates her poetry from beginning to end, and is especially central to her first two collections. Part of the challenge for Espanca consisted in the fact that, in real life, she acted as a muse to several of her male contemporaries. As she wistfully reminisced toward the end of her life in "Lembrança" [Recollection], "So many poets sang me in their verse" [Tanto poeta em versos me cantou!].[3] Such hypervisibility as a poetic object, however, was a hindrance to her positioning as a poetic subject and, concomitantly, her recognition as an exceptionally talented woman in her own right. After her premature death in 1930, her image remained a powerful source of inspiration for male and female writers alike right up to the present day including, as will be shown in subsequent chapters, Agustina Bessa Luís, Natália Correia and Hélia Correia. Regrettably but perhaps predictably, this was not matched with any in-depth analysis of her poetry for at least half a century.

Admittedly, Espanca's life-story does read like a soap-opera script, for she was born out of wedlock, was twice divorced and married three times.[4] At a time when it was still most unusual for women to study, she not only completed her secondary schooling in the provincial town of Évora, but later moved to Lisbon to enroll at university, an unexpected move as she had married in the meantime. Her letters and early poetry document her steadfast efforts, from 1916 onwards, to gain access to publication.[5] The relocation to Lisbon in 1917 certainly opened up the possibility of at least intermittent access to minor literary circles, through her male university fellow students, especially the poet Américo Durão, like her born in the Alentejo. Her first collection *Livro de Mágoas* [Book of Sorrows] came out in 1919. Although she gave up her university studies the following year, Espanca remained committed to her poetic career: her second collection, *Livro de "Soror Saudade"* [Book of "Sister Longing"] was published in 1923. After moving to northern Portugal as a result of her third marriage, her already tangential involvement with the literary life of the capital virtually ceased, with the exception of her one-off publication of the eponymous sonnet "Charneca em Flor" [Heath in Flower] in *Europa* in 1925, directed by Judith Teixeira, as well as several contributions in *Portugal Feminino* in the course of 1930.[6] Espanca's verses consistently reflect a wish to escape a narrow view of traditional female roles and being fixed by the male gaze.[7] Her work thus bears witness to her struggle to articulate her own, increasingly dissident, conception of "genius" in a culture which was not geared toward viewing women as potential "first-class" poets.

Espanca died on the eve of her birthday, in December 1930, as she was about to turn thirty-six, almost certainly by taking her own life. The publication of her third volume of poetry a few weeks later, *Charneca em Flor* (1931) [Heath in Flower] projected her into the limelight. A seminal article by the influential António Ferro, where he described her as gifted "poetess-poet" [a poetisa-poeta], gave a boost to the well-meaning efforts of Guido Batelli, the retired Italian professor who had helped her to publish *Charneca em Flor*, to promote her as a talented but ill-fated poet, in other words a genius in the Romantic vein. Several other works appeared posthumously in the aftermath of this success.[8] Since it is primarily as a poet that Espanca made an unprecedented impact in twentieth-century Portuguese letters, this chapter will focus exclusively on her poetry.

WALLED IN GRIEF: *LIVRO DE MÁGOAS*

From its incipit, her debut collection *Livro de Mágoas* (1919) displays the anxiety of female authorship. Much like Virginia Woolf's brilliant articulation of the double bind facing women artists, through her haunting image of an imaginary Judith Shakespeare, Espanca perceives herself as some sort of poor relation.[9] In her case, the famous older sibling against whom she pitches herself is Antó[nio] Nobre, the most influential late nineteenth-century poet in the early part of the twentieth century, (in)famously dismissed by Teixeira de Pascoaes as "the greatest Portuguese poetess" [a maior poetisa portuguesa]. But in *Livro de Mágoas,* she engages with Portuguese male literary tradition more broadly, including canonical authors such as Luís de Camões and Antero de Quental. As she struggles to position herself against prevailing images of womanhood, whereby women were perceived merely as muses and not as creators in their own right, it is small wonder that feelings of loneliness and despair pervade the volume from beginning to end.

In the opening sonnet "Este livro" (131) [This Book], which is indirectly constructed in dialogue with Nobre's influential 1892 collection *Só* [Alone], Espanca claims that her book grew inside her, "I bore it in my womb" [trouxe-o no meu seio], thereby echoing Nobre's assertion in his own incipit, "I bore it from a womb" [trouxe-o d'um ventre (19)].[10] This early reference to metaphorical pregnancy is most telling. Espanca may have had a more complex set of meanings than Nobre in mind, especially if we consider the miscarriage which, according to some biographers, she experienced in early 1918.[11] Her inability to reproduce is likely to have affected her, at least subconsciously, given the extent to which at the turn of the century a woman's main function was still generally understood as biological procreation rather than artistic creation. Her failure to carry to term must have compounded her feelings of isolation and exclusion as a woman, but by the same token provided the impetus to develop a carefully crafted image of herself as a *poète maudit,* into which were woven the untold complexities of being female.

As she embarks on a journey which privileges creation over procreation, her perceived abnormality in relation to prevalent gender norms remains a heavy burden at this stage. Five sonnets, "Pior Velhice" [The Worst Old Age], "Pequenina" [Young Girl], "Dizeres Íntimos" [Intimate Sayings], "Tédio" [Tedium], and "Velhinha" [Old Woman] convey her anguish about her destiny being intrinsically different from that bestowed on other women. For instance, in "Pior Velhice" (149), her failure to enjoy the promise of a carefree existence leaves her stranded, "a woman shipwrecked by Life" [náufraga da Vida]. Is attributed to an ill-fated destiny, implicitly linked to poetic vocation.

> Life which adorns and crowns the brow of woman
> With pure white roses at her birth,

On my mystic brow of madness, placed
Only the fading passion flowers of martyrdom!

[A Vida que ao nascer enfeita e touca
D'alvas rosas, a fronte da mulher,
Na minha fronte mística de louca
Martírios só poisou a emurchecer!] [12]

Her madness may lead to recognition if not consecration as a mystic prophet/poet, but it comes at a heavy price since it withers her femininity, is a source of martyr-like suffering, and may have fatal repercussions.

According to Battersby, "since the woman artist does not stand in the same relation to tradition as the male, her face can only emerge clearly by playing two separate games. She has to be positioned in two different, but overlapping patterns: the matrilineal and patrilineal lines of influence and response."[13] Given the disjointedness and scant visibility of matrilineal lines of influence in the Portuguese canon at that point in time, Espanca resorts, by virtue of necessity, to positioning herself instead in relation to a broad historical canvas enshrining traditional expectations of femininity. The face that emerges when attempting to place her within such a lineage confirms her estrangement as a female anomaly. Yet she feels equally an outsider in relation to male literary models.

The sonnets which deal with her metapoetic quest and problematic engagement with male literary tradition are similar in number to those where she portrayed herself as unfeminine. Most are likewise tormented in tone. Two in particular, "A um Livro" (150) [To a Book] and "A Maior Tortura" (143) [The Greatest Torture], vividly foreground her inability to emulate canonical male role models. "A Maior Tortura" is dedicated "To a great poet of Portugal" [A um grande poeta de Portugal], which according to Dal Farra must have been Durão.[14] Nevertheless, the choice not to identify the individual artist by name means that, above all, female creativity has to assert itself in dialogue with a generic category, that of the male genius.

The sonnet starts off by portraying Florbela as a distraught and forsaken being, in what is a bid to claim for herself the credentials of a Romantic poet/genius. Yet, in the first tercet, the explicit comparison between herself and the male poet, "I am like you, a doomed laughter!" [Sou, como tu, um riso desgraçado!], merely leads her to highlight a fundamental difference, that of talent, as the sonnet reaches its close.

But my torture is yet greater:
Not being a poet as you are,
To cry out my Grief in a single verse! . . .

[Mas a minha tortura inda é maior:
Não ser poeta assim como tu és,
Para gritar num verso a minha Dor! . . .]

In other words, Espanca was acutely aware of the asymmetries between herself and her male canonical role models. In this instance, nonetheless, she provocatively claims supremacy for herself in terms of the magnitude of her suffering owing to what, on closer inspection of the variations between the draft of this sonnet and its published version, turns out to be her female lineage and gender. Indeed, in the draft version, the poem featured three words in capitals: "Torture, Poet and Grief" [Tortura, Poeta and Dor], all in the last stanza.[15] In the subsequent published version, only one of these three words, Dor, retained a capital. The most revealing change from the earlier draft, however, is that Espanca rewrote the second stanza extensively in order to identify her sorrow as a specifically female legacy, adding two new capitalized words in the process. The final published version thus became, "My poor Mother so white and cold / Gave me Sorrow to drink with her milk!" [A minha pobre Mãe tão branca e fria / Deu-me a beber a Mágoa no seu leite!] in a rare reference to her biological mother. Her poignant perception of her maternal antecedents stands in a sharp contrast with Nobre's beatified view of his own in his introductory "Memória" [Recollection], "Oh mothers of Poets! Smiling in their chambers, / That are virgins before and after giving birth!" [Oh mães dos Poetas! Sorrindo em seu quarto, / Que são virgens antes e depois do parto!].[16]

The three capitalized words in the revised version thus become Mother, Sorrow and Grief [Mãe, Mágoa and Dor]. This shift of emphasis demonstrates that Espanca did not attribute her inability to articulate her predicament merely to the fact that she was a beginner and the canonical poets she measured herself against were not, but that her gender intervened in the process of trying to emulate their poetic authority.

This impression is further confirmed if we bear in mind that, immediately after 'Este livro,' in "Vaidade" (132) [Vanity], the second sonnet of this debut collection, Espanca tries to imagine herself as a hypothetical female poet, "the chosen Poetess" [Poetisa eleita], with an ill-fated outcome. This attempt to do so is the first and last in her entire poetic output and is shown to be completely doomed to failure.[17] Her heady escalation to power is emphasized over the first three stanzas through the anaphora "I dream that" [Sonho que]. As José Rodrigues de Paiva perceptively noted, this clearly echoes Antero de Quental's celebrated sonnet "O Palácio da Ventura" [The Palace of Fortune], which began with the statement "I dream I am an errant knight" [Sonho que sou um cavaleiro andante].[18]

The female poet's ambition reaches a climax in the third stanza as she visualizes herself as

> Someone in this world . . .
> The one with learning, vast and deep,
> At whose feet the whole Earth bows!
>
> [Alguém cá neste mundo . . .
> Aquela de saber vasto e profundo,
> Aos pés de quem a terra anda curvada!].

Her dream equates her with the power of a modern-day Virgin Mary ("At whose feet the whole Earth bows"). Furthermore, through a daring appropriation of Camões, as she voices the wish to own the (male) "Learning, vast and deep" ["Saber, alto e profundo"] evoked in Canto X of *The Lusiads,* she is envisaging herself as someone who would not merely be a procreator of male poets (as Nobre and many other would have it), but a creator, a Poetess or Poetisa in her own right, endowed with poetic authority.[19] Her ambitions, however, lead only to bitter disappointment and nothingness in the concluding stanza (admittedly in keeping with the original ending present in Quental's "O Palácio da Ventura"). Where she differs from her predecessor, however, is in the breaking up of the line on the printed page in the first edition, which graphically suggests her being literally torn apart.

> I wake up from my dream . . .
>   And I'm nothing! . . .
>
> [Acordo do meu sonho . . .
>   E não sou nada! . . .]

As such, any attempt at self-definition can only lead to a portrayal of herself as adrift, like in the next sonnet, "Eu . . ." (113) (I . . .) where she becomes the female equivalent of the Nervalian "Unhappy One" [El Desdichado]: adrift and grieving. Symptomatically, the closing verses highlight the virtual impossibility for her to be anything other than a figment of male literary and cultural imagination: "I am perhaps the vision Someone dreamt" [Sou talvez a visão que Alguém sonhou], a sketchy vision not found by the presumably male, demiurgic, Pygmalion-like "Someone" [Alguém], leaving her in a no-man's-land.

In a sense, in order to be readily "found," Florbela had to fit into pre-existing cultural stereotypes. This fact may account for the way in which, thereafter, she chooses to construct an image of herself as a silent princess or nun. That she should fall back on these century-old fixed images is understandable: both were readily recognizable representations of women who differed from everyday women, and, as has already been stressed, whenever Espanca sets up a comparison between herself and "normal" women, it is primarily to highlight her feeling of having been cast in a different mould. Furthermore, in previous centuries, both princesses and nuns were among the few females likely to be literate. Nuns, at least officially, were not enmeshed in the corporal business of procreation. Arguably, nor were princesses, since in contrast to queens, usually represented as mothers, they were portrayed as innocent, virginal maidens.

"Castelã da Tristeza" (134) [Chatelaine of Sadness] depicts her as an imprisoned princess, waiting in vain for liberation from her metaphorical castle of sorrow. In a dramatic moment of introspection, Espanca realizes, "The silence weeps . . . nothing . . . no one comes . . ." [Chora o silêncio . . . nada . . . ninguém vem . . .], thereby negating the possibility of any fairytale "happy ending." Even more bleakly, "Lágrimas Ocultas" (136) [Hidden Tears] stages her as a silent, petrified nunlike figure, whose tears are not seen by a single soul, "No-one sees them fall within me!" [Ninguém as vê cair dentro de mim!]. Finally "A Minha Dor" (138) [My Sorrow] features her imprisoned in a metaphorical convent: not only is she walled up, she is practically buried alive, because once more her pain remains completely unheard by the outside world. As the close of the sonnet poignantly foregrounds: "And no one sees or hears me . . . no one . . ." [E ninguém ouve . . . ninguém vê . . . ninguém . . .].

The extreme pathos of her situation as a trapped maiden in this sequence of cornerstone sonnets alternates with "Tortura" (135) [Torture] and "Torre de Névoa" (137) [Tower of Mist] two sonnets which describe her poetic quest. "Torre de Névoa" also sees her walled up, but in this case able to climb up an imaginary tower to enter in dialogue with "the dead poets" [os poetas mortos] a pantheon of unnamed canonical male poets. There are predictably several of them while she is entirely on her own. In a rather paternalistic fashion, they call her "crazy naive child" [criança doida e crente] and point out that she is deluded, like they once were. Their curt rejection of her right to dream leaves her once more bereft of any hope, while nevertheless signaling her utterly 'tragic' poetic vocation. While her ambiguous poetic initiation is, up to a point, reminiscent of "Tormento do Ideal" [Torment of the Ideal (132)] by Antero de Quental, her poetic consecration, unlike his, depends on a double marginalization.[20]

As a whole, then, the collection portrays extreme isolation, compounded by Espanca's inability to find a kindred soul in the human world. Only in the natural world can she can find an echo of her sadness, embodied for instance in the night-time song of the nightingale of "Alma Perdida" (151) [Lost Soul] a motif with a long female lineage.[21] Even so, her sorrow surpasses all others found in nature, as "Mais Triste" (159) [The Saddest Thing] underlines: "Do they not see that I am . . . I . . . in the end, / The saddest thing among all those that are sad?!" [E não vêem que eu sou . . . eu . . . afinal, / A coisa mais magoada das que o são?! . . . (93)]. "Mais Triste," as its title indicates, also surpasses previous cultural articulations of grief and, in so doing, provides the ultimate challenge to Nobre's famous closing statement in his introductory "Memória" that his was "the *saddest* book that exists in Portugal" [o livro *mais triste* que há em Portugal (our italics)].[22]

As the collection reaches its end, in what is yet another echo of Nobre (131), the poet is perceived by others as the morbid embodiment of a "Sexta-Feira de Paixão" [Good Friday], in "Impossível" (162) [Impossible]. This all-pervasive feeling of doom had already been encapsulated in another religious image in the earlier "Mais Triste" where she defined herself as a dark Night "as sad as Extreme-Unction" [triste como a Extrema-Unção].[23] While those around her advise her to be content with her (female) lot, far from taking heed of their well-meaning advice, in the parting words of this final sonnet, she bitterly complains that

> The woes of Anto are known to all!
> And mine . . . to no-one . . . My Sorrow will not fit
> Into the hundred million verses that I could write! . . .
>
> [Os males d'Anto toda a gente os sabe!
> Os meus . . . ninguém . . . A minha Dor não cabe
> Nos cem milhões de versos que eu fizera! . . .]

The incommunicability of her infinite "dor" may be linked to the fact that, as the title of this sonnet seems to imply, it was all but impossible for the utterances of a female artist to be recognized as inspired poetry in the cultural context of the day. But, Espanca goes even further in her attempt to turn the tables on the status quo: in the closing section of *Só,* significantly entitled "Males de Anto" (173) [The Woes of Anto], Nobre had knowingly committed both religious and literary heresy by claiming himself to be a greater sufferer than famous religious figures such as Job and Christ himself, as well as (implicitly) Camões. The allusion to Anto's suffering, then, becomes a pretext to reaffirm the supremacy of her own plight, especially if we consider that here Espanca may also be indirectly engaging with Camões and his famous "Canção X," where he had masterfully voiced his grief, while paradoxically claiming that

I was long ago undeceived that my laments
might prove a remedy. But he who suffers
per force must cry out, if his grief is great.
I will cry out. Yet how weak and feeble
is my voice for the outpouring of my soul;
not even crying out lessens my grief.

Já me desenganei que de queixar-me
não se alcança remédio; mas quem pena,
forçado lhe é gritar se a dor é grande.
Gritarei; mas é débil e pequena
a voz para poder desabafar-me,
porque nem com gritar a dor se abranda.[24]

Likewise, Espanca's final statement "Os meus . . . ninguém . . . A minha Dor não cabe / Nos cem milhões de versos que eu fizera!" may on the surface foreground her inability to transmit her woes onto paper but, in fact, becomes an undeniable proof, not only of the greatness of her suffering itself (in keeping with Camões' blueprint), but also of her growing poetic skill in emulating the literary masters of the past: for, indeed, she manages to artistically condense into two short lines an intensity of despair that had taken both Camões and Nobre many pages to articulate in their seemingly endless torrential outpouring of confessional verse. As such, it signals her awareness that her place in literary tradition could only be secured, initially at least, by engaging with the legacy of canonical male-authored texts, while superimposing her own lapidary discourse of difference onto it.

However, although *Livro de Mágoas* despondently locates Espanca in some sort of vacuum, like a latter-day Antigone haughtily if perhaps involuntarily walled alive in grief, and concludes by stressing the failure of her repeated attempts to reach a different way of relating to the outside world, the inexplicable solace she finds in being different (and concomitantly in being her own person despite the pressure to conform to society's expectations) repeatedly comes to the fore. Dream, in other words, the visionary desire to see herself as potentially someone other, alienates her from reality, and often alienates her from herself too. But it is also potentially redemptive. Quite aside from confirming her credentials as a poet in Romantic vein, a genius, only by delving so intensely inside her inner world can she begin to harness the strength to articulate a challenge to (man-made) reality as she knows it. In this respect, one poem within the collection deserves to be singled out, "Languidez" (153) [Languor], since it provides the stepping stone for a more daring rejection of her social and sexual invisibility, which was to become her hallmark in subsequent collections.

"Languidez" depicts the female speaker as occupying an in-between space between day and night. The possibility of her insertion within this metaphorical literary landscape (a setting which is ever so revealingly characterized as "the evenings of Anto" [as tardes d'Anto]), necessitates, in a truly staggering fashion, a transgendering. It would seem that only by projecting a male image of herself can she fully commune with the privileged sphere of sorrow inhabited by mystic poet/prophets, the "hours of grief in which I am a [male] *saint*" [horas de dor em que eu sou *santo!*' (our italics)].

Once she has momentarily secured integration, albeit on male terms, she shuts her eyes to reality as she knows it, enabling her to come to life again: in the tercets she feels her mouth come alive with "silent kisses" [beijos mudos], while her hands begin to sketch "dream gestures in the air" [gestos de sonho pelo ar]. The focus on bodily and sensory experience is subversive since it is in blatant contradiction with the premise of saintly chastity. Both the mouth and hands (which are grammatically feminine in Portuguese) are extremities of the body which mediate between the self and the outside world. Needless to say, they are also able to serve a multiplicity of purposes. The mouth can be used for both kissing and for speaking out. As for the hands, they can reach out to others, but may equally function as the instrument used in writing. It is as if, by shutting her eyes (the most intellectual of our senses) to the reality which initially surrounds her, Espanca could start to experience empowering new sensations, which stems from her own recentered body.

This focus on her material core self opens up fresh possibilities still barely voiced here, but rather conjured up in a dreamlike fashion amidst ellipsis. Indeed, throughout *Livro de Mágoas,* the tentative nature of Florbela's musings is often reflected in the abundant use of ellipsis, a predilection inherited from nineteenth-century Symbolist poetry, especially that of Verlaine, a poet featured in an epigraph (the other being Eugénio de Castro).

On the surface, then, a linear reading of the collection leads to an overwhelmingly negative impression. By virtue of being female, Espanca considers herself mostly debarred from the genealogy of genius. She is a freak of nature, barren and misunderstood. One of her rhetorical strategies becomes "excessive femininity," as she endeavors to cast herself as a hypervisible figuration of the silent, imprisoned female: the princess or nun who becomes, by extension, a metaphorically dead body. Several poems depict this Antigone-like tragic posture. The other, arguably more subversive, strategy, is the rethinking of herself through her senses, which provides her with a self-centered apprehension of reality, as featured in the lone "Languidez." Perhaps predictably, given the overwhelming preponderance of the male gaze in the world she lived in, her self-definition as princess or nun would be seized

upon by several of the male poets around her, to the detriment of the possibly more empowering, self-centered one. Nevertheless, in the next collection,
while the starting point would be her image as envisaged by her male peers,
her engagement with it would gradually lead to its collapse. In so doing, her
attempts to reclaim herself through her material body would increasingly
come to take precedence.

THE UNDOING OF THE NUN:
LIVRO DE "SOROR SAUDADE"

A landmark moment in Espanca's turbulent journey toward the construction of selfhood is provided in the title of her second collection, *Livro de
"Soror Saudade"* [Book of "Sister Longing"] (1923), especially if we dwell
on the significance of the generally overlooked fact that the name "Soror
Saudade" appears in quotation marks in the first edition.
   At the most basic level, the quotations marks visibly indicate from the
outset that the label of Soror Saudade was not of her own devising, but rather
was attributable to a fellow university student, the poet Américo Durão, a
fact explicitly confirmed soon after, both in the epigraph and in the opening
eponymous sonnet " 'Soror Saudade' " (167) ['Sister Longing'], also symptomatically encased in quotation marks in the first edition. On a deeper level,
however, the use of quotation marks unobtrusively points to a disturbing
discrepancy: it conveys her awareness of only existing in the public realm as
the figment of someone else's imagination, thus signalling the gap between
her socially assigned identity and her hidden (yet equally real) one. Subliminally, her apparent deference, bordering on the ironic through excessive iteration, already suggests the need to reject her existence "in-between quotation
marks" for a more authentic one, predicated on her own first-hand experience.
   The spiritual sister that Durão idealized, confined within convent walls,
was by definition inaccessible. While his disembodied female vision is apparently embraced by Florbela in her opening sonnet, already therein she explicitly states that, as a direct consequence of her identification with such an
image, "with this you made me much sadder" [Com ele bem mais triste me
tornaste]. Her provisional acceptance of a nunlike performativity may lead
her to visibly conceal her female sexuality but, whereas in the previous collection her hypervisible disembodiment could be read at face value, as this collection progresses, it becomes increasingly difficult to do so. In other words,
the veil and the habit may conceal the body, but simultaneously they emphasize concealment and therefore become unwittingly all the more revealing,

pointing to, if only through absence at this stage, the material body and its potentially disruptive sexuality. Already in this opening sonnet, Espanca's mask as "Soror Saudade" becomes invoked as a magic protection against her own, more complex apprehension of herself "in evil hours of fevered anguish" [Nas horas más de febre e de ansiedade]. As a result, the viability of this one-dimensional and provisional portrayal of a mystical Soror Saudade, briefly re-enacted in "Ódio?" (193) [Loathing?] becomes dramatically called into question in the sonnet which comes immediately after, the ironically titled "Renúncia" (194) [Renunciation]. It further culminates in its outright rejection in the sonnet which closes the collection, "Exaltação" (203) [Exaltation].

Indeed, "Renúncia," under the guise of extreme renunciation, functions as an impassioned denunciation: it questions the inhumanity of confining a woman of bones and flesh, endowed with an unspoken yearning for freedom and sexuality, to a metaphorical convent of Sadness where she will wither away until the hour of her death. By enacting an excessively submissive stance, "Forever sequestered, / Eyes closed, frail hands in a cross . . ." [sempre presa, / Olhos fechados, magras mãos em cruz . . .], Espanca is in fact parodying extreme self-denial, especially if we bear in mind that in the second stanza she allows her thoughts to momentarily wander to the life-giving kiss of nature, which floods her cell with light: "Nature is like an ardent kiss . . . / My cell is like a river of light . . ." [É como um beijo ardente a Natureza . . . / A minha cela é como um rio de luz . . .]. As such, the self-defeating implications of her self-abnegation are ironically thrown into relief in the paradox of the closing lines: "Fill your mouth with earth and ashes, / O my youth in your full flower!" [Enche a boca de cinzas e de terra, / Ó minha mocidade toda em flor!]. From the point of view of the prevailing patriarchal order (and her up to now internalized assumptions), the living promise of the female blossoming youth must be abruptly curtailed by a self-imposed death-like sentence.[25] But reading in-between the lines, the prospect of being metaphorically buried alive, given the violence it entails, becomes a politically charged way of questioning "the symbolic constraints under which liveability is established," in a way that is reminiscent of the untenable choice faced by her famous predecessor, Antigone.[26]

Significantly Espanca is engaging in this collection, by virtue of necessity, not just with one, but with several different textualizations of her as a metaphorically dead body, present in the poetry (some published, some unpublished) of her male contemporaries. Poe famously asserted that "the death of a beautiful woman is, unquestionably, the most poetical topic in the world."[27] This was a topic that certainly fed the imagination not only of Américo Durão, but also that of a cast of other minor poets, including her university peers Boto de Carvalho and Vasco Camélier. Their poetry reveals the extent of Florbela's iconic status, as they enshrined her as a desexualized, symptomatically dead (or virtually dead) female body. Boto de Carvalho, for instance, had referred to her 'mãos de Morta' in the 1919 poem he dedicated to her, "A Princesa Incompreendida" [The Misunderstood Princess].²⁸ Significantly, this second collection features a sonnet where she alludes to having been named "Princesa Desalento" (198) [Princess Melancholy] (Boto de Carvalho had in fact described her as "Princess Desolation" [Princesa Desolação]).²⁹

As in the case of Durão, her literary response enables Florbela to articulate a more complex apprehension of herself in the process. In the opening line of her sonnet, she characterizes her soul as "pained and pale and sombre / like the tragic sighs of the wind!" [magoada e pálida e sombria, / Como soluços trágicos do vento!], in other words, grief-stricken but unable to articulate her predicament in words.³⁰ However, by the tercets, under the cloak of Princesa Desalento, she starts to enact what constitutes, from a male-centered perspective, a sinister subjectivity: she roams free, "at the dead of night, she wanders" [Altas horas da noite ela vagueia], signalling her refusal to be meek and compliant or remain imprisoned within the confines of the house or in silence. In the closing line, by communing with moonlight, she can by proxy go on to haunt a former lover, casting the ghostly imprint of "the shadow of a cross on your door" [A sombra duma cruz à tua porta], in a mute accusation.

Since unrequited love leaves the speaker almost bereft of identity, Espanca repeatedly focuses on the battered female ego in order to endow it with new meaning and value. This woman-centered perspective also enables her to reformulate the premises in often unequal male/female unions, by acknowledging and owning (if not always voicing) her feelings. For instance, in "Nocturno" (188) [Nocturne] the uncaring male lover seeks to nail her violently into the missionary position "You traced on me the arms of a cross, / and to them you nailed my youth!" [Traçaste em mim os braços duma cruz, / Neles pregaste a minha mocidade!]. Yet, as the next stanza shows, the female poet can never be pinned down, be it literally or metaphorically: "My soul [. . .] Tonight is a water lily on a lake / spreading its white wings upon the waters!" [Minh'alma (. . .) É nesta noite o nenúfar dum lago / Estendendo as asas brancas sobre as águas!].

A particularly successful destabilizing of an asymmetrical love relationship occurs in "Esfinge" (185) [Sphinx] when the poet compares herself to an earth-bound heath, awaiting the daily visit of the sun in order to achieve her dreams of union. The depth of her silent emotions is evoked through her portrayal as a dreaming sphinx, symptomatically a mythical creature who does not talk, lying awake at night.

> And, awaiting you, while the world sleeps,
> I would lie there, quiet-eyed and brooding . . .
> A gazing Sphinx, on the vast plains . . .
>
> [E, à tua espera, enquanto o mundo dorme,
> Ficaria, olhos quietos, a cismar . . .
> Esfinge olhando, na planície enorme . . .].

This image implies that because of her eerie, other-worldly nature, associated with the moon, her innermost core remains inaccessible to the superficial male sun. Thus, as her inner world remains private, her ongoing mute gaze implies that the intense emotions experienced by the sensitive female may often not be understood. Yet, in mythology, the riddle of the Sphinx constitutes a challenge that needs to be deciphered, since otherwise the unsuspecting victim will be devoured. Her choice of title then reflects, at least on a subconscious level, the destructive power that could potentially arise out of a woman-centered perspective.

A different strategy in the journey toward female empowerment is to reframe the premises by questioning female over-reliance on love altogether. For instance, although in her fourth sonnet, "Fanatismo" (171) [Fanaticism], she declares to her lover "Because you are like God: the Beginning and the End!" [Que tu és como Deus: Princípio e Fim!], her blind acceptance of male supremacy is indirectly called into question by the very ironic excess of the title "Fanatismo," as well as showing how this trajectory of annihilation inexorably leads to the "End." Later in the collection, she dismantles the myth of Prince Charming in "Prince Charmant," (183) questioning the cultural assumptions handed down through fairytale stories and "happily ever after" endings, through denial of the existence of "Mr Right": "You never find the One you are waiting for!" [—Nunca se encontra Aquele que se espera!]. In "A Vida" (195) [Life], a sonnet which perhaps not coincidentally comes immediately after "Renúncia," she becomes vocal in her rejection of received wisdom about love necessarily entailing a life-long commitment, bluntly stating "I could not love you my whole life" [Amar-te a vida inteira eu não podia].

Another strategy deployed to great effect by Espanca is to revise prevailing expectations about appropriately "feminine" expressions of love. In "Horas Rubras" (196) [Red Glowing Hours] the sonnet which immediately follows on from "A Vida," she focuses on the sensual dimension of relationships,

breaking long-held taboos in order to allow for the expression of female desire. She portrays herself as both spiritual in essence and sexually available,
thus collapsing boundaries, "I am flame and white snow and mysterious . . ."
[Sou chama e neve branca e misteriosa . . .], and playfully making the first
move: "And I am, per chance, on this sensual night / O my Poet, the kiss
you are seeking!" [E sou, talvez, na noite voluptuosa, / Ó meu Poeta, o beijo
que procuras!]. The kiss, situated at the interface of the material and immate-
rial world, encapsulates the conflict harbored within the mind (and body) of
the female speaker. The artist is male, while the female's role is seemingly
only to offer herself to the male gaze as a desirable *objet d'art*. Nevertheless,
as she destabilizes customary female passivity, gender roles are shown to be
susceptible to revision. This poem is, moreover, only one of many stages as
the collection unfolds in an ongoing journey of empowerment that culminates, arguably, in the altogether more revolutionary "Da Minha Janela"
(200) [From my Window].

Until "Exaltação" (203) [Exaltation] was added at the very last moment,
"Da Minha Janela" was the penultimate piece, since the original intention
was for the collection to end with "Sol Poente" (201) [Sunset].[31] "Da Minha
Janela" is remarkable for the way in which sexual feelings are projected onto
the natural landscape: in an extraordinary reworking of pathetic fallacy, nature comes to metonymically represent the sexual act itself. We witness how,
at sunset, the male sun becomes ever closer to merging with the boundless
sea, where waves break "with whispered, troubled sighs . . ." [num soluçar
aflito e murmurado . . .]. In the third stanza, sunset projects an in-between
light, described as

> O my charming verse of Samain,
> Not yet daylight, already you're moonlight,
> Like a white lilac whose flowers wither!
>
> [Meu verso de Samain cheio de graça,
> 'Inda não és clarão, já és luar
> Como um branco lilás que se desfaça!]

Arguably, this diffuse poetic light is precisely the answer to Espanca's un-
fulfilled earlier wish in "Vaidade" (132) that "a verse of mine sheds light /
Enough to fill the world at large!" [um verso meu tem claridade / para encher
todo o mundo!].

Indeed, here the female speaker's apprehension of reality from her van-
tage-point (from my window) is fully endorsed, as the (male) sunset is
morphed into (female) moonlight to illuminate the world in a previously

unknown way, precisely through the imaginative power of a poetic art which
seems to be halfway between being man-made ("my verse of Samain" [Meu
verso de Samain]) and infused with the hallmark of female exceptionality
(being like the Virgin Mary "full of grace" [cheio de graça]). This process
of redefinition culminates in a metaphorical description of the sexual act of
unprecedented daringness, given that the latter becomes viewed from the female perspective.

> Love! I carry your heart in my breast . . .
> It pounds within me like this sea
> In an endless, never withering kiss! . . .
>
> [Amor! Teu coração trago-o no peito . . .
> Pulsa dentro de mim como este mar
> Num beijo eterno, assim, nunca desfeito! . . .]

It is hardly surprising then that, even before "Exaltação" (203) was added at
the last minute, the draft version of the collection ended with the rather less
controversial "Sol Poente" (201), where the closing lines depicted an active
male sun "deflowering" [desfolhando] the mouth of a reassuringly passive
female speaker.

Ultimately, however, the gradual undoing of the nun-image (and, more
ambitiously, of man-made theology), which was the central intent of Espanca, culminates, in the definitive published version of *Livro de "Soror Saudade,"* with the closing sonnet "Exaltação"(203). The exaltation here
evoked, far from being of a religious nature, instead becomes "sinfully" self-
centered. The sonnet begins with the life-affirming exclamation "To live!"
[Viver!], signaling an outright rejection any previous self-abnegating stance.
It may also be read as a radical refusal of being enshrined by her male peers
as a metaphorical dead body. By the end of the first stanza, an alternative
religious genesis has been inscribed as we are provocatively told "God made
our arms for grasping! / And gave us mouths of blood for kissing!" [Deus fez
os nossos braços pra prender, / E a boca fez-se sangue pra beijar!]. While
God still features in line three as the subject at the beginning of the sentence,
by line four in the Portuguese original, the female body has taken on a life
of its own in a wholehearted embrace of sensuality.

Sensuality is empowering because it constitutes an alternative instrument
of knowledge, which opens up previously unattainable worlds. These include, as the end of the second stanza explicitly states "Glory! . . . Fame! . . .
The pride of creating!" [A glória! . . . A fama! . . . O orgulho de criar!].
Espanca is fully aware that her embracing of the senses, coupled with her

unseemly public display of craving fame, goes deeply against the grain. Both were widely perceived as unbecoming to a woman and bound to result in her marginalization from mainstream society. However, as she was already in practice both unable and unwilling to fit into existing man-made images, including those disseminated by her fellow poets, she opts instead to triumphantly proclaim her difference, embodied through her "ecstatic, pagan kisses! . . ." [beijos extáticos, pagãos! . . .].

In other words, as *Livro de "Soror Saudade"* draws to a close, far from retaining the appropriately modest "feminine" identity originally bestowed upon her from the outside, Espanca subversively redefined herself as completely disenfranchised from society. In so doing, her radical stance brings her closer to a community of outcasts. With newfound authority, now the speaker, she can address all fellow poets in words that can be heard publicly, unlike what had happened in the earlier "Torre de Névoa" (137), as indicated through the mark of direct discourse: "O bohemians, tramps and poets/ How truly, Brothers, I'm your Sister! . . ." [Boémios, vagabundos, e poetas: / —Como eu sou vossa Irmã, ó meus Irmãos! . . .]. At this point, she completely spurns the identity bestowed on her as a religious sister, claiming for herself an alternative kinship: she is the sister of outcasts and poets, a fact which enables her at long last to consider herself on a par with male writers. Admittedly, there are several of them, whereas she remains very much on her own. Nonetheless, while she may still have to contend with double marginalization from the perspective of the world at large, she feels she has achieved some parity at long last.

Espanca's jubilant proclamation of her hard-earned sense of equality, which manages to retain her birthright to sexual difference, is fascinating. In this respect, it is illuminating to read *Livro de "Soror Saudade"* not only as a creative response to male depictions of her, but equally as a progressive work in a female context. For in practice it reclaims the right to produce love poetry as a positive choice, precisely at a time when women's poetry increasingly became narrowly and often patronizingly dismissed as such by male critics.[32] Indeed, not only does it pre-empt the sexist implication that love poetry, at least at the hands of its female practitioners, was a lesser mode of self-expression, more radically it even goes so far as to propose sensual love as an alternative instrument of knowledge. This trend would culminate in the justly famous sonnet of *Charneca em Flor* [Heath in Flower] "Ser Poeta" (229) [To be a Poet] where self-expression, poetic expression, and expressions of love become inextricably intertwined, as Espanca claims for herself, in an ingenious reworking of Camões, the right to be both a talented poet *and* a loving woman.

WHEN THE SKY BECOMES THE LIMIT: *CHARNECA EM FLOR*

Espanca did not publish anything else in book form during her lifetime but, according to a letter to J. E. Amaro, a manuscript bearing the title *Charneca em Flor* was at an advanced stage of composition by May 1927.[33] It is almost certain that her beloved brother's untimely death, less than a month after this letter was sent, would have made any publication plans grind to a halt. Three years later, in the summer of 1930, the opportunity to publish a now significantly increased collection arises when a retired Italian professor, Guido Battelli, contacts her after reading some of her poetry featured in *Portugal Feminino*. Six months later, at the time of her death in December 1930, an expanded *Charneca em Flor* (1931) was at the final stages of proofreading, all but ready to go to press.

The defiant voice which had begun to surface intermittently in *Livro de "Soror Saudade"* reaches an almost epic dimension in this posthumous work. Setting the tone, the eponymous "Charneca em Flor" (209) constitutes a reworking of the earlier "Renúncia," spelling out a profane orgasmic communion with nature. One of the most relevant, yet little known, facts about this ground-breaking opening sonnet is that it was first published in 1925 in *Europa*, a magazine directed by the most controversial woman writer of the modernist period, Judith Teixeira.[34] Teixeira's second collection of poetry, *Decadência* [Decadence] had been seized in 1923 by the Governo Civil de Lisboa, at the time of the scandal involving Botto and Leal.[35] That Espanca should have chosen to subsequently associate her name with that of Teixeira confirms both her willingness to push boundaries and her awareness of the disruptive power of sexuality.

In the sonnet, after shedding her nun-like clothing, which is described as "my shroud, my woollen habit" [a minha mortalha, o meu burel], the poet gradually experiences a reawakening, as her entire body comes to life: "I'm the barren heath in flower!" [Sou a charneca rude a abrir em flor!]. Her stripping off is both literal and metaphorical, for it entails shedding layers of man-made assumptions about women, which had kept her imprisoned in a virtual death. Her pagan "resurrection" is immediately followed by "Versos de Orgulho" (210) [Verses of Pride] where, in sharp contrast with the earlier "Vaidade" from *Livro de Mágoas*, Espanca asserts her individual identity, in the self-affirming verse "Because I am *I* and *I* am Someone!" [Porque eu sou Eu e porque Eu sou Alguém!]. Significantly, in the two tercets, she is able to redefine the entire world through a subjective apprehension of reality, which entails it being perceived firstly as the Eden-like blossoming landscape of her poetry, "The garden of my verses all in flower" [O jardim dos meus versos todo em flor], and secondly, and equally subversively perhaps, as her all-encompassing union with her lover: "It is your arms nestled in my arms, / The Milky Way sealing the Infinite" [São os teus braços dentro dos meus braços, / Via Láctea fechando o Infinito].

A later sonnet in the collection, "Eu" (215) [I], also further engages with previous self-definitions as it cancels out the despondent, similarly titled early version from *Livro de Mágoas,* "Eu . . ." where the poet's existence had been suspended, as was graphically inscribed in the ellipsis. Now, the poet charts an alternative course, in which her "desire to live" [ânsia de viver] becomes central to her self-definition. If, on the one hand, such yearning allows her to live life on her own terms, on the other it still leaves her to be defined by the reflection of herself she finds in her lover's gaze: "I found my gaze in yours, / And my mouth on yours!" [E achei o meu olhar no teu olhar, / E a minha boca sobre a tua boca!]. In other words, this sonnet implies that the female poet is still reliant on a male lover in order to reach completeness. As such, retrospectively at least, its foregrounding of sexuality as the main source of self-knowledge may seem problematic. Nevertheless, at the time of publication, its explicit eroticism was certainly daring.

Charneca em Flor features some of the most accomplished and sensual love sonnets ever written in the Portuguese language. It is noteworthy that a number of them engage with canonical European male literary tradition in the broadest sense, going back as far as classical tradition. For instance, the suggestive "Passeio ao Campo" (216) [Walk in the Countryside] stages a seductive woman who incites her lover to make the most of the passing moment, in a superb reworking of the "collige, virgo, rosas" motif, which successfully gives voice and agency to the female poet. This process reaches its most brilliant variation in 'Se Tu Viesses Ver-me' (218) [Ah, If You'd Come This Evening], where the waiting woman subverts social rules to become an active desiring being. In a convoluted statement, a series of conditional and temporal subordinate clauses proliferate to take over the entire sonnet, playfully leaving the sentence unfinished.

Elsewhere in the collection, female agency is established through extensive engagement with Camões, widely regarded as the greatest Portuguese love-poet. As Isabel Allegro de Magalhães perceptively points out "Supremo Enleio" (226) [Supreme Bliss] provides a textual counterpoint to Camões's "When supreme pain takes hold" [Quando a suprema dor muito aperta].[36] Likewise, as several critics have noted, the seminal "Ser Poeta" (229) provides an inspired reworking of one of Camões's most celebrated sonnets, "Love is a fire that burns but is not seen" [Amor é fogo que arde sem se ver].[37]

Espanca's bid for literary empowerment reaches its paroxysm in the middle sonnets of *Charneca em Flor,* where the body of the poet becomes part of a ritual of seduction. In "Volúpia" (238) [Desire], for instance, Espanca projects herself as endowed with an endless capacity to entrap her lover. The first stanza states unambiguously that she is seized by a profane insight, predicated upon her body, which enables her to triumph over her socially assigned lot: "in a pagan ecstasy that conquers fate" [num êxtase pagão que vence a sorte], she experiences a newfound and empowering awareness of her ability to shape her own destiny. The sonnet then asserts her power to undo conventional perceptions, as she depicts herself as a (grammatically feminine) lone cloud, improbably sweeping the wind in its wake: "the cloud that swept the north wind away" [A nuvem que arrastou o vento norte]. Quite aside from being a complete reversal of our normal apprehension of physical reality, this image cancels out that offered in the earlier "Eu. . . ." This enables her to celebrate the intoxicating power of her body in a sacrilegious, deliberately shocking, reworking of the central mass rite: "My body! It carries a strong wine within: / My kisses of evil and desire!" [— Meu corpo! Trago nele um vinho forte: / Meus beijos de volúpia e de maldade!]. Accordingly, by the close of the sonnet, her bewitching, Salome-like dance casts her passive male lover as a mere prey.

In "Ambiciosa" (234) [Daring Woman] her lack of concern for the feelings of a string of successively discarded male lovers may simply appear to constitute a role-reversal of the traditional male predatory stance, bordering at times on the sadistic.[38]

> If the claws of my hands sank
> Into a throbbing blood-drenched love . . .
> — How many savage female panthers killed
> For the pure joy of the kill!
>
> [Se as minhas mãos em garra se cravaram
> Sobre um amor em sangue a palpitar . . .
> — Quantas panteras bárbaras mataram
> Só pelo raro gosto de matar!]

Yet if, as Natália Correia convincingly argues, Espanca's later poetry provides a reworking of the myth of Diana, her amoral stance can arguably be read as the product of a conscious need to perform an almost cannibalistic cultural appropriation and role reversal, in order to destroy all false male idols.[39] Thus, not only does the poem conclude with the recognition that human love cannot ever satisfy her quest, it cannot but cast some doubt on the absolute standing of any male divinity, as implied in the lowercase spelling of

God: "The love of a man?—Such well worn ground! [. . .] / A man?—When I dream the love of a god!" [O amor dum homem?—Terra tão pisada! (. . .) / Um homem?—Quando eu sonho o amor dum deus!]. If so, this undoing of any male absolute would signal the relative place that male others, any putative god included, ultimately come to occupy in her journey towards self-definition. As the first tercet already intimated, this leaves her at the center. Yet paradoxically she can only visualize herself as a tomb-like inscription amidst nothingness: "My soul is like the tomb stone / Raised on a lone mountain" [Minha alma é como a pedra funerária / Erguida na montanha solitária]. It is tempting to see in this image an echo of Antigone's fate: undoing Creon's authority, but still doomed to die. Yet ultimately both stand as timeless symbols which question, as Butler argues, "the symbolic constraints under which liveability is established" (p.55) .

In a world where the supremacy of male gods has been displaced, Espanca increasingly looks to herself as a source of value. She comes to see herself as endowed with unrivalled demiurgic power, precisely by virtue of being a woman capable of both creation and procreation, at least theoretically. As such, in "Crucificada" (235) [The Crucified Woman], the subversion of the religious theme of crucifixion, a necessary precondition for resurrection, provides a powerful re-enactment of the earlier "Nocturno" (188) scene, where Espanca had portrayed herself as being nailed in the missionary position, while nonetheless already planning her escape route through her quietly but tellingly outstretched wings. In this later sonnet the poet, initially presented as crushed, "crucified in myself, on my arms" [Crucificada em mim, sobre os meus braços], re-emerges triumphant and able to engender eternal life: "You'll be, of another Mother, born again!" [Nascerás outra vez de uma outra Mãe!]. The ability to give everlasting fame to her lover, a reworking of yet another literary *topos* here given a female twist through the unexpected conflation of creation and procreation,[40] culminates in "Mais Alto" (240) [Higher]: as Espanca visualizes herself as a Turris Eburnea, in a sacrilegious reworking of the Assumption of the Virgin Mary, only the sky becomes the limit, and she becomes endowed with the power to redeem mankind.[41]

If the sonnets we have just examined perform a series of gendered role-reversals and appropriations in terms of female literary imagination, it is clear that marginality often becomes an empowering space for the poet, *faute de mieux*. Espanca's nonalignment enables her to carve out a space for herself as subject, most memorably perhaps in "Sou Eu!" (249), [It is Me!] and in the sonnet which immediately follows it, "Panteísmo" (250) [Pantheism].

"Sou Eu!" contains a revised self-definition which differs markedly from either of the previous sonnets titled "Eu," in that the poet is no longer dependent on either a lover or higher being in order to achieve a sense of her own worth or self. In the opening stanza, the speaker defines herself as "pagan," and is able to release her dreams to flow freely amidst an idyllic natural landscape, as birds come to rest on her shoulders. The harmonious flow of this initial stanza contrasts with the unexpectedly defiant declaration of the second stanza, which forcefully proclaims that all attempts to bury or silence her have been in vain: "In vain they buried me amid the rubble / Of vainly carved cathedrals!" [Em vão me sepultaram entre escombros / De catedrais duma escultura vã!]. This implicitly equates her with the dimensions of a pagan goddess, historically crushed by the advent of Christianity but not completely defeated.

But, contrary to what might have been expected, although Espanca is determined to recover an alternative cultural memory, never quite suppressed, it does not result in her complete liberation from prevailing cultural parameters. In the second half of the second quatrain, mathematically and thematically the turning point of the sonnet, the male sun looks on aghast, while the female clouds empathize with her plight, acknowledging her as their sister: "the blond sun beholds me, / And the weeping clouds call me sister!" [Olha-me o loiro sol tonto de assombros, / E as nuvens, a chorar, chamam-me irmã!]. The implication seems to be that the rigid enforcement of asymmetrical roles for men and women in contemporary mainstream society means that suffering still remains Florbela's socially assigned lot. The shadows which haunt the sun are nevertheless a surreptitious indication that not all is well. Furthermore the tears shed by the grammatically feminine clouds may prefigure change, if we bear in mind that, according to Chevalier and Gheebrant, clouds are "the symbol of metamorphosis" (le symbole de la métamorphose).[42]

In the first tercet, change is paradoxically evoked by recalling a remote past, from which we are told that Espanca brought the magic of her verses [a magia dos meus versos], in a timely reminder that social and gendered roles are not cast in stone, but rather historically conditioned and sedimented over time. Nevertheless, the last tercet concludes that the poet is now cut off from this magic world of primordial harmony, in other words, reduced to being a shadow of her former all-powerful self. In today's world, she seems destined to seize "the hurtful thorns and none of the roses!" [Os maus espinhos sem tocar nas rosas!], blindly grasping thorns without ever being able to reach the perfection of the roses. In a context, where artistic fulfillment and recognition was still routinely denied to women, the poet, having lost the magic powers of a pagan goddess, is doomed to become once more a martyr, like Jesus weighed under a crown of thorns but, unlike him, without hope of salvation for the time being.

Yet, crucially, in the sonnet which immediately follows, "Panteísmo"

(250), dedicated to her university friend Boto de Carvalho, she overcomes this feeling of exile in order to envisage herself once more as a goddess. Although her starting point is again an image of herself as embodied in male poetry (classical poetry in this instance), "I feel I am light and color, rhythm and glow / From a triumphal verse by Anacreon" [Sinto-me luz e cor, ritmo e clarão / Dum verso triunfal de Anacreonte!], this embodiment merely acts as a prelude to her anthropomorphized body coming to life and swelling to take over the entire natural landscape. In so doing, she becomes able to incorporate within her previously consecrated male deities. The latter become as innocent as sleeping children, having been reabsorbed into her mother-earth womb: "My soul is the deep tomb / Where the dead gods sleep, smiling!" [A minha alma é o túmulo profundo / Onde dormem, sorrindo, os deuses mortos!]. It is revealing that, once more, the gods (here in the plural) are spelt only with a lower-case, signalling their loss of status as absolutes. As the dead outside world has shrunk to fit inside her, her tomb-like (or perhaps womblike?) soul provides a powerful undoing of the center/margin dichotomy.

A metaphorical reading of this poem suggests that, in terms of creative imagination, Espanca has come full circle, at long last. Initially, her dream of being the "chosen Poetess" [Poetisa eleita] seemed overly ambitious in a patriarchal context; yet a decade later, by reformulating the premises, her divine right to absorb, neutralize, and incorporate male canonical tradition within her is asserted. Somehow, one cannot helping thinking that there is a fitting poetic justice in the fact this was the last sonnet that she proofread before her untimely death.

In the context of a collection which, as a whole, repeatedly reformulates received wisdom in order to empower the female poet, it may seem rather perplexing that the last piece, prior to the sequence of ten sonnets in the last section under the aegis of Camões's famous line "It is a longing for nothing but to long" [É um não querer mais que bem querer], should be "Teus Olhos" (254) [Your Eyes].[43] For this sonnet engages with the fact that the poet appears once more willing to be defined by the male gaze, with fatal consequences. The eyes of her lover, depicted as "medieval graves" and "eternal cathedrals" [campas medievais/ catedrais eternas] act as the deadly mirror of cultural memory. In the closing stanza, they explicitly engender her and give her the status of a fully fledged woman (although this turns out to be an unreality) so that, in fact, the momentum of the poem leads inexorably to her demise in the closing line.

> Cradle coming from heaven to my door . . .
> Oh my bed of unreal nuptials! . . .
> My dead woman's sumptuous tomb! . . .

> [Berço vindo do céu à minha porta . . .
> ó meu leito de núpcias irreais! . . .
> Meu suntuoso túmulo de morta! . . .]

In other words, through the male gaze, she is ritualistically created, shaped, and "fixed" and finally magnificently entombed as a female dead body on which the male poetic imagination can feed. Espanca's choice to end the main thrust of the collection with this particular sonnet is puzzling, so much so that we need to consider whether it was intended to be read ironically. Several clues may support such an interpretation. Firstly, the lack of dedication (in contrast to the nine other sonnets which immediately preceded it) means that the nameless "tu" becomes universal in significance, like any male lover whose gaze "petrifies" the willing female, moulding her into *history*, in a linear trajectory of dispossession leading to death. Secondly, the underlying irony becomes more obvious if we bear in mind that the poem's final close-up on the woman's deadly entrapment emphatically turns out to be a *mock* closure in the context of the collection as a whole.

As such, the collection's extended conclusion consists instead of the sequence of ten sonnets introduced, by way of epigraph, by Camões's famous line, "It is a longing for nothing but to long" [É um não querer mais que bem querer].[44] Espanca, in keeping with her famous predecessor, textualizes the irrational highs and lows of love, through her own lived, subjective experience, something of which Camões would no doubt have approved. What is of particular note is that, while the series starts off with variations on the all-encompassing nature of love, superb and wide-ranging as they may be (Sonnet IV [259] being one of the most often anthologized), from Sonnet VII (262) onwards the sequence suddenly veers off course. Simply put, the lover is left behind. In fact he is presented as dead, something which gives the female creator the freedom to reflect on the meaning of life and death, uninhibited by anyone.

On one level, one simple explanation for the change in focus, somewhat unexpected within a self-contained sequence, may be found in her correspondence. When Espanca first sent the complete manuscript of *Charneca em Flor* to Battelli, she declared it amounted to fifty-two sonnets. Moreover, she clarified that the last section, totaling six sonnets, should be introduced by Camões's famous quotation.[45] This evidence suggests that the last four sonnets, precisely the ones which no longer center on love, were in fact last minute additions (and compositions?). Given that this decision constitutes a deliberate authorial intervention, its full implications must be considered.

Sonnet VII (262), the turning-point moment, deserves careful reading, a fact of which at least some of her contemporaries were aware: it was featured in Botto and Pessoa's 1944 anthology of modern poetry, the only piece by a woman to be included.[46] The poet, as she thinks ahead to the time of her death, euphemistically evoked as "when I depart for the Land of Light" [Quando eu partir para o País da Luz], wishes she could merge with the natural world to become "the shadow of a soothing twilight" [A sombra calma dum entardecer]. Nevertheless the closing tercet expands on this metaphor in a rather curious way: embodied in a serene dusk, her shadow would become like a shroud covering the heroic body of her dead male lover/soldier, who is depicted as "placed in a cross" [posto em cruz]. This image indirectly constitutes an inversion of the earlier "Nocturno" (188) scene, where she had been the one crucified, only later going on to celebrate the ability of the self-sacrificing poet to re-engender her male lover, for instance in "Crucificada" (235). Here, likewise, Espanca portrays the female speaker as rising onto a higher plane, reborn through the power of poetry. Were we to consider the possibility that the dead lover/warrior conjured up here may be the most famous lover/soldier in Portuguese literature, the great Camões himself, the sonnet would effectively have succeeded in showing how Espanca can leave his dead shell behind, having artistically risen above him.[47]

The last three sonnets in this series alternate between proclaiming her lust for life (Sonnet VIII [263] and Sonnet X [265]), and a momentary feeling of crushing failure (Sonnet IX [264]). It may not be entirely a coincidence that the identity of the dispossessed speaker of Sonnet IX is clearly female, as foregrounded by the feminine adjective "haunted" [assombrada] in the closing line. This gender marker notwithstanding, the poet envisages herself as a (male) knight throughout, stripped of all symbols of royalty. She moreover sees herself as surviving a shipwreck but, unlike her famous predecessor, Camões, is unable to save her possessions "I threw myself into the sea and saved none" [Deitei-me ao mar e não salvei nenhuma]. This metaphorical scenario may encode her awareness of the asymmetrical fates seemingly allotted to male and female writers in the literary canon. In other words, the failure of the knight at this juncture becomes explicable precisely because s/he is female.

By contrast, however, in the sonnets on either side, which are devoid of explicit gender markers, Espanca spurs herself on with invincible enthusiasm to conquer new worlds. In particular in Sonnet X (265), the sonnet which closes both the series and the collection as a whole, her impetus to go beyond the world as it is known suggests that she may be in dialogue with Camões once more. The first stanza elaborates on her wish to push back further the boundaries of the known cosmos that lies under stars, sun, and moon, as she imagines an ever-expanding sea in perpetual flux:

> I would like the stars to be higher,
> Space more vast, the sun more creative,
> The moon brighter, greater the sea,
> The waves more rippling and more beautiful;
>
> [Eu queria mais altas as estrelas,
> Mais largo o espaço, o sol mais criador,
> Mais refulgente a lua, o mar maior,
> Mais cavadas as ondas e mais belas;]

The aesthetic beauty conjured up by this boundless cosmic vision provides a reworking of the earlier tortured "Da minha janela" (200) where the outside world was in the throes of an agonizing sense of pain, mirroring her own. Here, by contrast, Florbela can confidently go on to state her desire to open more windows, in the second stanza.

> Wider, torn wide open the windows
> Of the souls, more rose gardens blossoming,
> More mountains, more winged eagles,
> More blood on the cross of the caravels!
>
> [Mais amplas, mais rasgadas as janelas
> Das almas, mais rosais a abrir em flor,
> Mais montanhas, mais asas de condor,
> Mais sangue sobre a cruz das caravelas!]

Tellingly, as she pushes herself to the limits in her journey toward previously undiscovered worlds, the images she conjures (i.e., torn open, blossoming, bleeding) can be read as metaphorically inscribing a range of bodily female experience, a fact arguably supported by her choice of predominantly grammatically feminine words throughout the stanza.

As the final tercet indicates, only then will she have accomplished the task of living life fully and at the end of her earthly journey be able to rest in peace, "as a child asleep in its cradle!" [como dorme num berço uma criança!]. The return to the innocence of childhood, aside from allowing her to come full circle, may here also allow her to supersede gender dichotomies, as a gender neutral (albeit grammatically feminine) child.

SUICIDE AS POETIC AUTHOR(IZ)ING

If in *Charneca em Flor* material death was often recast as a prelude to potential artistic rebirth, in the posthumously published collection *Reliquiae*

(1931), Espanca often seems to envisage death simply as the ultimate female refuge, most famously perhaps in "Último Soneto de 'Soror Saudade'" (292) [Last Sonnet of "Sister Longing"], "Deixai Entrar a Morte" (300) [Make Way for Death], and "À Morte" (301) [To Death].[48]

In "Deixai Entrar a Morte" (300), she welcomes death, specifically because it provides a respite from a life marred by illegitimacy, "What am I in this world? The disinherited" [Que sou eu neste mundo? A deserdada]. As she goes on to stress, directly addressing her biological mother in the tercets, her progenitor must have endured an unbearable plight, both physical and emotional, while carrying her in her womb. The reference to her mother's own ill-fated birth evokes a more collective predicament, namely that of female suffering reproduced across several generations.

A subsequent sonnet, "À Morte" (301), addresses Death directly as a welcome motherly presence. Death not only provides solace, but is believed to have the power to overturn ill-fate, in a way that her biological mother was never able to: "in you, within you, resting in your lap / There is no sad fate, nor ill fortune" [Em ti, dentro de ti, no teu regaço / Não há triste destino nem má sorte]. This fantasizing of a return to the womb, via death, becomes tantamount to a conscious refusal to continue living life on male terms.

"À Morte" has often been interpreted as Florbela's parting words. Nonetheless, "Último Soneto de 'Soror Saudade'" (292) might equally be regarded as a literary testament of sorts, given its title. Here, the female poet, once more embodied in the excessively disembodied Soror Saudade, shows herself expecting nothing from life and feeling only contempt for a man-made world ("ugly the world" [feio o mundo] "the men hollow" [os homens vãos]). As a result, she knowingly chooses death over life. Curiously this becomes articulated as a sign of allegiance to her dead brother, to whom the sonnet is dedicated: " 'And, until death, she prayed, without lament / for *One* who had been lost upon the way!'" [E, até morrer, rezou, sem um lamento, / Por *Um* que se perdera no caminho!]. Although Espanca has been repeatedly accused of incestuous desire for her beloved brother, it is our contention that it would be more productive to read this statement as inscribing an Antigone-like last resort preference for death over life, insofar as the virginal Soror ultimately refuses, like her famous predecessor, to carry on aquiescing to sterile man-made discourses.

Espanca wrote more in the final year of her life than she had in the preceding three years. She was a regular contributor to *Portugal Feminino,* where she published both poetry and short stories; she also worked earnestly on the proofs of *Charneca em Flor* and kept a diary. There is no doubt that to the very end she wished for "Glory! . . . Fame! . . . The pride of creating!" [A glória! . . . A fama! . . . O orgulho de criar!] ("Exaltação" [203]). But, as

Anthony Soares argues, ultimately she paradoxically channeled her desire of creativity and fame through suicide, which "becomes another creation, but one where the author is erased."[49] Drawing on the words of Bronfen, "suicide implies an authorship with one's own life, a form of writing herself and writing death that is ambivalently poised between self construction and self-destruction."[50] It is unquestionable that, at least in terms of critical reception, suicide becomes a crowning act of authorship in Espanca's writing of the self, even if (or precisely because?) it meant bodily self-erasure. It enabled her to join an illustrious cast of canonical Portuguese male 'geniuses' which included Camilo Castelo Branco, Antero de Quental and, closer to her own times, Mário de Sá Carneiro. And it potentially places her among a striking female lineage within the Western canon, whose names in the twentieth-century alone would include among others Virginia Woolf, Sylvia Plath, Alejandra Pizarnik, Alfonsina Storni, and Marina Tsvetaeva.

In a specifically Portuguese context, given that suicide subsequently became, to a large extent, a taboo subject during the dictatorship, Florbela Espanca's self-willed death turned out to be the ultimate gesture of defiance, even more so than she could have ever predicted. As such, similarly to that of Antigone more than two thousand years before her, her self-immolation raised the thorny question of the need to envisage new "terms of liveability" in twentieth-century Portugal.[51]

Ten Sonnets by Florbela Espanca

Translated into English by Richard Zenith

Vanity

I dream I'm the chosen Poetess,
The one who knows and says everything,
Whose inspiration is pure and perfect,
Who in one verse can put infinity!

I dream that a verse of mine sheds light
Enough to fill the world! And delights
Even those who die of longing! Even
Those with a deep, dissatisfied soul!

I dream I'm Someone in this world . . .
The one with knowledge vast and deep,
At whose feet the whole Earth bows!

And when I ascend to heaven, dreaming,
And when in the heights I find myself flying,
I wake up from my dream . . .
And I'm nothing!

Chatelaine of Sadness

Proud and armored with disdain,
I live alone in my castle: Sorrow!
The light of every love runs by it . . .
And no one has ever entered my castle!

Chatelaine of Sadness, do you see? . . .
Whom?! . . . (My gaze always questions.)
I scan, in the distance, the sunset's shadows . . .
The silence weeps . . . nothing . . . no one comes . . .

Why do you cry, chatelaine of Sadness
All dressed in white, reading a book of hours
In the mottled shade of the stained-glass windows? . . .

At night, leaning over the parapets,
Why do you softly pray? . . . Why do you yearn? . . .
What dream do your real hands caress?

My Sorrow

My Sorrow is an ideal convent
Full of cloisters, shadows, vaults,
Whose darkly twisting stone reveals
Meticulously sculpted lines.

With agony the bells toll,
Telling their sorely felt affliction . . .
All of them make funereal sounds
On striking the hours day in, day out.

My Sorrow's a convent where there are lilies
Whose violet hue is steeped in suffering,
Their beauty such as no eyes have seen.

In that sad convent where I dwell,
Night and day I pray and weep!
And no one sees or hears me . . . no one . . .

Renunciation

I long ago placed my youth in the quiet
Convent of Sadness. Forever sequestered,
There it spends its days and nights,
Eyes closed, frail hands in a cross . . .

The Moon outside, Satan, tempts me!
It blossoms into shimmers of Beauty . . .
Nature is like an ardent kiss . . .
My cell is like a river of light . . .

Shut tight your eyes! See nothing at all!
Turn yet paler! And, resigned,
Throw your arms round a greater cross!

Make the shroud that wraps you colder!
Fill your mouth with earth and ashes,
O my youth in your full flower!

From my Window

High sea! Vanquished waves
That break with whispered, troubled sighs . . .
Immaculate, weightless flight of gulls,
Like snows emerging on the hilltops!

Sun! Falling bird, still flapping
Its wounded wings while gasping for breath . . .
To you, sweet tortured sunset, I lift
My hands in inward prayer, weeping!

O my charming verse of Samain,
Not yet daylight, already you're moonlight,
Like a white lilac whose flowers wither!

Love! I carry your heart in my breast . . .
It pounds within me like this sea
In an endless, never withering kiss! . . .

Exaltation

To live! . . . To drink the wind and sun! . . .
To lift up to the sky our throbbing
Hearts! God made our arms for grasping!
And gave us mouths of blood for kissing!

The always red-glowing flame on high! . . .
The always straying wings that soar
Still higher, ready to uproot the stars! . . .
Glory! . . . Fame! . . . The pride of creating! . . .

Life's honey and life's bitterness
Dwell in the lake of my eyes like violets
And in my ecstatic, pagan kisses! . . .

The heart of carnations fills my mouth!
O bohemians, tramps and poets,
How truly, Brothers, I'm your Sister!

Heath in Flower

The tremor caused by painful things
Fills my breast by some strange charm . . .
Beneath the scorched heather, roses
Sprout . . . I stanch the tears in my eyes . . .

Yearning! Spread wings! What do I harbor
Within? I hear silent lips
Whisper to me mysterious words
That ruffle my being, like a caress!

Invaded by this anxious fever,
I throw off my shroud, my woollen habit,
And cease, O Love, to be Sister Longing . . .

My eyes are burning with love's ecstasies,
My lips smack of sun and fruit and honey:
I'm the barren heath in flower!

Ah, if you'd come this evening

Ah, if you'd come this evening to see me
At that hour of magic weariness,
When softly night begins to fall,
And hold me tightly in your arms . . .

When I recall the taste I tasted
On your lips . . . your footsteps' echo . . .
Your laughter like a spring . . . your hugs . . .
Your kisses . . . your hand in mine . . .

Ah, if you'd come when my lovely, mad lips
Trace the honeysweet lines of a kiss
And are like red silk, singing and laughing,

And are like a carnation in the sun . . .
When my eyes close, full of desire,
And my arms reach out to you. . . .

It's Me!

to Laura Chaves

Over the fields, over the knolls,
Over the hills that cradle the morning,
I scatter my glowing pagan dreams
While birds alight on my shoulders . . .

In vain they buried me amid the rubble
Of vainly carved cathedrals! Dizzy
With wonder, the blond sun beholds me,
And the weeping clouds call me sister!

Far echoes of waves . . . of universes . . .
Echoes of a world . . . of a distant Beyond,
From where I brought my verses' magic!

It's me! It's me! The one who, like no one,
Plucked from life with anxious hands
The hurtful thorns and none of the roses!

Make Way for Death

Make way for Death, the Illuminated
Who comes to take me away from here.
Fling wide open all the doors
Like flapping wings of birds in flight.

What am I in this world? The disinherited,
Who with her hands seized all the moonlight,
The dream, the earth, the sea, all life,
Then opened her hands, and found nothing!

O Mother, dear Mother, why were you born?
Why, tell me, amidst such agonies
And horrid pains did you carry me

Inside you? . . . Just so that I could be
The bitter fruit that in evil hour
Was given birth by a lily's womb! . . .

2
Irene Lisboa: Minding the Gender Gap

There is irony and weariness in my eyes

Há nos meus olhos ironias e cansaços.
> —José Régio, *Poemas de Deus e do Diabo*

I thought of the organ booming in the chapel and of the shut doors of
the library; and I thought how unpleasant it is to be locked out; and I
thought how it is worse perhaps to be locked in.
> —Virginia Woolf, *A Room of One's Own*

IF, AS THE PRECEDING CHAPTER OUTLINED, FLORBELA ESPANCA STRUGGLED
to achieve recognition as a talented writer in the first quarter of the twentieth
century, from the 1930s onwards the political climate of Salazar's dictatorship placed additional constraints on women writers. Research by Ana Paula
Ferreira has convincingly shown the ways in which its authoritarian, family-
oriented ethos, which enshrined women's reproductive rather than productive capacities, was undoubtedly detrimental to their visibility and concomitantly to their critical appreciation.[1] Although women did continue to
publish, the extent to which they were excluded for their differences at the
point of reception is telling: for instance, only a handful made it into anthologies and literary histories, which have such a prominent role to play in the
shaping of the literary canon. This may be explained by sexist assumptions
on the part of male literary critics, be they overt or latent, and is furthermore
compounded by the fact that female writers did not fit seamlessly into dominant literary schools. Most crucially, their works were often not reprinted,
making them virtually inaccessible to the wider public in the long run and
hindering the creation of a female literary tradition.[2]

One particularly relevant case study is that of Irene Lisboa (1892–1958).
Widely perceived as the most exceptional woman of her generation, she cou-
rageously opted to finance the publication of her works when publishers
were not forthcoming, and steadfastly refused to produce a novel, despite
ongoing pressure from influential male counterparts from the *Presença* gener-

70

ation, such as Régio and Gaspar Simões, with whom she corresponded extensively during the 1930s.[3] Her nonconformist attitude meant that she
attracted scant critical attention until Paula Morão's doctoral thesis in the
late 1980s began to recover her from near oblivion,[4] paving the way for a
critical edition of her oeuvre in the early 1990s.[5]

This chapter examines a selection of Lisboa's works from the 1930s
through the 1950s, arguing that her unwillingness to fit into existing literary
molds is a rhetorical strategy through which she seeks to question universaliz-
ing and essentialist assumptions which effectively disempower women writers at the various stages of literary production. Ultimately her writings expose
the concept of "genius" itself as gendered.

Irene Lisboa was born in 1892 and came of age during the very year in
which the old monarchy gave way to the progressive, if shortlived, new Republic. This coincidence seems fitting on a symbolic level for, despite the
odds staked against her in early life, her adult trajectory is that of an emancipated woman: educated, financially independent, and single. Born out of
wedlock to a young peasant mother (a story which bears some resemblances
to that of Florbela Espanca), she was raised, from the age of three, by her
elderly father and his long-term companion, who became her godmother.
His subsequent marriage to a much younger woman, and ensuing favoring
of his legitimate family, led to her complete displacement as a teenager. Neglected, mistreated, and eventually disowned from the paternal home, Lisboa
was left to fend for herself in Lisbon, in the company of her ailing elderly
godmother.

Despite this inauspicious start in life, she completed secondary schooling,
trained as a primary school teacher, and went on to become an expert in the
field of primary education. After more than a decade as a classroom teacher,
she spent three years studying in Switzerland, France, and Belgium (1929–
32), where she completed advanced training. Upon her return to Portugal,
she was promoted to the job of Inspectora-Orientadora and was active in
disseminating her research in the field of progressive educational theory and
practice, through several articles in *Seara Nova,* under the male pseudonym
of Manuel Soares.[6] In particular, her theoretical and practical writings outlined the importance of drawing for child development and anticipated the
field of modern-day art therapy. Her liberal ideas earned her the opposition
of the Salazar regime, led to a desk job in 1938, and culminated in her virtual
dismissal in 1940, when still in her professional prime, she was given no
realistic option but to accept early retirement at the relatively young age of
forty-eight.

Her first literary work, *13 contarelos* [13 Insignificant Tales], a self-
published volume of short stories for children, dates from 1926, the year

which marks the end of the Republic and the start of a new military regime, during which Salazar first rose to prominence. After a ten-year hiatus, her return to literary activity occurred in a transformed political landscape, after the consolidation of Salazar's Estado Novo, with two collections of poetry under the male pseudonym of João Falco, in 1936 and 1937. Although all her works published between 1936 and 1940 bear this male signature, her debut poetry collection *Um dia e outro dia . . .* (1936) [One Day and Another . . .] is subtitled "diário de uma mulher" [A Woman's Diary] while her actual diary *Solidão* (1939) [Solitude] features the subtitle "notas do punho de uma mulher" [Notes Penned by a Woman].[7] Thus, the discrepancy between the individualized male signature and the anonymity of the "uma mulher," whose identity is relegated to the subtitle almost as a footnote, an anonymity further compounded by the use of the indefinite article, flags up the paradox of female authorship in both cases. The speaking subject is clearly a woman, but it appears that her voice can only come into the public domain through embodiment in a male persona.

The subtitle of Lisboa's first collection, "diário de uma mulher," is thought-provoking on other counts too, since the autobiographical genre is normally associated with prose writing. Her brand of poetry is very different indeed from that of both her immediate predecessors (the *Orpheu* generation) and her peers (the *Presença* generation, known as the "presencistas"): it makes predominant use of *vers libre*, to be sure, but an almost nonpoetic kind of blank verse, which contrasts with the rhetorical outpourings of the likes of Fernando Pessoa's famous heteronym, Álvaro de Campos, or her more immediate contemporary José Régio. Her disregard for overblown rhetoric is epitomized at the outset of her second poetry collection, *Outono havias de vir* (1937) [Autumn, You Had to Come], when she teasingly declares in the epigraph "Call verse what seems like verse to you and call everything else prose" [ao que vos parecer verso chamai verso e ao resto chamai prosa].[8]

Her ongoing disruption of readers' expectations is accentuated even further in the diary *Solidão* (1939) and the autobiographical novella *Começa uma vida* (1940) [A Life Begins], as she chooses to explore both her inner world and the world around her through less established prose genres than the canonical novel.[9] Given, on the one hand, the authoritarian dictatorship and, on the other, the regimented literary programs endorsed by her male contemporaries, which included major "presencistas" such as Régio and Gaspar Simões but also, from the 1940s onwards, the major neorealists, her choice of form may be perceived as a rejection of male discursive methods in favor of fluidity, hybridity, and nonlinearity. In other words, it signals an attempt to articulate experiences from a consciously marginalized position.

Such marginal location would be heightened in *Esta cidade!* (1942) [This City!] and *Apontamentos* (1943) [Sketched Notes], since these works resolutely position themselves outside mainstream literary practice, not only because of their unclassifiable nature in terms of genre, but also because of their status as self-published texts.[10] Her choice to publish again under her own name, for the first time since the publication of *13 Contarelos,* is nonetheless indicative of a renewed sense of ownership of female authorship.

A (B)LOG OF ONE'S OWN

In her first collection of poetry, *Um dia e outro dia* . . . Lisboa displays considerable skill in the way she invites her readers to question their expectations. For instance, the fact that she provocatively attributed the same title, "outro dia" [another day], to a succession of poems suggests that they may be so indistinguishable as to be interchangeable, thus undermining the linear premises of a "grand narrative." In terms of playing with readers' expectations, the most striking moment in the first section comes when the surface monotony of a series of "outro[s] dia[s]" is unexpectedly interrupted with a poem entitled "outro dia, na praia" (151–52) [another day, on the beach]. The variation in the title immediately draws attention to it as an exception. The different location, a natural space, might suggest an opening, but in practice it merely acts as a backdrop in which traditional gender roles appear to be reconfirmed. Yet as we shall see, over the course of five stanzas, fixed roles become subtly called into question through excessive iteration.

In the opening stanza, the male Sun is felt to have invincible powers to "dominate, / possess / and weaken" [dominar, / possuir / e enfraquecer], to such an extent that the identity of the vulnerable female poet would dissolve into no more than an inanimate, flat stretch of sand. The second stanza describes her as being metaphorically penetrated "The Sun [. . .] domineering, hot and invading, takes care of my body" [O sol (. . .) dominador, / quente e invasor / toma-me conta do corpo]. The reiteration of the concept of domination, coupled with the adjective "invasor" or "invading," stresses asymmetrical power relations, whereby the female body is colonized. Lisboa briefly resists this metaphorical intrusion, expressing in the third stanza the wish to write and think, which she equates with an attempt to triumph over the Sun: "I wanted to write, to think . . . / Nonsense! / I wanted to defeat the sun . . ." [Queria escrever, pensar . . . /Tolice! / Queria vencer o sol . . .] But her attempts are in vain for, as the fourth stanza indicates, he is "King and lord" [Rei e senhor . . .]. In response to his purposeful "firm hand which brings down / and sets on fire the body / which exposes itself to him"

[Mão firme / que abate / e incendeia o corpo / que se lhe expõe], dissidence is perceived as impossible.[11]

In the last stanza, Lisboa surrenders entirely. But, tellingly in fact, she begs "Sun! / Master me, lull me to sleep! / Turn me into the sister of sand" [Sol! / vence-me, adormece-me! / irmana-me com a areia] in an overblown plea to become putty in his hands. Her voluntarily capitulation into nothingness is so explicitly self-defeating that it becomes difficult not to read it as a spoof. If read out of context, the poem may inscribe femininity as bodily destiny. But if we situate it within the collection as a whole, as it was indeed meant to be understood, it is difficult not to interpret it ironically. Not only does this piece take up all the clichés of the male Sun as king of the universe and the woman as passive, its language encodes violent and asymmetrical power relations to such an extent that it becomes an oblique, satirical comment on men's unchallenged supremacy. This supremacy occurs at the expense of women, yet, as Lisboa lucidly implies, is ultimately perpetuated with their complicity.

By contrast, several earlier "outro[s] dia[s]" show the extent to which Lisboa seeks to bypass, question, and undo the existing gender gap, by mapping out alternative perspectives. Typical in many respects is a long "outro dia" (72–81) early on, where Lisboa addresses the rain:

> I vaguely recalled
> some banal sentences,
> used in everyday language,
> dedicated to you.
> And in reality I thought
> that they weren't yet sufficient,
> that new ones should be invented . . .
>
> [vagamente me lembrei
> de certas frases banais,
> entradas na linguagem,
> que te têm dedicado.
> E, realmente, achei
> que ainda não bastavam,
> que outras mais
> deviam ser inventadas . . .] (73–74)

In so doing, in what may be an indirect allusion to Verlaine's famous "Il pleure dans mon coeur," and its subsequent Portuguese reworkings, the poet is engaging with literary tradition in order to highlight its inadequacies.[12] Yet, despite her bid to renew old motifs, Lisboa feels unappreciated as a

writer. As a result, she is led to ponder on her perceived lack, wittily highlighted through a series of neologisms, created using the negating prefix "in":
"incultura" [lack of culture], "incortesia" [lack of courtesy], "insistemática"
[unsystematic]. Ironically, the one existing word starting with an 'in' featured in the course of the poem is "inferioridade" [inferiority].

Nonetheless, despite her (excessively reiterated) deficiencies, she goes on
to stress that she will not give up the right to put across her point of view.

> *However,*
> now that I yield myself without fear
> to the *lack of systematization,*
> to the *lack of intelligence,*
> to the banality
> and to the very vulgarity
> of writing badly [. . .]
> I distance myself without regret
> from those with culture and knowledge.

> [*Porém,*
> hoje que me dou sem rebuço
> à *insistematização,*
> à *ininteligência,*
> à banalidade
> e à propria vulgaridade
> de escrever mal (. . .)
> sem pena me aparto
> dos cultos e dos sabedores] (77) (our italics)

This wry assertion of her right to "write badly" or "escrever mal," intended
to prompt readers to consider the validity of prevailing definitions of what
might be classified as "good" writing, leads her to part company from those
endowed with knowledge. This she does "without regret," "sem pena," a
witty *double entendre* in Portuguese since it also means "without a pen." As a
result, even when considered to be part of a lesser world, described as worm-
like, she still yearns to

> . . . affirm,
> to shout even!
> that the vegetating world
> of worms of my ilk
> has the right to exist

> [. . . afirmar,
> bradar mesmo!

que o mundo vegetativo
dos vermes da minha conformação
tem o direito de existir](79)

Although her right to speak up despite her supposed inferiority is here confidently stated, in another "outro dia" (142–48), she enters in dialogue with herself and her readers, seemingly doubting the point of producing the kind of dissonant poetry that she so carefully crafts.

Is there any value
(most probably not!)
in striking sounds without music,
in telling, repeatedly,
that which is not of interest to anyone else?
that which does not produce accords?

[Haverá algum valor,
(decerto não há!)
em ferir sons sem música,
em contar, repetir
o que a mais ninguém interessa?
o que não suscita acordos?] (144)

As her rhetorical question probes the wholesale value of her enterprise, which does not lead to consensus or "acordos," the bracketed negative comment "most probably not!" (decerto não há!) early on confirms that, from the perspective of the literary establishment, her aesthetics of dissonance are most likely devoid of value. But this excessive assertion undoes itself, serving to raise doubt in her own mind, and possibly in that of her readers too. This is all the more the case given that, in the next stanza, the importance of her dissident aesthetics becomes inscribed in an adversative conjunction (recalling the strategic one-line "Porém" of the earlier poem).

But there has come a time
in my life,
a time of inconformity
and exaltation,
when I need to speak out. . . .

[*Mas* uma hora chegou
da minha vida,
hora de inconformação
e de exaltação,
em que preciso de falar . . .] (144) (our italics)

While the use of the word "exaltação" is reminiscent of Florbela's ground-breaking sonnet "Exaltação" discussed in the previous chapter, this statement also stands out for its use of the verb "falar" (to speak out) as opposed to "escrever" (to write). According to conventional perceptions, writing would presuppose more skill than speaking. But "falar," recalling the earlier "bradar" or "cry out," is a strategy of survival for the female self, which eschews man-made rhetoric. It thereby disrupts consecrated binary oppositions such as writing versus speaking.

This exemplary poem concludes over its three closing stanzas with a discussion of whether the label of "true" artist (i.e. potential genius) is applicable to Lisboa. Firstly she states

> Ah, I'm not an artist, oh no,
> a woman who can master
> and cultivate a gift . . .
> I am merely,
> a human being,
>
> [Ah, não sou artista, não,
> senhora
> e cultora de um dom . . .
> Sou um ser humano,
> apenas,] (148)

The next stanza, however, questions the (gendered) parameters which determine genius: "But . . . / are artists only those who invent fiction?" [Mas . . . / artista é só aquele que cria a ficção? (148)] not least through the subtle but effective use of her trademark adversative "Mas . . ." or "But . . .", to speculate on the validity of existing definitions, here heightened by the use of ellipsis. Her probing into fixed ideas of what constitutes an artist is so skillful that, by the closing line of the poem, when she states categorically "No, I'm not an artist!" [Não, não sou artista! (148)], she has in fact subverted ingrained assumptions, having made her readers wonder who and what determines artistic value. As such, this final exclamation must be read, at least in part, ironically. Indeed, the strategic dislocation of the negative "Não" to the beginning of this closing sentence, in a chiasmus-like mutation from the first outpouring "Ah, I'm not an artist, oh no" [Ah, não sou artista, não (148)], subliminally draws attention to the way in which any seemingly definitive assertion is susceptible of revision, raising the possibility of precisely the opposite statement being equally true.

There is no doubt that Lisboa was deeply aware of the constraints and

pitfalls of writing as a woman in an overwhelmingly male-dominated landscape. As she declares in yet another "outro dia" (181–83),

> Because my aesthetics
> (and those of others?)
> are the consequence,
> the very real reflection,
> of my cramped life
>
> [Porque a minha estética
> (e a dos outros?)
> é a consequência,
> o real reflexo
> da minha acanhada vida] (182)

As she foregrounds the influence of life circumstances (including gender) on
aesthetic practice, the bracketed question, interrupting the flow of the sentence, interrogates the universality of man-made aesthetics and unobtrusively
implies that they, too, may be simply the product of external historical con-
tingencies.

In the second section, where poems do not bear the title "outro dia," the
poem "princípios de julho" [Beginning of July] (220–24) goes one step further, inscribing the impossibility of truly being/thinking/writing like a man:
"if only I were / or could be . . . / that untroubled prose writer!" [Se eu
fosse, / ou pudesse ser . . . / aquele tranquilo prosador! (222)]. Instead, Lisboa
vividly conveys her feeling of being torn apart:

> as if inside myself
> there were two . . .
> two ablaze
> inside my single body . . .
>
> [como se em mim
> duas houvesse . . .
> duas que se conflagrassem
> no meu único corpo . . .] (223)

This passage inscribes the impossible choice facing female creators, incisively
described by Battersby as follows: "a woman who created was faced with a
double bind: either to surrender her sexuality (becoming not *masculine*, but
a surrogate *male*), or to be *feminine* and *female*, and hence to fail to count as
a genius."[13] (italics in the original).

However great the lure of attempting to become a "surrogate *male*" may be, Lisboa is aware of its empty promises. Accordingly, the second section of *Um dia e outro dia* . . . concludes with "princípios de agosto" [Beginning of August] (233–34), a poem where she voices her fantasy of becoming omnipotent, in charge of the world and able to define its perimeter.

> If only I
> could renegate myself
> and be reborn! [. . .]
> With my hand stretched out,
> trace a circle;
> sit inside it
> and survey the world from there . . .
> a circle
> which I myself could expand,
> or reduce. [. . .]
>
> [Quem me dera
> poder renegar-me
> e renascer! . . .
> Com a mão estendida
> traçar um círculo;
> nele me sentar
> e dele ver o mundo . . .
> Círculo
> que eu própria alargasse,
> ou reduzisse . . .] (233)

The understated irony of the line "or reduce . . ." [ou reduzisse . . .], in the light of her use of ellipsis to convey a reductionist way of mapping out the world, is especially witty. As a result, the end of the poem portrays male demiurgic impulses as both unattainable and limited in scope. For Lisboa is acutely aware that, if her wish to deny her gender came true, she would merely join the conformist ranks of the male literary establishment, whose mastery (senhorio) she caricatures as stilted creativity (conformação).

> My [. . .]
> never attained
> field of repose,
> *conformity,*
> and *mastery!*
>
> [O meu (. . .)
> nunca alcançado

> campo de paz,
> de *conformação,*
> e *de senhorio!* (234) (our italics)

In those circumstances, bound by her "acanhada vida" by virtue of being female, and therefore liable to "fail to count as a genius" (to recall Battersby's postulation), yet completely unrepentant, Lisboa opts to carry on as the outsider, denouncing the existing status quo through her almost invisible irony. In so doing, she is fully aware that she risks being misunderstood. Indeed, her second collection, *Outono havias de vir,* features an arresting poem, aptly titled "A ironia" [Irony] (316), where she lucidly reflects on what is at stake when she enacts intellectual resistance.[14]

> I'd like irony, my irony, to be so controlled
> and intelligent, so discreet, so independent and
> so dry that it would *go almost unnoticed.*

> [A ironia, a minha ironia, queria-a eu tão medida
> e inteligente, tão rebuçada, tão independente e
> tão seca mesmo, que *mal fosse percebida.*] (316) (our italics)

It is possible to read additional ambiguity into the last phrase, insofar as it might be taken to mean both "hardly understood" and (in a more pedestrian word by word reading) "misunderstood." Indeed, as Lisboa goes on to stress, she relishes being misunderstood.

> I'd like my quiet and almost serious irony to be my fortress.
> It fell asleep, my besiegers would say
> (what a marvelous word: besiegers!)—
> those on the outside who comment on intentions, intimacies.

> [Que a minha ironia calada e quase séria fosse o meu baluarte.
> Adormeceu diriam os sitiantes.
> (Sitiantes, rica palavra!)
> Os que estão de fora e comentam intenções, intimidades.] (316)

In other words, the assailants, who may be taken here as referring to the male critics who presume to pass comment on female authorial intentions, are likely to see her as harmlessly asleep. Yet from the fortress of her irony, the beleaguered woman writer is in fact protected from their intrusion and can plot her escape, freely poking fun at their "marvelous words" or "ricas palavras" which she can, as brilliantly evidenced here, appropriate and turn on their head.

Lisboa's poetry shows her profound awareness of the extent to which the "vocabularies of aesthetic praise and those of sexual difference" are inextricably intertwined.[15] Through her devastating use of irony, she deliberately resists these vocabularies and the sexist assumptions which underpin them, in a way that was entirely pioneering for the period. Perhaps unsurprisingly, the majority of male critics (with the possible exception of José Gomes Ferreira) failed to appreciate her true intentions. After twice attemping to challenge prevailing assumptions about literary worth in the context of a canonical genre, that of poetry, Lisboa refrained from publishing any other verse collection. Instead, she went on to negotiate her marginal position through less canonical prose genres.[16]

MINDING ONE'S OWN BUSINESS . . .

Solidão, still published under the pseudonym of João Falco, is Lisboa's first venture into a more conventional diary format insofar as, unlike *Um dia e outro dia . . . ,* it is actually a prose-work. Given the relative scarcity of diaries in Portuguese literature at that point in time, this format still allows her considerable freedom to innovate. For instance, *Solidão* does not feature one of the fundamental ingredients of the diary: dates for individual entries. Yet Lisboa does not completely spurn chronological time markers either (two out of three of the overarching sections are in fact dated, even though they are not featured in chronological order), but her tendency to break conventional rules in order to tell *her*story is much in evidence throughout. In this context, the importance of the opening fragment must be emphasized, as it attempts to map out Lisboa's woman-centered aesthetics, in dialogue with canonical male-authored literature.

The opening sentence of *Solidão,* "How sad is the pleasure that a woman may find in crying for her/self, in saying without rebellion 'my cold house, my cold house . . . my inhospitable world . . .'" [É triste o gozo que uma mulher pode ter de se chorar, de dizer sem rebeldia: 'Minha casa fria, minha casa fria . . . Meu mundo inóspito . . .' (15)] clearly foregrounds gender (uma mulher) as a constitutive element of the self. It furthermore explicitly links femaleness with suffering and tears. This echoes one of most famous narratives in the Portuguese literary tradition, the sixteenth-century novel *Menina e Moça* [Young Girl and Maiden] by Bernardim Ribeiro, where female destiny was emphatically equated with tears through the mouth of its first-person female narrator. Closer to Lisboa's own times, it is also reminiscent of Florbela Espanca's privileging (and eventual subversion) of "dor" or "sorrow" as a specifically female mode of apprehending reality, inscribed in her inaugural *Livro de Mágoas*.

Lisboa is aware that "se chorar," crying for oneself, as if mourning for a lost self, or "dizer sem rebeldia" [saying without rebellion], only leads at best to the articulation of an all-pervasive sense of displacement. Thus, the speaking self becomes exiled both within "the cold house" [a casa fria] and without "the inhospitable world" [o mundo inóspito (15)], leaving her bereft of a sense of belonging and, by extension, identity. As she brings this opening fragment to a close, Lisboa objectifies herself by comparing herself to a metaphorically doomed house: "I look at myself like a dark house. That window which I sometimes attempt to open towards the sky, clumsily shuts itself at once" [olho-me como a uma casa escura. Aquela janela que às vezes quero abrir para o ar, logo desastradamente se cerra (15)]. This image suggests her entombment, calling to mind once more Espanca's hyperbolic figurations in her inaugural collection of the imprisoned princess/nun, walled up in a metaphorical convent of grief (for instance in "A Minha Dor" [138], "Lágrimas Ocultas" [136]). Any attempt to open a window of communication with the outside world results in defeat, silence, and near-complete obliteration.

But significantly, half-way through this fragment, Lisboa does emphatically stress that, for all its seeming inefficacy, she will not give up on the right to lament herself, "I lament myself, I want to lament myself" [eu lamento-me, quero-me lamentar (15)]. This constitutes an empowering assertion in a cultural context in which women were expected to bear their crosses silently. The role of the lament as a speech act becomes thus invested with a positive value, for despite implying an almost masochist suffering, it also becomes the flagship of someone who remains endowed with a voice against all odds. As such, the confessional outpouring becomes a reaction against the threat of silencing which might otherwise lead to asphyxia or even aphasia. The fact that this potentially empowering streak is articulated half-way through, rather than at the end of the fragment as a logical conclusion, disrupts linear progression and, by extension, historical fatality.

In this context of seeking to find her own voice as a woman (writer), it is revealing that the first explicit literary allusion, as early as the third page of *Solidão,* is in fact to Florbela Espanca. Lisboa's engagement with Espanca despite of, or perhaps because of, the fact that her deceased peer was a writer who, at that point in time, had already begun to be rejected by the dictatorship is most significant. In her second collection of poetry, Lisboa had already made a wry oblique reference to her predecessor in the poem "Passeios" [Walks], summarily dismissing Florbela as "flower-like," in other words, as precious and elitist.[17] Here, likewise, Lisboa's main purpose seems to position herself beyond her dead contemporary: "I started to read Fb's sonnets, which I hadn't read for quite a while. The woman is truly a Parnassian, lascivious and measured. She is a worker of intricate verse and a sensualist. Her grief is luminous, dazzling, coherent and elegant" [pus-me a ler os sonetos da Fb., que há muito tempo não lia. Esta mulher é realmente uma parnasiana, lasciva e medida. É uma delicada trabalhadora do verso e uma sensualista. A sua dor é radiosa, iluminada, coerente e elegante (17)]. Lisboa notes the sensuality which springs forth from Espanca's verses, but abundantly qualifies it with words implying self-restraint and artifice. In other words, Espanca's aesthetics act only as a springboard to enable Lisboa to clarify her own dissident poetics, as she strives instead toward spontaneity and simplicity: "I aspire to the most *extraordinary* art, that of unveiling the disorder of the mind, its confusion [. . .] but simply, spontaneously" [ambiciono a mais *extraordinária* arte, a de pôr a nu a desordem do espírito, a confusão (. . .) mas châmente, espontaneamente (17) (our italics)]. Lisboa's own definition of genius, which goes against the grain, is curiously stated in specific opposition to a female forerunner, whose thought she still perceives, perhaps unjustly, as being entirely imprisoned in man-made form and language.

Espanca's style is not the only feature of her writing with which Lisboa takes issue. While her predecessor intermittently found empowerment through love, (admittedly a physical love which subversively recentered her sense of self through the body as seen in chapter 1), Lisboa resolutely rejects the notion of a romantic happy ending altogether. A few pages later, this rejection is expanded on in connection with yet another female writer, Katherine Mansfield (identified only by her initials, K.M. in the text). As she disagrees with the romantic ending of one of her English-speaking predecessor's diary fragments, Lisboa rewrites the love-script in order to stress the disjunction between male and female expectations of love (39–41).

If Lisboa does not find immediate affinities with her female predecessors, equally revealing is another outpouring shortly after, where her gender is shown to curtail the path to creativity: "And I, a woman, a whole living being, leaning aimlessly against the porch on a doorstep! Far from me all correspondences. Far away or impossible!" [E eu, uma mulher, um ser íntegro, vivo, encostada para ali à ombreira de uma porta! Longe de mim todas as correspondências. Longe, ou impossíveis! (42)]. Lisboa describes herself as condemned to remain marginalized, literally on the doorstep. Her problematic access to love, culture, and language is here flagged up through what may be an indirect reference to Baudelaire's landmark sonnet, "Correspondences," and seems to rest specifically on the fact that she is "uma mulher," an anonymous (albeit fully-fledged) woman. In other words, man-made culture denies her poetic access to (self) expression on equal terms.

It is evident that neither the Western male literary canon nor any sketchy female tradition, be it Portuguese or English-speaking, can afford Lisboa an unproblematic entry-point into literary practice. As such, the first part of the diary concludes with a four page-long interpellation addressed to an "Amigo" (58–62) (Male Friend) whose identity is not disclosed. Lisboa responds to his (less than favorable) critical appreciation of the manuscript she had sent him to comment on. Although at first she seems to agree with him, it becomes apparent that she is both unable and unwilling to change her style: "To write is to persist, to go on persisting" [Escrever é teimar, teimar (62)].

As if to illustrate the extent of this gender gap, the second section of her diary features a self-contained piece, entitled "Pastoral" (69–74), in which Lisboa adopts the voice of an alter-ego, an illiterate shepherdess. In what constitutes, whether consciously or not, a brilliant reworking of Pessoa's heteronym, Alberto Caeiro, and his "Guardador de rebanhos" [Keeper of Sheep] from a gender-inflected perspective, the uneducated shepherdess laments her lover's inconstancy, thus drawing attention to the asymmetrical social and cultural positions of men and women.[18]

Lisboa's awareness of a gendered artistic conflict manifests itself particularly acutely in the third and last section of *Solidão,* for instance, as she dwells on three separate occasions on the work of Thomas Mann (86, 118–19, 121). Despite clear admiration for his artistic achievements, she pointedly remarks that his work reveals "an opposition, a conflict between the *man* and the *artist*" [uma oposição, um conflito entre o *homem* e o *artista* (italics in the original) (121)]. By contrast, her own artistic practice does not shy away from incorporating herself in her texts, as both woman and artist. Ultimately, then, Lisboa is clearly unwilling and unable to surrender her gender allegiances in order be counted in as a "surrogate *male*" (to recall Battersby's formulation), preferring instead to take issue and mock the idiosyncratic and inconsistent tendencies of male critics at the point of reception.

This she does cogently in an often quoted discussion where she addresses the vexed question of the validity of distinguishing between male and female artistic practice (136–38). Lisboa rejects any simple sexual dichotomy predicated upon biological premises, which so often leads to double standards in critical reception. Firstly, as she points out with a compelling argument, many men might fall under the category of "mentally feminine": "It wouldn't be the law of sexual physiology that divides, since many men would come under the category of *mentally feminine"* [Não seria a ordem fisiológica sexual que dividiria, porque muitos homens entrariam na categoria de *femininos mentais* (137) (italics in the original)]. Secondly, she indicates that these categories are in any case man-made: "men, always accustomed to divisions and definitions, separate themselves from women, even in the field of intelligence, without reason!" [os homens sempre habituados às divisões e definições, se separam das mulheres, mesmo no campo da inteligência, sem razão! (137)].

Finally she adduces the names of two well-known American women writers, coincidentally both born the same year as her, although she does not refer to this fact. The first is Agnes Smedley, an American political activist, and author of three books on China throughout the 1930s, who would go on to write her most famous work *Battle Hymn of China* in 1943. Lisboa pertinently asks "Don't the physical and social conditions of our lives per chance actively influence our mental structures?" [As condições físicas e sociais da vida não influirão activamente na nossa estrutura mental? (138)] going on to make the point that Smedley "is likely to have gone to war like a man" [devia ter feito a guerra como um homem (138)]. Although she does not draw further inferences from this fact, the implications are clear: once women are given access to the public sphere, their language, style and subject-matter may well change accordingly. In other words, for better or for worse, biology is emphatically not destiny.

Lisboa then moves on to analyze Pearl Buck's novel *The Mother*. While she singles out its many qualities, this work is clearly not the kind of artistic achievement that Lisboa has any desire to emulate. Nevertheless, she uses it to argue that "it is surely not this feeling of order, of reality and of clarity that is ordinarily considered typical of *feminine art*" [não é seguramente este sentido de ordem, de realidade e de nitidez que de ordinário se considera apanágio da *arte feminina* (138) (italics in the original)]. It is worth noting that, just over two years after this fragment was written, Buck would go on to win the Nobel Prize in 1938, the first American woman writer to do so. For it suggests that, just as Lisboa had sensed, Buck was writing in a "universal" style, one which could therefore be readily appreciated and rewarded by a Nobel jury.

Through the example of these gifted women writers who, plainly put, can write like men, Lisboa is questioning the flawed premises of an essentialist worldview. The closing paragraph of her discussion is the most revealing. Smedley and Buck are not, according to Lisboa, to be pigeon-holed as exceptional in a putative parallel female universe: "If they are exceptional minds, they should be so in the world at large" [Se são espíritos de eleição, sê-lo-ão no mundo em geral (138)]. In other words, she deconstructs man-made criteria for the definition of genius, since it conveniently excludes women from greatness and the literary canon on the basis of biology.

One significant problem for Lisboa and by extension all other Portuguese women of her generation, however, stemmed directly from the ideology promoted by the emergent dictatorship which made social mobility through education (a possibility from which many women such as herself and Espanca had benefited in the closing years of the monarchy increasingly difficult. According to Lisboa, in the more equalitarian theoretical discourse of the First Republic, social difference had been primarily regarded as a contingent historical accident (and presumably this is an argument that, by extension, could be applied to gendered differences too). By contrast, under Salazar, it has become perceived as a fatality.

> they make me feel that there is invagination and inbredness in my inferiority, that it is insurmountable! [. . .] Poor me . . . and countless others like me! [. . .] totally wiped out the innocent mirage of knowledge being universal, of education being equal, of the mind being free, and of avenues being open . . .
>
> [fazem-me sentir que há invaginação e ingenitismo nesta minha inferioridade, que é insuperável! (. . .) Pobre de mim . . . E de tantos outros como eu! (. . .) Apagada de todo a inocente miragem de a ciência ser universal, a instrução igualitária, livre o espírito, abertos os caminhos . . .] (130–131).

Through the proliferation of nouns with negative prefixes, all of which do actually exist (invaginação, ingenitismo, inferioridade, insuperável), Lisboa subtly deconstructs the dictatorship's retrograde ideology, concerning not only social class, but also by alluding to its misplaced insistence on women's "special" status, on the basis of their physical differences. For, as is well known, the 1933 Constitution had infamously proclaimed all Portuguese citizens to be equal before the law, except for women "because of differences inherent in their nature and in the interest of the family."[19]

As Lisboa sees it, this double-tier citizenship also prevents women from entering the literary arena on anything remotely resembling equal terms. Towards the end of *Solidão,* she becomes ever more scathing in her appraisal of the male literary establishment, whom she caricatures relentlessly as follows.

> When I see men of letters together, I have the impression that, being *forced by a barren milieu to write for one another,* they form an excessively close-knit and amiable coterie of critics. And at once the world appears to me to be so insipidly geometric and unvarying . . . so dehumanized and systematic . . .
>
> [quando vejo juntos homens de letras tenho a impressão de que eles, *forçados por um meio pobre a escrever uns para os outros,* formam uma demasiado apertada e amável sociedade de críticos. E logo o mundo me aparece tão insipidamente geométrico e invariado . . . tão desumanizado e sistemático . . .] (156–57) (our italics).

This passage makes it clear that men of letters do not allow or even envisage room for difference. Lisboa positions herself, implicitly because of her gender and possibly her conflicted class-allegiances too, as being outside their narrow homosocial bonding (here comically described as "unvarying" or "invariado"), which she regards as lacking in real humanity.

In the light of her dissident aesthetics, it is perhaps unsurprising that Lisboa opted to self-publish, under her own name, her next two volumes, *Esta cidade!* (1942) and *Apontamentos* (1943). It may well be that she had no choice: after all, having been dismissed from her job in 1940, she was a *persona non grata* in official circles.[20] Her incisive criticism of the male-dominated mechanisms of publication, dissemination, and critical reception culminates in a little-known story "Um dito" [A Remark], the last but one story in *Esta cidade!*

In this thought-provoking tale, Lisboa deals with the problematic position of an aspiring female writer, Sara, who approaches a well-known male critic hoping that he will help her to secure publication for her first work. He is described as "elegant, clever and *prescriptive*" [elegante, esperto e *normativo* (57) (our italics)]. Since his name, Mourão, is not disclosed until later in the story, he can be seen as a "type," a representative of his profession as an eminent "man of letters." Although he listens to her reading out her work, he criticizes it dismissively, "as though he were addressing a child" [como se se dirigisse *a uma criança* (57) (our italics)], unhelpfully telling her that it seems to take place in the clouds. Nevertheless, she persists and asks if he will introduce her to a publisher. At a subsequent meeting in a bookshop, he appears to exude unquestionable authority, "he welcomed her with all the affability of a *house proud host*" [acolheu-a com toda a gentileza de um *dono de casa* (58) (our italics)]. All these descriptions are loaded with irony, especially since he confidently goes on to propose as a model the very book which he himself had written. It is abundantly clear that because Sara is female, her access to the publishing sphere is severely curtailed owing to her gendered asymmetrical position, her lack of experience and contacts, and furthermore, her style of writing, which does not reproduce dominant modes of expression.

Eventually "chance put her in the path of some *condescending* publisher" [um acaso a pôs no ençalco de qualquer editor *condescendente* (59) (our italics)]. The adjective condescending stresses uneven relations of power, implying that the publisher is looking down on her and doing her a favor. Moreover, the narrator points out that the gendered dynamics enacted between the male-dominated literary world and the now published Sara continue to be played out without any significant structural change, as epitomized in the next encounter between the powerful male writer and Sara several years later. Mourão is kneeling down by a bookcase, looking for a Greek book and the notes he had scribbled in its margins twenty years previously. His kneeling down could potentially indicate a power shift. But it does not, as his arrogance allows him to ensure that he promptly regains the upper hand.

He fired off abruptly: Young lass, did I not encourage you to publish your first book? You remember it, don't you?

[Desfechou-lhe subitamente,
Eu não animei a menina a publicar o seu primeiro livro? Está lembrada, não está?]
(62–3)

The choice of words "desfechou" ironically implies foreclosure as well as an arrow being fired. The fact that he patronizingly calls her "menina" or "young lass" furthermore repositions him on a superior plane. As such, it is impossible to publicly disagree with him, rendering his question merely rhetorical. Inside her mind, however, Sara knows that he is mistaken in his recollection, having failing to provide any support whatsoever.

As the story draws to a close, Sara notices how younger men will learn from Mourão and eventually reproduce the pattern so that the situation will remain unchanged. By contrast, the mute female writer is left helpless, listening to them: "Sarah, who had nothing to say, carried on listening to them" [Sara que não tinha nada a dizer, continuou a ouvi-los (63)]. This predicament is one affecting all dissident women writers, for it is shown in the course of the story that some women can in fact achieve success, so long as they stick to appropriately feminine compositions, which can then be easily dismissed as second-rate (57). Nonetheless, the irony of the statement "who had nothing to say" [que não tinha nada a dizer] (not because of want of things to say, but because she does not have a receptive audience) problematizes the monolithic nature of exclusively male discursive public spaces.

In other words, in this short story, Lisboa is denouncing the ways in which the mechanisms of both publication and subsequent critical reception are almost entirely in the whimsical hands of the male establishment. A simple throw-away male remark, "um dito," can be taken at face value and make or unmake a reputation. Yet, ultimately, even though Mourão is described as a modern-day Socrates early on in the piece, and symptomatically surrounded by a host of eager male disciples, from Lisboa's dissident perspective the wisest person in the tale is unquestionably Sara, as the name she chose for her protagonist surreptitiously encodes.

HISTORY DOES NOT TELL OF THE WEAK?
['DOS FRACOS NÃO REZA A HISTÓRIA'?]

Insofar as official history is often overridingly constructed as *his*tory, Lisboa considered it essential to travel down the alley of memory in order to unravel the complex social and psychological processes through which her adult, gendered self had come into being. Such a revisiting of the past occurs primarily in her two autobiographical novellas, *Começa uma Vida* (1940), located toward the beginning of her literary career, although she was already forty-seven at the time, and *Voltar Atrás Para Quê?* (1956) [Why Go Back in Time?] published two years before her death.[21] These twin texts bear witness to the dismal long-term repercussions of Lisboa's gradual displacement from the paternal house, as illegitimacy becomes a shaping factor in her life.

Solidão had registered her misgivings about the project of committing her memories to paper (118–19). Several fragments made reference to her stepmother (a kinship label she could not bring herself to acknowledge in print) and the latter's own mother, but they constitute bitter outbursts of raw resentment and hatred (37–39, 93–94, 159), a vivid indication of the deep emotional wounds they had inflicted on her. She seems more distanced from her blood family, to whom she only refers on external prompts in the third section: a law book leads her to evoke her father (147–49), while a chance encounter with a mutual acquaintance acts as a pretext to discuss her sister (154–56). This avoidance of painful recollections, alternating with momentary violent outbursts, suggests the difficulty she experienced in revisiting the trauma of her early formative years. Yet by the time she comes to publish her novella in book form, she has managed to transfigure her material artistically. The result is a small masterpiece.

Começa uma Vida opens with words uttered by a three-year-old Irene. She has just been separated from her biological mother, an uneducated country girl, in order to live with her elderly father, a lawyer, and his long-term companion, a wealthy elderly widow, who became her godmother.[22] She abruptly rejects her substitute mother figure: "Get out of here! This house does not belong to you!" [Vá-se embora daqui! Esta casa não é sua! (19)]. The irony of this statement lies in the fact that, in reality, the house is certainly not Irene's, nor will it ever be, given her precarious position as an illegitimate daughter. In fact, as she recognizes soon after, "The house into which I was being received by my godmother was hers" [a casa em que a madrinha me recebia era sua (19)]

The novella spans her childhood formative years, roughly from the ages of three to thirteen. These take place at the turn of the century, in the closing years of the monarchy and provide a vivid portrayal of the almost feudal relations between social classes including, predictably, the unequal relations of power between landowning men and female servants. Yet as Ellen Sapega convincingly argues, this may also reflect the situation under the dictatorship and be a thinly veiled indictment of its backward attitude to women, after the short-lived interlude of the more progressive Republic.[23]

As Lisboa explores her feeling of nonbelonging, of remaining outside as an observer, what emerges is the predicament of the young child, stemming from her lack of solid bonding to any one mother-figure. Later on, while she may feel embarrassed by her elderly parental figures and by her unsuitable clothes in comparison to her school friends, she becomes simultaneously aware of her privileged status in relation to the lower social strata. Her description of Luísa, a laundress, is especially revealing.

> All these familiar creatures, with a slight air of disqualified, insignificant relatives, led sad but unfortunately all too common existences. In order to survive, they sought support from those more favored by fortune [. . .] But once the main link with this friendly family and its beneficial support was broken, everything disappeared into poverty . . .

> [Todos estes entes familiares, com um ligeiro ar de parentes desclassificados, secundários, tinham umas tristes vidas, infelizmente bem normais. Encostavam-se aos mais favorecidos para poder viver (. . .) Mas quebrada a cadeia principal daquela família amiga, do bom sustentáculo, sumiu-se tudo na miséria . . . (70)].

The precarious situation of Luísa shares many parallels with her own, so that, tellingly, the allusion to the breakdown of the family unit prefigures not only the servant's, but also Irene's own downfall later on.

As the narrative progresses, the self-centered behavior of her father comes to the fore. It includes a new liaison, which will result in the gradual displacement of Irene's godmother, and perhaps even more damagingly, financial improprieties which enable him to secure legal ownership of the rural estate. In other words, the house which at the outset did indeed belong to Irene's godmother, by the last page of the novella is no longer the old lady's property. In an ironic twist of fate, we learn that she had surrendered it to her long-term companion in exchange for the promise that Irene and her younger sister would be recognized as his legitimate heirs. But since this promise was never made good, in effect both the older and the younger female generation are completely stripped of their rightful belongings.[24]

At this point, the novella abruptly draws to a close in two paragraphs. Although Irene states "this period of my life, which was so decisive for me, is one I would like to describe accurately" [este período da minha existência, que para mim tão decisivo foi, é que eu estimava saber bem descrever], she cannot even begin to make sense of it: "But I won't be able to! It is beyond me, it exceeds my understanding" [Não o saberei! Ultrapassa-me, excede-me o entendimento (79)]. Readers endowed with outside knowledge of her biographical circumstances or of the sequel *Voltar Atrás Para Quê?* can surmise that her father's remarriage entails for her a complete loss of the relative stability of her former life. But the trauma inflicted on her has been such that she is left unable to articulate at any length these acutely painful memories: "Everything that surrounded me made me miserable or rejected me, expelled me from family life. I spent two very unhappy years in this situation . . . I lived downtrodden and adrift, without the love of anyone" [Tudo quanto me rodeava me acabrunhava ou me repelia, me expulsava da vida comum. Dois anos bem infelizes passei nesta situação . . . Vivi muito rebaixada e desorientada, sem o amor de ninguém (79–80)].

It would be many years before Lisboa could bring herself to describe in greater detail these two traumatic years in *Voltar Atrás Para Quê?*, published sixteen years later in 1956. For the time being, what remains evident is the irony of the title *Começa uma Vida,* "a life begins," as the account of the dawn of her life ends in bleak uncertainty, with the sensitive teenager deprived once more, and ever more dramatically, of a supportive family environment and love.

Although this tale is ostensibly about the past, it may also figuratively share parallels with Lisboa's own professional situation at the time of writing: she had been up to then tolerated by an emergent authoritarian dictatorship, but on a whim was about to be cast aside by the regime as an ideologically unsound daughter. Indeed, as Lisboa did not fit the mold, it was easier simply to de-authorize her on the grounds of intellectual illegitimacy to the nationalist project. Needless to say, as Salazar became ever more narrow-minded in his pronouncements about women, all "illegitimate daughters" become potential casualties of the regime. The novella vividly portrays the vulnerability a non-negligible proportion of women across different social strata and generations such madrinha, Luísa, and Irene.

In *Voltar Atrás Para Quê?* Lisboa delves once more into her past, in order to recall in greater detail the two traumatic years (twenty months to be precise) she spent in the rural estate in the company of her father, his new wife, and the latter's mother. The process is so harrowing that, in sharp contrast to the earlier first-person account, she can only go ahead by giving a fictional identity to herself and all those surrounding her.[25] Accordingly, the sequel makes use of a third-person narrator, the fictionally named Açucena da Felicidade Pais: the floral name White Lily implies purity and whiteness, but any dreams of happiness, encoded in the middle name Felicity, remain bitterly out of reach, given her lack of "Pais" or parents hyperbolically foregrounded in the surname. A further fictional element is the death of her younger sister, which enables Lisboa to revisit her plight with a heightened sense of isolation. Furthermore, with her godmother, Dona Felismina, now living in Lisbon, Açucena/Irene is left completely unprotected in the rural estate at the mercy of the ruthless plotting and social climbing of his father's new wife, Esperança [Hope] and the latter's mother, Dona Adélia.[26]

Açucena/Irene's gradual displacement from her father's affections becomes evident early on, as the text details increasing humiliation at the hands of both her father and the two women. Esperança's first pregnancy heightens her complete lack of status as an illegitimate daughter, a fact poignantly experienced when the new baby, also female, is referred to as "little heiress" [morgadinha] in front of her. Her negation as a person comes through in a series of other episodes denoting major stigmatization, such as being left drenched in blood when she has her menstruation. Talking about menstruation so openly is a major taboo breaker, and here Lisboa shows the extent to which social exclusion is predicated upon the abjection ascribed to the female body.

Symbolically, Açucena/Irene is an orphan. In fact, the text contains references to Victor Hugo's *Les misérables*, which put her indirectly on a par with the abuse experienced by the young Cosette, although the parallel is never made explicit. Throughout the text, her dirty and increasingly ragged clothes become a visible sign of her destitution. But unlike Cosette, she does not ever have a providential Jean Valjean father-figure to come to her rescue or indeed a mother-figure. As a result, her plight leads her to suicidal thoughts, in front of a well, in an unconscious aspiration to return to the maternal womb.

In a desperate attempt to rehabilitate her battered self-esteem, she accepts the courting of a local boy, Júlio. When she is caught with him, she hides in trees which are anthropomorphized and endowed with maternal qualities such as "the pear tree full of arms" [pereira, cheia de braços (106)]. By contrast, when she attempts to go back to the paternal house later that night, it transpires her father has locked her out. Her downfall culminates with expulsion, as she is sent away to live with her godmother in Lisbon. She is taken there by Esperança, pregnant once more, a fact which confirms the position of the legitimate wife within the household.

Açucena/Irene's dramatic exclusion from the paternal home represents a turning-point, however: in Lisbon, under her godmother's wings, she can resume her schooling and begin to flourish. Nevertheless, when she reaches majority at eighteen, her father's attorney presents her with a document to sign. The agreement would give her a small monthly sum, barely enough to live on. But to add insult to injury, it is only available as a trade-off for for agreeing to leaving her father's surname out of her signature, a gesture tantamount to acknowledging publicly her illegitimacy. She tears the paper in an uncontrollable fit of indignation. She dryly comments, "One does not die from want, or for lack of food, or of cold, in one's own land, when one is only eighteen" [Não se morre à míngua, de fome nem de frio, numa terra conhecida e com dezoito anos (139)]. The implication, however, is that, whereas material survival is possible, emotional survival is much more challenging.

The negative effects of Açucena's extreme alienation reach out into the narrative present, leaving the ageing narrator floundering as she ponders the unanswered question foregrounded by the title: "voltar atrás para quê?" Why indeed go back in time? The narrator constantly hovers between the impulse to deny any therapeutic value to her account and the urge to speak out. When, at the beginning of her narrative, she first recalls the women who so nearly destroyed her, her repressed pain is unleashed against them with unprecedented violence: "damned old woman" [maldita velha!] (20)] and "bitches!" [cadelas! (22)].

Approximately one third of the way into her account, Lisboa despondently asks what is achieved by naming and shaming those who so nearly destroyed her. The answer, surely, lies in the fact that her story confirms her survival instinct, which enables her to rise above the ghosts of the past and allows her to focus on "the river and the fresh air and the countryside too" [a ribeira e o ar e o campo também (51–52)], all of which are life-affirming. This realization is especially significant, as it takes place immediately prior to her father beating her, an episode which leaves her on the brink of committing suicide. The cathartic value of writing thus lies in enabling her to transcend her past and counteract a death wish which remains ever present. Verbalization has a therapeutic value since, through active re-membrance, the mature self, however bitter, can outlive countless humiliations and become "grounded" once more in the present, even if only to get on with the difficult business of living as an mature sixty-two-year-old woman.

At the outset, the narrator had stated that she was going to describe only two years, but in fact the narrative encompasses five years, a necessary strategy for the survival of the speaking subject, who would otherwise have remained figuratively almost totally alienated from society and powerless. By the end of her autobiographical account, Lisboa is better equipped to put to rest the ghosts of the past. This she does in the closing scene, which stages a chance encounter in Lisbon with the former maid, Delmira. Delmira, after years of mistreatment, left the family estate without any financial reward.

Her situation echoes on many levels that of Irene, but being more emotionally detached from the past, Delmira can be openly critical of the ageing
patriarch, of Esperança and Dona Adélia, and even of Dona Felismina's former maid, Ana, all of whom connived to lure the old lady back to the rural
estate and left her there, to die alone and in poverty. She describes the death
and solitary burial of Dona Felismina. For Lisboa, the choice of concluding
her account with the burial, albeit seen through the eyes of a third party, is
an empowering device, insofar as it allows her to metaphorically bury the
past by proxy.

Lisboa dramatically foregrounds the stark events which threatened to en-
gulf her during her formative years and left her crippled for life. It is tempting to read her tragic life-story as emblematic of a wider curse experienced
by women across the social spectrum, under a dictatorship which repeatedly
de-authorized them. Irrespective of social class, women like Dona Felismina,
Delmira, and Açucena/Irene are all displaced and deprived of what is right-
fully theirs. There is another option open to women, however: to collude
with patriarchal structures of power, although in so doing, they inevitably
become oppressors of other women. This is the route successfully chosen by
the likes of Esperança and Dona Adélia.

Ultimately, however, the illegitimate daughter's narrative stands as a powerful indictment of their choice. Her account shows the violence which is
necessary in order to achieve a seamless family. On a broader collective level,
her portrayal of the disowning of illegitimate children stands as a clear denunciation of Salazar's monolithic discourse of "Deus, Pátria, Família"
[God, Fatherland, Family].[27] Moreover, the plight of the ostracized daughter
highlights both the exclusion of the silent majority of women from the social, political, and cultural landscape during the dictatorship and, worse still,
their perceived inability to redress the balance.

Metaphorically speaking, Lisboa's autobiographical novellas may also reflect the stark choices available to women writers: stick to suitably anodine
feminine themes that reproduce "legitimate" ideology or be excluded. Lisboa's trajectory of survival against all odds, then, not only bears witness to
the difficulty of attaining recognition on a personal level, but arguably also
on a literary one.

CONCLUSION

Irene Lisboa remained virtually unread by the wider public both during
her lifetime and for many decades after. She herself was wryly aware of her
marginal status: "I had half a dozen pleasant, charming, readers. (Men of

letters, naturally). And I remained forgotten and on my own" [Tive meia dúzia de leitores, simpáticos, graciosos. (Letrados, já se sabe.) E continuei esquecida e solitária].[28] Her ironic reference to "men of letters," in the bracketed comment, conveys a scathing appraisal of the male critical establishment with its narrow definitions of literary worth and genius.

In many ways, Irene Lisboa was ahead of her time. Her daring attempts to venture outside readily legible "feminine" modes of expression, and to map out uncharted territory by exposing and resisting a massive gender gap led at best to a *succès d'estime,* but not widespread recognition. Yet, in her lucid analyzes of the processes which perpetuated gendered definitions of genius, conditioned critical reception and ultimately excluded women, she inscribed her rejection of the man-made rules under which she was expected to operate. Arguably, through her ongoing articulation of an agonizing sense of marginalization, magnified through her resourceful handling of self-published material, she found a degree of empowerment.

As such, in her rethinking of the complex relations between gender and genius, she is a noteworthy heir to Florbela Espanca, despite her own thoughts on the matter. In retrospect, she can also be seen as a precursor of subsequent writers of prose fiction such as, among many others, Maria Judite de Carvalho, Maria Velho da Costa (whose novel *Irene ou o Contrato Social* published in 2000 recuperated her symbolic image), and Lídia Jorge, whose work will be discussed in chapter 6.

A Poem by Irene Lisboa

Translated into English by Richard Zenith

Irony

Irony, that witty device that makes us laugh
about things we feel like crying over . . .
That little dog on a leash that jumps, audacious and restrained, . . .
I'd like that irony, my irony, to be so controlled
and intelligent, so discreet, so independent and
so dry that it would go almost unnoticed,
its lighthearted laughter seeming like acquiescence, its
reticence like simple doubt, its politeness like acceptance.
I'd like my quiet and almost serious irony to be my fortress.
It fell asleep, my besiegers would say
(what a marvelous word: besiegers!)—
those on the outside who comment on intentions, intimacies.

My dear sweet irony, my little dog, your voice is a
brief and unmusical, almost harsh bark
that's pure sport.
Or if it isn't, because imperfectly trained,
I wish it were!

3
The Case of the Missing Body: Allegories of Authorship in Agustina Bessa Luís

> Woman does not, at present, have any historical memory other than that
> which is loaned to her by man.
>
> [A mulher não tem por ora memória histórica senão aquela que lhe é
> emprestada pelo homem.]
>
> —Augustina Bessa Luís, *Vale Abraão*

> Romanticism turned the artist into a demi-god: the genius. Woman, by
> contrast, became simply "Other." The occasional female creator could
> be countenanced; but being a creator and a truly feminine female were
> deemed to be in conflict.
>
> —Christine Battersby, *Gender and Genius*

INTRODUCTION—THE MOTHER OF ALL MATRIARCHS?

A LEADING FIGURE IN THE PORTUGUESE LITERARY ESTABLISHMENT FOR
more than six decades, Agustina Bessa Luís occupies a very different place in
the national imaginary from that of either Florbela Espanca or Irene Lisboa,
who struggled for recognition, for many years, in the male-dominated cultural contexts of their day. Bessa Luís is easily the best-known and most pro-
lific of Portugal's twentieth-century women writers. Born Maria Agustina
Ferreira Teixeira Bessa Luís, on October 15, 1922, in Vila Meã, near Amara-
nte in northern Portugal, many of her works evince profound ties with the
Douro region and the city of Oporto. She began writing in the 1940s and
her published works date from 1948 to the present day, including more than
thirty novels, as well as literary criticism, short stories, novellas, biographies,
plays, film scripts, and numerous literary prizes, including the Camões Prize
in 2004. Spanning the pre- and postrevolution eras, the majority of her writings fall into the period after the Portuguese revolution of 1974, although
she belongs chronologically to the generation of writers who emerged during
the New State dictatorship (1933–74). From the perspective of feminist

97

scholarship and analysis of canon history, it is all too easy, on one level, to regard Bessa Luís as the ultimate "extraordinária" or "exceptionalist," the woman writer who transcended gender to achieve unassailable canonical status. The work which heralded Bessa Luís's breakthrough in 1954 was her novel *A Sibila,* which broke onto a literary scene increasingly dominated at the time by Marxist neorealism. It was awarded the Delfim Guimarães Prize while it was still only in manuscript form, and went on to win the Eça de Queirós prize. It also came to be canonized as a standard text on the Portuguese secondary school literature curriculum.

The reputation that Bessa Luís acquired was largely bound up, initially, with the positive reception of *A Sibila* as well as with the support of influential critics and literary historians such as Óscar Lopes.[1] The various descriptions of her work, in the different revised editions of *História da Literatura de Portuguesa,* the classic literary history of Portugal by António José Saraiva and Óscar Lopes, enable us to trace a revealing and symptomatically ambiguous trajectory into, and out of, gender specificity as her canonical status came to be progressively consolidated. In the first edition of 1954 Bessa Luís was one of only five women included.[2] However, somewhere between the first edition and the volume's second edition of 1956, Bessa Luís effectively stopped being classified as a "woman writer" and became instead simply a very notable writer.[3] By the third edition of 1965, she was back in the "women's section" of the volume, but clearly set apart from her contemporaries on account of her more "universal" appeal.[4]

In the first edition of this *História,* she had figured alongside Florbela Espanca, Irene Lisboa, Maria Lamas, and Maria Archer as part of the "boom of female personalities breaking with the traditional affectation of Portuguese women's sensibility and posing their problems more openly" in a process that is generalized as "literary emancipation."[5] In the second edition of the *História* in 1956, however, when *A Sibila* had been in print for two years, she was no longer considered part of the female literary emancipation process at all, but rather appears in a general, modern fiction part of the volume, as "without a doubt, the most notable personality of recent years, for the exuberance, albeit still rather uncontrolled, of her dramatic and poetic powers of evocation."[6] In this instance, she is totally separated from the description, in a different section of the volume, of the "development of literature authored by women."[7] This feminine lineage starts with Florbela Espanca and goes on to include Marta Mesquita da Câmara, Virgínia Vitorino, Fernanda de Castro, Maria Lamas, Maria Archer, Irene Lisboa, Adelaide Félix, Rachel Bastos, Natércia Freire, Ilse Losa, Celeste Andrade, Patrícia Joyce, and Maria da Graça Azambuja.

Following the triumph of *A Sibila* in 1954, then, Bessa Luís appears progressively to supersede the concerns of gender and sexuality, securing a paragraph of her own in the second *História da Literatura Portuguesa*. In the third edition, in 1965, Bessa Luís does interestingly figure in the "women" category once again. However, she is specifically praised this time for being a "story teller with much of her imagination seeking to structure itself in the existential novel."[8] Thus, the scope and existential depth of her work clearly place her above other female authors whose focus on women's political issues is deemed to confine them to "the sociological aspect of the phenomenon."[9] In this context, she is constructed as the exemplary ideal of a woman writing "beyond feminism" on universal humanist and existentialist themes, and thus she finds herself paternally authorized and institutionalized by the *História da Literatura Portuguesa* at a very early stage of her career.[10] However, as the foregoing will argue, universalism notwithstanding, the power dynamics of sexual difference and the gendering of Portuguese cultural memory are rarely if ever absent from her literary preoccupations. Indeed, for the purposes of our study, Bessa Luís constitutes a key transitional figure, moving from women's conventional exclusion from canonical literary history, to women's successful negotiation of a leading position in the mainstream, albeit by dint of a kind of double agency, simultaneously revealing, yet also ironically reinventing, an originary suppression of female cultural memory, as the predominant aesthetic guiding her own creative project.

Given Bessa Luís's early elevation by the establishment to a category of her own, set apart from overtly feminist writers such as Maria Lamas, it is not very surprising that she proved a problematic maternal figure for the more radically politicized women writers of the 1960s and 1970s. This is particularly evident in the Three Marias' *Novas Cartas Portuguesas* in 1972. The Marias' very sparing references to real women forebears such as Florbela Espanca and Agustina Bessa Luís had a significant role to play in symptomatizing the radical antimaternalism and the deconstruction of genealogy, both literal and literary, that were central to their collaborative work. In this scenario, Agustina Bessa Luís seems to represent, for the Marias' generation, the curse or blight of the phallic mother's literary legacy as it is lived under patriarchal conditions. The single, intertextual reference that the Marias make to Agustina Bessa Luís is to a short story, "A mãe de um rio" [The Mother of a River] published in the collection *A Brusca* in 1971 but written, as the preface indicates, sometime between 1958 and 1967.[11]

In this allegorical tale, the mythical wise woman of the title, the "mãe de um rio" or "mother of a river" is said to be more than a thousand years old. Echoing Celtic myths as well as Greco-Roman antecedents in Ceres and Proserpine, she is an ancient goddess in charge of wisdom, water, and harvests. She has golden finger tips and is feared but also revered by the villagers who depend on her. As she grows weary of her role she loses touch with the peasants and their lives become morbid, hunger-stricken, dark, and barren. Meanwhile, a dreamy, motherless village girl, Fisalina, is aware that she has always felt set apart from others around her, and she takes a suitor from outside her community. In trying to leave and marry outside, she is breaking local law. She goes to seek advice on the true nature of her desires from the ancient Mother of a River.

In her cryptic response, the Mother of a River complains that she has little contact with the affairs of humans, and that even she, as the ancient guardian of the truth, needs to be replaced. She takes Fisalina to a magical underground wellspring where she dips her fingers into the water, only to discover later that the Mother of the River has disappeared and that she herself has now gained the same golden finger tips. Initially proud of her distinction from others, she returns to her home "cured" of her previous love, and rejects her former suitor. She keeps her hand a secret, but when her golden fingers are accidentally discovered, she is stoned and driven away from her village. Retreating into the hills, she lives in isolation, for a further thousand years, becoming a replacement for the "mother of a river" until she too can trick someone into taking her place.

Lamenting the treacherous maternal genealogy, which Bessa Luís's story seems to endorse for the female creator, one of the Three Marias in *Novas Cartas* appeals to Agustina as if she were the "Mother of a River," to defend the wholeness of the female writing body as well as the Marias' own female writing collective: "I find that we are merely repeating Agustina Bessa Luís's story called 'The Mother of the River' (O Agustina, you who are so alone and so independent, so much your own woman!). Let us hope that our hands will not be crippled or our bodies shattered as in Agustina's story, that those who love us for what we are and do will not divide themselves by dividing us" (53) [eu acho que estamos só fazendo a mãe do rio. (ó Agustina só e só) que não nos tolha a mão e o corpo *roto*—que/quem amar agora o que fazemos não seja dividido a dividir-nos" (50)]. As the Marias suggest, the gift-turned-curse of the golden fingers evokes exclusion from society, the loss of an incarnate female existence for the woman who thus "becomes" the phallus. In Lacanian terms, the Mother Goddess's betrayal of Fisalina subjects her to paternal Law, under which she may symbolize eternal wisdom and memory for others, only at the expense of her own corporeality and expression, as she demarcates culture at the defining edge of the community. In this respect, Fisalina discloses the impossibility of the physically embodied, desiring woman, speaking her own culture outside the terms mandated by patriarchal symbolic law.

The mythical "deformity" of the phallicized female body, marked by the immobilized hand of Fisalina, is destined to recur in different guises throughout Bessa Luís's works, notably as Quina's birthmark in *A Sibila,* and as Ema Paiva's crippled left foot in *Vale Abraão [Abraham Valley].*[12] Unpalatable models though they may have been to the Three Marias, early prototypical figures such as Fisalina and The Mother of a River lay down significant paradigms for Bessa Luís's ongoing preoccupation with the "gifted" or exceptional woman and her troubled relation to female sexual embodiment and creative subjectivity.

As Silvina Rodrigues Lopes has indicated, two particular female types that seem to reecho this message reappear time and again through Bessa Luís's vast opus.

> One is the figure of the "matriarch," virile, powerful and vengeful, who can guarantee order and prosperity. The other, who is not exactly a fully fledged figure as such because she borders on the sublime, derives from the notion of the unclassifiable. She is the woman who is capable of foresight and passivity, tedium and pride.

> [Uma é a figura da "matriarca," viril, poderosa e vingadora, capaz de garantir a ordem e a prosperidade. A outra, que não é inteiramente uma figura porque ronda o sublime, origina-se na ideia do inclassificável. É a mulher capaz do pressentimento e da passividade, do tédio e do orgulho.][13]

Underlying this dichotomy is the familiar opposition, noted by Christine Battersby in her work on female genius, between being physically masculinized (virile, powerful and vengeful) and being physically incorporeal (sublime, ethereal and unclassifiable). Rather than insisting upon the sexual embodiment of woman as the writing subject, as the Three Marias famously did, the four Bessa Luís works that we discuss here all focus, in different ways, on this exclusion of the female body from language, as the Lacanian lack that forms the defining edge of culture. This gives the impression, at times, of an almost ritually reenacted mourning for the lost origins of female creativity, and for the impossibility of voicing female cultural memory outside of paternally authorized language. Thus, Bessa Luís appears to repeatedly kill off the very object that she textually mourns, namely, the possibility of women's historical cultural memory and tradition.[14]

Battersby has observed that, "a woman who created was faced with a double bind: either to surrender her sexuality (becoming not *masculine,* but a surrogate *male),* or to be *feminine* and *female,* and hence to fail to count as a genius."[15] This rather bleak scenario effectively reinforces women's manichaeistic choice between the silence imposed by an "impossible" female tradition (Fisalina's inability to live out her "individuality" within the confines

of society) and the ventriloquism required by complicity with an alien, masculine one (the Mother Goddess's imposition of a paternal symbolic ordering that speaks for and through Fisalina). At the same time, however, Bessa
Luís's treatment of sexual mythologies is characterized by an all-pervading
sense of irony and it is this that provides the most reliable clue to her subtextual critique of women's exclusion from dominant culture. As Isabel Pires de
Lima has noted in a short but highly astute assessment of Bessa Luís entitled
"Agustina, the subversive conservative" [Agustina, a conservadora subver-
siva], "it is always by means of irony, that she moves towards the denunciation, that is central in her work, of patriarchal and phallocentric power
which, within Judeo-Christian tradition, dominates the many women that
people her novels."[16]
    The remainder of this chapter will explore this trajectory of ironic denun-
ciation across Bessa Luís's work, through a comparative reading of four well-
known works from three different decades: A Sibila from 1954, Florbela Espanca and Fanny Owen from 1979, and Vale Abraão from 1991.[17] We will
argue that the course these novels trace may be productively mapped onto
the dichotomy of women's two opposing choices as defined by Battersby (the
surrogate male exceptionalist and the noncreative feminine female) but also
onto a possible resolution, or at least a productive third choice, which entails
reading Ema Paiva's self-textualization through death in Vale Abraão, as a
tentative allegory of female authorship. In both A Sibila, and Florbela Espanca, Bessa Luís's fictionalized biography of the woman poet, we witness
women being represented as surrogate males in order to pursue their ego
ideals. In Fanny Owen, we observe the fate of the hyperfeminine female as
Romantic Muse, who is sacrificed to the sexual ambiguities of the male genius ideal, and thus fails to be recorded as creative in her own right. Finally,
in Vale Abraão, we discuss the production of the "woman as writer" from a
pastiche of the Emma Bovary tradition that effectively disestablishes the "paternal law" of canonical Flaubertian realism by undercutting the symbolic
sexual identifications upon which both genius and genealogy depend.

A SIBILA—PROMOTING THE PROMETHEAN WOMAN?

A Sibila is a highly fragmented, achronological novel, which draws its co-
herence from the story of the Teixeira family, explored through three generations of women: the mother, Maria da Encarnação; her second daughter,
Joaquina Augusta or Quina, who becomes the sybil of the title; and Quina's
niece Germa, the daughter of her brother Abel. Following the fall, rise, and
impending decline of the Casa da Vessada, the Teixeira family homestead

before, during, and immediately after Quina's lifetime, the novel begins with the nostalgic associations of the niece Germa's memories as she recalls the origins of the household starting from the date over the door, 1870. Germa has just inherited the house and estate but she is unlikely to maintain it according to rural farming traditions, the way Quina did. She is an unmarried intellectual, who lives in the city and prefers the "aristocracy of the mind" [aristocracia do espírito (191)]. Concluding the events of her family history as she sits in Quina's old rocking chair, it is stated at the beginning of the novel and reiterated at the end in retrospect, that this young female intellectual, Germa, has been narrating her memories of Quina's life to her cousin, Bernardo Sanches, a few years after Quina's death. As the younger, rurally bred generations migrate to the city, the future of the Vessada is uncertain. The fact of Quina's death at the age of seventy-six implicitly brings the time span of the story full circle, up to the period of the novel's composition in the 1950s.

Most readings of this work focus, to some degree, on the novel's nostalgic, Proustian reconstruction of disjointed memories and associations which evoke a remote time and place, always on the verge of disappearing.[18] As a classic piece of rural nostalgia, it understandably appealed on one level to Portuguese urban folk memory. As Catherine Dumas has noted in an insightful close reading of A Sibila, its most significant temporal structuring device is indeed that of female genealogy down three generations.[19] At the same time, the corresponding role played by memory in this work is far from straightforward, not least because it does not simply map onto a temporal unfolding of female genealogies. Germa is not in fact, as is implied in the novel's conclusion, a consistent or authoritative agent of memory transmission. The novel is not narrated in the first person, and the third-person narrative voice deployed through the novel is actually multiple and ambiguous. Frequently adopting the highly moralistic, aphoristic omniscience that is characteristic of Bessa Luís's prose, this third-person narrative goes far beyond the scope of Germa's possible field of focalization, particularly regarding events that occurred before her birth.[20] Thus, the framing of this third-person novel between the introductory statement, "and suddenly, Germa began to speak about Quina" [e, bruscamente, Germa começou a falar de Quina (9)] and the near final phrase " 'it was so terrible!' said Germa" ["foi tão terrível!" disse Germa (245)] spoken in the novelistic present after Quina's death, indicates that this is not a simple renarrativization of Germa's memory. Rather it is an evocation or a remembering of the role that memory *itself* plays in creating a nostalgic aura around the past. In this sense, the use of Germa's act of pseudoretrospection draws attention to the status of memory as an aesthetic device, rather than actually enabling the reconstruction of a biographical life story through a connecting thread of memory united in a single, first-person narrating subject. The genealogical continuity linking Quina and Germa, as aunt and niece, is not therefore narratologically sustained at the level of a poetics of memory. Germa has literally inherited Quina's estate, the Vessada, but the continuation of any conscious aesthetic or expressive legacy, through the transmission of cultural memory between the two women, is far less clear-cut.

The perspectives of the two women, Quina and Germa, are frequently shown by the narrator to overlap, but they are not represented as being aware of this overlap. Their unknowing proximity to each other, as perceived by the third-person narrator, serves rather to reinforce a Romantic nostalgic vision of undifferentiated female "pastness," firmly controlled nonetheless by third-person narrative mastery. Thus the image of an unspoken, inchoate connectedness between the two women feeds into a quasi-mystical representation of Portugal's rural, preurban past in terms of intuitive, prerational "feminine" knowledge or sybilline thought. In the view of influential critics such as Eduardo Lourenço, this feminine mysticism placed the book at the service, not of women themselves, but rather of a national literature urgently requiring regeneration in the face of the Marxist neorealist movement, which according to Lourenço writing in 1963 "had largely paralysed the national imagination for the last fifteen years."[21] Lourenço's classic interpretation of *A Sibila* reclaimed it therefore as the cornerstone of a new Romanticism or "neo-romantismo" devoted to lyrical exploration of the "national literary subconscious."[22]

Bessa Luís's undoubted rehabilitation of a certain Romantic legacy in *A Sibila* leads to the repression of the maternal female body, as the biological laws of sexual difference exclude women from any aspiration to "genius," coded here as Quina's individualist ambition, her special status as a mystic, her desire to succeed. Thus, Quina's fate hangs on Romanticism's classic female double bind, the "incompatibility . . . of creative potency and marriage."[23] Quina cannot find personal expression or social status outside the terms of her paternal legacy, remaining a single, celibate "masculinized" woman, committed to the maintenance and expansion of the Vessada, and channelling her sexuality into mysticism as a sybil. However, she finds herself condemned to chaos, ridicule, solitude, and affective failure when the needs of the maternal body reassert themselves in later life. In this context, Laura Bulger has pertinently remarked of the novel that "the issue of Quina's sexuality remains, perhaps deliberately, to be explored."[24]

The social and cultural masculinization of Quina is suggested from the outset by her close relation to her father, Francisco Teixeira, a notorious local seducer and wastrel. As the undervalued, second daughter, Quina ultimately wins her father's respect by becoming a pragmatic hard worker. The close identification between father and daughter is described as "an almost ironic complicity" [uma cumplicidade quase irónica (23)]. The turning point in Quina's life comes at the age of fifteen when she miraculously survives a serious and prolonged childhood illness. Her fevered murmurings, and the fact that she has a mysterious birthmark on her arm, are taken by superstitious friends and neighbors to indicate a magical quality, giving rise to the naïve local perception that Quina is endowed with supernatural powers. Adroitly capitalizing upon the mythology of the sybil or wise woman, Quina subsequently becomes widely respected as a mystic, counselor, and adviser. Sublimating her sexual energies into her business dealings, she becomes the most prosperous member of her family, growing rich through extreme parsimony and careful management of rents, as she skillfully outmanoeuvres her siblings to acquire financial ascendancy.

The option of marriage represents the risk of Quina losing control over her wealth, land, and property.[25] Thus, Quina's aspirations for material gain and personal renown are represented throughout as defeminizing, denaturing behavior, as they require a rejection of marriage and maternity. Her state of "virilization," her overidentification with her father and her loathing of marriage ultimately lead to her monsterization. She is described as usurping the founding power of Old Testament patriarchy, the power of God, since "her ambitions proliferated like the tribe of Abraham, until they filled the entire earth" [as suas ambições proliferaram como a tribo de Abraão e encheram a terra inteira (59)].[26] As the biblical tone of the narrative suggests, Quina's desire to excel in a male domain, to possess the phallus, will not go unpunished. Her castigation is expressed, precisely, as a loss of embodiment, a perversion of her maternal destiny. The sybilline birthmark on her arm resembles a burn mark, figuratively associating her with "the freedom of Prometheus" [a liberdade de Prometeu (170)], who stole fire from the gods, just as Quina has usurped the masculine power of knowledge by becoming the financial head of the household. Her fall from prelapsarian innocence takes the form of trying to acquire sexualized maternal knowledge, beyond the "natural" age of motherhood, at the age of fifty-eight when she is beset with the desire to adopt an orphan child, Custódio, a beautiful but mentally slow boy, who is the illegitimate son of her friend's manservant.

Germa offers the alternative possibility for continuity of her aunt's legacy, but Quina is alienated from her own sex and despises all women on principle, since "all of her life she had struggled to overcome her own condition" [toda a vida, ela lutara por superar a sua própria condição (98)]. The tense and cautious relationship between the two women is sharply contrasted with the close bond formed between Quina and Custódio. Fated like Prometheus to have her gizzards pecked out while eternally chained to a rock, Quina's experience of maternal love rebounds on her, however, when an idle and dissipated Custódio pursues the family wealth to which he has no entitlement. Quina's rational judgment is described as hopelessly impaired by her attempt to combine business and adoptive motherhood, through an extended metaphor in which the phallic tower or "keep," the self-image based on wisdom and profit that she has built, is suddenly demolished by her emotions. When Quina offers Custódio a home, the omniscient third-person narrator observes censoriously

> Here we have Senhora Joaquina Augusta of the House of the Vessada, granted the title of "dona" on account of the properties she has accumulated, the wealth she has acquired through lucrative investments. . . . She was a fortress of prudence, in which her vanity was the keep. But she was nothing but a stupid little woman, with a weak and foolish heart the day she accepted that child into her home, and unconditionally adopted him.

> [Eis aqui a Senhora Joaquina Augusta, da casa da Vessada, a quem o seu acréscimo de propriedades e riquezas em rendosos dinheiros conferia já o título de dona. . . . . Era uma fortaleza de prudência cuja torre de menagem era sempre a vaidade. Mas não passara duma mulherzinha inteiramente ignara, tola e vulnerável de coração no dia em que aceitou em sua casa aquela criança e incondicionalmente a adoptou (135)].

The resurgence of Quina's female physical desire is represented in increasingly violent terms. Her passion for her dead father, enshrined in the house of the Vessada itself, is Oedipally transferred to Custódio, variously described as a father, son, and lover. Custódio mounts a campaign of emotional blackmail to get Quina's will changed, promising to maintain the household as she would want in her father's memory. Yet Quina ultimately resists Custódio's manipulation, the main estate of the Vessada is left to Germa as legal convention dictates, and Quina dies a bitter, solitary death. Even though he inherits other minor properties, Custódio feels disaffiliated. Forced to leave the Vessada, he melodramatically cuts his own throat. It is the narration of this suicide episode that brings the text full circle back to the opening passage of the novel in which Germa was talking about Quina to her cousin, Bernardo Sanches.

Reviewing her aunt's life from the narrative present, Germa ultimately contemplates for herself a similarly rigid dichotomizing of body and mind, of physical and mental fulfillment. If Quina's collective memory for future generations can only be recuperated and transmitted as either pseudomasculinity or mystical sublimation of physical desire, the narrator asks whether Germa will ever "translate the voice of her sybil" [traduzir a voz da sua sibila" (249)], whether her ego ideals as an artist will find anything of value in Quina's fatalistic legacy of individual power. There are clearly Nietzschean overtones to the Promethean revolt that Quina undertakes, as a form of sacrifice before, and sacrilege against, the male gods.[27] The novel may be taken, at this level, as a statement that all genius, all defiance of the law of the gods, requires sacrifice and suffering. But in Bessa Luís's *A Sibila,* the law of the gods that is broken is precisely the law that governs the "naturally" separate spheres of sexual difference and the power and knowledge pertaining to each. In her aspiration to the absolute, it is the sexed laws of genius that Quina breaks. For Bessa Luís, the spirit of genius is assumed male-sexed to begin with, so the sacrificial Nietzschean pact entered into by the would-be woman genius requires her to usurp the power of the male gods and be punished, in kind, by becoming "like a man," by loss of the right to live the maternal body, even socially. Left poised then between the two impossible options suggested by Quina's life, the closing passage implies that Germa may well remain silenced and inexpressive, "hermetically sealed into the circle of aspirations that she has not been able to specify and to accomplish" [hermeticamente fechada no círculo de aspirações que não conseguiu detalhar e cumprir (249)].[28]

It is not hard to find in *A Sibila* an exemplary, antifeminist parable against women's overachievement.[29] Nor is it difficult to link this negative parable for women with the novel's canonical success in the 1950s and after. As noted above, *A Sibila* became a classic on Portuguese school syllabi, and remained for several decades, including after the Revolution, the female-authored novel most likely to be read by Portuguese school children. Yet, as Óscar Lopes astutely observed some decades later, the modern woman of the postrevolution 1980s was unlikely to identify with Quina or Germa. He expresses the doubt that "without some explanatory glossing, the Portuguese woman of the next generation would want to see herself in this tormented book."[30]

FLORBELA'S RESISTING BIOGRAPHER

Something similar could be said, with rather different implications, for Bessa Luís's *Florbela Espanca,* an account of the life and death of the famous woman poet that was first published in 1979. This work is an interesting genre hybrid. Avowedly a fictionalized biography, it is clearly heavily researched, and it includes reprints of some of Espanca's poetry as well as a biographical time-line and photographs of its subject.[31] Beyond that, however, the book eschews the conventional scholarly apparatus of footnotes, bibliography, and referencing that would place it unambiguously in the academic literary biography genre. Further, the construction of Florbela herself as an exceptional figure, carries many important resonances with fictional female characters such as Quina in *A Sibila,* written more than twenty years earlier. In contrast to Natália Correia, who as we will see in chapter 4 recreates the mystical aura of Florbela Espanca's poetic genius, the better to identify herself with it, Bessa Luís tends rather to deauratize and demythologize her subject. Indeed, she claims she experienced the legacy of writing about Florbela as a troubled and unwelcome imposition, a feeling she shares with the younger writer, Hélia Correia, to be explored in chapter 5.[32]

Bessa Luís's Florbela Espanca is reconstructed very much in the mold of one of her exceptional, gifted women characters. Revealing aspects of both Fisalina and Quina, she is cursed by her exceptionalism, and this curse is manifested in the nonmaternal body, in the virilization that is visited upon women who seek the status of a poetic genius that is firmly sexed as male. As Catherine Dumas has astutely pointed out, Bessa Luís treats poetry in this work as a form of sublimation that is peculiar to male sexuality, and therefore not available to women whose "natural" link to maternity makes them unable to distance or abstract themselves from the inescapably physical materiality of the female body. As Bessa Luís remarks of Florbela:

> She is without doubt a great poetess. Her genius is not feminine, as it never is in poets. Poetry is not feminine. . . . Poetry partakes of the nature of perversion, which always takes the form of sublimation; poetry is just a sublimation that gets appreciated. It is not feminine, though. The eternal feminine is a state of maturity that goes beyond the personal. Woman never sees herself as alienated from her own body, and therefore constrained by her sexuality. She attains the absolute in maternity; man seeks the absolute through sexual aspiration and therefore through the process of sublimation.

> [É, sem dúvida, uma grande poetisa. O seu génio não é feminino, como nunca o é nos poetas. A poesia não é feminina. . . A poesia participa do carácter da perversão, que é sempre uma sublimação; a poesia é apenas uma sublimação apreciada. Não é, portanto, feminina. O eterno feminino é uma maturidade suprapessoal. A mulher nunca se define como isolada do seu próprio corpo, e portanto constrangida pela sua sexualidade. Ela atinge o todo na maternidade; o homem busca o todo no objectivo sexual, e, por conseguinte, no processo da sua sublimação.] (27)

If sublimation cannot be female and therefore women cannot attain it through poetry, this makes Florbela either masculine in her abstract aesthetic contemplation of the body (hence Bessa Luís's comparisons of Florbela, via the critic José Régio, with Don Juan), or an excessively desiring hysteric who fails to sublimate extreme emotion successfully into "true" poetry. Nor can she simply bridge the "maternal deficit," after the fact of genius, by some other means. The figure of the overreaching, masculinized genius evidently cannot simply reconstruct socially the essentialized maternal body that she has forsaken in the pursuit of fame. Thus, Quina the sybil is punished by the gods for her "unnatural" Oedipalized love of Custódio, and Florbela is presented by Bessa Luís as incestuously and fetishistically loving her younger brother Apeles, a role in which she is tellingly likened to Antigone, the famous grieving sister of Sophoclean drama (135).

Furthermore, where the suicidal neurosis that kills Florbela is rooted in her perverse physical pathology, in what Battersby would call her "misplaced sexuality," namely her failure to truly "be" a woman, alongside her inability convincingly to "ape" the men, the act of suicide itself loses its auratic force in the narrative of Romantic genius.[33] It is no longer the ultimate sublimation of desire beyond the body, but rather the absolute failure of such a sublimation in Florbela's case. She is crowned with the word "poetisa" in the statement above not as a "gift," as Natália Correia would view it, but rather as a consolation prize. In Dumas's reading of *Florbela Espanca*, Bessa Luís absorbs Florbela into the maternal embrace of her own fiction, her own acts of artistic sublimation as the following indicates:

> Agustina Bessa Luís portrays this reality and its sublimation, making Florbela into a myth. She portrays them, . . . with all the affection the subject of the biography inspires in her. . . . Marked by the image of gestation, the poetry of Florbela is absorbed into the poetics of the novelist-biographer who herself becomes part of this very same poetics.

> [Agustina Bessa Luís pinta a realidade e a sua sublimação, fazendo de Florbela um mito. Pinta-as, . . . com toda a simpatia que lhe inspira o sujeito biografado. . . . Marcada pela imagem da gestação, a poesia de Florbela é absorvida pela própria poética da romancista-biógrafa que participa também desta mesma poética.][34]

Given that Florbela herself is so substantially defeminized by Bessa Luís casting her in terms of Don Juanism and hermaphroditism, we would ask how consistently this maternal, gestational mother-daughter association is sustained. On what grounds is Bessa Luís's biographical narrator seeking common cause with Florbela, as a sexually conflicted female writing subject? It is noteworthy in this work how far Bessa Luís's biographical voice retains the intellectualized, aphoristic, and gnomic third-person narrative distance

that is characteristic of her prose fiction style. Perhaps the most telling feature of *Florbela Espanca* is its resistance of all temptation to eulogize, in contrast to Natália Correia's paeons of praise to Florbela, as we will see in
chapter 4 and Hélia Correia's thoughtful revision in chapter 5, of Florbela's
critical ill-treatment by the canon. The license enjoyed by the novelist enables Bessa Luís to retain a position of mastery over her creation that resists
both the emotive pull of the biographical subject, and feminine (or feminist?) identification through eulogy. In this sense, the consciously unclear
and ambivalent *genre* boundary of this text, between literary biography and
historical fiction, may also be read as indexing an unclear *gender* boundary
as regards Bessa Luís's own gender positioning as putative biographer in respect of former generations of female literary influence. The possibility
opened up by the biographical format for feminine self-recognition in the
mirror, through the "other woman of letters," the historical interarticulation
of a mother and daughter poetics of continuity, is constantly resisted. In this
sense, *Florbela Espanca* seems to represent a slightly uneasy experiment in
Bessa Luís's opus. Certainly her biographical studies are substantially out-
numbered by her vast novelistic output, in many of which, dialogues with
the great male prose writers of European tradition assume central importance. For example, an attempt to "outmaster" the master of Portuguese Romantic fiction on his own terms is clearly central to the novel *Fanny Owen,*
one of Bessa Luís's best-known literary historical romances, published in
1979, the same year as *Florbela Espanca.*

FANNY OWEN—WRITING ON THE HYMEN, DECENTERING SEX

In this novel, Bessa Luís makes no attempt to rescue the Romantic heroine
from her death in the watchtowers of the male-authored canon. Nor does
she claim a voice for suppressed female authorship under Romanticism. She
does, however, contest the narrative mastery of Portuguese and other European Romantic traditions authored and protagonized by men, thereby decentering the "natural" masculinity of the genius text by exposing the
dynamics of sexual difference on which it rests. The voice of the narrator in
Fanny Owen engages in overtly ironizing dialogue with the Romantic "father
figure," Camilo Castelo Branco (1825–90), who has remained one of Bessa
Luís's most significant and lasting literary interlocutors, including in her
1994 collection of essays and creative texts, *Camilo. Génio e Figura.*[35] In her
literary and critical exchanges with Camilo, Bessa Luís bears out Elizabeth
A. Fay's important assertion, in relation to the English Romantics, that many
women writers did, in fact, find a voice within the possibilities offered by

Romanticism, most significantly, by adopting positions of critique. This afforded them a means of participating in Romanticism as traditionally defined by the works of male writers, while at the same time marking their difference from some of its key beliefs.[36] As Fay puts it, "women writers, . . . needed to have a complex relation to Romanticism, one which allowed them to absorb and yet dissent from its main precepts."[37]

Bessa Luís's novel *Fanny Owen* was originally produced as the basis for a script for the Manoel de Oliveira film *Francisca* (1981), which portrays the relationship between Camilo and Fanny Owen, a real historical figure who was one of his female muses.[38] It is significant that Bessa Luís does not focus here on the literary legacy that was left in reality by Ana Plácido, the most famous of Camilo's lovers, but also a Romantic woman writer in her own right. Her literary reputation was for a long time overshadowed by her role in Camilo's dramatic life, although recent work is beginning to explore Plácido's biography and work in more detail, and she figures prominently in Bessa Luís's critical essays and dramatic writings collected in *Camilo: Génio e Figura*.[39] By choosing to focus on Fanny Owen for her novel on Camilo, Bessa Luís appears to select a more clear-cut case of the masculinization of creative genius leading to the silence, absence, and editing out of the female writing subject in Romantic tradition. Certainly, as the case of *Florbela Espanca* also revealed, recuperations of real literary women have not assumed the critical centrality or importance for posterity that Bessa Luís accorded fictional and intertextual dialogues with male writers.

Written in the form of a literary historical novel, with strongly critical and scholarly overtones, *Fanny Owen* retells and revises one specific part of Camilo's real life story. The rather distant analytical tone of Bessa Luís's novel brings it close to formal literary criticism, openly exploring its own sources and references in its attempts to redraw certain boundaries, to cannibalize and consume the narrative of male genius. The history of Camilo's relationship with Fanny Owen is a fairly well-documented, if contested, set piece in the history of Romanticism.[40] He is known to have met, and possibly fallen in love with, Fanny Owen, the daughter of Colonel Hugo (or Hugh) Owen, a Welsh port wine manufacturer, and a Brazilian mother, living in Oporto in the second half of the nineteenth century. However, Fanny subsequently eloped with Camilo's close friend from college days, José Augusto Pinto de Magalhães. The events surrounding this episode are detailed in Camilo's own writings, particularly his diaries in *Duas Horas de Leitura* (1857) and *No Bom Jesus do Monte* (1864) referring to a visit to the famous Roman Catholic basilica and shrine in Braga. As Maria de Fátima Marinho has noted, his entries for June 7, 1849 and 1854 serve as Bessa Luís's source texts.[41] She also draws on the diaries of her other key protagonists, José Augusto and Fanny herself, as well as on Camilo's fictional variants of their story. In *Fanny Owen,* Bessa Luís produces a series of resisting readings of Camilo's accounts of the affair in which he portrays himself in the first person as an innocent and neutral party. The effect of her reworking is to wrest narrative authority from Camilo, casting him as an ultraromantic, somewhat demonic, central character in her own novel, written in a style that partly pastiches his own. As Magalhães has aptly remarked, "Agustina Bessa Luís reveals herself to be more like Camilo in this novel, than Camilo himself" (136).[42] Bessa Luís explains in her preface, "I used a collage effect, and nearly all of his [Camilo's] speeches are authentic, things that he himself wrote in novellas, in fragments, on pages where he jotted down his thoughts" [Usei a *colagem,* e quase todas as suas falas são as autênticas, que ele escreveu, em novelas, nos dispersos e nas folhas em que anotava os seus pensamentos (7)].

The key difference between Bessa Luís's version and Camilo's in *No Bom Jesus do Monte,* as most critics have noted, is that she paints Camilo's role in this intrigue in a considerably more negative light than that in which he depicts himself, adding an aggressive, at times sexually ambiguous, rivalry between the two male friends. The symbolic encoding of desire in this novel works metonymically through the circulation of texts that take the form of letters, diaries, creative fiction, poetry and, as we will see, body parts. Bessa Luís's revision of Camilo's accounts leaves little doubt that Camilo sought to sow discord between the couple, handing José Augusto letters, which Fanny had addressed to himself (i.e., Camilo), who subsequently pretended they had been destined for a man named Fuentes. According to Bessa Luís, Fuentes may even have been a fictitious figure whom Camilo invented, as an alibi to deflect public attention from his own instrumental role in dividing Fanny and José Augusto (182). In the context of canonical Portuguese Romanticism, her critique of Camilo remains quite daring even for the 1980s, and it certainly attracted some refutation from establishment positivist scholars in Oporto.[43]

Whether the specifics of Bessa Luís's revisionism withstand scholarly scrutiny or not, the issue at stake here is the way in which she uses Camilo's source texts to write her own critical narrator into the position of mastery that was beloved of mainstream Romantic males.[44] In so doing, she reveals how particular constructions of the masculine and feminine body are central to, and underwrite, the sexual dynamics of writer and written in the Romantic canon. At the same time, she exposes the considerable gender ambivalence and ambiguity at the heart of these sexual constructions as they work in particular ways toward the rhetorical elevation of the genius male.

In Camilo's own accounts of his time with the Owen family in 1853, he asserts that his friend José Augusto was initially attracted to Fanny's sister, Maria, but later switched his attentions to Fanny herself. José Augusto eloped with Fanny in 1853, although Camilo claims he tried to dissuade him from doing so. After the elopement José Augusto was sent a series of potentially compromising letters which Fanny herself had supposedly addressed to a former male friend or lover, thought to be the Spanish man named Fuentes. These letters fuelled José Augusto's doubts about Fanny's past fidelity and affections for him, the marriage turned cold, and he subsequently kept Fanny cloistered in his Douro mansion, O Lodeiro, where she died of consumption in 1854. Camilo himself was widely accused at the time of having sent the letters out of jealousy and revenge, although he vigorously denied it. Following Fanny's death, José Augusto died from an opium overdose, believed to have been accidental.[45] In his subsequent writings, Camilo drew on the lives of Fanny and José Augusto and the mysterious circumstances of their deaths, even making it public that the autopsy which José Augusto had had performed on Fanny's body revealed her to be still a virgin at the time of her death. The question of her virginity, the posthumous intactness of her hymen that symbolizes the sexual rivalry between the two men, ultimately comes to metonymize the battle for narrative authority that is here fought, quite literally, over a woman's body as inscrutable text. The narrative authority that emerges from the battle between the men, however, is ultimately shown to rest on a decidedly ambivalent, shifting, and unstable inscription within heterosexual masculinity.

Fanny Owen, the disputed object of the two men's passion, is constantly described, through their observing gaze, as an incorporeal Romantic muse. Thus, recalling Bessa Luís's gendered description of poetry in her work on Florbela Espanca, Fanny functions predictably as the aesthetic medium by which men experience the inspiration of the sublime. Never allowing her to figure as a real, embodied woman, the two men perceive her in terms of the awe-inspiring sphere of nature, and the Romantic opposites of maternal angel and femme fatale. The narrator describes Fanny as the "libidinal fulcrum of the entire plot" [pólo libidinal de toda a intriga (223)]. Repeatedly compared to Lotte in Goethe's *Sorrows of the Young Werther,* Fanny is represented as if at one remove, in the act of being constructed by the consolidated gaze of European male Romantic tradition. As the narrator puts it, "in addition to her biological condition, woman has been elevated to this mission of reconciling opposites, through the production of symbol" [para além da sua condição biológica, a mulher elevou-se a essa missão de conciliadora de opostos, pela produção do símbolo (105)].

For José Augusto, who has recently lost his mother, this takes the explicit form of a Lacanian eternal "Feminine," the illusory maternal mirror that appears to reconcile the contradictions in his own perceptions of identity and reality. Bessa Luís's narrator remarks,

> José Augusto was very much engaged in making Fanny a symbol. That is, in driving away the disorder of the unconscious, through the conscious function of symbol. So Fanny became for him a means of salvation, whilst Camilo was imposing his law on the truth and invading the field of the unconscious in which José Augusto was left struggling.

> [José Augusto estava extremamente empenhado em fazer de Fanny um símbolo. Isto é, em afastar a perturbação do inconsciente através da função consciente do símbolo. Assim, Fanny tornou-se para ele um método de salvação, à medida que Camilo ia impondo o seu direito sobre a verdade e invadindo o campo do inconsciente em que se debatia José Augusto]. (104)

It is in this role as the increasingly fantasized and unreal point of negotiation between the two men, that Fanny bears interesting comparison with Marta, the heroine of Mário de Sá-Carneiro's modernist prose classic 1914, *A Confissão de Lúcio*.[47] Marta also has little existence in her own right, serving rather in this work to contain, transmit, and transform the sexual tensions that are generated by the highly ambiguous homoerotic relations between the two artistic male friends at the center of the novel, Lúcio and Ricardo.[47]

For Camilo, moving in a similarly constituted love triangle, both Fanny and José Augusto are ambiguously cast, at different points, as objects of his desire.[48] Thus, in Bessa Luís's constellation linking the woman and the two men, the shared idealization of Fanny persistently fails to stabilize male sexual identification. Interestingly, for our purposes, this nonstabilization and nonconsummation of sexuality is spoken, or rather coded, in terms of male "genius." The term "genius" or "génio" repeatedly recurs "out of place" in the novel, in contexts which relate it, not to literary creativity, but to moments of sexual or affective crisis. In this sense, the very term "genius" functions as a kind of code for sexual ambiguity and male homoerotic desire, recalling Elfenbein's assertion that the "potential intersection between genius and sexual transgression shaped the careers of men and women producing literature."[49]

Only on the verge of her death does Fanny openly express her own physical needs. Even then, her plea seems to take the form of rhetorically rehearsing the impossibility of physical fulfillment because of José Augusto's genius, as she cries, "I want to conquer you, José Augusto. Possess you, steal you from everyone and from yourself. From your genius . . . from your genius" [eu quero vencer-te, José Augusto. Possuir-te, roubar-te a todos e a ti próprio. Ao teu génio . . . ao teu génio (209)].[50] Spoken in the context of Fanny's own sexual frustrations, and with the ellipsis deliberately implied in the three suspension points, José Augusto's "genius" here could refer not only to his own "transgression" making him unavailable to Fanny, but also, more suggestively, to a competing relationship with Camilo, possessively claimed here as "your," that is, José Augusto's, genius. José Augusto's rather prosaic response to the outburst above is to think regretfully about an alternative wife he could have had, who would not have made major physical or emotional demands. She would have been a female relative, "a young widow whom he had almost courted. She was rich and healthy; she could give him children and help him to pay off his loans. What else could one expect of a woman?" [jovem viúva, que ele quase cortejara. Era rica e saudável; podia dar-lhe filhos e ajudá-lo a pagar as suas hipotecas. Que mais se podia inferir de uma mulher?" (209). This reflection is rapidly superseded by a nostalgic memory of Camilo in happier times.

After José Augusto's own death, the narrator states, "without Fanny, what was a simple bohemian affection, between Camilo and José Augusto, would not have become obsessive to the point of extreme behavior, such as handing over the compromising letters" [sem Fanny, aquilo que foi uma simples afeição de boémios, entre Camilo e José Augusto, não crescia em obsessão até acções exorbitantes, como a entrega das cartas comprometedoras (223)]. On one level, this implies that heightened passion for Fanny has caused Camilo's rivalry to go beyond all sanctioned norms in breaking the pair up. However, it could also signal that Camilo's desire for José Augusto has required his direct intervention in the couple's romantic future and physical consummation, the ploy with the letters. The narrator's prefacing of this observation with a comment on the "simple bohemian affection" between the two men inclines toward the latter reading. Furthermore, Camilo himself has previously been referred to as a "little Plato" who all his life had to "cover with a dirty mantle that friendship that had seemed to him capable of casting the very gods down from Olympus" [cobrir com um manto sujo aquela amizade que lhe tinha parecido capaz de precipitar os próprios deuses de Olimpo (206)]. This is emphasized again when Camilo finally turns his attention to another young male companion, José Vieira de Castro, who adores him and whose "intimacy had replaced that of José Augusto" [intimidade substituíra a de José Augusto (226)].

Read in this context, the consummation of love between Fanny and José Augusto, as a married couple, appears as having to be prevented at all costs, so that Camilo's own ambiguous desire can be kept in play. The turning point for Camilo comes when Fanny, the key to this triangulation of desire, threatens to escape her objectified position and to take control of her own corporeal identification as a woman, by arranging to elope with José Augusto in defiance of her family. As she flees her restrictive bourgeois relatives, she precipitates crisis for, and between, José Augusto and Camilo by making them realize that she is not merely part of the "choirs of asexual angels" [coros dos anjos assexuados], but literally, "a fearsome woman" [uma mulher temível" (201)]. The realization of her embodied sexuality is also the potential realization of their own in relation to each other.

The failed romance and death of Fanny appear to feed Camilo's literary aesthetic project in the manner of Lacan's famous assertion whereby "the symbol manifests itself first of all as the murder of the thing, and this death constitutes in the subject the eternalization of his desire."[51] However, the death of José Augusto will also serve Camilo's art. Crucial to disclosing this aestheticization process, the transition from sex to text, is the fetishization of Fanny Owen by both men, as dead virginal body and missing female-authored text. Camilo's incriminating letters apparently lead José Augusto to doubt Fanny's honor and to become estranged from her. Fanny's early death from consumption, the classic repressive demise of the Romantic heroine, appears to be hastened by her unhappy marriage, confined to José Augusto's northern mansion during his prolonged absences. The truth of Fanny's previous life (the possibility of former lovers) is ostensibly made into the irresolvable enigma at the heart of the novel. However, the relations between the two men also become further enigmatized in the process of interrogating Fanny's past. José Augusto unsuccessfully searches both Fanny's dead body and her diary for clues to her history.

After her death, Fanny's corpse becomes a fetishized work of art, kept in a glass-lidded casket in the church at Vilar while her heart is removed and preserved in alcohol in the chapel of José Augusto's estate at Lodeiro. Where the dead body is fetishized and exposed to view as an artistic object, it functions, in conventional Freudian terms, as phallus substitute to reassure the male subject who, fearing castration and/as death, must simultaneously, ambivalently disavow and remember the lost phallus through attempts at its substitution.[52] According to Elisabeth Bronfen "the fetishist's attitude toward feminine sexuality and toward death is a duplicitous compromise that . . . replaces or augments an 'object of desire' in an effort to restabilize a conception of self dependent on the image of an 'adequate' other, put into question by the unwelcome perception that the feminine body is neither phallic nor immortal."[53]

In this respect, José Augusto clearly uses the dead body of Fanny, which he repeatedly visits in the chapel at Vilar, as a fetish to ward off the fear of castration and death. To use Bronfen's terms, he transfers this realization of the " 'inadequate body' on to another site, on to that 'something else' which has taken the place of the 'lacking part' . . . the doubly 'castrated' body of a dead woman embalmed as a self-reflexive reduplication, as its own auto-icon."[54] However, a further act of fetishism occurs here through the post-mortem examination that José Augusto has performed to determine Fanny's past sexual history. While José Augusto ostensibly does this as a matter of personal honor, it is Camilo who makes public in his writings the account of Fanny dying a virgin. It is he who turns the hymen into a public symbol. By insisting that this be the official record on memory, Camilo displays the unexpected presence of an intact hymen in a married woman, much to the detriment of his friend's masculine reputation as a husband and "morgado" or landed male heir. Through this virginal hymen-centered reading, the "feminized" phallic lack that is the dead body of Fanny is effectively, retro-spectively, associated with and displaced onto the body of José Augusto. In-sofar as Fanny's virginity points to the absence of male heterosexual consummation by José Augusto, he is thus preserved "intact" from hetero-sexual relations in Camilo's fictionalized memories of him.

Furthermore, in contrast to Fanny's allegedly virginal body as "unwritten hymen," the dead corpus of writing that she leaves behind in her diary has been unexpectedly filled or intruded upon by the phallic male pen. A single word regarding a former lover, in her diary, has been crossed out and altered. The phrase "the man that now detests me" [o homem que hoje me detesta] has replaced "the man that now torments me" [o homem que hoje me ator-menta (219)]. What is more, some pages have subsequently been ripped out, further emphasizing the inverse parallel of the intact hymen and the violated text. This raises the question as to who edited her diaries in the intervening years, before they are known to have come into Camilo's own hands six years after they were written (211; 219). As Bessa Luís's narrator implies, the miss-ing pages and some of the diary alterations point to editorial intervention by Camilo himself.[55]

The lesbian feminist critic Mary S. Gossy has written powerfully and com-pellingly about the fictitious meanings that attach to the hymen in the social and literary critical economies of patriarchy. For Gossy, "the hymen is fic-tionalized and made to tell the story of the phallus marking woman as object; stories of marriage/copulation or virginity, or both; but never neither—that is, never the story of a hymen indifferent to the phallus."[56] In poststructura-list and psychoanalytical criticism, this has found important parallels in the compulsion to fill with interpretation those "vaginal" gaps and ellipses that emerge in the weave of textual signification.[57] It is no accident, therefore, that Camilo's penetration and part destruction of Fanny's diary text, writing on the metaphorical hymen, is implicitly bound up with maintaining his own account of Fanny's virginal past. At the same time, it also leaves José Augusto's place in the patriarchal, heterosexual order dephallicized and over-

written by another man. The body of the virginal woman who did not officially belong to the patriarchy has become, metonymically, a text that now
does. Sexual possession of Fanny has been transmuted into textual possession, the condition of (men's) symbolic language and culture. And Camilo,
as genius writer, has come out of the tragedy empowered.

Following the death of José Augusto, the story of the two lovers richly
inspires Camilo's own literary work. However, Bessa Luísa's narrator has intervened in this process by reediting the story of Camilo's two "original"
interventions in Fanny's written exchanges, his misdirection of the love letters, and his possible diary editing. Further, by operating her own form of
revisionist "post-mortem" on the iconic works of the now dead Camilo, fill-
ing the gaps and ambiguities of his originals with her own interpretations
and hypotheses, the narrator discloses a powerful counterphallic desire for
the fetishized corpus of Camilo's texts. In this process, she reveals Fanny's
disembodiment functioning purely instrumentally as the means by which
the sexually fluid identities of male Romantic genius are kept in circulation.

Rather than recuperate a single scholarly "truth" about this episode of
Romantic literary history, *Fanny Owen* forms a series of ever-receding absences. But the silencing of female subjectivity in Fanny's altered and ob-
scured diary is turned here into a highly visible absence. Without ever
writing herself into existence, Fanny acquires a kind of eloquence insofar as
she symptomatizes the discursive conditions governing the absence of wom-
en's creative genius from the Portuguese Romantic canon. And the aesthetic
process by which the woman writer is edited out and overwritten in the literary history of Romanticism is clearly interrogated, albeit subtextually, for the
gendered fictions that it generates in forging the transgressive masculinities
that get named as "genius."

The question of the historically absent, or hijacked, female body-text,
forms the basis for one of Bessa Luís's best-known and most daring engagements with male-authored tradition, in *Vale Abraão* in 1991. If *Fanny Owen*
discloses a masculine textualizing of and through the dead female body, *Vale
Abraão* reincorporates the Madame Bovary tradition as a "dead male text."
Like *Fanny Owen, Vale Abraão* was made into a film by Manoel de Oliveira
in 1993.[58] Indeed, the novel was written at the request of Oliveira, who suggestively described it at the time as "a vision, a kind of 'remake' of the Flaubert character" [uma visão, uma espécie de 'remake' da personagem de
Flaubert.][59] In this cinematographic "remake" text, Bessa Luís points beyond
the rigid sex dichotomies whose transgression brings tragedy in *A Sibila,* and
beyond the sexual ambiguities of Romantic genius masculinity in *Fanny
Owen.* Drawing more fully than in these previous works on the ludic and
comic potential of postmodern pastiche, simulacra and sexual dragging,

Bessa Luís moves in *Vale Abraão* toward a more overtly gender-conscious challenge to the cornerstones of European realism.

Vale Abraão or Madame Bovary c'est quoi?

In *Vale Abraão,* Bessa Luís tells the story of a twentieth-century provincial northern Portuguese Emma Bovary, updating Gustave Flaubert's foundational realist tale of adultery. Bessa Luís's novel is played out as a self-conscious Flaubertian mirror-text with constant allusions, on many levels, to Emma Bovary.[60] Ema Paiva enjoys compulsive affairs, and indeed knowingly and self-ironically inhabits the *persona* of Emma Bovary in the public eye, pursuing rather more sexual adventures than Emma Bovary's paltry two, and proving to be a destructive force in the lives of men. She thus assumes the socially aberrant role of the adulteress for her own purposes, repeating her adulterous mores long after their ability to shock or provoke crisis has subsided. Eventually, the very mythology of the symbolic legacy she inhabits, outpaces her body's ability to sustain it in the public eye.

Key to our reading is the way in which Ema Paiva's partial and resistant textual mirroring of Flaubert's Bovary enables her to produce her own autobiographical textuality, her own dissident rewriting of the realist "model," through the inscription of her body into a series of mythical narrative and cultural precedents that progressively displace the Bovary "original." In this respect, an important point of reference for our reading is Elisabeth Bronfen's analysis of *Madame Bovary,* in which she indicates that Emma's adultery and death, inspired by her excessively literal readings of Romantic fiction, are intimately bound up with the act of life-writing and memory (the very form that we saw suppressed in *Fanny Owen's* diary), and therefore with the historical construction of female authorship itself. Thus *Madame Bovary* may be read as a kind of "suicidal autobiography" in a process of "voluntary fading before the text she writes," so that, according to Bronfen, "as Emma writes herself out of existence to become the romantic heroines she has been so possessed by in her reading, she does so almost exclusively in the order of the body. . . . Her self-textualization engenders a form of self-obliteration while at the same time suicide generates texts and constructs the dead self as author."[61]

Performing various literary and mythical feminine roles for herself and her audiences, before a series of actual and figurative mirrors, the Portuguese Ema Paiva certainly reproduces aspects of Emma Bovary's literary self-textualization as dead romantic heroine, using the self-conscious construction of her own female body to prescribe her own future memoir. For Bessa Luís, however, there is a crucial variation of focus and scope. In *Vale Abraão*, this process of self-authoring through death is characteristically not merely individual but rather, as the link back to the Bovary realist paradigm suggests, it connects with a universalized suppression of women's cultural memory, resulting from their historical absence or marginality in relation to male literary traditions. Thus, her Ema does not stop at representing a modern, self-ironically overperformed Emma Bovary as pastiche. She also takes on the guise of a simulacrum, an image that covers the "empty space" in western literary tradition, in which no female Flaubert exists.

The position that Ema ultimately reproduces, then, is not only that of the would-be romantic heroine or the suicidal realist heroine. It is also an allegory of the would-be realist woman writer, seeking to fashion an authorial self, out of male-authored canonical antecedents. As several critics have noted, the Bible's patriarchal order of Abraham is clearly invoked in Abraão de Paiva, the mythical founder of the valley, and the family into which Ema will marry, despite coming from the sinister left bank of the river, and having a crucially deformed left foot, which connects her from the beginning with the distaff side of genealogy, the occluded facet of culture.[62] Central to the novel's metatextual process of resisting male realist genealogy is the heroine Ema Paiva's relationship to her actual dead mother, who comes to metonymize the absence of a genealogical legacy for women writers, the symbolic lack of the cultural Mother.[63]

In common with most realist adultery novel heroines, Ema has lost her biological mother an early age.[64] For Bessa Luís, then, this classic maternal deficit finds itself expanded to include the collective cultural suppression of all female historical memory, the exclusion of the female body as agent of cultural expression. Left without an adequate female role model, or any ongoing female lineage, Ema is raised by her Aunt Augusta.[65] Thus Ema is described as living as if in a "desert of meanings" [num deserto de significados (210)]. Refusing to close the imaginary with the symbolic cut of phallic language, Ema remains in a permanent state of dissidence. This is directly linked by the narrator to her lack of induction by the mother, into the workings of patriarchal symbolic law, stating that:

> If her mother had lived with her another ten years, she would have transmitted the meaning of woman to her, as she who is constructed to bear children, which would not then have come as a surprise to her. But was this criterion really appropriate to its object? . . . No language is definitive and Ema always proceeded on that basis.
>
> [Se a mãe tivesse vivido com ela mais dez anos, transmitia-lhe o significado de mulher, a que é construída para parir filhos, o que não constituiria surpresa. Mas

seria esse critério apropriado ao objecto? . . . Nenhuma linguagem é definitiva. Ema procedia dentro dessa noção (211)]

As Bronfen points out, Emma Bovary's response to her mother's death was one of "aestheticisation, the first instance of her self-authorship against death and under its auspices."[66] For Ema Paiva, the image of her dead mother laid out in her wedding dress in the beautiful "oratório" of the house at Romesal is similarly destined to recur throughout *Vale Abraão*, framing the heroine's aesthetic self-recognition in the trappings of death, but also marking points at which she fails, or refuses, to be installed in the patriarchal symbolic order.

Like her French near-namesake, Ema marries the widowed local doctor Carlos Paiva but soon grows bored with provincial living as a bourgeois doctor's wife, and resents the imposition of motherhood. Prone to fantasizing romance she is ripe for seduction at the first society ball she attends at Jacas, the home of her neighbors, Pedro and Simone Lumiares, as she meets a young businessman Fernando Osório and has an affair with him. This and Ema's other sexual liaisons, and her destructive cruelty toward men, become an obsessively repeated, almost symptomatic pretext for her own cultural identity quest. The narrator poses particularly starkly the dichotomy that Ema faces regarding her lack of symbolic repertoire.

Ema was a woman who survived innumerable failures in the ranks of the female past. Men built their castles and shut themselves away in them and reigned as best they could over their servants, including their wives and concubines. But women were left comparing themselves to a plant or a dog. There were some who could not bear this, and they found the easiest thing was to act like men.

[(Ema) Era uma mulher que sobrevivia a um sem-número de fracassos nas fileiras do passado feminino. Os homens construíam castelos, fechavam-se lá dentro e reinavam de qualquer maneira entre os seus serviçais, incluindo as esposas e as concubinas. Mas as mulheres tinham que se comparar a um cão, ou um vegetal. Havia algumas que não aguentavam isso, e o mais simples era parecerem-se com homens]. (96)

In light of her quest for cultural identity through transgression, Vesúvio, the family estate of Ema's first lover, is gradually transformed from being a trysting place to being a space in which Ema can contemplate herself. Consequently, Fernando Osório's importance to Ema long outlives their actual sexual affair. The form of mirror-gazing in which she engages there, relates directly to her lack of any individual or collective ancestral memory as a woman. As the narrrator remarks, "woman has no historical memory, for the time being, other than that which is loaned to her by man" [a mulher não tem por ora memória histórica senão aquela que lhe é emprestada pelo homem (142)]. Ema's response to this is to seek some form of retrospective feminine identification through her imagined affinities with the "borrowed" female ancestors of Fernando Osório. This leads her to become fixated on the unnamed "Senhora," Osório's long-dead but once powerful grand-mother, whose portrait hangs in the house at Vesúvio. Ema talks to her pic-ture and admires the legends of her astute, hard-headed business deals and mastery of men. Yet her attempt to establish a retrospective genealogy of shared "female" cultural forms fails. She realizes that she shares only a sense of hostility with the old women on the Vesúvio estate, the "bruxas" or witches, driven by the envy that she also discerns on the face of A Senhora (152–54). The female intergenerational legacy that she finds under the sign of patriarchy in the male property of the Vesúvio, with its treacherous mir-rors and portraits, is only one of women's alienation, separation, and mutual destruction, as they survive and rule by adopting pragmatic phallic identifi-cations.

Resisting the authority of virilized, desexed or masculinized cultural iden-tity, Ema's "self-Bovarization" expands to include acting out a whole range of iconic, fatal, hyperfeminine roles in myth and fiction, associated with the "innumerable failures in the ranks of the female past" [sem-número de fra-cassos nas fileiras do passado feminino (96)] that the narrator describes her as surviving. These acts of self-representation are bound up with the media-tions of two men. The aristocratic Pedro Dossém, her *pagem* and fashion adviser, stage-manages her social performances. Her neighbor from Jacas, Pedro Lumiares, is her intellectual and philosophical guide and confident. It is with Lumiares as her appreciative audience that she performs the roles of other dead, textualized female heroines of western cultural mythology.

> She would act out roles as if she were in the theater. . . . She would laugh and make gestures with such artistry and amusement without ever seeming ridiculous or banal, that Lumiares would eclipse himself to yield all the space to her, aware that Ema wanted the love of all men at that moment and that to that end, she would give her own life to hear applause, . . .: she was Dido, crowned with a tower of gold. . . .: she was Iphigenia, sighing for her childhood in the shadow of her father. . . . She was the duchess of Praslin, vengefully trailing her chestnut silken skirts across the carpet of her boudoir.

> [Ela actuava como no teatro, . . . Ria e gesticulava com tal arte e desenfado, sem ser jamais ridícula ou banal, que Lumiares se apagava para lhe deixar todo o espaço, consciente de que Ema queria o amor de todos os homens nesse momento e que, para isso, seria capaz de dar a vida pelos aplausos. . . .: era Dido, coroada duma torre de oiro, . . .; era Ifigénia, suspirando pela infância na sombra do

pai. . . . Era a duquesa da Praslin, vingativa e arrastando as saias de seda castanha nos tapetes do seu boudoir.] (194)

It is also Lumiares who coins her nickname of Bovarinha in the diminutive and who points out to her that "the Bovary woman was a man" [a Bovary era um homem" (236)]. Thus, becoming the new Bovary does not establish a clear model of femininity, and the diminutive affords an ironic differentiation from the "original" given Ema's quest to exceed the role rather than reduce it. This theatricalized dialogue between Ema and Lumiares, quoting and questioning the sexual boundaries of the roles Ema inhabits, will effectively install her in a citational rather than a mimetic order of staged performance. Ema's compulsive need to repeat and reproduce, again and again, the hyperfeminine performances of the dead and hysteric women of western culture (echoing her melodramatic need for relations with multiple men) spills over into the realm of dragging and pastiche. As such, these roles fail to cohere into any essentially sexed body. As noted above Ema has never been disciplined to a sanctioned feminine role in the symbolic order as wife and mother. But nor does the consciously constructed Bovaresque role of adulteress establish her reliably as femme fatale, hysteric or "Other" of culture, at the edge of language. Her never complete, never closed consolidation of sexuality increasingly works beyond the operations of Lacanian law. Particularly crucial to how we read the regulation of paternal law, and thence the dissident nature of Ema Paiva's sexual self-authoring in this novel, is the ambiguity surrounding her eventual death.

The death of the adulterous heroine, even if by suicide, is conventionally seen in mainstream western realist tradition as the act of necessary, ritual punishment, the expulsion of dangerous alien matter that reestablishes the social order.[67] In this respect, it corresponds to what Bronfen has called the "sacrifice of a body necessary for the founding of a social community" remarking more specifically, following Julia Kristeva, that "the sacrificed feminine body stages a triumph over the violence of the death drive as dynamizing force which needs to be contained and rejected, and serves as a confirming mirror which guarantees the stability of the social construction of the world."[68]

In the final chapter of the novel, Ema visits Vesúvio for the last time. Falling into the river by accident, she drowns when she is dragged down by the weight of the boot she wears to disguise her deformed left foot.[69] However, her deliberate carelessness with the rotted planks of the landing stage, and her decision not to struggle in the water, make the social meaning of this death indeterminate, somewhere between a suicide and an accident. Certainly, it is unrelated to any immediate sexual transgression and does not have, for example, the contributory force of social condemnation that had pursued the debtor Emma Bovary. Nor is there any ground for reading it as a punishment, in the manner of Eça de Queirós's heroine Luisa, in *O Primo Basílio,* who dies of a fevered exhaustion brought on by the strain of deceiving her husband. Rather the death is bound up with the particular nature of Ema's identity fictions and the fact that she can no longer transgress social law, because its force is no longer active.

When she falls asleep on the day before her death Ema realizes that she is no longer a spectacle being watched by others, as she comments, "noone is paying any attention to me, it is no use pretending otherwise . . . Who am I?" [ninguém me liga, não vale a pena fingir outra coisa . . . Quem sou Eu?'" (293)]. She has lost her power to shock, offend, or dazzle an audience, to mark her sexual identity by exceeding social limits. On her final visit to Vesúvio she prepares to leave the house, feeling curiously disconnected from the image she projects, so that "it was as if she were leaving the stage where she was acting in a play not to her liking but where the crowds were convinced of her role" [era como se deixasse um palco onde fizesse uma peça não do seu agrado mas que convencia a multidão do seu papel (299–300)].

Ema's final act of self-inscription does not mimic the Bovaresque suicide of an unsymbolizable "hysteric." Emma Bovary, as Bronfen describes her, "collides her body with deanimated textual feminine bodies but writes with her body so that it can be read as a text of her emotions."[70] However, Ema Paiva's constantly rehearsed and reworked identifications with the hysteric body of western cultural history do not only operate, as Bronfen puts it, as "dead letters or inanimate figures, metaphorically killing herself [Emma] into an inanimate work of art."[71] Rather they are repeated performances, permitting her to register an ambiguous, unreliably "female-sexed" body as a dynamic, mobile space in cultural memory.[72] As Teresa Salado points out, "de la transtextualité à la transsexualité, il n'y a qu'un pas (une lettre), qu'Agustina Bessa Luís n'hésite pas a franchir, faisant passer le motif de l'androgynie du registre de la suggestion à celui de la nomination."[73]

Staging the hysteric's desire again and again in overlapping guises, Ema's performances of iconic dead heroines in western culture effectively play on the impossibility of emulation. And the dissident potential of this impossible emulation is bound up with the absence of social paternal law. Butler's examination of the discursive limits of sexuality famously takes issue with the Lacanian paradigm whereby sexual subjectivity is installed in the signifying chain of symbolic language and culture through the necessary and absolute force of paternal law and prohibition, with the problematic result that any "recourses to the body before the symbolic can take place only within the symbolic."[74] Instead, Butler focuses on the reiterable and therefore phantasmatic process by which bodies assume "sexual" identification, such that "sex" is produced as an illusionary effect after the fact of its repeated naming. Thus, for Butler, " 'sexed positions' are not localities or constructions" reflecting a "prior reality." Rather they are repeated, citational practices of norms laying claim to authority, after the fact of their instantiation. They are instituted "within a juridical domain" that is dependent precisely on the authority-producing effect of iteration, rather than deriving from any construction of gender that refers back to a material, universal or biological precedent.[75] Nor does the Lacanian paternal law itself exist in any sense other than that induced by its own authority-producing repetitions. For Butler, the resistant potential within sexuality relies on the fact that this form of " 'identification' is thus *repeatedly* produced, and in the demand that the identification be *reiterated* persists the possibility, the threat, that it will *fail* to repeat."[76]

In this context, Ema's persistent and repetitive cultural citations, her compulsion to assume transgressive roles that no longer transgress (i.e., that "*fail* to repeat" successfully,) represent an unloosening of the bounds of absolute sexuality as determined by paternal social law and mimetic (realist) language. Where Ema's death is neither a social punishment nor a ritual sacrifice for the community's good, this is because there is no operation of absolute law, in the Lacanian sense, no force of prohibition creating order and language as its "outside." And her sexual outrages and performances do not, therefore, consolidate a fixed sexual identity as "Woman." Rather they merely reveal the means by which this fiction creates itself and its authoritative effects. Furthermore, this reiterative deconstruction of sexual normativity in *Vale Abraão* affords a new consideration of the role that sex plays, but need not in fact play, in territorializing and deterritorializing myths of artistic genius.

By adopting a performative, citational view of "Woman" in the male-authored realist tradition, Bessa Luís shows how the force of the law which installs Ema's adulterous desire as an act of transgression has progressively lost its meaning over time. The body here has been emptied out of any belief in an essential sexual identity or any absolute law of prohibition installing it reliably in culture. The "authority-producing" effect of social law within realist tradition has simply worn itself out. Ema's repeated performance of the adulterous overstepping of law, her arrogance and excess in knowing no boundary to her affairs, is the very thing that has removed its force as transgression. As the narrator remarks,

Society cast no blame upon her, in so far as its own means of survival were not threatened. On the contrary: Ema was left in peace because scandal favored what may be termed the work of salvation. When a group of people finds itself incapable of true confrontation, when everything points toward immediate solutions favoring comfortable urban prosperity, the spirit of scandal is called upon and rushes to intervene.

[a sociedade não lhe atribuía culpas, na medida em que os seus métodos de so-brevivência não se achavam ameaçados. Pelo contrário: Ema era deixada à von-tade porque o escândalo favorecia o que se pode chamar obra de salvação. Quando um grupo se acha incapaz de afrontamentos verdadeiros, quando tudo concorre para soluções imediatas a favor duma rentabilidade urbana de bem-estar, o génio do escândalo é reclamado e corre a intervir]. (142)

The performance of excess, of scandal, of outsider status, is seen as period-ically socially necessary and desired, reciprocally creating the effect of the social "law" that outlaws it. No absolute cultural, aesthetic outside (the fe-male muse, the female body, the female character) can be reliably inscribed "as nature" by the laws of prohibition and transgression in which the intelli-gibility of sexual difference is grounded, and which underwrite the essential-ist, sexually embodied paradigms on which genius, read as (sexed) exceptionalism, rests.

In this respect, the novel's woman writer character, Maria Semblano, pro-vides an important counterpoint to Ema's process of sexual self-authorship. She is described as Ema's double since, "the two women possessed a double personality" [as duas tinham uma dupla personalidade" (176)].[77] Through the figure of Semblano, *Vale Abraão* effectively ends with two competing cycles of authorship that prevent closure. Semblano is about to publish an-other novel, and she says of herself, "no one emulates a beautiful life better than I do" [ninguém imita melhor que eu uma bela vida" (305)]. This work is explicitly linked to Ema's own story. We are told that she would have found Semblano to be "soulless" [desalmada] in her advocacy for "the de-feated, the guilty, the unjust and the sad" [vencidos, culpados, injustos e tristes (305)]. Ema is not, in the end, to be enclosed either in the moralistic regimes of realist positivism or in the cautionary tales of Maria Semblano. In the closing lines of *Vale Abraão*, it is the dead Ema's word that prevails in respect of her memorialization. Semblano had wanted Ema to be buried and forgotten at Romesal, her childhood home. However, the narrator remarks instead that "Ema would say that this was not for her and that she was fine as she was—at the bottom of the Vesúvio" [Ema diria que isto não era para ela e que estava muito bem como estava—no fundo do Vesúvio (305)].

It is no accident that the place of Ema's (self-)reflection, eventual death, and memorialization is the river at Vesúvio. This is described as being the place where sexual identities are laid down, not through the fixation of mir-

rored reflections, but through the collective ritual effect of cultural sedimen-
tation, the progressively iterated transformation of memory into social
authority. It is significant that Ema herself had previously contemplated the
river in the following terms.

> Romesal, which revolved around happiness and curses, seemed to have cast itself
> into that abyss which was Vesúvio, not in order to lose itself but rather to form
> part of a mysterious store of memory. The dark waters of the river at Vesúvio
> seemed to contain a huge pile of facts, which had been thrown there in the rituals
> of ancient peoples who allowed young men and virgins, jewels and flowers, to
> sink to the bottom of lakes, not just as a sacrificial rite but also, and most particu-
> larly, as the politics of constructing memory.

> [O Romesal, com o seu eixo de imprecações e alegrias, parecia precipitar-se na-
> quele abismo do Vesúvio, não para se perder, mas para fazer parte dum misterioso
> fundo da memória. As água negras do rio, no local do Vesúvio, pareciam conter
> uma pilha imensa de factos, precipitados ali com o ritual dos antigos povos que
> deixavam afundar-se nos lagos virgens e mancebos, e jóias, e flores, não apenas
> como rito sacrificial, mas sobretudo como política de construir a memória. (142)]

The result of Ema's death by drowning in the memory space of the Vesúvio is thus not a refounding of patriarchal community through female sacrifice. Nor does it represent acquiescence with any law that "requires" her
death. Rather it marks the disestablishment of the male-authored mimetic
realist community in literary history. Where Ema is no longer "a Woman"
and Flaubert is no longer "a Man," the multiple performances of Ema in
Vale Abraão cannot mark any female reclamation of the realist genius text.
Rather they suggest the superannuation of the need for any such paradigm at
all, making it merely an authority-producing effect in the history of literary
canonicity, the death of any inevitably or reliably sexed law of genius itself.

4
Matriarchal Precedents: Thus Spoke Natália Correia

In order to embody the Motherland [Natália Correia] surrounded herself
with the wisdom of men . . . That knowledge that is expressed over time
and through writing, she drew from the masculine mind, but that other
way of knowing, the wisdom we associate with mystery, that manifests
itself in art and mysticism, she drew from within herself, through the
natural bond of the womb to the belly of the earth, from her talent as a
pythoness.

[Para incarnar a mátria [Natália Correia] rodeou-se da sabedoria de
homens. . . . O conhecimento que se exprime ao longo do tempo e da
escrita foi buscá-lo à mente masculina, o outro saber, o do mistério, o
que se manifesta na mística e na arte, extraiu-o de si própria, pela natural
ligação do útero ao ventre da terra, pelo seu talento de pitonisa.]
—Clara Menéres, "O Veludo, o Útero e a Rosa"

We are pieced back to the string which leads back, if not to the Name-
of-the-Father, then, for a new twist, to the place of the phallic-mother.
—Hélène Cixous, "The Laugh of the Medusa"

INTRODUCTION—PENNING THE PYTHONESS

IF THE EMBODIED FEMALE SUBJECT SEEMED ELUSIVE AND ENCODED IN AGUS-
tina Bessa Luís, she is everywhere in evidence in the taboo-breaking works
of Natália Correia. Born in the same year as Agustina Bessa Luís, Natália
Correia became one of Portugal's most famous and spectacular public figures
in twentieth-century literature, politics, and the arts, widely associated with
her cult, and personal embodiment, of the Portuguese *Mátria* or Motherland. In order to construct and disseminate this national matriarch position,
she consciously maintained a challenging intellectual dialogue with the great
men of Western philosophy and literature. As the foregoing discussion will
demonstrate, Correia's panoply of masculine interlocutors ranged from the
classics, in Sophocles and Euripides, via modern philosophical and psychoanalytical thought, in Friedrich Nietzsche and Sigmund Freud, to the experi-

mental theater of Brecht and Artaud. In order to explore the shifting construction of the Mátria and of women's culture that Correia presents in her interrogation of male-authored canons and aesthetic legacies, we focus our principle analysis on four works from different genres: the dramatic poem *O Progresso de Édipo* [Oedipus's Progress] (1957), the play *A Pécora* [The Whore] (1983), the novel *A Madona* [The Madonna] (1968), and poems from the collection *O Armistício* [The Armistice] (1985).[1] *A Madona* published in 1968 and *A Pécora,* published in 1983 but initially written in 1966, both stem from the same period, the late 1960s, affording a certain synchronic perspective. Extensive cross-reference is also inevitably made, however, to the many other essays, poems, anthologies, and works of journalism that are inspired and informed by Correia's woman-centered philosophy of *Matrismo,* the cult of the Motherland, and by her debates with 1960s and 1970s feminism in the UK and the USA.

Correia's most specific and persistent manifestation of a personal Motherland concerned her own native birthplace of the Azores, where she was born, in Fajã de Baixo on the island of São Miguel in 1923.[2] She died in Lisbon in 1993, having assumed throughout her life a series of different public and literary roles, as playwright, journalist, essayist, polemicist, publisher, critic, translator, politician, broadcaster, opponent of the Estado Novo, literary salon hostess, and presiding doyenne of Lisbon's Botequim bar. In these various capacities, Correia made a career from being the "extraordinária" *par excellence* of late twentieth-century arts and politics in Portugal, although of a considerably more iconoclastic nature than Agustina Bessa Luís. Arriving in Lisbon from the Azores to study in 1934, Correia became involved in antifascist opposition as a young adult in the 1940s, joining the communist-linked MUD (Movimento Unitário Democrático) in 1944/5. She began to publish in earnest in the 1950s and was particularly influential in the development and dissemination of Portuguese surrealism during that period and after, editing the important anthology *O surrealismo na poesia portuguesa* in 1973.[3] Interestingly, this is the role for which she is primarily recorded in Portuguese literary histories of this period, rather than for her more politicized writings on gender.[4]

Correia's work was targeted by Salazarist censorship on several occasions, for breaking sexual taboo and satirizing national mythology. She caused a particularly notable furor with the censors when she edited her *Antologia de Poesia Portuguesa Erótica e Satírica* in 1966 for which she was tried and condemned in 1970 to a three-year suspended prison sentence.[5] Her satire on Sebastianism, *O Encoberto,* published in 1969 was also censored and only staged in 1977.[6] Indeed some of her most important dramatic work was not published or performed until after the 25 April Revolution, most notably *A*

Pécora, written in 1966, but first staged in 1989, and *Dom João e Julieta,* originally written in 1957 but not published or staged until 1999, after Correia's death.[7] In the 1970s, she was also instrumental in publishing, with Estúdio Cor, Portugal's most famous case of feminist literary resistance during the twentieth century, the Three Marias' *Novas Cartas Portuguesas.* Correia gave depositions of support at their trial and the poet Maria Teresa Horta, the most overt and longstanding political feminist of the Three Marias, became Correia's protégée.[8] In the 1980s, Correia supported the decriminalization of abortion. This led to a particularly renowned intervention in the debates of 1982, when she wrote, and declaimed in the Portuguese parliament, a satirical poem denouncing the antiabortionist CDS MP João Morgado for hypocrisy and naivety.[9]

In addition to pursuing her own literary resistance to the regime, Correia supported leading oppositional male writers such as David Mourão-Ferreira and Urbano Tavares Rodrigues. In the early 1970s, Correia became a co-owner of the Botequim Bar, an important political and artistic meeting place during and after the Revolution, particularly among supporters of democratic pluralism, such as the future president, António Ramalho Eanes. Having distanced herself considerably from her early procommunist radicalism, Correia was elected to Parliament in 1979 as an independent on the PPD (Partido Popular Democrata) lists, and reelected in 1987 again as an independent, this time on the PRD (Partido Renovador Democrático) lists, furthering her already close association with Ramalho Eanes. She only left political office in 1991 at the age of sixty-eight.[10] The television programme *Mátria,* which Correia devised and presented for the national channel RTP, started transmission in 1986 and ran throughout the late 1980s. Focusing on key female figures of Portuguese mythology, culture, and national history, this television show consolidated Correia's status as both a household name and a visual embodiment, through her own dramatic persona, of the Portuguese Mátria.

Culturally elitist and steeped in esoteric mythology, it would be far too easy in retrospect to associate Natália Correia's Matrismo solely with essentialist strands of gender conservatism. As Luís Adriano Carlos points out in a tribute ten years after her death, the concept of a mystical Motherland has a mixed and complex history which he reads, in the Portuguese patriotic context, through the seventeenth-century Jesuit, Padre António Vieira and his associations of the Motherland with the earth, and the Fatherland with heaven.[11] Certainly, the Motherland has most conventionally been mobilized by nationalist cultural history, in the cause of male patriotic identifications.[12] Yet, as Carlos indicates, Correia seems more inspired by anti-Christian pagan roots and surrealist conceptualizations of the inchoate feminine, than by

Vieira's Neoplatonic Christianity. Indeed, Correia made a point of being notoriously difficult to pin down, and her far from unitary vision of Matrismo actually varied and shifted considerably across time, context, and artistic medium. The questions that she continues to pose most acutely for a consideration of women's literary and cultural genealogy in Portugal are: how far did she ultimately reterritorialize a strategic Mátria space that could serve as inspirational legacy, and symbolic resource, for literary daughters and feminine cultural production?; how far did her attempt to appropriate and redefine the Mátria as Portuguese cultural paradigm, actually constitute for women writers a workable paradigm shift? We will argue that through her writings over several decades, Correia actually deployed the Mátria as a plural, flexible matrix for maintaining a very personal form of political stance in defence of women's cultural specificity, the feminine symbolic and women's sexual freedom in the face of patriarchal Catholic morality. At the same time, this stance inevitably drew some of its cover story from the more ostensibly conservative mappings of maternalist national regeneration.

Matrismo against Feminismo

Not surprisingly, Correia's Mátria seems to operate in its most unitary form, where it does mobilize a spirit of place connected to putatively national sentiment. This discourse has tended to predominate in official, national memory of Correia's work privileging her public persona and her poetry. Among the many public tributes since her death, a particularly telling one was held in 2000 at the Museu Nacional de Traje [National Museum of Clothing] in Lisbon, alongside an exhibition of her wardrobe and accessories, crystallizing across time her unchanging public aura, based on flamboyance of dress, long cigarette holders, and heavy eyeliner designed to resemble Queen Nefertiti. The museum director, Madalena Braz Teixeira, described Correia in her opening speech as "the only woman capable of simultaneously being and representing the deepest and strongest female spiritual link between the pre- and post-April Revolution periods."[13]

This primal image of Correia as embodiment of changeless feminine spirituality finds emblematic expression in her poetic construction of the Azorean motherland, her portrayal of a "mother island."[14] In the "Mãe Ilha" [Mother Island] section of her *Sonetos Românticos* (1990), Correia's vision takes the form of a daughter's hymn of love to the mother, addressed to her mystical, as well as biographical, Azorean mother, as she declares "with pasture and wave I will merge true / Island in the gentle blue of the mother waiting" [ao pasto e à onda me unirei sincera, / Ilha no manso azul de mãe esperando

(247)].[15] In the closing stanza, the Azorean maternal space of eternal return also becomes a metonym for Portugal, as her mother's death leads her to ask, "to what deep sea was the skiff bearing you? / Not to the end" [a que pélago o esquife te levava? / Não ao termo (249)]. The image of a body borne after death to deep sea, the "pélago" that also forms a pun on the islands or archipelago, in an "esquife" that evokes both skiff and coffin, conjures up Fernando Pessoa's Arthurian visions in *Mensagem* of the last Avis King, the dead Dom Sebastião, the Encoberto or Hidden One, lying asleep on an island from which he will one day return. For Correia, however, the death of the heroic mother serves as a simple reminder of the circularity of life and of the mother as the gentle first principle of all beginnings, rather than of a fated Sebastianic return to rescue an embattled nation.

Fernando Pessoa also affords an important source for the "vaguely esoteric mysticism" that Paulo de Medeiros identifies in Correia's published diary records of the 25 April Revolution, *Não Percas a Rosa* [Don't Lose the Rose].[16] In this discussion, Medeiros helpfully elucidates Correia's female appropriation of Fernando Pessoa's male nationalist symbolism, via his future-oriented image of the "Rose of Life." For Medeiros, this affords the "title of a diary [*Não Percas a Rosa*] in which she regards the personal as the collective, and comes to engender the Nation."[17] Medeiros describes this mysticism as the route Correia chose to follow out of the morbidity of Portuguese nationhood, regarded as being in chronic decline from the nineteenth century onwards, and thrown vividly into crisis by the 25 April Revolution. Both Christianity and Marxism were perceived by Correia as the nation's equally illusory opposite poles. Given that her poetic vision of the Motherland was so heavily invested in Portuguese national revival, it comes as no surprise that Correia took pains, in her journalistic and other writings, to dissociate her concept of the Mátria explicitly from the term "feminismo" as such, particularly as manifested in British and North American political activism during the 1960s and 1970s.[18]

In this respect, Correia follows in the discursive tradition, identified by Graça Abranches among others, in which early twentieth-century pre-Republican feminists insisted on espousing a "true feminism" [feminismo verdadeiro] that they defensively distinguished from the false feminism [feminismo falso] of the emancipated "masculinized" British.[19] Indeed, the very insistence with which Correia's Mátria was defined in opposition to the outside, seems to suggest that Matrismo expressed a Portuguese nationalism that Correia's feminism used as an alibi. Even more indicative in this regard is Correia's excoriation in her *Breve História da Mulher* [Short History of Woman] of the "English feminists that always were asexual" who disrupted the Miss World Beauty Competition in London in 1970 and were condemned by Correia for being "inappropriately ugly."[20] In this context, Correia's emphasis on natural femininity, heterosexual complementarity, and the maternal metaphor seem designed to preempt the charges of unnaturalness and masculinity (read lesbianism) that were still conventionally leveled at British and American emancipation feminism in the 1960s and 1970s. Predictably this takes an even stronger form in Correia's response to radical separatism, evident in her attack on what she calls the "parthenogenetic" feminist art of Valerie Solanas with her S.C.U.M. (Society for Cutting Up Men) Manifesto and her notorious shooting of Andy Warhol.[21] In defending her literary and theoretical conceptualization of Matrismo here, Correia obviously sought to draw a line between the type of classical metaphors she favored for her aesthetic assertion of women's culture, such as the dilaceration of Pentheus by the *bacchantes,* and the horrific literalization of such figurations, proposed by Valerie Solanas in her Society for Cutting Up Men.[22] Yet, as Maria Teresa Horta points out in her preface to Correia's *Breve História da Mulher,* Correia's appalled fascination with Valerie Solanas betrays precisely "a sort of mirror effect in which Correia saw herself reflected to some extent."[23]

Asked by the journalist Antónia de Sousa to define Matrismo in a 1983 interview, she gave the following summary:

Woman must follow her own cultural tendencies which are intimately linked to the paradigm of the Great Mother, who is the great and eternal reserve of Nature, precisely so that she can impose them on the world, or at least integrate them into the rhythm of society, as a vital way out of the serious problems that have been created by masculine rationalism. The paradigm of the Great Mother is where I see woman's cultural origins; that is why I call it matrismo and not feminism.

[A mulher deve seguir as próprias tendências culturais, que estão intimamente ligadas ao paradigma da Grande Mãe, que é a grande reserva, a eterna reserva da Natureza, precisamente para os impor ao mundo ou pelo menos para os introduzir no ritmo das sociedades como uma saída indispensável para os graves problemas que temos e que foram criados pelas racionalidades masculinas. É no paradigma da Grande Mãe que vejo a fonte cultural da mulher; por isso lhe chamo matrismo e não feminismo.][24]

As Correia had indicated already ten years earlier in her preface to the 1973 anthology *A Mulher,* she believed that the ancient power of women as mother goddesses, "the natural order of the cycle of mother-rule" had been historically defeated by the rise of patriarchy, leading to the "separation of what was once unified in the unitary sphere of magic-matriarchal societies."[25] This paternalist victory she particularly associated with the misogyny of the Olympian Greeks, dividing the world into spirit and flesh, psyche and soma, and negatively associating woman with the natality, mortality and materiality of the flesh, not with the gifts of the intellect or the spirit.[26]

Clearly underpinning many aspects of Correia's Matrismo, as noted above, are the late nineteenth- and early twentieth-century social anthropological works subscribing to mother-right theories. In this respect, Luís Adriano Carlos has identified an important influence for Correia's matriarchy theories in the work of the British anthropologist Robert Briffault, whose 1927 text, *The Mothers,* Correia cites in the preface to the *Antologia de Poesia Portuguesa Erótica e Satírica* in 1966.[27] As a late exponent of the mother-right theory made famous by Johann Jakob Bachofen, Briffault believed that ancient matriarchal and matrilinear societies had once enjoyed primacy in the arrangement of society, but had been historically defeated and superseded by the forces of patriarchy.[28] In exploring the historical origins of the family, Briffault and Correia emphasized the need to return to the maternal, reproductive order to combat the decline of society and civilization through father-law.

This matriarchalist line of thinking in anthropology, which had begun with Bachofen's *Das Mütter-recht* in 1861, was already largely discredited by the time Briffault published his three-volume magnum opus, *The Mothers,* in 1927. In a famous debate with Bronislaw Malinowski, Briffault's work was termed the "swansong" of mother-right theory.[29] Briffault's work and Bachofen's are conventionally taken as the beginning and the end of the much larger nineteenth- and early twentieth-century process of debate on the origins of the family, in which the primacy of matriarchy was pitted against, and often used to decenter, the "naturalness" and inevitability of patriarchal rule. Academic analysis of this debate has tended, as the historian Ann Taylor Allen points out, to focus on the principle male protagonists in the arena, and to emphasize the fact that it did eventually lead to the reinforcement of paternal law and patriarchal formations, most emblematically in Freud's Oedipus theory. In this context, Allen makes an important case to the contrary, drawing on the vibrant interventions that feminist and antifeminist women made during this period in their discussions of the history and prehistory of the family. She thus argues that "the very conception of patriarchy as a historical phenomenon, contingent on time and place, provided the basis for the emergence of a feminist critique of male supremacy, in both the past and the present, that has continued throughout the century."[30]

Correia was writing some decades later than the turn of the last century period that affords the main focus for Allen. However, her interest in the mother-right theories that emerged from, and informed, debates on the prehistoric origins of the family did open a number of important theoretical and aesthetic directions for her work enabling her to contest, albeit in coded ways, the naturalness and supremacy of the paternalist metaphysics that governed New State Portugal. Her focus on classical myth and prehistory had the advantage of placing her deliberations at an apparently safe distance from overt or recognizable historical references to Portugal's New State present. At the same time as she displaced the natural, universal rule of patriarchy, she also vigorously embraced a discourse of antihistoricism. In this, as in much of her maternalist aesthetics, a significant interlocutor and sparring partner was undoubtedly Friedrich Nietzsche, who had also been influenced by Bachofen's mother-right theories.[31]

SAYING YES AND NO TO NIETZSCHE

Several critics have noted Nietzsche's overt presence in Correia's thought from her earliest writings onwards. As António P. B. F. Dinis points out, she was inspired by his critique of morals and his rejection of Alexandrian historicism, and it would not be an exaggeration to say that she saw herself as a dissident, female disciple of the great German philosopher. Her exuberant cult of polytheistic paganism clearly drew on the Nietzschean death of god.[32] Correia's poetry collection *O Armistício* famously calls for the "decrucifixion" of Christ. In a similar vein, but in prose, her humorous short story, "Where has Baby Jesus gone?" [Onde Está o Menino Jesus?], describes a little girl liberating a talking, humanized Christ-child figurine from the Christmas crib, leaving him free to become a Zarathustra-like "eternal child-god" playing in the meadows, the "real Baby Jesus" [Menino Jesus verdadeiro] described by Pessoa's famous pagan heteronym Alberto Caeiro.[33] While her *matrista* countertheology underpins most of Correia's thought, the most significant recurring influence on the literary aesthetics that she created to express it was, as Dinis notes, Nietzsche's *The Birth of Tragedy*. In this work he elaborates his theory of the competing and complementary Greek principles of the Apollonian and Dionysian, which informed his pre-Olympian ideal of Greek tragedy in the works of Sophocles and Aeschylus in the fifth century B.C. These warrant brief elucidation here as they are central, not only to Correia's aesthetics, but specifically to her conceptualizations of the relations between gender and creativity.

Where Apollo represented order, reason, form in art, light, visuality, dreams, and prediction, the opposing principle of the Dionysian was named after the sexually ambiguous god of male femininity, the god of wine and pleasure, who was associated with the realm of darkness, chaos, the formless,

and the nonvisual art of music.[34] Thus, while the Apollonian brought ratio-
nality, knowledge, morality, moderation, and distinct human individuation,
Dionysus stands for the merging of all differences back into a primary, mythical, and deindividuated universal whole, at one with nature and open to
nonrational forms of wisdom. For Nietzsche, the Greeks' greatest tragic art
required the active competition and fusion of the two elements. The vitality
and energy of the Dionysian must therefore infuse and inspire the tragic
drama which nonetheless cannot be cast into an artistic form at all without
the opposing force of the Apollonian.[35]

In *The Birth of Tragedy,* Nietzsche asserted that the era of supreme Socratic
rationalism, and the theater of Euripides which banished the Dionysian principle from his art, marked the end of the great age of Greek Attic tragedy as
he saw it, in which tragic heroes such as Oedipus had, in various forms,
reenacted the drama embodied in Dionysus. Nietzsche perceived the truly
Dionysian state of suffering as related to human individuation, separation,
and disunity, following the myth in which Dionysus was torn apart as a child
by the Titans.[36] Yet this dismemberment of Dionysus also carried the possibility of rebirth and reunion, so that art would become "the joyful hope that
the spell of individuation is to be broken, as the presentiment of a restored
unity."[37]

As Christine Battersby and other, feminist and nonfeminist, critics of
Nietzsche have pointed out, his Romantic feminization of creative genius is
not unproblematic for feminist politics and women's writing.[38] His effemi-
nate Dionysian masculinity effectively hijacks the vocabulary of maternal
gestation to describe the sublimation of biologically male procreative energy.
As Battersby puts it, "for Nietzsche, women and men are necessarily and
eternally involved in a power struggle—a struggle that favors woman, as long
as she does not seek to fight man with his own weapons and on his own
ground. In the sphere of culture (and even of speech) women must lose
out."[39]

Correia's response to this power struggle, however, involved enjoining the
battle on the master's stylistic terms with an appropriately Nietzschean degree of rhetorical excess and aphoristic duelling, rather than meekly accepting women's exclusion from the spheres of speech and culture. Drawn by
Nietzsche's energetic, polytheistic paganism, as well as his return to the essentially mythical order of art, beloved of the surrealists, and his rejection of
the metaphysics of presence, Correia forged her own personal vision of an
eternally recurrent Dionysian feminine that could be the driving force of
artistic production by women. Thus, her poetic and public self-embodiment
as a female literary creator chose to literalize the Dionysian metaphor, as
cast by Nietzsche, back into a visibly female, material form. The Dionysian

principle thus becomes an actual woman artist in her work and is given the privilege of predominant speech.

Commenting on the appropriation of Nietzsche for deconstruction and thence poststructuralist feminism, Battersby rightly sounds a warning note that this "anti-metaphysical metaphysics conserve[s] (via Nietzsche) the patrilinear traditions of Romanticism—which reassigned the vocabulary of female power to *males*."[40] Correia, however, imitates Nietzsche's style of writing at the same time as she exposes, as mere metaphoric imitation, as an artificial and reversible act of borrowing, his appropriation of her gender. Furthermore, she does this in terms that conspicuously usurp his aphoristic rhetoric. This was not without risks, as we will see in relation to her novel *A Madona,* below, and also in her more direct theoretical dialogues with Nietzsche, such as the 1974 set of meditations, *Uma Estátua para Herodes* [A Statue to Herod].[41] This provocative and controversial thesis rails against the Portuguese cult of child worship and compulsory procreation. Here she engages directly with the German philosopher's own words in the notorious passage of *Thus Spoke Zarathustra,* "Of Old and Young Women," where he exhorts woman to be man's plaything and "discover the child in the man!" stating "the man's happiness is: I will. The woman's happiness is: He will."[42] Correia's reaction to this takes the characteristically Nietzschean form of reversing the terms of his sexed equation as she writes, "woman's happiness is: I will! Man's happiness is: she will! I deliberately invert a Nietzschean maxim here" [a felicidade da mulher é: eu quero! A felicidade do homen é: ela quer! Propositadamente inverto um axioma de Nietzsche]."[43] Through counterfactual inversions such as these, Correia springs the Nietzschean gender trap at least wide enough for a female countervoice to expose the latent misogyny of the original.

In the same work, *Uma Estátua para Herodes,* Correia launches a more direct attack on Nietzsche's association of intellectual activity with women's sterility and masculinization. Here, Correia blames Germanic traditions of misogyny for this "enclave of stupidity in the territory of his extreme astuteness" [enclave de estupidez no território da sua extrema argúcia.][44] Although Correia does not cite or source Nietzsche directly here, Dinis ventures to place the above remark in dialogue with Nietzsche's infamous statement in *Thus Spoke Zarathustra* that "everything about woman is a riddle, and everything about woman has one solution. It is called pregnancy."[45] However, the Nietzschean pronouncement to which she responds here seems equally, if not more, likely to be the following remark from *Beyond Good and Evil:* "When a woman has scholarly inclinations there is usually something wrong with her sexually. Sterility itself disposes one toward a certain masculinity of taste; for man is, if I may say so, 'the sterile animal.'"[46]

Correia's response is as follows:

Conceiving and giving birth are, for woman, functions inherent to her nature and, although this nature possesses its own psychic specificity on account of this, it is not deprived of the gifts of intellectual enquiry, nor of artistic creativity, which materialize in distinct cultural forms from those pertaining to male culture.

[Conceber e parir são para a mulher funções inerentes à sua natureza que, se por esta propriedade apresenta uma especificidade psíquica, não é privada dos dons da especulação intelectual e da criação artística que se objectivam numa composição cultural diferenciada da cultura masculina].[47]

Here Correia emphasizes the specificity of woman's reproductive biology as responsible for the underlying difference of her psychic and intellectual activity. Female artistic creativity and culture become, in this scenario, a Nietzschean-inspired sublimation of maternal (uterine) physical energy for women, in a gender reversal of the sublimation which Battersby showed to be biologically virile in origin for Nietzsche. The question that must be asked here is how far Correia's vision of an "other" feminine culture merely reformulates what Luce Irigaray would later term the "other of the same"?[48] Furthermore, as Luisa Muraro notes, this vision of "woman made to man's measure" can still function as the eternal symptom of disintegration and unity, for an exclusively male modernist malaise.[49] Certainly, Correia's creative feminine intellect remains eerily isomorphic here with the Nietzschean maternal metaphor, as historically propelled by the masculine imagination.

This is one of the central issues posed in *O Progresso de Édipo. Poema Dramático* [Oedipus's Progress. A Dramatic Poem], Correia's first known published work for theater, written in 1957.[50] In this short play, she sets out to subvert the classic paternalist paradigm of Oedipus in a satirical, maternalist reversion of Sophocles that draws its artistic inspiration and authority explicitly from Nietzsche.[51] In her version, Correia has Jocasta deliberately blinding Oedipus as a way of maintaining the primal mother-child bond, the return to a Dionysian unity, reasserting itself against the "natural" laws that prohibit incest.[52] Nietzsche's *The Birth of Tragedy,* section nine, dealing precisely with Sophocles' *Oedipus,* provides Correia's epigraph to the play.

Wherever prophetic and magic powers break the spell of present and future, the inflexible law of individuation, and above all the real enchantment of nature, this must have been brought about by a monstruous transgression of nature—as in this instance incest.[53]

[Quando por uma força mágica e fatídica, se rasga o véu do futuro, se espezinha a lei de individuação, se faz violência ao mistério da natureza, há-de ser a causa qualquer monstruosidade anti-natural como o incesto.]

This statement, in the original context, effectively glosses Nietzsche's observation regarding those cultures in which a wise magus must violate the laws of nature by being born of incest as he affirms that "Dionysian wisdom is an abomination against nature," drawing support also from the original Sophoclean statement by Tiresias that "wisdom is a crime against nature."[54] Thus Oedipus violates natural law by cracking the riddle of the sphinx, which then sets him on course for the "unnatural" crimes of patricide and incest. In deference to these Nietzschean intertexts, Correia constructs the tragedy of a Dionysian wise man. Her Oedipus achieves a transgressive, anti-natural wisdom that goes against rational Apollonian knowledge and therefore precipitates his destruction, in a "fall" that is contradicted by the title of the play as *O Progresso de Édipo,* Oedipus's Progress.

In a short prologue to the play, a figure named the "autor" declares "it would have been better to have torn out the eye that one day deciphered the sign of the doctrine in its entirety! It would have been better never to have known" [melhor fora ter arrancado os olhos que um dia decifraram o sinal da doutrina inteira! Melhor fora nunca ter sabido (9)].[55] As with the oracle of Apollo which predicts the fate from which Oedipus flees in Sophocles, Correia's apparently prophetic statements about blinding have a specific twist. In her version, Oedipus will be blinded twice, first by his father and then by his mother. The play opens as Oedipus arrives in Thebes crowned with glory because he has unmasked the sphinx. For this reason Tiresias tells him he will commit a crime against nature, advising him not to use knowledge or do battle with those who have predicted his fate. Declaring his defiance of predestination, Oedipus asks Tiresias what the Thebans want of him. Thus, embarking on the path that will lead to his crime against nature, he hears that he must free the Thebans from the tyranny of King Laius because his name was the answer to the riddle of Apollo, in which "he who shall avenge Thebes will descend into hell through the passageway of his own veins and, when he rises to the surface again, will be innocent as a god" [aquele que vingar Tebas descerá aos infernos pelo corridor das suas próprias veias e quando vier ao cimo será inocente como um deus (15)]. Accepting the challenge, Oedipus defeats Laius, who then blinds his predestined successor.

When the now-sightless Oedipus first encounters the queen, Jocasta, the sound of her voice recalls his childhood, arousing Oedipus's distant memories of maternal milk. As the chorus points out, it is Jocasta's destiny to marry Laius's killer so Jocasta leads him away to his wedding with her and feeds him from her own breasts, drawing him back into the chaotic, darkness of infancy and maternal union. Jocasta, however, increasingly regrets that Oedipus cannot see her. She fears that their love depends on her being invisible to him, and therefore undifferentiated. Asked where he thinks he "saw" Jocasta for the first time, Oedipus observes that they have always been part of each other, as if she were mingled with his blood. In the scene that follows, we learn that Jocasta and the people of Thebes are making offerings to Apollo for Oedipus's sight to be restored, to repay him for their deliverance from a tyrant.

When his eyes are opened, Oedipus runs toward Jocasta who stands bathed in golden light but the chorus tells us "there is a shadow on this stain of light" [há uma sombra nesta mancha de luz (31–32)]. This reference to a shadow on the "stain of light" takes up and inverts Nietzsche's own reverse image of the sun spots that heal the eye when he states, in *The Birth of Tragedy,* "the Apollonian qualities of the mask are the necessary results of a glance into the terrifying inner world of nature, bright spots so to speak to heal the eyes which have been damaged by the sight of the terrible darkness."[56] Here the darkness threatens to intrude once again and to overwhelm the Apollonian qualities of healing light and visuality. As Oedipus falls into Jocasta's arms, he realizes that she is his mother. Stricken with guilt by the knowledge that ends his innocence, Oedipus hands his sword to his mother so that she can kill him honorably in a fitting Apollonian conclusion to the tragedy, as he remarks:

> With a single blow I have undone the sacred bond of the family. Not a single branch have I left in place. When you plunge the tip of this sword into the breast of your son, you will be punishing at a single stroke, the patricidal man that left you widowed, the incestuous son that dragged you into crime, and the murderous brother that made your children orphans.

> [Dum só golpe eu desatei o nó sagrado da família. Nem um ramo deixei de pé. Quando mergulhares a ponta desta espada no peito do teu filho, punirás duma só estocada o parricida que te fez viúva, o filho incestuoso que te arrastou ao crime e o irmão assassino que provocou a orfandade dos teus filhos.] (33)

Jocasta, however, refuses to instate any "natural" paternal law or taboo on incest by killing him. Nor, as in the Sophoclean original, does she hang herself. Instead, she takes the sword from Oedipus and blinds him all over again. The problem is posed, as the author's opening comments show, in terms of knowledge against wisdom, the separation and naming of acts versus their formless undifferentiated non-naming. The play closes with the statement that their act of love only constitutes a sin or prohibition where they can see it and name it as such. As the chorus comments, "previously there was no sin because no one knew what name to give to his crime" [dantes não havia pecado porque nenhum deles sabia que nome dar ao seu crime (33)]. By returning Oedipus to his prior state of blindness, Jocasta facilitates his passage, his "progress", back to the status of the Dionysian wise man. The chorus narrates this final act of violence from off-stage, concluding with the question, "can they let sin be dead and buried and then afterwards return to a state of innocence? And if they do return? Will the world have to invent another name for chastity?" [poderão os dois pôr uma pedra sobre o pecado e regressarem depois à inocência? E se regressarem? Terá o mundo de inventar outro nome para a castidade? (34)]

The question that remains with this open ending is how far Dionysian darkness, the wise state of innocence, can ever be wholly restored, once the rational knowledge of form, law, and name has been experienced. On the other hand, can the brightness of Apollonian individuation and law ever be free of the encroaching threat from the Dionysian shadow? The play's most daring move is to make an actual female protagonist, Jocasta, who is wholly absent from Nietzsche's *The Birth of Tragedy,* into the agent of those Dionysian forces that mount the play's central challenge to Freudian and Sophoclean paternal law.[57] The result is a restoration of sexual symmetry. Both Oedipus and Jocasta have played both the Apollonian and the Dionysian roles at different points in the drama.

If Correia reclaimed *Oedipus Rex* for the maternal agency of Jocasta in her *O Progresso de Édipo,* her 1968 novel *A Madona* returns to the themes of Greek classical tragedy, this time to rework the myth of Pentheus and the Bacchae, made famous in Euripides' *Bacchae.* Here, too, her prose style is heavily overladen with the densely figurative and aphoristic language of Nietzsche's *Birth of Tragedy,* to the point of directly redeploying many of his metaphorical tropes. Adopting the *A Madona* title with overt pagan irony, so as to unpack its multilayered mythical contents, this novel follows Nietzsche in his condemnation of the Socratic and Euripidean triumph of Apollonian reason which, for him, saw the death of Greek tragedy with Euripides' plays. It is noteworthy in this context that in her journalism, Correia described Valerie Solanas, the American feminist author of the S.C.U.M. Manifesto, as being one of the bacchantes, who dilacerated Pentheus in Greek myth and Euripidean drama. Insofar as Correia casts a real-life antagonist, Valerie Solanas, in 1970 in the mythical bacchic role that her fictional heroine Branca ultimately rejects in *A Madona,* this novel invites reading as Correia's counterposition to the brand of radical feminism she identifies with Solanas.[58]

MAKING THE MADONNA MANY

When *A Madona* was published in 1968, it was received as an iconoclastic statement on art and gender, as well as being closely read as a *roman à clef,* by Correia's contemporaries.[59] Offering a more sustained allegory on Nietzschean art and creativity than that attempted in *O Progresso de Édipo,* the novel operates through the first person narration of a young Portuguese woman, Branca, who acts as principle protagonist and, like Jocasta, as the embodied female power that underwrites Nietzsche's Dionysian metaphor. The novel is set in the 1960s and is structured as a cyclical first person *Bildungsroman,* involving a departure from, and a return to, the heroine's home. Given the strongly autobiographical overtones of the novel and descriptions of the settings, critics such as Regina Louro have plausibly identified the novel's Portuguese location as Correia's homeland of the Azores, set in contrast here to a journey of discovery across continental Europe.[60]

Central to Branca's trajectory in the novel is this trope of the originary rural "home" to which she eventually returns, the landed estate in Briandos, which she leaves to go and develop her adult identity and sexuality in Paris and other European capitals. As António Quadros points out, the orgies that Branca attends in Paris function as sites of Dionysian disintegration, from which her future sense of direction will emerge.[61] She later also visits London, the Netherlands, Denmark, Sweden, Switzerland, and Italy. The temporal structure of the novel constantly switches between past and present, and between ancient mythical and contemporary discourses, evoking elements of Branca's childhood history. We learn that much of Branca's personal narrative history has been inspired by the "prehistory" of her mother. She had been humiliated throughout her life by her husband, a powerful landowner and judge, whose love affairs ultimately caused his death while having sex with a mistress. Branca's mother tries to take public revenge on her husband, by donning a celebratory red dress for his funeral, but is hidden away by her family who declare her mad and force the child Branca to connive at the drugging of her mother.

Branca's departure for Paris is largely motivated, therefore, by revenge for the humiliation of her mother. She leaves behind in Briandos a young huntsman Manuel who is attracted to her. Much of the novel is addressed posthumously to a "tu" who represents, on one level, Manuel, but in a typically Nietzschean drive away from individuation, he also merges with mythical images of Mankind, Dionysus, Christ, Branca's father, and her lover Miguel, who is likened to Correia's "decrucified Christ" descending from the cross (100). On her travels, Branca becomes involved with two different men, the neurotic, sadistic, and overintellectual Portuguese, Miguel, with whom she lives in Paris, and the disembodied and ethereal Danish antinuclear campaigner Lars Nielsen, nicknamed o Anjo, whom she first meets in London. When the two men fight over her, Branca leaves Paris and travels through other European capital cities encountering alternative spaces, cultures, and sexualities in a journey which ultimately leads her home to Briandos in winter, at the time of the full moon. There she embarks on a passionate physical relationship with the huntsman Manuel. Ritually abusing and humiliating him like a slave, in revenge for her father's maltreatment of her mother, she finally drives him to despair and suicide. Miguel comes to find Branca in Briandos and the novel ends as they return to Paris together, the creative Dionysian / Apollonian balance of their antagonistic relationship precariously restored through the ritualized death and implied rebirth of Manuel, who is restored to unity with the earth.

In writing *A Madona,* as in her poetry collection *Mátria* of the same year, Correia sets out to regenerate, from her Azorean ideals, a mystical Portuguese culture for the future, threatened by the rise of rationalism, science, and an impending nuclear Doomsday, which she associates with the Northern European capital cities, London and Paris in the 1960s.[62] Quadros tellingly describes Miguel as "the image of the Western intellectual, whose greatest achievement is the invention of the atom bomb, whose spirituality is literary, arid, encyclopaedic and self-sufficient, whose rationalist trajectories have led him into meaningless angst, to the notion of the absurd, to nihilism, to self-destruction through literature that has become corrupted either by turning in on itself or by making political choices that ultimately lead to tyranny."[63] Correia represents Northern Europe's enlightenment and the Cold War clash of the superpowers as responsible for the terminal decline of the West in the late twentieth century, through the triumph of the Apollonian extremes embodied in science, technology, and rationalism.[64] Like the mother-right theorists, Correia also blames what she calls "the paroxysms of male genius" on the defeat and exclusion of the matriarchate by the world historical triumph of patriarchy.[65] Significant here is the fact that Miguel, the typically rationalist "Western intellectual," is actually Portuguese, not Northern European. He becomes a potential avatar of (Salazarist) Portugal, as a nation that must be saved from itself by a Dionysian return to its own originary unity. Indeed, it is possible to identify images of Salazarist platonic rationalism in both Branca's father and Miguel, recalling what Adriano Carlos refers to in Correia's work as "the rational economist (read Salazarist) Father [who] represses the nocturnal world of the instincts, nature and debauchery."[66] Correia's apocalyptic nuclear Northern Europe, the place where Branca meets Miguel, is thus set against the desired idyll of the rural Azores signified by Briandos, the return to the Mother.[67]

On a figurative level, the conflict of reason and emotion, the Apollonian and the Dionysian, is played out in the novel through two interrelated sets of references: the myth complexes surrounding the dilaceration of Pentheus by the Bacchantes; and the dismembering and restitution of the body of Dionysus/Osiris. The novel's blurring of recurrent mythical referents produces a complex, surrealist amalgam of quasi-archetypal figures as individuation is overturned, and shadowy figures merge back into the originary, nostalgic unity that constantly permeates Branca's memory of Briandos. Regina Louro has also interestingly noted Branca's return to the maternal home as reflecting the Persephone myth, although it is Branca's relations with men that ultimately shape the novel's conclusion.[68] In this newly coined myth cycle, the destruction of the Penthean "father" leads to the restitution of the male body through maternal agency, conveyed as the eternal return embodied in Branca and associated with the mystical conception of genius. It is the Greek myth of the bacchantes, made famous in the Euripidean drama *Bacchae,* that underpins Branca's and her mother's relations with the father, as the women take revenge against the age of male rationalism and law embodied in Pentheus, the king of Thebes. In this story, the people of Thebes enrage Dionysus by refusing to accept his status as a god. In revenge, Dionysus drives the city's women, acting as the *maenads* or bacchantes, into insane, drunken behavior. Pentheus is influenced by Dionysus to try and observe the women but is ripped to pieces when he is found out, and his own mother Agave carries his severed head to Thebes. Pentheus's family are then banished from Thebes.[69]

In *A Madona,* Branca imagines her father, a former law-giver or "desembargador," being destroyed as revenge for the humiliation of the mother. Thus Branca gradually assumes the mythological role of the maenads, the servants of Dionysus. She visualizes her mother as Agave awakening the sleeping maenads, and later exhorting the women at the funeral to take their revenge on their faithless "bloated consorts" [inchados consortes (40)] by tearing them to bits. As she departs for Paris, Branca imagines that she is urged on by the haunting voice of her mother, a voice that subsequently recurs, impelling her in highly Nietzschean rhetorical tones, to return to Briandos.

> Go forth! . . . Go forth! . . . The hour has come! Go and join the downtrodden daughters of the night, your sisters! Go together and rouse the Great Mother to the drum beat of your blood! Shatter the glass tomb in which the laurel-crowned tyrant has imprisoned your righteous anger! The hour has come! Unleash your fury exiled in the crystals of millennial slumber! Your hour has come!

[Vai!.. vai! . . . chegou a hora! Vai unir-te às humilhadas filhas da noite, tuas irmãs! Ao som dos tambores do sangue ide acordar a Grande Mãe! Quebrai o vidro tumular em que o tirano coroado de louro aprisionou a sua augusta ira! Chegou a hora! Libertai a fúria exilada nos cristais do seu sono milenário! Chegou a hora!] (14 and 142)

She later imagines her mother dressed in red, serving up pieces of the father's body as ritual communion hosts to the maenads, each part of the broken mirror of her past reflecting her fragmented self back to her.

Interwoven with this narrative of revenge and dilaceration are the cyclical fertility and regeneration myths of Dionysus and Osiris, the tales of wholeness restored, and the return to original unity. Once again, this relates to the process that Nietzsche celebrates as deindividuation, exemplified in the story where the Titans tear Dionysus to pieces as a child. Correia also incorporates related images surrounding the Egyptian fertility god Osiris, the pieces of whose body were scattered across Egypt by his brother (father) Set's jealousy, only for his sister and wife Isis to seek out and rejoin all of the pieces to make him whole again. Isis succeeds in binding the pieces to recreate Osiris, the only missing element being the phallus, which has been thrown into the river and eaten by fish. Isis thus fashions him a new phallus, attaches it to him, and breathes life back into him by flapping a bird's wings.[70] Other versions detail the resurrection of Osiris, pieced together by Isis and her sister, with the help of the embalmer Anubis, and brought to life by Isis flapping her wings over him.[71] These resurrection myths afford a series of interlocking references for Branca's relations with Manuel, Miguel and o Anjo, as well as her father.

As a direct, symmetrical parallel to Branca's destruction of Manuel, Miguel also undergoes an experience of ritual dismemberment which entails a woman's revenge. Overcome with literal nausea when he is faced with a leg of lamb for dinner at Branca's home in Briandos, Miguel is prompted to describe his experiences in Paris of cruelly manipulating two sisters, his beautiful lover Monique and her mentally retarded sister Cécile, in order to provoke the latter's jealousy. Cécile takes revenge by murdering her sister Monique, cutting off her legs and serving them in a stew to Miguel who had always admired them. Miguel is thus tricked into participating in a typical Bacchanalian ritual, involving the eating of human and animal flesh, or the meat of an animal believed to be the god Dionysus.

Miguel's narration of this experience precipitates Branca's final decision to leave Manuel who then commits suicide in a gesture that effectively regenerates Branca's sexuality, leaving her free to return to Paris with Miguel. As Branca explains to Miguel, "I felt that if I destroyed him [Manuel] I would finally achieve my real consummation as a woman" [sentia que se o (Manuel) destruísse me consumava realmente como mulher (147–48)]. Silencing the destructive bacchantes of ancient memory, and the separatist rejection of men that they imply, she tells Miguel, "I am as vital to you as is the womb to the seed of the fruit seeking to be born" [sou-te necessária como o útero à semente do fruto que quer nascer (150)]. Manuel's sacrificial death and the fulfillment of Branca's pact with ancient maternal memory are linked with the awakening of the creative spirit in winter when, "the body dries up. The spirit wakes from its sleep and stiffens like the thoughts of a philosopher or a monk's scorn for the flesh. And the spirit of genius is born. The technique of cruelty" [o corpo seca. O espírito desperta da sua sonolência e inteiriça-se como as ideias de um filósofo ou o desprezo do monge pela carne. E nasce o génio. A técnica da crueldade (152–53)].

Sacrificing the original, savage male in the figure of Manuel the huntsman, who must die and be reborn, Branca asserts her own sexual and maternal identity as death goddess and is therefore able, like Isis, to recreate Miguel's (creative genius) phallus and like Rhea to rebuild the dilacerated Dionysus. The destruction of Manuel enables the restoration of Miguel's artistic vision, as a writer whose phallic genius is "refashioned" by Branca. Manuel, whose name also echoes Emmanuel or Christ, possesses a rifle that is explicitly associated with sexual potency making him a fertility god, killed, buried and resurrected. In a conclusion that closely reflects the novel's opening passage, Branca declares that she has paid her dues to Ereshkigal, the Sumerian or Babylonian Death Goddess and so "I shall seek the fragments of my son and lover scattered over the face of the Earth. Until the skies rain milk" [vou procurar os pedaços do meu filho e amante espalhados por toda a face da Terra. Até que os céus chovam leite (181)]. In rescuing rationalist man (Salazarist Portugal) from himself, by reconstructing his creative phallus, the burden of rectifying historical imbalance falls, as with Jocasta, on the female side of the pairing. "Man," in this process, is refashioned as sexually and artistically potent by the symbolic agency of Woman as Mother Goddess.

Excluded from, yet rhetorically shoring up, this rebirth of mystical Portuguese home-space from Miguel and Branca as "original" artistic pair are the novel's homosexual characters, o Anjo and Elsa. Both of them are Danes, associated with urban decadence in London and Denmark. Homosexual encounters provide here the "outer limit" with which Branca and Miguel both experiment. Thus, homosexuality is presented in disturbingly distopian tones as the sterile, morbid space of nonreproductivity, the "other" against which heterosexuality must struggle to define itself, as guarantor of a living and vital future. In a sadomasochistic battle between o Anjo and Miguel, the latter physically dominates the former, confining him to the "grotesque drama of pederasts" [drama grotesco dos pederastas (126)]. For Miguel, homosexuality is the excessively natural "animalized" option against which the Dionysian wise man must rebel, as he rails against the Greek Olympian "fake homosexuals. The dangerous clay from which warriors and tyrannical idealists are made" [homossexuais contrafeitos! A perigosa argila de que são feitos os guerreiros e os idealistas tiranos (126)]. For Miguel, only women can stimulate men's artistic sense of the sublime.

It is this turn away from homosexuality that marks Miguel's heterosexual return to a "proper" reproductive rebalancing of sexual and creative forces with Branca, and by analogy his "return" to a truly Portuguese spiritual homeland. Branca, in her turn, is driven by Miguel's battle with o Anjo to undertake her own sexual odyssey as she leaves both men, and travels first to Italy and then to Scandinavia where she is tempted by lesbianism. When she almost yields to the advances of a Danish woman Elsa, she represents her stereotypically as a solitary lesbian having "the soul of an abandoned puppy" [alma de cachorro abandonado (133)].[72] Branca soon disclaims the experience and turns away repelled. In their two-dimensional functionality and the "service" they perform for the novel's all too binaristic central couple, these representations of the gay man and the lesbian woman recall Judith Butler's description of the spectral images that the heteronormative symbolic creates out of its own terms, by way of stabilizing itself. Butler observes "the binarism of feminized male homosexuality, on the one hand, and masculinized female homosexuality, on the other, is itself produced as the restrictive spectre that constitutes the defining limits of symbolic exchange. Importantly, these are spectres produced *by* that symbolic as its threatening outside to safeguard its continuing hegemony."[73]

As noted earlier, Correia's use of mythology undoubtedly borrows from the lexicon of male-authored anthropological and philosophical debate on matriarchy, shaped by Briffault, Bachofen, Nietzsche, and Jung, and profoundly underpinned by nostalgia. If as Luisa Muraro aptly reminds us, these "myths that have come down to us are a scenario already 'staged' by patriarchy," women characters such as Branca and Jocasta work to alienate and estrange this patriarchal "staging" by mounting their own counterdemonstration of a female mythology authentically embodied by women.[74] In this sense, then, the authority they mobilize derives from inhabiting the rhetorically "real" biological femaleness that will reveal the male speaker's metaphorical femininity to be a mask. Asserting, through the biological difference of the specifically maternal body, the authority from which to recapture the feminine gender mask for women, it can be claimed that Correia reinforces rather than destabilizes the mask's sexual referent in the phallicized female body. Voicing the hyper-femaleness of the Mother Goddess archetype to call the bluff on Nietzsche's "feminine," is a move that ultimately risks digging his latent sexual essentialism in even deeper.

If Branca's relation to men and to male creativity corresponds to that of Isis, the mother who refashions the phallus (or genius) for Osiris, she only possesses it herself precisely on the condition that she play the maternal role, and like the original Christian Madonna, on the condition that she reproduce a son. Thus, the creative value afforded the woman in this scenario is only, retroactively, held in place by their ability to reproduce, or inspire, a male. And any transmission of power to the symbolic "daughter" as daughter (the rejected lesbian Elsa perhaps?) is far less clearly identifiable than Branca's liberation of the wronged mother. In this sense, insofar as she stands in relation to man as the necessary "reminder" of the regenerative function of matter, she still accepts the position that is historically freighted toward the incarnate and the somatic, in the dualist opposition with rationalism. And the sublimation of sexual energy, which has historically been a masculine domain, remains the primary artistic force.

Replaying the Actress and the Bishop

If Correia seeks, in *Édipo* and *Madona,* a rewriting of the symbolic paradigms that will rebalance the sexed forces of nature and creativity, she mounts a more radical challenge to the gendered mind/body dualism of Platonism and Christianity in her historically-based works for the theater. In this respect, the debt owed by some of her dramatic works to Bertolt Brecht and his concepts of epic and gestic theater, and alienation effect, proves of central importance. A case in point to which we now turn, and which stems from the same period as *A Madona,* is her play *A Pécora,* focusing on the opposing stereotype to the Madonna, that of the Whore. Written in 1966, it was first published in 1983 and was not performed until 1989.[75] Correia notes in the preface that she rejected the suggestion of her friend, David Mourão-Ferreira, to whom the play is dedicated, that she align it with a male-authored devotional tradition and evoke the renaissance playwright Gil Vicente, by calling it *O Auto da Paixão de Santa Melânia.* Instead she insisted on the play's more provocative, and less respectable lineage, by recuperating the pejorative term *A Pécora,* meaning literally, "the whore."

The play's opening scene declares itself in the stage directions to be set in the late nineteenth century, the era associated with the rise of Republicanism, in a disclaimer probably designed for the censors. In point of fact, the drama ranges freely through telescoped references to both Republic and New State periods, its historicity carefully inscribed in its figures, choruses, and images, while maintaining only the loosest, antirealist narrative chronology. The setting throughout is, similarly, a readily identifiable metaphor for Portugal, the fictional realm of Gal. The action of the play centers on the process by which a prostitute called Melânia is called upon to act out the role of a virgin saint, only to be trampled to death by the holy faithful when she threatens to destroy the illusion.

The opening scenes of the play invoke the liberal anticlericalism of the First Republic personified in the Regedor who does not believe the protestations of two shepherd children that they have seen visions of an angel, in an overtly satirical reference to the New State cult of virgin worship at Fátima. The Regedor sets out to destroy the holy "oratório" that provides Gal's main source of revenue and is consequently dethroned and killed by the entrepreneurial, atheistic villain Teófilo Ardinelli, who sees the commercial potential of religious worship. Established as the de facto ruler of Gal, who profits from the holy oratory, he becomes the play's dominant character, working with a masculinized, bourgeois woman, Dona Zenóbia, who becomes his wife. When he visits the brothel of Mme. Olympia, Ardinelli meets again his ex-fiancée, Melânia, the "whore" of the title. Now working as a trainee prostitute called Pupi, it transpires that she has been seduced and left pregnant by the parish priest, Padre Salata, in the guise of the "angel" that the two shepherd children claimed to have seen. Her subsequent hasty disappearance to the city, to join the brothel, has been glossed as an assumption into heaven, witnessed by the two shepherds. This gives Ardinelli the idea of using her to act out the role of the Virgem Melânia in a series of staged and fraudulent apparitions, which will make the shrine at Gal a famous center for pilgrimage and mass worship, as well as enriching Ardinelli and his complicit church associates with the sale of holy merchandise.

The dramatic centerpiece of the play is a mass public ritual that is performed to greet the apparition of Santa Melânia, at which the lame, the dumb, and the sterile are miraculously healed, sins are forgiven, and the adherents of scientific liberalism abandon their skepticism and turn to worship, making the play a clear double assault on Christianity and on the docility and failure of Portugal's enlightenment humanism. Thirty years later, during the festival of Melânia's canonization, the life of the real Melânia (now once again Pupi the prostitute), is shown to be degenerate, impoverished, and exploited. Her much younger lover and gigolo Paco, o Abutre [Paco, the vulture] has turned his attentions elsewhere, having exhausted all of Melânia's funds. Desperate for the money to buy him back, she tries to blackmail Ardinelli into paying her the profit he has made out of her, by threatening to reveal to the world her true identity and history. Taking Paco with her to confront Ardinelli, Melânia is betrayed once again, when the latter buys off

Paco by making him a member of the firm that runs the shrine, and continuing to exclude Melânia from her share of the income. Rejected by Paco in the quest for a respectable old age, and reduced to abject poverty, the real Melânia dies confronting the hysterical pilgrims at the play's closing religious ritual with the truth, as she protests that "your holy saint is a whore" [a vossa santa é uma puta (165)]. But she is savaged by the crowd and trampled to death under the feet of the religious procession which has assembled to celebrate her canonization by bearing her iconic holy image across the stage.

In her treatment of gender roles, Correia makes specific use here of Brechtian epic theater techniques to register her critique of the Catholic symbolic in terms relevant to women. In so doing, she effectively historicizes the oppression of women in an antirealist mode. Her dramatic technique invites a rereading of Brechtian epic theater through a feminist political lens, and useful insights may be drawn here from Elin Diamond's work on Brecht and performance theory in *Unmaking Mimesis*. Key to Diamond's recuperation of Brecht here is her insistence on articulating the politicization of gender ideology and the operation of sexual desire, with the critique of class ideology foregrounded by Brecht. Thus she contends that "understanding gender as ideology—as a system of beliefs and behaviour mapped across the bodies of women and men which reinforces a social status quo—is to appreciate the continued timeliness of *Verfremdungseffekt*, the purpose of which always is to denaturalize and defamiliarize what ideology—and performativity—makes seem normal, acceptable, inescapable."[76]

In practice, this alienation effect classically relies on the actor, as historical subject, conspicuously distancing him or herself from the role played in such a way as to split and interrogate the identificatory gaze of the spectator and to expose not only the constructedness of the role, but also the social and ideological conditions that have shaped it as a role, as a "not natural" state of being. For this reason, *A Pécora* is structured as a series of metatheatrical "performances within the play," taking the form of Melânia's fraudulent apparitions, the prostitutes' song and dance routines, the learned fakery of the "professional" beggars at the shrine, and the eerily staged mass rituals of the Catholic Church. Through these framed performances, the roles of both prostitute and virgin are revealed to be a series of cultural and economic constructions. Thus, we witness Melânia being carefully trained on stage to act as both virgin "saint" and cunning "whore" in a sequence that juxtaposes the two roles to comic effect, effectively placing the emphasis on the commodification of her body. She acquires the skills to play the "saint" by repeating back, in the manner of Catechism, the descriptions of her role fed to her by Ardinelli in the following exchanges, as her face grows increasingly ecstatic and beatific.

ARDINELLI: God has declared your flesh undefiled.
MELÂNIA: God has declared my flesh undefiled . . .
ARDINELLI: . . . so that virtue may defeat the weight of matter
MELÂNIA: I have defeated the weight of matter
ARDINELLI: . . . and defy the laws of gravity
MELÂNIA: I have defied the laws of gravity

[ARDINELLI: Deus declarou a tua carne impoluta
MELÂNIA: Deus declarou a minha carne impoluta . . .
ARDINELLI: . . . para que a virtude vencesse o peso da matéria . . .
MELÂNIA: Venci o peso da matéria . . .
ARDINELLI: . . . contrariasse a lei da gravidade
MELÂNIA: Contrariei a lei da gravidade] (76)

At the conclusion of this saintly "rehearsal" scene, Melânia has become so delighted at her own talent that she hitches up her skirt and dances a spirited can-can revealing her stockings and suspenders. As Diamond notes, with Brechtian alienation theory, "the actor must not lose herself in the character but rather *demonstrate* the character as a function of particular socio-historical relations, a conduit of particular choices."[77] The "character" of Melânia at this point switches abruptly between two, usually distinct, iconic images, saintly ecstasy and sexualized dance spectacle. The normal Catholic separation of the sacred and the profane, the shrine and the brothel, is thus opened up to interrogation here in terms of its gender ideology. Melânia's already objectified prostitute's body is shown being commodified once again, this time for the male gaze of the pilgrim. At the same time, the lack of sanctioned choices and social roles for Melânia herself, as a desiring female subject, is made evident by her ecstatic emotional display. Exceeding the limits that either role would seek to impose on her, Melânia's hysterically dancing body deconstructs the boundary between the two roles, pointing to the ideologically veiled continuity and complicity between Church and sex trade that divide her body between them, prefiguring the fate she will meet literally when she is torn to pieces at the end of the play.

This operation of gender ideology is developed further in the scene when Melânia is supposed to be inducted into brothel life. Mme. Olympia shows her a "manequim" or tailor's dummy, Mik, the model of the prostitute that can be made to represent anything, and to bear any imprint from the "master" who has paid for it. As she remarks, "Mik is a shadow. She can receive any face. She is disembodied sensuality. Pure lust. Mik is never cowardly. She has no limits. I would say that in her arms you can experience infinity" [Mik é uma sombra. Pode receber qualquer rosto. É a luxúria descarnada. A pura volúpia. Mik não é cobarde. Não tem limites. Eu diria que nos seus braços se conhece o infinito (47)]. As Mme. Olympia speaks, the stage directions tell us that she circles the dummy pretending to work on it in the manner of a sculptress perfecting a masterpiece. In this visual image, the generic female body is separated from the prostitute "character" constructed upon it so that "body" and "character" become subject, once again, to the shifting and changing forces of historicization and ideological debate.[78] Trying to interpellate Melânia into a smooth representation of the time-honored prostitute's profession, Mme. Olympia warns her to humbly remember that she is merely a woman, but Melânia refuses replying "less than that. I have already said that I am worse than a rat" [menos do que isso. Eu já disse que sou pior do que um rato (47)]. In this exaggeratedly masochistic self-abasement, Melânia's conscious performance of an "abject self" exceeds and comments upon the prostitute's social significance. Furthermore, the singularity of the (male) spectator's gaze at the "prostituted body" is split in three directions in this scene. Melânia comments upon Mme. Olympia's comments upon the inanimate female dummy as the ultimate fetish object.

It is no coincidence that the play's other use of a manequim or dummy figure occurs in the closing scene depicting Santa Melânia's canonization, in the form of the painted statue borne aloft by the faithful as they trample its referent, the body of the living Melânia, underfoot. Diamond has emphasized the importance of Brechtian *gestus* to her feminist theory of performance, recalling that *gestus* classically refers to those contradictory and conflicted gestures, words, actions, and tableaux on stage by which the "social attitudes encoded in the play text become visible to the spectator."[79] The gap between Melânia's words and those of the pilgrims performs a feminist *gestic* function in the closing tableau-like scene. An agonized Melânia addresses the crowd screaming at the icon of herself "that woman there is the fake . . . made of wood . . . a painted image. It was an artist who gave her that immortal face . . . The real woman . . . is lying mangled in the dust in a pool of blood" [Essa é a falsa . . . de madeira . . . pintada. Foi um artista . . . que lhe deu esse rosto imortal . . . A verdadeira . . . jaz no pó desfeita em sangue (169)]. As the crowd marches over her dead body, it intones "with this flesh without stain / the Lord God fell in love / sending Melânia, the pure / an angel from above" [da carne sem mácula/Deus se enamorou/E à casta Melânia/um anjo mandou (169–70)].

The spectator's experience is gestically divided here between the changeless practices of a Catholic Church that ritually unites around the reified female body, and the growing assertion of a desiring female subject who resists reification as virgin or whore. Melânia's insistence on fulfilling her own sexual need for Paco in her old age is significantly what dictates her actual need for money. When she tries to unmask Ardinelli's fraud and reclaim her own identity, she is killed by the crowd. In counterpoint to this affirmation of Melânia's sexual embodiment, the play affords a strong critique of official fascist matriarchy, manifested in the stereotypical figure of Ardinelli's masculinized wife, Zenóbia, whose sexual jealousy instigates much of Ardinelli's cruelty to Melânia. In this context, the play's competing interpretations of "perverse" and "liberated" female desire operate within, but also beyond, the economics of class to bring about Melânia's downfall, affording a significantly gendered revision of the Brechtian model.

As Diamond claims, *gestus* provides insight not only into the "fable" of the play itself, but also into the "culture which the play, at the moment of reception, is dialogically reflecting and shaping."[80] This raises important questions regarding the culture in which *A Pécora* was received when it was actually performed, under democracy in 1989, more than twenty years after it was written, in the climate of antifascist resistance in 1966. In the preface to the 1990 second edition, Correia notes that she waited to publish this play that had languished "in the drawer" [na gaveta], during the dictatorship. She did not, however, like most writers in that position, bring the play out straight after the 1974 Revolution. In this sense, she effectively dissociates it from the rise and the fall of the New State dictatorship that originally inspired it. Its production on stage in 1989 simultaneously locates it in relation to a much wider, more diverse, vector of historicization related also to the agendas of the second-wave feminist struggle and sexual liberation still being enjoined throughout the 1980s, most obviously in Portugal's abortion campaigns. If the ostensible "fable" of the play in 1966 was clearly antifascist, the culture it reflected and shaped in its 1980s staging context rather emphasized the irreducibility of sex and gender struggle to the old Marxist resistance paradigms of class. Correia's critique of Catholic ideology clearly affords a feminist countermemory of national history and ideology, at the same time as she reworks, from a gender perspective, the overmastering influence of classic Brechtian techniques in resistance theater.

A WOMAN TOO DIVINE

If Correia did much, as we have seen, to revise and appropriate the feminine icons of the patriarchal symbolic, most notably the Madonna and the Whore, as well as rehabilitating the female figures of matriarchal mythology, we ask in our conclusion how her reworkings of myth played out in relation to the genealogies of actual Portuguese women writers, both forebears and descendants. In her critical work on Florbela Espanca, Correia tellingly recreates the poet's antecedents in terms of classical mythology. If Agustina Bessa Luís's Florbela was, as we have seen, all too human in her weakness and neurosis, Natália Correia's Florbela is all too divine. This is particularly evident in Correia's preface to Espanca's *Diário do Último Ano* [Diary of the Last Year], a work that is often scrutinized for insights into her suicide. Here Correia represents her fellow woman-poet as the untouchable virgin huntress and moon goddess Diana, ultimately committing suicide because her brother/twin Apollo, whose name evokes Espanca's brother Apeles (killed in an aviation accident), has been struck down in full flight to the sun. Viewing the three-times married Espanca as a physical "virgin," made poetically fertile through mythical union with Apollo/Apeles, the brother enjoyed to the exclusion of her husbands, Correia's Florbela also clearly has echoes of Antigone, a link that will be further explored in the theater writings of Hélia Correia, which Natália inspired. As Clara Crabbé Rocha implies in her review in 1982, however, Natália Correia's vision of Espanca in this preface also involves promising much more than is really present in Espanca's diary.[81] It effectively entails a considerable appropriation of Florbela for Correia's own paganist agenda of Matrismo. It also writes Florbela into the role of sacrificial cornerstone on which women's literary heritage is built, as Correia interpellates the other woman writer into her own polytheistic pantheon of poetesses.

This is even more evident in Natália Correia's poem in the cemetery of Vila Viçosa, "At Florbela's Tomb." Here Florbela becomes the "Princess whose bones now wear marble" [Infanta de ossos. No mármore que os veste] who once "shivered at the slightest breeze" [tu que a um sopro de ar estremecias] but now, "proud and mythic in the country / of cold stones" [no país das lajes frias/soberba e mítica] does not even notice a spider roaming over her tomb.[82] Cast in stone, Florbela and her poetic legacy become immune to indifference, pettiness, and mortal decay, a women's monument and icon through the transmutation of the flesh into marble art.

In the poem "In the Temple of Florbela-Diana" (223), subtitled "the castrator," Florbela is described as the hieratic, untouchable goddess, as "a medium and daughter / Of Venus, she goes to serve the moon" [Venérea e mediúnica / Vai ao serviço em que a tem a lua (223)]. In this poem, the ephebes castrate themselves and take their offerings to the temple of Diana, where "the legend of Florbela, Artemis / Of the Alentejo, turns them into stags" [onde em veados os transforma a lenda / De Florbela, a Artemisa alentejana (224)]. Thus, as with Isis and the Mother Goddesses in *A Madona*, Florbela's legend, her auratic image, both takes and restores the creative phallus of the male hunter. While this clearly reverses the subservient admiration with which Florbela prostrated herself before male poetic genius in some of her early poems, it also reduces her to a phallic singularity projected by the masculine imagination, and it appears to occlude the worship of female daughters in favor of emasculated men.

One much-commented critical device with which Natália Correia connects women from the past and future with herself is her insistence, as already noted, on recuperating the famously negative suffixed term "poetisa" or "poetess" to reaffirm women's poetic identities positively.[83] Thus she declares in her preface to Florbela's *Diário*, "Yes, I shall call her a poetess. To pay homage to female poetic genius by making its gift masculine is an outrage to a poetry that seeks to feminize the world with the magic of its lunar clarity" [Sim, chamar-lhe-ei poetisa. A homenagem que distingue o génio poético feminino com o prêmio de lhe masculinizar o estro ultraja uma poesia que quer feminizar o mundo com a magia da sua claridade lunar (11)]. She similarly demanded that the "poetisa" title be applied to herself, and she influenced Maria Teresa Horta in the next generation to do likewise.[84]

However, this putative lineage of poetesses, the hieratically chosen "ultrafeminine" order, appears rather to mark out the scarcity of actual women poets in her edited anthology named *A Mulher*. This collection covers paintings and poems celebrating women in Portuguese literature, from eighth-century jesters, through Dom Dinis, António Nobre, and Mário de Sá-Carneiro, through Correia's fourth husband Dórdio Guimarães, to the 1940s. The only two women poets out of the ten writers featured are Florbela Espanca and Maria Teresa Horta. As a result, the term "poetisa" resonates in this context, not only with the biologistic assertion of the feminine suffix but also with its discursive history of female exceptionalism, the shadow of the "extraordinária" cult, of one woman per generation, the worship of the Mother Goddess in the singular.

It remains a compelling irony in Natália Correia's career that this declaredly antifeminist defender of the Mátria should have mothered, in her role as a publisher and critic, the ultimate antimaternalist rebel daughters in the form of the Three Marias and their *Novas Cartas Portuguesas*. Their specific poetic, as opposed to political, debt to Correia remains to be fully evaluated. Certainly, the lasting wealth of Natália Correia's work lay in its very multiplicity and contradiction, its refusal ever in fact to simply cohere into the "single origin" maternalist discourse with which she came to be most often publicly and nationally associated, at the expense of more complex, differentiated readings. Alongside her poetic identification as a regenerated national Mátria, she fostered a Nietzschean antihistoricism and a rejection of metaphysics that interrogated the historical master discourses of the New State and the moral hegemony of Christian tradition. This antihistoricism was inventively recycled by future generations, as evidenced in *Novas Cartas*

Portuguesas with its multiple feminine personae, its breaking of sexual taboo, and its refusal of evolutionary or teleological temporality.

In this respect, Correia dealt a powerful body blow to the naturalness and inevitability of paternal families and patriarchal power as sustained by Portuguese fascism, even as she consciously and polemically flirted with the risk of enshrining a new phallic matriarchy in their place. Her insistence on saving a decadent, nihilistic modern civilization through a new consideration of male and female relations, setting up what Muraro calls "an ethical world of men and women together" seems to anticipate, in many respects, the philosophical preoccupations of Luce Irigaray in her essay the "Universal as Mediation."[85] And like Irigaray, Correia made a provocative contribution to future debates on female literary genealogy, salvaging the prehistoric Mother through matriarchal myth, yet complicating the daughters' actual accession through the Mother Goddess's ongoing complicity with the phallic son. If her comments on women's essential nature and the "innate" creativity of the mother now seem anachronistic and restrictive at times, her ludic use of this "feminine" sign to expose the limits of paternal law still makes her one of Portugal's most important precursors of the postmodern and poststructuralist aesthetics that women increasingly claimed as their own, as we will see, in the closing decades of the twentieth century.

Two poems by Natália Correia

Translated into English by Richard Zenith

At Florbela's Tomb

Princess whose bones now wear marble . . .
Over it a spider roams indifferently.
And you, who shivered at the slightest breeze,
still proud and mythic in the country
of cold stones, don't even notice.

Cemetery of Vila Viçosa, June 9, 1986

In the Temple of Florbela-Diana, The Castrator

At night in a lonely tower, a tiger
At her feet, Florbela combs her hair.
Burning candles tell of her kindred
Wanderer's soul, covered by stardust.
The temple calls her. A medium and daughter
Of Venus, she goes to serve the moon.
Doe of the goddess who demands her tunic,
The moonlight strips her till she's naked.
Her myrtle flesh languidly spreads
Scented spasms across the night.
Wrapped by that fragrant, moonstruck cloud,
Ephebes in pastures and on threshing-floors
Castrate themselves, then take the offering
Of their bleeding parts to Diana's temple
Where the legend of Florbela, Artemis
Of the Alentejo, turns them into stags.

5
Giving Up Whose Ghost in
the Works of Hélia Correia?

> For a male, art is already *displaced* sexuality; for a female it is already *misplaced* sexuality.
>
> —Christine Battersby, *Gender and Genius*

> Gothic-marked narratives always point to the space where the absent mother might be.
>
> —Susan Wolstenholme, *Gothic (Re)Visions*

WHITHER WUTHERING HEIGHTS? A GOTHIC BEGINNING

WHERE THE LOSS OF MATRILINEAL CULTURE AFFORDED IMPORTANT, IF CON-trasting, sources of theoretical reflection for Agustina Bessa Luís and Natália Correia, the fear of an excessive, all too present, maternal lineage has tended rather to haunt Hélia Correia's writings post-1974.[1] In common with many women writers of the postrevolution generation, Correia has resisted, as being too essentialist and reductive, any radical or feminist maternal legacy and the sexing of her texts as "escrita feminina," a subject which led her into disagreement with Maria Teresa Horta in the 1980s.[2] At the same time, she has often been placed by critics, feminist and nonfeminist alike, in maternal lineages. Agustina Bessa Luís is probably the most frequently-cited Portu-guese influence model for Correia's work. As Miguel Real indicates, in a *Jor-nal de Letras* review in 2006, "departing from Agustina, the current matriarch of the Portuguese novel, it is not difficult to unwind the thread of a generational cluster which, among those women authors that have achieved recognition for the quantity and quality of their texts, passes through Maria Velho da Costa and Lídia Jorge, taking in Hélia Correia and ending up with Inês Pedrosa and Clara Pinto Correia."[3] Certainly, as the foregoing analysis of her 1991 novel, *A Casa Eterna* [The Eternal Home], will show, her neo-Romantic and Gothicist trends do place her aesthetics in a recognizable rela-tion to Agustina Bessa Luís. Furthermore, her play *Florbela,* considered here alongside *Perdição. Exercício sobre Antígona* [Perdition. An Exercise on Antigone] draws direct inspiration from Natália Correia.[4]

The common ground between Hélia Correia and Bessa Luís that we will explore here focuses on the way in which both writers deploy Gothicism to ironic and subversive ends.[5] In Correia's case particularly, this can also be traced back to English literary influences. She has acknowledged, for example, drawing important inspiration from her youthful readings of Ann Radcliffe and from an ongoing attachment to Emily Brontë.[6] Furthermore, as we will see, a specific tension between Romantic and Gothic narrative modes affords an important marker, as it does in Bessa Luís's work, for locating the gendering of creativity in Correia's works. Indeed, Susanna Becker has usefully observed that "feminine gothic texture, with its complex subject processes, might be seen as dramatisation of gender construction."[7]

In an unpublished lecture delivered at Rutgers University, New Brunswick, in 1998, Correia states, "I think that all my life I have been in love with Emily Brontë's *Wuthering Heights*. . . . I have been to Haworth, the Brontë's homeland, and could almost touch their feelings with my fingers, could almost hear them think."[8] In this talk, Correia draws on her experience of reading Brontë to articulate her view of transcendent, disembodied literary genius, arguing for the "primitive divinity" of the act of reading itself, the search for the always enigmatic and unattainable core of the genius-text.[9] To illustrate this, she brilliantly anatomizes the ways in which Emily Brontë holds readerly desire at bay, barring the readers' metaphorical entry to the house of fiction that is also literally the house of Wuthering Heights to which Lockwood is rudely refused admission in the novel's famous opening passages.[10] Thus, she claims, we the readers seek to pass through the text's "forbidden field of light" only to find that we are left masochistically worshipping this very prohibition to do so, and finding true illumination, the fulfillment of desire, only in death.[11] The spirit of genius described here belongs, much as in Romantic tradition, with the ineffable, the sublime, and the sphere of Nature.

Yet Correia's own subject positioning in this text is, in fact, curiously dispersed between the "excluded" but admiring reader, worshipping this Romantic genius from afar, and the identification of the fellow woman writer, seeking some form of model for her own work, as she wishes to walk in Brontë's footsteps, to be in her physical space. This latter sentiment is even more prominent in her 2008 short story "Doroteia," published in parallel textual versions in Portuguese and English. In a concluding authorial footnote, Correia explains, "something in the rather Gothic theme that emerged, demanded that I write this in English. Although you cannot see it, it all starts in Haworth with my friend Emily Brontë."[12]

Housing the Eternal Maternal

As we noted in our discussion of masculinized genius in Bessa Luís's *Fanny Owen,* the unsolvable enigma, the symbolization of the "spirit" of genius, is commonly associated with the inscription of the "eternal feminine," the place of desire and lack. For Correia, however, writing "in parallel" with the spirit of Emily Brontë as (female) genius par excellence, this pattern undergoes a gender reversal, a blurring of sexual boundaries. It is this that we intend to explore in relation to her fourth novel, *A Casa Eterna.* Here, the enigma which propels the text concerns a woman's quest to "find" the elusive genius artistic male who is always beyond reach, and whose absence in fact creates the space for a female Gothic subtext to emerge.[13] In this work, which won Correia the Máxima literary prize, a female journalist visits Amorins, the native village of Álvaro Roíz, a fictional, famous, and recently dead male poet that she admired. She is driven by the need to ascertain what happened in the dying moments of the poet, with whom, it is implied, she had had some form of relationship. It is the written account of this quest that constitutes the material of the novel, for which the unnamed female journalist acts as the first-person narrator. There is an increasing implication that the circumstances surrounding Roíz's death were somehow suspicious or mysterious, despite the fact that he was returning to the village of his birth because he knew he was terminally ill. The narrator sets out ostensibly intending to uncover some facts by conducting and recording oral interviews with a series of local inhabitants, friends, and family of Roíz, regarding what they might have known, seen, or witnessed. A distinction is drawn between her project to trace his last days, and that of a Paolo, an Italian liberal humanist scholar in Lisbon who is seeking the definitive biographical data that will unlock Roíz's poetic works.

On her increasingly labyrinthine journey through his native village and surroundings, the narrator is constantly foiled in her attempts to connect Roíz's family history and early years in Amorins, with the events of his demise, or the meaning of his writings. Her partial success in tracing some of his genealogy to the wild and womanizing Spanish Roíz family, and the provincial aristocratic Baião dynasty, proves ultimately unreliable. The notoriously roistering behavior of Álvaro Roíz's father Pedro has produced illegitimate children, one of whom is thought to have been Agostinho Rosa, a traveling salesman, whom the narrator interviews. Where genealogy proves slippery and unreliable, the trail to a family-motivated killing is further impeded, as the text takes on the Gothic texture of the unsolvable enigma. It turns out that several people could have had motives to kill Roíz. His childhood friend Santoro, the successful returning emigrant, is envious of Roíz, and intended to buy up and convert his former home, Quinta Viçosa. Filomena the childhood friend who was his first lover, and Estelinha the prostitute who sexually initiated him, both had their reasons to resent him. Agostinho Rosa retained childhood jealousy of the man he thought was his socially superior half brother. The pretentious Antonieta Sotto has been humiliated by the drunken behavior of Roíz at the literary party she hosted in his honor. And the old family servant Perpétua Dimas had wanted to marry the dying Roíz to her niece, Lizette, for his money. The doctor claims he died of a heart attack but is defensive over the matter of an autopsy. Roíz's sister Anabela did not appear to mourn him and his coffin was left closed at the funeral.

The narrator ends up collecting a series of conspicuous red herrings as the mystery remains and deepens, finally degenerating into the collective popular fantasy of a cheap boarding house whodunit, in which all her fellow residents participate over supper at the Pensão where the narrator is staying. She finally admits to Agostinho Rosa, her would-be detective side-kick, that she has no concrete "história" to tell about Roíz's death at all, only a verbal labyrinth leading nowhere. Yet throughout this process, the dynamic of the plot gradually shifts from the question of resolving the mystery to the subject of narrative authority. This process reaches its climax in the narrator's encounter with o Ruço, the local taxi driver and slaughterer of animals, who was the last person to see Roíz alive. His name "o Ruço" refers to his red hair, pointing to his status as a typically Gothic "suspect" figure, because his physical appearance marks him as different. The narrator drives through the night to pressure o Ruço into revealing what he really knows, but he tells her nothing, other than indicating with the word "também" that others may also have accused him of the killing. As he points out he had no real motive to murder Roíz, other than perhaps theft. Nothing can be pinned on him or on the other key suspect, Perpétua Dimas. Meeting an impasse and finally abandoning her detective trail, the narrator follows o Ruço's advice to simply invent what appears to be a suitable fictional ending for her account of Roíz's life.

The story progressively becomes, then, the tale of a woman writer, rewriting the male writer as third person "personagem," from within her own fantasy and imagination in an act that redoubles and shadows his original spirit of genius. As with the Brontës and their "spirit of the place," this shadowing or doubling of the male genius takes the form of following in his footsteps, breathing his air, visiting the places where his physical presence would have walked. When she arrives in Amorins at the beginning, the narrator writes, "I am with him in the square at Amorins. I am, like a child in the sand, looking for his trail so that I can place my feet in the exact spot that he placed his. Carrying a suitcase and feeling very cold. The act of making him into a character now means not finding him, and weaving a kind of gloss around him" [estou como ele no largo de Amorins. Estou, como uma criança na areia, procurando-lhe o rasto para colocar os pés exactamente onde ele os colocou. Segurando uma mala e tendo muito frio. Transformá-lo agora em personagem é não o encontrar e tecer uma espécie de glosa à sua volta (25)]. Thus, it is precisely the absence of his physical presence that inspires the narrator's writings or "glosa." To walk the earthly trail left by his genius is to follow the body in the negative, in its absence, to trail the sublimation and disembodiment that is associated with poetic genius.

In the narrative aesthetic that this produces, as Isabel Allegro de Maga-lhães has aptly observed, a strong stylistic and spiritual proximity is represented between the two writers, one living, and the other dead.[14] However, where both are inevitably refracted through the single lens of the living narrator, there can be no mutual or equal reciprocity in this proximity. Indeed, the dead Roíz progressively becomes the textualized *objet d'art* of the female narrator. It is in this immortalizing act of sealing him into a piece of art that she effectively, in Elisabeth Bronfen's terms, "deanimates" or "dematerializes" him. Becoming a phantom that lives on through the narrator's imagination, Roíz provides what Bronfen calls "the proof of the textual superceding bodily existence."[15] By the same token, Roíz's supposed "memories" of the places where the narrator goes to find him are recorded only as her acts of textualized imagination and desire.[16] This double perspective also affords a doubling of gender perspective, such that the narrator is able to take a critical, authoritative view on the male gendering of the artistic process. As Wolstenholme notes, in relation to the British female Gothic, "doublings serve the function of distancing which allows a degree of mastery."[17]

As Roíz becomes increasingly the creature of the female narrator's fiction, the narrative of his ethereal, unreachable genius, the spirit that drives the narrator's quest, is interwoven with his shambolic, roistering, ancestral life story as she retells it. This opens up a parodic, alternative perspective on his greatness in the manner of what Becker terms a typically Gothic "mirror text" or "mirror plot."[18] As Becker notes, the Gothic genre's antirealism and tendency toward excess, as a strategy of defamiliarization, make it a powerful tool for parody, particularly in its more modern variants, with its strategies of repeating, reversal, exaggeration, and expansion.[19] In this sense, the Gothic mirror text's distorted representations of the "whole" echo the narrator's warnings to the reader at the end, that Roíz's story has become literally, a distorting mirror at a fairground, an "espelho deformante numa feira" (211).

As the narrator follows in Roíz's footsteps and imagines his thoughts, other female bodies persistently and obscenely intrude upon and distort her retelling of his past. The long-buried women and matriarchs of Roíz's past, the marginalized, repressed, and unremembered of patrilinear history, start to reemerge. As the narrator admits at the beginning, in a near throwaway line recounting her first meeting of Roíz in his Lisbon salon, "it is almost always a horrible business admitting the vulgarity of a body into the authorship of writing by a genius" [é quase sempre um passo horrível admitir um corpo, uma vulgaridade, na autoria de uma escrita genial (20)]. Yet a whole host of "vulgar bodies" belonging to rustics, idiots, servants, and rejected females, do, in fact, begin to populate the pages of the novel, further complicating the Romantic textualization of Roíz as genius. If Roíz himself is somehow disembodied, the ever-retreating absence whose physical trace must remain unfindable and dematerialized for his genius text to stay intact, the displacement of this somatic burden onto the excessively embodied, hysterical experiences of the women, traces a parodic, parallel history of "female genius in the negative," delineating the terms of women's exclusion.

Roíz's female relations, lovers, servants, and forebears are represented as suffering hysteria, insanity and sexual excess, starving, tortured and incarcerated, usually in the domestic context of marriage, sexual relations, and childbirth.[20] And this often violent abjection of the female body is shown, in turn, to be related to the historical suppression of matriarchy. Roíz himself has been the fading scion of a small-time rural aristocracy in decline. As the narrator discovers, his patriarchal lineage had been locked in battle with a powerful, underlying matriarchal culture, the Baião family that was progressively supplanted. Thus, we learn that Roíz's financially prosperous father Pedro, descended from a long line of romancing Spanish Bohemians, was obliged to marry his mother, the exotic, Germanically-named Hermengarda, and settle with his mother's family when he got her pregnant, after meeting her at a traveling circus. The idealized, romantic future of silk and roses that she had dimly envisaged ended rapidly with her first brutal, sexual encounter, converting her from childlike innocence to near nymphomania. Eventually, Hermengarda's exaggerated sexual desire, in the face of male neglect and infidelity, drives her to insanity and self-starvation. She sadomasochistically locks herself away in the attic for life, her only presence in Álvaro Roíz's memory being the sound of her heels in the room overhead pacing between door and window, as she haunts the house and all her descendants, the first of the text's many mad women to take refuge in the attic.

Carolina Sotto, a distant relation of the Baião family, fears that Hermengarda's madness has been passed down to her, as she too is confined at home with her children. Álvaro's father, Pedro, meanwhile has enjoyed a series of sexual affairs, including with his mad cousin Maria Carmelinda. An ex-nun who also enjoyed a wild life in the *fado* clubs with Pedro, Carmelinda came close to being locked away as a deranged alcoholic. Roíz's own first sexual conquest, Filomena, is similarly described as a sad bloated old doll, "half dead and half alive" [morta-viva (127)] as much a prisoner as Hermengarda, confined behind the walls of her home for good after Roíz has left her (59; 127). In this instance, a Gothic interpretation is playfully suggested to the reader, when we are informed that her life story "seemed rather like a gothic tale, the one about the good vampire and the maiden" [parecia de algum modo um conto gótico, do vampiro bondoso e da donzela (62)].

The Gothicized women that punctuate the narration of Roíz's genius are thus represented as monsters, lunatics, hysterics, and outcasts in relation to the dominant history of a patriarchal lineage. This lineage seeks to perpetuate itself through a female body that nonetheless refuses to be reliably domesticated.[21] As Becker has noted, Julia Kristeva's concept of the abject is particularly pertinent for understanding how the threat of excessive female sexuality and procreativity actually operates in Gothic and horror genres. Kristeva's famous concept of the "abject" refers to the "outside" that always also marks out a limit on the inside, the threat of social danger and subjective disintegration, possessing a simultaneous capacity to induce both fascination and horror in the subject.[22] Separation takes place from the abjected figure of the double-faced good and bad Mother, with the Mother constituting the primal physical matter that has to be held at bay. In this sense, the Kristevan subject is caught between loss of boundary and boundary construction, as its oppositional relation to the abject marks out an ambivalent, fluid space of simultaneous revulsion toward, but also desire for, the Mother, thus questing toward meaning, while simultaneously dreading its loss.[23] Kristeva significantly links the historical rise of social purification rituals based on abjection, with periods in which excessive matrilinearity threatens to overpower patrilinear patterns of kinship.[24] As she puts it, "fear of the archaic mother turns out to be essentially fear of generative power. It is this power, a dreaded one, that patrilineal filiation has the burden of subduing. It is thus not surprising to see pollution rituals proliferating in societies where patrilinear power is poorly secured, as if the latter sought, by means of purification, a support against excessive matrilineality."[25]

Roíz's failing patrilinear family has endeavored to suppress the influence of an older matrilineal network, the heritage of powerful matriarchal foremothers.[26] The family estate of Quinta Viçosa is neglected and is cared for only by an ancient, embittered servant. Roíz's legacy of degeneracy is alleged to have been matrilineal in origin, passed down through his maternal grandmother, Carolina Baião. The very name of Roíz's ancestral home, the "Quinta Viçosa," turns out to conceal a gruesome, female ancestral history.

We later learn that the name may have been a distortion of "viciosa" or vicious, referring to a particularly terrifying female ancestor in Roíz's maternal lineage, whom Santoro describes as "an evil sort of a woman, if you get my meaning, vicious" [má mulher, se me entende, viciosa (146)].

The Gothic mirror text projected by these suppressed, "insane", matrilineal women comes to demarcate an "unofficial" out of bounds, an extraliterary space for the radically female "Other," the beyond that Roíz alternately feared and desired. The women are also the bearers of the pluralized, organic narrative forms that characterize the Gothic. Forming an ever-growing network, the women tell multiple tales to each other, dispersing and fragmenting their narrative subjectivity in a female, oral genealogy of their own that resists containment in patriarchal houses or defined, transmittable texts. Thus, Carmelinda, the ex-nun, befriends a hatmaker who spreads the local news in the form of gothicized tales. Similarly, Filomena absorbs her own mother's stories of sexual scandal and excess which have been passed down from Roíz's mother, Hermengarda (75).

Recalling the false trails left in nineteenth-century English Gothic fiction, the local stories that the narrator hears from them are inconsequential tales that lead nowhere, told for their own sake from the margins of society, by women, rustics, servants and idiots.[27] Far from yielding any meaning about Roíz's death, this spontaneous oral discourse affords the presymbolic speech matter that the narrator must then shape into the representational forms of literary convention. This nostalgic scene of "natural" orality, associated with the maternal body, provides the raw material for poetic expression. Thus, the people's meandering testimonies to the narrator come to be valued for their rhythmic beauty, not their signification.

In the culmination to this aesthetic process, the narrator's conclusion describes o Ruço watching Álvaro Roíz as a child returning to the water, the weir beloved from his childhood where he drew inspiration for his poems and where his dead body had allegedly been found. In this metaphorical return to the womb, Roíz reencounters the mermaids that he fantasized in infancy, so that:

He looked at the women that lived in it, at the gilded mirrors in which they combed their hair. [O Ruço] saw how they held him in their lap and sang to him. And scarcely had they uttered the words, than the things they named would appear and explode in the air, above the child. He saw that he wanted to grow without leaving this behind, to grow up just enough for them to tell him their secret.

Olhou para as mulheres que lá viviam dentro, para os espelhos de metal doirado onde elas penteavam o cabelo. [O Ruço] viu como o seguravam no regaço, cantando. E, mal diziam as palavras, as coisas nomeadas apareciam e estoiravam no ar, sobre a criança. Viu que ele queria crescer sem se afastar, crescer apenas o suficiente para que lhe transmitissem o segredo. (242)[28]

In the passages that lead up to his death, Roíz experiences latently homoerotic final moments with o Ruço, before he is finally at one with the "welcoming loins" [lombo acolhedor (242)] of the mother. His feminization as an artist, returning to the wellsprings of poetry, evidently evokes on one level the disavowal of masculinity beloved of Romantic, outsider figures, the association of a feminized homosexuality with genius. It is no accident, as Magalhães rightly observes, that the novel tips a Nietzschean wink to the reader, in the naming of the cat, Zarathustra, bequeathed to the narrator by Roíz. As the ending suggests, with its cyclical return to the womb, Roíz's creativity has always been grounded in the feminine body, in those very embodied, but silenced, female histories that have progressively taken over the reconstruction of Roíz's past.[29] In this context, the attic space which is conventionally, as we saw above, an enclosure for the mad or hysterical female, is made instead into the liminal space of Roíz's own terror and eventual transfiguration.

The repellent physicality of the servant women at Quinta Viçosa, with their world of narrative folklore, had previously frightened and paralyzed Roíz, so that "he would flee from the attic, terrified of those great bodies, that came at him with their smell of warmth and badly washed flannel clothing" [fugia do sótão, assustado com aqueles grandes corpos, que lhe atiravam com um cheiro a quente e a roupas de flanela mal lavadas (120)]. The nighttime darkness, complicit with the women, spreads out to follow him in all directions becoming "the huge listening ear of his grandmother" [o imenso ouvido da avó (120)], the recurrent fear not only of matrilinearity, but of women overhearing him, of women absorbing and consuming his words. However, as the narrator describes his final visits to the family home and to Perpétua Dimas, she represents Roíz moving beyond his fear of the feminine, as "he had surely now passed through the mirror: the female world did not frighten him any more, nor did it lead him to bury his head, loving the crime and the beautiful phrases that imitate it" [tinha decerto atravessado o espelho: o mundo feminino já não o assustava, não o levava já a esconder a cabeça amando o crime e as belas frases que o imitam (117)].

Forcing Roíz to pass through both the mirror and the Gothicized mirror text, the narrator unleashes a silenced world of suppressed "Mothers" who are also, crucially, mothers to her own text, in which she "remothers" Roíz and ultimately rematerializes/rebirths his masculinity. In this process, she shows that his fear and desire of the maternal body, of his own superseded and half-buried matriarchal past, inescapably underwrite his own writing subjectivity. His history as a dead writer thus finds itself regrafted onto a pervasive, oral matrilinearity. At the same time, the ancestral "other" women that the narrator constructs as Roíz's abjects and border zones, effectively serve to intimate the narrator's own gender conflicts, her own historical alienation from female body matter, as a woman finding her literary voice under the overarching sign of male literary genius. Read in this context, Correia's treatment of the feminine/masculine artistic interface between Roíz and the narrator, approximates to Susanne Becker's concept of how split subjectivity works in the feminine Gothic, creating an "interrogatory" text, where different, contradictory levels of narrative cannot be reconciled. These different, irreconcilable levels reveal the covert operations of gender ideology, which addressing these contradictions then works to subvert.[30]

The *Casa Eterna* of the novel's title ostensibly refers to the opening epigraph from the *Book of Ecclesiastes,* the return to one's "eternal home" at the moment of death, the return to the womb, but it also, on another level, evokes the eternally inescapable "house" of male canonical literary history.[31] The narrator's gendered doubleness as a female writing subject-in-process, drawing her inspiration from the master narrative of masculine literary "greatness" affords her a strategic position of mastery regarding the female body's abjection from the essentially patrilinear histories that inform Portuguese literary tradition and canonicity.[32] Yet, these lost matriarchal structures are significantly not bound into a cycle of repression and return, women taking revenge on the historical victory of patriarchal rule, such as we witnessed in Natália Correia's work. Rather, for Hélia Correia, as for Julia Kristeva, the mother is that fluid space of simultaneous revulsion and desire that cannot, by definition, be completely eliminated, no matter how much she is cast out. The female narrator in *A Casa Eterna* shows how the double borders of abjection structure not only women's ambivalent position on the borders of male canonical literary history, but also men's anxious, fragile, and fearful conditions of belonging to that history, premised as they are on the illusion of suppressing that which never truly goes away.

If *A Casa Eterna* makes its point through a gothicized story of haunting, the two plays we move to consider now also deploy the double perspective of the specter, to explore women's cultural memory loss in the symbolic ordering of literary history. *Florbela* and *Perdição. Exercício sobre Antígona,* published as one edition in 1991, the same year as *A Casa Eterna,* show the real Portuguese woman poet Florbela Espanca, and the paradigmatic Sophoclean heroine, Antigone, commenting from beyond the grave on the mythologies associated with their own lives and deaths.[33]

ANTI-ANTIGONE—A STAGE BETWEEN LIFE AND DEATH

Both of these dramas engage, in different ways, with powerful literary foremothers.[34] Hélia Correia claims in the preface to the plays that she did not want to write either of them. The reworking of Florbela Espanca mythology was produced at the strong exhortation of Natália Correia, to whom *Florbela* is dedicated. She also, perhaps less consciously, follows in Natália Correia's footsteps by undertaking a gendered revision of Sophocles as did Natália in her *O Progresso de Édipo*. Although Hélia Correia's two plays were not staged as a pair, she invites a comparative reading of the print versions, by posing a question on the back cover about the points of connection between them.[35] There she asks, "what might Florbela and Antigone have in common?" [que haverá de comum entre Florbela e Antígona?] before sketching an answer to her own question as follows:

> Perhaps the fact that in both cases boredom inspired greatness? Let us suppose that Antigone was not a heroine but a young girl who had had a violent experience of life and had developed an addictive taste for pure folly. Florbela lasted longer and wrote poetry. But she too seems to have found the ultimate form of illumination in death.

> [Talvez o serem casos em que o aborrecimento inspirou grandeza? Suponhamos que Antígona não foi uma heroína, mas uma rapariga que tivera experiências violentas da vida e se viciou no gosto da pura insensatez. Florbela durou mais e escreveu versos. Mas parece também ter achado na morte o momento acabado da iluminação].[36]

As their publication in diptych and their appearance in the same year implies, certain common preoccupations run across the two plays. The most prominent of these is the linking of death or, more precisely, suicide with the two women's quest for individuation, fame, and notoriety, and with their troubled accession to adult female sexuality. In a lecture delivered at the Classics department of Coimbra University, Correia describes her Antígona in very contemporary terms of youthful alienation, leading to a doomed Warholian quest for fifteen minutes of fame.[37]

This desire to attain notoriety is heavily bound up with Antígona's arrested passage from adolescent sexuality to mature, maternal femininity.[38] Correia's Antígona, like her Sophoclean original, refuses to take up her maternal place in the Greek patrilinear kinship to which she is predestined through marriage to Hémon. For Correia, however, Antígona does not symbolize any heroic or redemptive defense of the household gods in the face of paternal law or political statecraft. She conspicuously does not love or revere

Polínices, the brother she buries. Her act of defiance against Creonte is a form of suicide that reenshrines her own ego. She deliberately engineers her own death as a means of rejecting her position in the Greek patriarchal sexual symbolic, making a statement, not in favor of kinship or affective values, but rather against the suppression of female individuality and identity that they imply, in other words, against the conditions of impossibility for a text of female genius.

In this capacity, her death becomes a comment on the limited conditions of life for the reproductive adolescent woman in Greek society. It is interesting to note in this context what Judith Butler has to say about the sexuality of the Sophoclean Antigone. For Butler, while Antigone does not actively embrace homosexuality, she does move "to deinstitute heterosexuality, by refusing to do what is necessary to stay alive for Haemon, by refusing to become a mother and a wife, thus scandalizing the public with her wavering gender, by embracing death as her bridal chamber."[39] Thus, her choosing death over life becomes a negative comment on the terms of social liveability for those not conforming to a paternal social symbolic. Her death-driven positioning outside of life, affords, as Butler puts it, "a perspective on the symbolic constraints under which liveability is established."[40] Correia's Antígona does much to reinforce this reading, insofar as her defiance of the state is so clearly suicide-driven, and her decision to die forecloses any possible attainment of adult sexual identity.

Having lost her birth mother Jocasta, Antígona has been raised by her nurse and by her aunt Eurídice, Creonte's wife. Eurídice tellingly remarks that Antígona always "had everything mixed up in her head" [tinha tudo trocado na cabeça (57)]. Antígona is clearly described as alienated from the typically circular existence of women in patrician Greece. She has been disillusioned early in life by her compliant sister Isménia, by the excessive maternalism of Eurídice, and by the dullness of women's lot, living as cheated wives and serial child-bearers for men who sexually prefer boys (34). Aware that royal wives such as her aunt are deprived of any fulfillment of desire, Antígona learns that women's only recourse to their own physical pleasure is through the secret Dionysian rituals that Eurídice enjoys with the bacchantes, and which do not appeal to her.[41] As her nurse and her aunt inform her, she can expect nothing good from her future life if she lives: "all that remains, my dear, is a life lived between weaving, the stores and the hearth" [fica uma vida filha entre os teares, o armazém e a lareira (34)].

The question of what is "liveable," of what can be expected of life, is posed particularly acutely in this play by its textual layout and staging as a visual enactment of the embodied versus the disembodied. Hence, the page and also the stage space are divided into two categories, the "Vivos" (who are collectively masculine and feminine) and the "Mortas" (who are only feminine). Through this device, Correia makes her now dead Antígona interrogate and criticize in retrospect the living Antígona's life, choices and meanings as she travels to the underworld accompanied by her faithful nurse. The comments that Antígona makes, blur the two time zones of life and death, transforming the "living" action into a reiterated, doubly specularized performance, as the audience watches Antígona in death, watching herself in life. A third level comes into play in *Perdição*, through the world of the soothsayers characterized by Tirésias who mediates between the two worlds, and through the Dionysian bacchantes who introduce and punctuate the action with chants and rituals.

It is through this double staging structure that Antígona's statements about herself become a form of life-writing, a form of reflexive artistic creativity, a self-representation. It is the act of death, and of commentary from beyond the grave, that makes her paradoxically into the narrator of her own life. Realizing that her life would have been lived in the tedium of the "gyneceum," she declares from her perspective in death, "I experienced the happiness in small things that is the lot of women. The belt with the shiny, jewelled clasp. A crown of daffodils in my hair" [conheci a pequena alegria das mulheres. O cinto com o fecho onde brilha uma jóia. Uma coroa de junquilhos no cabelo (33)]. Her choice of suicide is questioned when the living Antígona asks her nurse "I could not live with them, and put up with all that peace and quiet, could I?" [eu não conseguiria viver com eles, suportar aquela paz? (57)]. The dead Antígona remarks that in comparison to death "even the wretched life of women is preferable" [é bem preferível a vida miserável das mulheres (57)]. The dead Antígona cannot make her living self hear that her death has been a terrible mistake, that "this field of nauseating flowers is all there is in the hereafter" [este campo de flores nauseabundas é tudo o que há depois (57)].

Making her life-writing in death into a statement about the limitations of the only available sexual symbolic, Antígona's situation raises some interesting parallels with the indexing of Romantic genius to sexual nonconformity, a concept productively elucidated by Andrew Elfenbein. He notes that both men and women writers laid claim to genius status, precisely by virtue of their decadent, unconventional lives, and their "unfitness" for domesticity. Thus he comments that, "a frequent strategy for such authors was to challenge contemporary codes of sexual propriety in their works and, in some cases, in their lives. They used transgressive sexual representations, especially those of same-sex eroticism, to mark their perceived superiority to authors who merely reproduced codes of sexual propriety."[42]

The defining irony of *Perdição*, concretely enacted in its split structure, arises from the fact that it is only by choosing the spectacular, scandalous option of early death, the transgression of her proper reproductive role, that Antígona can sexually differentiate herself from the undifferentiated female *bios* around her, sufficiently to have anything to say about her life, any possibility of life-writing at all. Paradoxically, it is only by virtue of being dead, that she has a life worth writing about.

Reading the play in this context, we attribute a more overtly critical, ironic and tragic perspective to the double-staging than that adduced by Isabel Capeloa Gil, in her inspirational reading of the play in terms of Derridian spectro-poetics. Gil describes the world of the dead and of myth being transmitted to that of the living, through phantasmatic figures and events, through simulacra.[43] One important effect of this spectrography for Gil's antitragic reading is the challenge it presents to the classic Lacanian image of Antigone as "mulher morta," the Woman as the absolute Other on the margins, whose sacrificial death therefore shores up culture. As Gil notes, given that the Lacanian concept of "Woman" is always already associated with death to begin with, the use of the Antigone myth to talk about women's death becomes ultimately pleonastic, a kind of (liberating) double negative that reflects back upon itself, so that the play's double staging of the living alongside the dead, produces the Derridian *"difference/diferral* proper to 'feminine writing' about the death of a woman and the canonical model of this discourse."[44]

At the same time, however, this "feminine voicing" is taken up throughout the play by the chorus of bacchantes which Gil describes as "a primitive female *ethos*" celebrating "the female quest for love and identity."[45] However, where this feminine is expressed in the "circular time defined by biological rhythm," the burden of unreflective biological matter becomes once again vested in woman.[46] Antigone as "Dead Woman" is, as Gil rightly observes, a pleonasm because the name Antigone in culture always already symbolizes death. Yet, the name "Antigone" does not signify only "the dead Woman" in western culture, as in Lacanian psychoanalysis. Her name may also etymologically connote, as Butler points out, "anti/gone" or antigeneration, the non-maternal, the refusal to embody a particular kind of future.[47] Only by being dead, that is by radically repudiating this essential female bios of sex and reproduction, does Antígona distinguish herself sufficiently in the public sphere, to have anything to say or, historically inscribe, about herself as something other than the Lacanian defining edge of culture. Furthermore, self-writing as a woman from a position afforded only by death, reduces the possibility of women's self-authorship to the level of a purely hypothetical act.

Antígona's staging of a "life-in-death" double time still leaves her aesthetically and critically suspended, as if walled alive into her own text, between the boundaries of "Vivos" (masculine) and "Mortas" (feminine). The pattern of recursive nonclosure and the repetition of pointless regret in her life commentaries closely echo Freud's definitions of melancholia as a stalled or impossible process of mourning. But it is an act of mourning for the stillbirth of her female creative self, not for the honor of her brother or her father's family.[48] The play's structural doubling, the life/death space on the stage, that can reach no closure on the value or meaning of her death, acts out the cumulative, repetitive and pathological symptom of an ongoing melancholia, with its characteristic traits of self-exposure and self-dramatization.[49] Where a gap between two impossibilities cannot be bridged, Correia's doubled Antígona stages what Freud terms "the conflict within the ego, which melancholia substitutes for the struggle over the object."[50] This mourning has prolonged itself into melancholia but it has also transformed itself into art. The result is an endless lamentation of fate, of that which cannot now be changed or undone but which, in the act of speaking this inevitability, takes on the form of Antígona's own artistic construction of herself, revealing the extreme false dichotomy of her limited choices.

Antígona uses her posthumous self-textualization to shift and reinscribe her place in the Western cultural symbolic. She is still a mythical name but she is a name that has now been transformed into an encoding, and a speaking, of women's historical exclusion from cultural subjectivity. By standing for sexual nondefinition, she rejects both endogamous and exogamous kinship as she refuses loyalty to her brother, and she forecloses sexual consummation with Hémon by transforming it into her own, not his, erotic fantasy of death. She thus refuses to be any version of the obedient Other, of pure matter, occupying the place of the Lacanian dead Woman, at the defining edge of speech and culture. Rather she makes her death a comment on the liveability of a woman's life outside the bio cycle of Greek state patriarchy. She can only write herself if she remains unsexed and therefore dead, through suicide, as protest against a woman's life. The splitting of the staging thus inaugurates an important and ironic question for women's expressive subjectivity in Western cultural tradition. If Antigone can only self-author from a position of death that marks her refusal of Western culture's sexual symbolics, how would sexuality itself have to be written differently to enable her as a woman to self-author, to inscribe herself, while remaining alive? To put it another way, and for future generations, how can a woman individuate herself sufficiently to have something to say about her life, while still remaining alive long enough to say it? It is this question that resurfaces in Hélia Correia's play about Florbela Espanca.

THE DEAD (WOMEN) POETS' SOCIETY

Dedicated to Natália Correia, who asked Hélia Correia to write a play on this subject, *Florbela* is a fitting tribute to the great female writer of the Mátria, dealing as it does with Woman's symbolic relation to death, not in Western culture as a whole, as characterized by Antigone, but specifically and "locally" in twentieth-century Portuguese literary tradition. Seizing the initiative of critically defining her genius outside of male literary history, Hélia Correia's Florbela challenges all attempts to "wall her up alive" into the male canon by staging a retrospective review of her own life, work and critics against a scenic backdrop of her own funeral bier. Like *Perdição, Florbela* focuses on the "exceptional," dissident woman and the sexual positioning that this exceptionalism implies. However, if Antígona is given no final opportunity in the play's temporal organization to answer back to Tirésias's mythical construction of her for posterity, *Florbela* in contrast is built around the famous woman poet's answering back to her canonical image, her "entombment" in literary history, her rendering as hysteric by male-authored schools of criticism.

Antígona's dialogue with her nurse is here transposed into the pairing of Florbela, as a child and an adult, with the unnamed "Guia," who is by turns her critical interlocutor and her spectator. This character is explicitly linked in the stage directions with women's memory. We are told that the Guia is an older woman but she is "clearly not human . . . she must have the androgyny of the angels, because she is an Angel, and women's memory because she is the Guide of a woman" [claramente inumana, . . . deve ter a androgenia dos anjos, porque é um Anjo, e a memória do feminino porque é o Guia de uma mulher (61)]. Mirroring the mythical bisexuality of Tiresias, the Guia is physically androgynous, and yet she is also possessed of female memory, because she is guiding a woman. In this role, the Guia informs Florbela, as a precocious child and subsequently as an adult, of her posthumous public image and her subsequent fate in the Portuguese critical canon. Florbela's sense of disembodiment and sexual self-alienation is purveyed through the widening gap, which the Guia reveals, between Florbela's obsessively cultivated self-image (constantly changing clothes, voice, *persona* and appearance on stage) and her mythical and often contentious recreation in the eyes of literary history. As Battersby has suggested, "for a male, art is already *displaced* sexuality; for a female it is already *misplaced* sexuality," and it is Florbela's critical historical fate pitched between these two poles that forms the central issue of the play.[51]

The dialogue between the Guia and Florbela moves progressively to undo

the disjuncture between female sexuality and writing subjectivity. Throughout the play, Florbela consciously assumes an abstract, self-idealizing, godlike
sexuality on stage, as she adopts and repeats a series of conventional, iconic
poses. These resemble the many images of her captured on film by her photographer father, but here they reverse the power of the paternal gaze by
acting out in a living, constructed and therefore changeable format, the images that he had frozen for history in stills photography. For this reason,
Florbela's dialogue with her past, mediated by the Guia, becomes an attempted construction of the "artist as woman" in which Florbela seeks to
relocate this historical "misplacing" of her sex and to decenter established
critical authority.

    If the reenactment of photographic poses deauthorizes the father's lens,
the critical Guia marks the place of the absent mother in Florbela's literary
genealogy, in a therapeutic process that resembles psychoanalytical transference. It is the Guia who acts as a mediating figure linking Florbela back to
her conflicted maternal history. In this sense, the play traces a trajectory away
from assimilation to paternal literary genealogy, toward some form of alli-
ance with a putatively female one. Holding up the mirror of critical history
to Florbela's self-perceptions, the Guia reflects back a dual poetic identity
that is caught between the desexualization demanded of women writers by
the male literary canon, and the possibility of a maternalized female cultural
memory. The refraction effect of this historical mirror dialogue with the
Guia as mother/critic is further underlined by the presence on stage of a
literal mirror in which Florbela constantly regards and revises herself in the
course of her conversations.

    Reviewing her own posthumous treatment by the critical canon, Florbela
is given the right of reply to the reviewers who have characterized her work
since she died and whom the Guia provocatively quotes to her by way of
inviting correction. This process of citation and reorientation of famous
quotes from established Portuguese critics, primarily men, allows Florbela to
generate her own alternative literary genealogy after the fact, in the absence
of either a real biographical mother that she knew, or a female-authored literary and critical lineage. Casting an ironic eye on the way posterity has represented her as hysteric and neurotic, she moves to achieve instead an
alternative literary historical lineage, in which a new form of cultural, symbolic maternity can be claimed through interaction with the Guia. As she
reenacts and rescripts her own construction for posterity, her living and dead
images gradually move toward merging in the conclusion to shape an altered
inscription in literary history, in which the absence of female genealogy in
the national canon can be more clearly seen.

    Florbela's literal deprivation of mothering is expressed, as with Correia's

Antígona, in terms of her unconventional kinship relations and her subsequent inability to conform to adult heterosexual "norms" of maternity and family life, despite her three marriages. Thus, Florbela describes her own biological origins in terms of a male parthenogenesis which has left her with no mother, no sexual fulfillment for herself as a mother, and an ambiguously crossed kin relationship with her only brother, Apeles.[52] In biographical terms, this relates to the probability that Florbela was the child of a housemaid she scarcely knew, whom her father had impregnated as a surrogate, since his legal wife could not have children. The latter died when Florbela was very young. Preferring to consider herself divinely intellectually spawned by the sole agency of her father, Florbela describes herself as "a goddess, born in the foaming wave of her father. Because my birth occurred without women. . . . I was Pallas Athena, born from an idea, from the overflowing personality of João Espanca. He needed to extend himself, to go beyond himself . . . Everything emanates from my father" [uma deusa, nascida na espuma de seu pai. Porque o meu nascimento se passou sem mulheres. . . . Eu fui Palas Atena, nascida de uma ideia, do excesso de personalidade de João Espanca. Ele precisava de se desdobrar, de extravasar de si . . . Tudo emana do meu pai (75)].

Analogous to this absence of biographical maternal lineage and female embodiment is the absence of female cultural memory. This is expressed through her troubled, marginal relation to the male modernist canons. On this subject, the Guia refers to the critic José Augusto Alegria's statement "the history of modern poetry can perfectly well be written without even mentioning the name of Florbela Espanca" [Pode perfeitamente fazer-se a história da poesia moderna sem citar sequer o nome de Florbela Espanca" (71–72),] as he goes on to include in his poetic history the names of Mário de Sá-Carneiro, Fernando Pessoa, Camilo Pessanha, and José Régio.

In her quest to join the illustrious cast of modernist men, Florbela remarks ironically on her attempts to emulate the sexual scandals, excesses, and ambiguities that hallmark the genius male as the exception, the outsider to society. Dying young, and on cue, through a highly scripted act of suicide, she claims that if she actually had, as was suspected, contracted syphilis, that would be the final proof positive of her genius (89). Yet her sexual nonconformity as a woman is precisely what makes her a threat, not a prodigy, for the patriarchal canonical establishment. As Florbela admits, she was taken seriously as a poet only by an aging Guido Battelli who created an ethereal image of her because "my body did not get in the way, it did not come between us" [o corpo não nos atrapalhou, não se veio meter no meio de nós (95)]. Only when her sexuality is neutralized can she be considered a true poet at all, and where she loses the aura of sexual transgression that marks her as social exception, she cannot count as a genius. In this context, the Guia cites the writer and critic Jorge de Sena's comment that she is not a genius at all, merely a notable "poeta."[53] Florbela contests her implicit masculinization, as she protests "so they want to make me into a man now, do they?! [querem fazer de mim um homem, já agora?! (89)]. In saying this, she evokes the long-standing debate, most famously enjoined by Natália Correia, in which the latter defends women's right to be sexually marked, in a positive sense, as poetesses or "poetisas."[54]

Florbela's answer to her male critics is to reframe and reclaim the established corpus of her own poetry, by rereading it as part of the play, just as she physically reframes her body in relation to its historical imaging on camera by her father. By bringing familiar passages back to life in the context of canonical critical debates, Florbela's refractive readings and self-citations inaugurate the possibility of a new cultural memory of Portuguese women's writing that can be pitted against the blindspots of conventional modernist history. This is confirmed in the Guia's final citation, against the male critics, of a passage from Natália Correia's famous preface to Florbela's diary, *Diário do Último Ano,* narrating her death through the images of Diana and Apollo. Although Natália Correia is not named explicitly, Florbela realizes, on hearing the words of this other great "poetisa", that her writing has been understood and transmitted to a future generation of creative women.

As she lays her living body next to her dead one on the bier, and the one blends into the other, the visual union of the two bodies effectively marks the shift that has occurred, through the play, in Florbela's positioning in Portuguese literary history. Her embodied and poetic identities are no longer separate. Through the concluding association with Natália Correia, who provides both the play's inspiration and its final critical word, Florbela is inscribed into an alternative Portuguese theater aesthetic that is, if not consistently revisionist, at least open to revisiting the historical exclusion of women as sexed subjects of culture. Florbela Espanca writing in the 1920s and 1930s is connected, through the term "poetisa," to Natália Correia writing her preface to the *Diário* in the 1980s and to Hélia Correia inscribing them both in her play in the 1990s.

At the same time, Hélia Correia's decision to engage with literary historical criticism, by using a circular dramatic structure, fractured temporality, and a double-staging of life and death, prevents these contingent connections from cohering into a fixed, unitary counterhistory, the domain of the matriarch. By the same token, the epilogue brings the play full circle, as the Guia meets again the infant Florbela with whom the play opened. The child is left calling in the dark for a "mother" to come and turn on the light. The search through obscurity for the lost foremothers, the missing history, clearly remains an ongoing quest in this conclusion, but it is a quest that can draw new symbolic authority from Florbela Espanca, Portugal's archetypal "dead woman poet", retrospectively installing herself into a renewed and vital vector of women's cultural memory.

6
Sexual/Textual Re-Visions in Lídia Jorge

In vain they buried me amid the rubble
Of vainly carved cathedrals!

Em vão me sepultaram
Entre escombros duma escultura vã!]
—Florbela Espanca, "Sou Eu!"

Take me, O eternal night, in your arms
And call me your son.
    I am a king
Who voluntarily renounced
My throne of dreams and weariness.

[Toma-me, ó noite eterna, nos teus braços
E chama-me teu filho.
        Eu sou um rei
Que voluntariamente abandonei
O meu trono de sonhos e cansaços.]
—Fernando Pessoa, "Abdicação"

In her frequently cited essay, "When we dead awaken: writing as re-Vision", Adrienne Rich asserts that "Re-vision—the act of looking back, of seeing with fresh eyes, of entering an old text from a new critical direction—is for us more than a chapter in cultural history: it is an act of survival. Until we can understand the assumptions in which we are drenched we cannot know ourselves. And this drive to self-knowledge, for woman, is more than a search for identity: it is part of her refusal of the self-destructiveness of male dominated society."[1]

In the Portuguese context too, it is perhaps no coincidence that the fiction produced by postrevolutionary female writers insistently revisits a recent past where women often had no voice, in order to make sense of the present, all the more so given the glaring asymmetries between the position of men and women up to the revolution of 1974 and beyond. The production of Lídia Jorge is exemplary in this context, and this chapter constitutes an attempt to

178

map out the ways in which her characters deal with re-vision as an act of survival.

Lídia Guerreiro Jorge (1946–) was born in the Algarve, went on to study at the University of Lisbon, and subsequently spent some years in the then-colonies (Angola in 1969–70 and Mozambique in 1972–74), before returning to the capital. In 1980 the publication of the highly acclaimed novel *O Dia dos Prodígios* [The Day of Wonders] marked her literary debut and was followed, over the next three decades, by more than another dozen titles, mainly novels, for which she was awarded a string of prestigious literary prizes. Although she is by training a secondary school teacher, Jorge regards writing as her main vocation. Her explanation of why she writes is simple: "I wrote because in truth nothing was set in stone, not even the literary genres which seem to have a whole indestructible ready-built structure holding them together" [escrevia porque na verdade nada se encontrava predestinado, nem os géneros literários para cuja a integridade há todo um edifício feito que parece indestrutível].²

As we shall see, in addition to questioning assumptions about the sacredness of established literary genres, her texts also challenge the notion of fixed gender roles within the family and society at large. In fact, in a 2002 interview, Jorge remarks that she is interested in exploring the dynamics of relationships, especially outside a traditional family context: "I am not so much concerned with the traditional family unit as with the relationships within the nucleus of love that is housed under the same roof" [Não me preocupa a célula familiar tradicional mas sim as relações no núcleo do amor albergado pelo mesmo tecto].³ Broadly speaking, her revisionist stance prompts her to revisit all manners of preordained structures, and in so doing, to give voice to women.

Notícia da Cidade Silvestre (1984) [Memory of the Sylvan City], the first work we discuss here, inscribes the struggle of a widowed working mother as she attempts to navigate her asymmetrical position in patriarchal society. This chapter then analyzes her two most famous novels to date, *A Costa dos Murmúrios* (1988) [The Coast of Murmurs] and *O Vale da Paixão* (1998) [The Migrant Painter of Birds].⁴ Both focus on two isolated female figures, their coming of age during the closing years of the dictatorship, and their fight for emotional survival. Their retrospective gaze, as they go over the traumatic events in their past, highlight their uncompromising "refusal of the self-destructiveness of male dominated society," be it in a war-ridden or in a more domestic context.

Jorge's revisionist impetus carries through in the play *A Maçon* (1997) [The Woman Free Mason],⁵ which by its very nature constitutes a public attempt to see afresh a historically important Portuguese female forerunner:

the early twentieth century Republican feminist Adelaide Cabete (1867–
1935). This thought-provoking recuperation, staging a postmodern displacement of historical fact laced with satire and parodic intent, foregrounds the
mechanisms which have allowed Cabete's remarkable life achievements to be
almost forgotten in modern-day Portugal.

HOW TO "BRING NEWS OF THE OTHER REALITY" [DAR NOTÍCIA DA OUTRA REALIDADE]: *NOTÍCIA DA CIDADE SILVESTRE*

Notícia da Cidade Silvestre depicts two women, Júlia Grei and Anabela
Cravo, and their struggle for material and emotional survival in Lisbon in
the late 1970s. The influential critic Gaspar Simões praised the novel, although he arguably misread Jorge's intentions by singling out Anabela, "the
impetuous woman who is the adventuress for the modern era, the era of
feminist society" [a rompante mulher que é essa aventureira dos novos tempos, os tempos da sociedade feminista], and downplaying Júlia: "next to her
Júlia Grei is nothing, in human terms" [ao pé dela a Júlia Grei não é nada,
humanamente falando].[6] By contrast, in a subsequent interview with Regina
Louro, Jorge passionately defended Júlia against the (male) misconception
that she was a doormat, deserving to be trampled on: "[Anabela] imitates
men: Júlia is the character through whom real change is channeled" [(Anabela) faz mimetismo do homem; Júlia é talvez a personagem por onde a
mudança passa realmente].[7]

When the novel begins, the recently widowed Júlia has to fend for herself
and her son, struggling to make ends meet.[8] Right from the opening lines,
we are left in no doubt as to her position of dependency: "if we had lived in
a house with a window, on the morning of our meeting, I would have sat at
the windowsill waiting for Anabela Cravo" [Se morássemos numa casa com
janela na manhã do encontro, eu teria ido pôr-me no parapeito à espera de
Anabela Cravo (19)]. Quite aside from the shocking realization that Júlia's
home (which turns out to be her deceased husband's workshop) is devoid of
proper windows, thus making her a prisoner in her own attic, this incipit
positions her in the traditional passive female occupation of waiting at the
window for the arrival of a miraculous "savior," albeit a female one in this
instance.

Júlia exists in a limbo, metaphorically living a living death, surrounded by
her dead husband's art work, namely his sculptures. Despite her precarious
circumstances, she shuns Anabela's advice of a lucrative marriage with the
eligible Saraiva, following instead her heart into a relationship with Artur,
the penniless sculptor, an inveterate traveler. This results in an unplanned

pregnancy, a backstreet abortion,[9] and ultimately, Artur's departure. Following the disappearance of Artur and Anabela in close succession, Júlia begins to juggle various potential suitors, including the old family friend Mão Dianjo and her boss Sr. Assumpção. The attempt to sell herself culminates in a spell of literal prostitution where, in a hallucinatory scene, she is nearly run over by a psychotic male driver. The main plot therefore vividly highlights, through a series of almost surreal episodes, the near-impossibility of material (and arguably emotional) survival for Portuguese single mothers at a time when the traditional family unit was undergoing unprecedented change. In so doing, it draws attention to the gap between the official democratic discourse of equality and everyday reality.

Jorge also shows the extent to which women's creativity is constrained by needs material: Júlia supplements her income by sewing rag dolls, although her creativity spills out into written forms of expression too. When the opportunity presents itself, in financial dire straights and emotionally desperate, Júlia decides to sell her diary, her yellow-backed notebook (*caderno de capa amarela*), during a chance encounter in the local bar Together/Tonight with a person, addressed only as "You" [Você] throughout. The mediating role of this impromptu anonymous literary agent is prominently recognized right from the outset: indeed, as is recounted in the second preface, both Júlia's musings and her letters are addressed, in the first instance, to him/her. Having bought the *caderno* containing Júlia's "memories," the mysterious person has effectively bought the "rights" to the story. As Hilary Owen points out elsewhere, this simple fact foregrounds varying entitlement in accessing publication.[10] We may also add that it recalls Irene Lisboa's scathing indictment of the widespread condescending attitude of well-meaning publishers or literary agents toward women writers, especially those who defy conventional norms and writing styles, in "Um dito" analyzed in chapter 2.

The awareness of the mechanisms through which actual publication (as opposed to "venue à l'écriture," which we shall examine in a moment) can be secured, in this instance where a diary is at stake, furthermore raises the issue of appropriation of someone else's life-story. In the preface, Júlia's nameless editor does in fact acknowledge that s/he chose, unilaterally, to rewrite the tale in a way that downplays the notebook. Nonetheless, s/he confidently proclaims that Júlia felt reconfirmed in, not stripped of, her identity as a person.

> [Júlia] would ultimately be surprised that the yellow-backed notebook should have played so small a role, and that, on the contrary, the papers she continued to send me by post, or through others at random, should turn out to be so important. But she added that she saw and recognized herself entirely [in the final product].

[(Júlia) haveria de vir a admirar-se que o caderno de capa amarela tivesse tido tão pouco destaque e que, pelo contrário, os papéis que me ia mandando pelo correio, ou por quem calhava, aparecessem com tanta importância. Mas acrescentou que se revia e achava, por inteiro]. (17)

Thus, while on one level the narrative draws attention to the central role of both speaking and writing in the construction of identity and self-definition, on another level, V's overarching presence throughout the story effectively denies Júlia the right to authorship on conventional terms. In effect, this highlights the assumptions and mechanisms through which women are traditionally excluded from dominant conceptions of productive genius. Indeed, prevailing definitions of literary genius do not take into account the often complex material situations under which women write. As Jorge herself indicated in an interview, "the number of women has been increasing, but yet comparatively little writing is being produced, due not to lack of talent, but to pressures upon their lives".[11]

Tellingly, in the first preface to the novel, the real author, Lídia Jorge herself describes "the testimony of Júlia" [o testemunho de Júlia] as "reproducing freely of a kind of spoken intimacy" [a reprodução livre de uma espécie de intimidade falada (11)], thereby turning on its head the traditional opposition between oral and written discourses, conceivably with the aim of encouraging her readers to consider what kind of words are deemed to have literary worth. Throughout the novel, we are repeatedly alerted to the discrepancy between the story presented for public consumption and the private story on which it draws, since Júlia's letters/papers are interspersed with and recount her personal memories *before* the main narrative tackles the same events. The fact that main text and the letter-sequence are out of step allows the private perspective to be disclosed first. Significantly it is through the latter that we discover how the suicide attempt and near-death of her son Jóia trigger a turning-point in Júlia's life, forcing her to focus with a sense of immediate urgency on his gradual recovery. This crisis also provides a catalyst for her own potential healing.

It is, however, in the main narrative that we are told that, while in hospital by Jóia's bedside, Júlia is overcome by an irrational and all-pervasive need to carry a knife with her, a tangible symbol of her pent-up aggression. Instead she starts frantically scribbling in her diary (296), something which she had already been doing for years and which may have been the only outlet for her repressed anger. As the novel draws to a close, these twin empowering acts, writing and carrying a knife, allow her to build up sufficient strength to stand up to the various persons who used and abused her over the years: Saraiva, Mão Dianjo, Sr, Assumpção, and finally Anabela. These confrontations culminate in a climatic scene where Júlia threatens her former friend with the knife, something which becomes tantamount to a liberating assertion that "Anabela would have to learn that the Earth moves in different ways" [Anabela teria de saber que a Terra se move de vários modos (320)]. In other words, at this point in time, Júlia ceases to be powerless: she is no longer bound by Anabela's gaze, her preconceptions and inverted sexism.

Although Júlia has to go through the assertion of freeing herself from the ghost of Anabela, pen and paper become ultimately more therapeutic than the phallic knife. As the story draws to a provisional close, then, unlike her former friend who arguably remains trapped in the "self-destructiveness of male dominated society" (to recall Rich's formulation), Júlia can find a degree of empowerment and a voice through the act of writing. Unlike the knife which, in the end, she chose not to use, paper is in fact endowed with qualities commonly associated with the feminine: "the blank paper seems to me like a soft piece of fabric, gentle, human and absorbing like a skin. Passive, plant-like, and other adjectives that are not worth listing" [o papel em branco parece-me um tecido doce, humano e envolvente como uma pele. Passivo, vegetal e outros adjectivos que não vale a pena enumerar (305)].

Not only does she no longer need a knife (which, in a symbolic gesture, she returns to the nameless Você), it is also implied that she no longer needs this "talking cure" facilitator doubling up as literary agent. To crown it all, she is now ready to give up her day job in a bookshop, where she had been at the receiving end of male-dominated culture and where the printed word had regularly been used by Sr. Assumpção to proposition her. It is significant that the novel should end with her about to give up her job in order to devote herself to full-time writing, for this signals a momentous shift from Júlia's role as passive guardian of the written word to active productive agent in her own right. Júlia lives on to tell her tale or, as she puts it on the very last page of the novel, "to bring news of the other reality" [dar notícia da outra realidade (322)].

Crucially, this "other reality" had already been vividly visualized shortly before, during the flash of inspiration which had signaled Júlia's liberating "venue à l'écriture," while her son lay helpless in his hospital bed, hovering between life and death. In an almost visionary trance, she had evoked the haunting certainty that, beneath the savage reality of the world as we know it, lies an uncharted and wild territory, full of promises: "she felt the certainty, at once happy and painful, that the other side of the main street was a primitive, sylvan place of which this side was only a barbaric recollection" [experimentava a certeza, ao mesmo tempo alegre e dolorosa, de que a outra margem da rua principal era uma zona silvestre de que este lado era apenas uma lembrança selvagem (297)]. Moreover, she understood this truth intuitively: "and this I understood not because I had crawled to visit it with the logic of my mind, but because those years of jousting and battling which would have sufficed to embellish twenty happy lives with upheaval, removing the monotony of permanent comfort from them, told me this through unvoiced words" [E percebia isso não porque tivesse ido lá de gatas com a cabeça do raciocínio, mas porque aqueles anos de cavalhadas que dariam para enfeitar de acidentes vinte vidas felizes, e retirar-lhes a monotonia do cómodo permanente, mo diziam por palavras não articuladas]. Significantly, her unvoiced, but frantically scribbled thoughts are then condensed into a poem, the form historically most closely associated with artistic inspiration.

Ultimately, though, it is her real-life, material experiences that enable her to achieve a kind of writing which will not simply reproduce male-dominated forms of culture. As such, a closer examination of the last page of the novel shows the extent to which Júlia is aware that "to bring news of the other reality" may entail a process of rebirth, and involve the breaking down of binary oppositions: "the paper is like a soft piece of fabric, gentle, human and absorbing like a skin. Passive, active, and other qualities that I do not need to name . . . As if from this fragile material, one could feel and bring news of the other reality" [O papel é um tecido doce, humano e envolvente como uma pele. Passivo, activo, e outras qualidades que não preciso de nomear . . . Como se a partir dessa frágil matéria, sentisse e pudesse dar notícia da outra realidade (322)]. In her bypassing of conventional "naming" and privileging of "feeling," Júlia (and through her, Jorge) is attempting to subvert existing hierarchies by redefining the path to knowledge and self-knowledge. Unlike Anabela, Júlia refuses to settle for the rules which prevail in the savage, urban juggle, and which, as the former's trajectory so clearly illustrates, only seem to lead to a dehumanizing "survival of the fittest." In that connection, it may not be a mere coincidence that during their last encounter Anabela becomes disparagingly described as a mutant, a monstrous creature: "a new race, another sex, another form of nature was announcing its arrival in Anabela Cravo as if the earth were laboring to give birth to another species of person" [uma nova raça, um outro sexo e uma outra natureza se anunciava em Anabela Cravo como se a terra se movesse para dar à luz uma outra espécie de pessoa (320)].

Júlia not only succeeds in overcoming a number of traumas, she is moreover able to rebuild her crushed sense of "self," with the help of empowering new friendships, including her potential companion, Fernando. Fernando, a man who seems in touch with his "feminine" side, offers an enabling presence: namely, it is thanks to his love and care that Jóia is able to run again freely. The novel, then, ends with a potential new beginning, hinting at the possible reconstitution of a new non-conventional family unit. Together, the three unlikely survivors may be able to build a better future, where the pattern of male dominance and the self-destructiveness of male-dominated society might be eschewed in favor of greater cooperation between the sexes. In a cautiously optimistic last page, Jorge shows that femininity and masculinity are fluid attributes, but that for as long as they remain interpreted in reductive ways,[12] the "sylvan city" [cidade silvestre] of her title will more readily continue to evoke an urban jungle than a promised city.

THE UNDOING OF MALE RHETORIC: *A COSTA DOS MURMÚRIOS*

If *Notícia* charted a potentially empowering "re-vision" for women in the immediate aftermath of the Revolution, *A Costa* goes further back in time, to provide a compelling exorcism of the traumatic effects of the colonial war in Mozambique. Structurally, it juxtaposes an anonymously male-authored tale "The Locusts" [Os Gafanhotos] with its exegesis by a female commentator: it thereby inscribes in its very structure the act of re-vision, all the more so given that Eva, the female commentator, featured only as one of the characters in the first tale.

In a pioneer article, Ana Paula Ferreira outlines the ways in which *A Costa* develops in gendered dialogue with Lobo Antunes' damning account of the colonial war in Angola, in *Os Cus de Judas* (1979).[13] Following on from Ferreira's article, Rui Teixeira de Azevedo and Margarida Calafate Ribeiro have examined how Lídia Jorge, effectively as the "token woman," engages with the (usually) male paradigm of the war novel.[14] Nevertheless, it would be unnecessarily reductive to see this novel as an act of revision simply within a well-established subgenre: like the rest of Jorge's literary output, *A Costa* displays the extent to which re-vision is indeed a necessary act of survival, by engaging with man-made culture in the broadest terms.[15]

The novel starts off with a thirty-page short story, "The Locusts," in which a wedding reception takes center-stage against a backdrop of war. But Jorge undermines from within the fairy-tale aura of this event through the use of a subtle but corrosive irony: not only is Ev(it)a Lopo not a virgin, she does not live happily ever after with Luís Alex.[16] In fact, his exhalted suicide brings the love story to an abrupt end, before she can bear him any children, thereby subliminally encoding from the outset the fragility of the national family project and undermining Salazar's supreme tenets of "God, Fatherland, Family" [Deus, Pátria, Família].

When Eva Lopo, the former Evita, steps out of the narrative frame in order to speak up, she evokes in greater detail events experienced twenty years previously and, through an extended commentary on the short story, questions the focus it adopted. While "Os Gafanhotos" did not altogether ignore violent events, most were downplayed or substantially rewritten even when not downright omitted.[17] Unlike the earlier carefully constructed tale, Eva places little emphasis on the fairy-tale wedding, proposing instead an alternative recollection, which details the lack of purpose of the lives led by the officers' wives as they while away empty days during their husbands' prolonged absences. Early on, the enormous war scar of Jaime Forza Leal, the ridiculously macho boss of Luís Alex, encapsulates what Eva regards as the anachronism of imperial discourses: "when the Captain walked by in his transparent shirt, I thought I was looking at the last man of the century to see himself in his scar" (59) [quando o capitão passava com a camisa transparente, eu imaginava estar a ver o último homem do século que se revisse na sua cicatriz"(63)].

Halfway through the novel, hundreds of secret photographs disclosed to Evita by Helena, Forza Leal's wife, provide disturbing evidence of the Portuguese army's killing of civilians. After this turning-point, Eva resolutely positions herself as a dissident voice, intent on probing imperialist rhetoric in subsequent chapters. She recalls how as a history student at the University of Lisbon, she had already been weary of manmade versions of history, with their reductive, linear view of time, which privilege the point of view of the dominant order. She evokes a former History professor, remembering the dogmatic intransigence with which he verbally shot down any alternative points of view. Her own concept of History, by contrast, allows her to develop the idea of simultaneity "in my concept of History there is room for the influence of invisible muscles" (203) [no meu conceito de História cabe a influência dos músculos invisíveis (196)]. As Maria Irene Ramalho points out, by then recovering from oblivion the "shameful" wound of Zurique's wife (a third-degree tear of the sphincter muscle during a labor which results in a stillbirth), Eva provides an ironic counterpoint to the "heroic" war scar of Forza Leal.[18] In practice, Eva is drawing attention to the nature of historical accounts: albeit seemingly factual, they are actually fictional constructs, which organize, include, and exclude with an unspoken ideological bias.

The dominant ideology which underpins discourses of Portuguese expansionism is relentlessly parodied in chapter VII when a blind Captain travels through Portuguese Africa to deliver a lecture pompously entitled "Portugal d'Aquém e d'Além Mar É Eterno." The lecture reproduces all the clichés of the Establishment regarding the integrity of the so-called "overseas provinces." The Captain's blindness could perhaps be a thinly veiled reference to the metaphorical "blindness" of Salazar, who in 1968 had been left disabled by a stroke, but who misguidedly continued to believe himself in charge of the nation until his death in 1970. The ideology embodied by the captain is comically called into question when he is prevented from making a proper conclusion by the sudden invasion of native locusts. Symptomatically, as Eva teasingly tells her readers, there is a record of the lecture in the Lisbon Military Archives, yet "obviously, no one will have noted, even in the margins, the fact that on that night a rain of locusts began falling on the city" (226) [obviamente que nem à margem se registou que nessa noite teve início uma chuva de gafanhotos sobre a cidade (216)], thereby once more challenging Eurocentric assumptions about which "facts" are preserved and transmitted to future generations.

In keeping with her protagonist's revisi(tati)on of History, Lídia Jorge parodies some of the most acclaimed poems from Pessoa's *Mensagem*, a collection which the dictatorship had swiftly appropriated in order to further its empire-building designs. Most memorably, she wittily conflates in her description of the hotel receptionist Bernardo, the emblematic poems "The Stone Pillar" [Padrão (51)] and "Portuguese Sea" [Mar Português (60)]:[19] "It was there, in the last port, that Bernard had been found. . . . The road had been difficult but worthwhile." (84) [Lá no *último porto,* fora encontrado o Bernardo. . . . Tinha sido uma senda difícil, mas havia *valido a pena* (86) (our italics)].

Later on, the black concubine of the mulatto journalist Álvaro Sabino becomes brandished as a parodic illustration of lusotropicalist harmony: "It made me imagine a postcard illustrating a particular notion of progress, of union between the races, created on the scaffolding of a house under construction already turned to rubble" (178–79) [Lembrava um postal que ilustrasse uma ideia especial de progresso, de abraço entre as raças, feito nos andaimes duma casa a construir já em escombros (174)], through what may be a deliberate misquoting of the orthonymic poem "The Scaffolding" [O Andaime].[20] Whereas Pessoa's poem concluded with the lines "I surrounded with scaffolding / The house as yet unbuilt" [Que cerquei com um andaime / A casa por fabricar], in Jorge's description the house being built is simultaneously presented as already in ruins, underscoring the futility of white men's colonizing of black women's bodies. The one-way myth of lusotropicalism is further deconstructed, given that Eva too becomes involved with Álvaro Sabino, thus breaking the ultimate racial taboo: a sexual relationship between a white woman and a mulatto man.

If, to recall the words of Adrienne Rich, "re-vision . . . is an act of survival. . . . It is a part of our refusal of the self-destructiveness of male dominated society," Eva (and, through her, Jorge) vividly foregrounds the extent to which the ideology of "Deus, Pátria, Família" led to Portuguese women's self-immolation. The absurdity of an entire generation of intelli-

gent women being indoctrinated to aspire to a sacrificial fate in marriage is
made abundantly clear: "they were already stretching their necks toward the
prospect of getting pregnant" (202) [já era para o engravidamento que esten-
diam o pescoço (195)].[21] Overall, marriages are portrayed as mostly dysfunc-
tional: the couples who withstand the men's return from the front are usually
the ones where women are either physically or emotionally battered, like the
anonymous wife of Pedro Deus or Helena. As the novel draws to a close, for
instance, Helena is confined to bed once more which, according to Forza
Leal's misogynistic assertion, is the place where women "naturally" belong
(254).

    In the final instance, the widowed Eva's bid to articulate a woman-cen-
tered representation of reality can in many ways be equated to a counter-
odyssey where women are no longer long-suffering Penelopes, awaiting their
menfolk. In the *Odyssey,* the Greek hero Ulysses (credited in Portuguese mythology with the founding of Lisbon, as enshrined in Fernando Pessoa's
Mensagem), journeys home to Ithaca from the Trojan war to recover his
house and his kingdom. Unlike the mythical hero, the more pedestrian Eva
cannot return twenty years later to her exact point of origin. But what she
can and does do is challenge the *Odyssey's* proclamation of the heroism of
war, which the general had so uncritically cited when confidently predicting
a Portuguese victory on the horizon: "'Let each man march to the front line,
whether he dies or whether he lives. Thus do war and battle kiss and whisper!'" (248) [Deixai que cada homem marche para a linha da frente—Quer
se morra quer se viva. Eis como a Guerra e a batalha *beijam* e *murmuram!*
(236)] (our italics). In that connection, we may wish to note that Jorge's
novel does begin with a kiss and end with a murmur, but the teleology and
expected triumphant outcome of the epic narrative is undermined in-between.

    Eva, then, challenges the male monopoly of truth through her ironic revi-
sion of several layers of imperialist discourses and ideologies. In the closing
pages of the novel, she furthermore provocatively contrasts her version of
Luís Alex's death with both those of the journalist and the nameless narrator
of "The Locusts" by reiterating "There was in fact a slight difference" (267)
[Houve de facto uma ligeira diferença (252)]. According to her, Luís Alex
does not commit suicide in a Russian roulette contest with Álvaro Sabino,
his rival in love, but meets an inglorious death in what, to all intents and
purposes, appears to be a simple car accident, rather than a tragic suicide.
On a broader collective level, her commentary on the destructiveness of the
war ethos is encoded in the parting shots of the novel, where the returning
(anti)-heroes are shown to be irreversibly physically and/or emotionally
scarred, in a lapidary rewording of Julius Caesar's famous assertion *veni, vidi,*

vici: "a ship was coming down the shore, filled with soldiers, on the way to the dock. Nobody was expecting them, they knew that now; they had already been there and come back. It was obvious that not all of them came back by dint of their own feet or of their own eyes" (274) [um navio desceu cheio de soldados, a caminho do porto. Ninguém os esperava, eles agora já sabiam, já tinham ido, já tinham voltado.—Nem todos obviamente voltavam por seus pés e por seus olhos (259)].

A Costa stages an intellectually much more confident protagonist than the earlier *Notícia*. Unlike Júlia, who was still dependent on the mediation of an unnamed Você, who took it upon him/her to edit her diaries, almost the opposite process takes place in *A Costa*. Indeed Eva repeatedly challenges the vision of events proffered by the male author of the short story and, through irony, undermines his extensive use of poetic license. More to the point, he is not afforded the opportunity to answer back, again in a role reversal to the relationship between Júlia and Você, where Você so clearly had had the last say in terms of editorial control. The reader is thus forced to evaluate the merit of their competing visions, and indeed the ways in which their insights themselves are relayed: Eva's oral account is placed on an equal footing to a written account, a subversive move in itself, undoing existing hierarchies. Through Eva, Jorge is pointing out how women's creative power within can be released without, but implying that it will not necessarily reproduce a "sublime" rhetorical mode.

Eva remains acutely aware of her ex-centric female position which, according to the dominant perspective, de-authorizes her. Yet, it is precisely because of her refusal to collude with or reproduce prevailing patriarchal war ideology and her ability to speak out that, unlike her husband and countless other war casualties, she can ultimately outlive the memory of the traumatic events in which she was involved. By problematizing the false dichotomy writing/speaking, Jorge is therefore rethinking "a whole ready-built structure that seems indestructible" [todo um edifício feito que parece indestrutível] and encouraging her readers to do so as well. On one level, Eva may encapsulate the double bind facing women creators outlined by Battersby: either to be a genius or to be female and to fail to count as a genius. Yet the ultimate paradox is that the female who created her, Lídia Jorge, surely cannot fail to count as a genius, given her inspired intertextual engagements with canonical male-authored discourses, from *The Odyssey* to *Mensagem* and beyond.

EXORCISING THE GHOST OF THE FATHER: *O VALE DA PAIXÃO*

In *A Costa,* in an attempt to challenge the symbolic ordering upon which the dictatorship had been predicated, Jorge portrayed the extent to which the ideology of "Deus, Pátria, Família" had led to the self-immolation of an entire generation of women and, by extension, of men too. Crucially, *A Costa* depicted the unsustainability of the traditional view of marriage, the bedrock of society. In many ways, *O Vale da Paixão* takes up where *A Costa* left off, by homing in on a female protagonist who locates herself both inside and outside a traditional family.

Since in *O Vale* the main character is primarily presented as a daughter, rather than as a wife (as in *A Costa*) or mother (as in *Notícia*), for the first time in Jorge's fiction, the trajectory of a female character from childhood through to adulthood is explored, albeit in a nonlinear fashion. The story is loosely structured around the memories of a handful of encounters between the nameless female protagonist, whose inner thoughts we follow intimately through the use of free indirect speech alternating with a first-person perspective, and her absent migrant "uncle" Walter whom, we soon surmise, is in fact her biological father. Born in the late 1940s, the illegitimate daughter's life straddles both the pre- and the postrevolutionary period.

It may seem slightly anachronistic, in sociological terms that, as late as 1998, Jorge should choose to depict an illegitimate daughter. After all, in the postrevolutionary era, where the traditional Portuguese family has gradually given way to an acceptance of cohabitation and of children born outside wedlock, by the late 1990s illegitimacy certainly no longer carried the social stigma it once did (and which Irene Lisboa's writing, and to a lesser extent Florbela Espanca's, had so poignantly illustrated). Nevertheless, the illegitimate daughter's life-trajectory allows Jorge to question the patriarchal model of the family in several ways.

Firstly, given that in *O Vale da Paixão* there is no longer a broader collective background of war, the many contradictions located within the family structure itself are magnified. Secondly, throughout the novel, Jorge's protagonist remains devoid of the single most important marker of individual identity: a name. Moreover her birth date and even her filial antecendents are falsified in her identity card. In so doing Jorge seeks to interrogate some of the "fixed" markers of identity we normally take for granted. Thirdly, by juxtaposing, through ironic excess, the twin parental figures of the absent biological father (Walter) and the literally but also metaphorically lame one (Custódio, Walter's elder brother whom her pregnant mother had been forced to marry in order to preserve the Dias family honor), she is disrupting the idea of a monolithic patrilinear genealogy.

The schizophrenic impossibility for the daughter/niece of colluding with the myth of a stable family unit can be seen to point to the growing fractures within the national family, as Ana Paula Ferreira has eloquently demonstrated.[22] More recently, Lígia Silva has convincingly explored how the unstable genealogy of Walter's daughter/niece may also be interpreted as a metonymy for the precarious position of women writers, both within and without the patriarchal literary canon, a point to which we shall return.[23] In this connection, we may wish to note that, in contrast to the proliferation of father-figures surrounding the protagonist, which include Walter, Custódio, and her patriarchal grandfather, Francisco, women are mostly relegated to roles of excessive conformity.[24]

Even though Walter was effectively disowned as a black sheep as family members closed ranks, the legitimacy of the patriarchal household is repeatedly undermined from within by his reappearances. The absent son/father becomes, as Paulo de Medeiros has incisively shown, a ghost-like figure, a "revenant" in São Sebastião de Valmares.[25] As such, he is endowed with the power to haunt the living, returning twice during his lifetime to his home village, in the 1950s and 1960s. If we take Medeiros' point one step further, Walter's most dramatic return is arguably his third, which occurs posthumously in a more obviously disembodied form, when he resurfaces in the postrevolutionary period (at an unspecified date, but probably in the late 1980s), in the shape of a package containing his last will: a worn-out soldier's blanket, accompanied by a brief handwritten note.

This traumatic event, occurring immediately prior to the start of the novel, acts as the trigger for the unfolding of the painful re-visi(tati)on and reappraisal of the past undertaken by Walter's daughter. For the adult narrator, the distressing, yet inescapable necessity of confronting her past, and more specifically her hybrid genealogy, becomes in itself endowed with therapeutic value as an act of survival. Unlike the previous two novels thus far analyzed, where it was implied that the female protagonists came through their ordeal through a dialogue of sorts, in this instance there is little opportunity for engaging in any "midwife" Socratic interaction, since the recollection of events takes place in the mind of the protagonist. The focus is instead on an obsessive, intense and individual mourning process.

According to Lídia Jorge, we are shaped by the physical environment in which we happen to be born: "No-one is born free from their native soil. It is not worth running away" [Ninguém nasce livre da terra. Não vale a pena fugir].[26] Although the illegitimate daughter may feel redundant in the household, "the superfluous person was me" (118) [quem estava a mais era eu (126)], when offered the chance of a new life abroad with her father, she is in fact unable to leave São Sebastião de Valmares. Her sense of belonging may not depend on any one member of her "official" family, especially not her mother Maria Ema. But it is certainly predicated on her familiar surroundings, the main reality at her disposal to help her to make sense of herself and to give her some feeling of security and continuity. Unlike Walter who, we are told at this juncture, is prone to escaping, "Walter will always think that by changing places, you change yourself" (136) [Walter pensará sempre que mudando de sítio se muda de ser (144)], his daughter is unable to run away, deriving instead a precarious sense of identity precisely from a conscious acknowledgment of her wounded self: "that everything comes from an ancient wound and that everything goes back to that. A crack" (136) [que tudo sai dum ferimento já feito e tudo aí regressa. Uma fenda (143)]. Her willingness to accept this preexisting birth fragmentation becomes the first step on the long and thorny journey toward a more integrated sense of self.

At fifteen, after her father's definitive departure, finding a way out of the limbo through the imaginary power of words becomes her choice strategy: "At the table in her room, emerging from that crack thanks to the power of words, she reads out loud to herself" (136) [Ela lê em voz baixa, na mesa do quarto, saindo dessa fenda pelo poder das palavras (143)]. The words she reads out, taken from the *Iliad,* conjure up a new dawn. Significantly, the *Iliad* recounts the story of Achilles, of his anger and determination to slay Hector. In other words, it may be that, to counter her position as an impotent illegitimate daughter, she is led to cast herself as the avenging (male) hero in the subsequent unfolding of her own story.

Similarly to the earlier Júlia, in order to come through her ordeal, Walter's daughter has to learn to express her anger and hatred. Like Júlia, she eventually gives up fantasies of phallic aggression, in this case her father's gun which she throws into the sea, in the course of her ten-year relationship with Dr. Dalila.[27] Later, as she takes to the pen and starts writing three short stories, which seek to defile her father's image in an act of almost sadistic revenge, her writing becomes the catalyst of a liberating expression of hatred toward him. Tellingly the stories are described as "not a loaded revolver, but three tales to hand over" (207) [três episodios escritos, para lhe entregar em vez do revólver (216)].

We only find out about the content of one story, entitled "The Fornicating Soldier" [O Soldadinho Fornicador], in which she caricatured Walter as an impoverished wandering soldier who fathers children in every port. Perhaps unexpectedly, he is presented as a later-day patriarch, in a way strongly reminiscent of his father Francisco Dias. The rich old man seeks to "find his legitimate descendants scattered among the coastal towns" (215–16) [encontrar os descendentes legítimos espelhados pelas cidades costeiras (224)], the very use of the word "legitimate" being heavily underscored by irony given his sexual antics. But his descendents have become mutants, making it impossible for anyone to identify them as legitimate heirs, because "they had interbred with other mammals" (216) [haviam-se cruzado com outros mamíferos' (224)]. The degenerate breed boards his boat for an uncertain destination and he is "followed by a nonhuman tribe with whom he could neither talk nor share out the spoils" (216) [era seguido por um bando inumano com o qual não podia dialogar nem fazer partilhas (225)]. The safe haven of an island, representing the possibility of a happy ending, remains completely beyond reach. This series of loaded images provides a damning reinterpretation of the official version of Portuguese overseas expansion.

Ironically, by the time Walter is tracked down in Argentina by his daughter, now a thirty-five-year-old, what comes across is that, in his pathetic mixing up of Spanish and Portuguese, Walter can be more readily identified as part of the adulterated Dias breed than as the all-powerful, arrogant lone male hero she had cast him as. But when she gives him the story to read, he takes the insult at face value: "only then did he sense that his daughter was offering him not sheaves of paper, but a mirror" (217) [Sentiu que em vez de papéis a filha lhe oferecia um espelho (225)]. This attempt to destroy him through literary aggression is only partially successful however, because, when provoked, a sinister ghostly Walter rises from the ashes "deathly pale . . . hung from his skeleton" (217) [lívido, . . . pendia do seu esqueleto (226)]. In retaliation, he throws her out, thereby locking them in a mutually destructive downward spiral: "It was growing light as it had twenty years before in Valmares, but everything was happening in reverse. . . . he was driving his daughter . . . away," (218) [amanhecia como vinte anos atrás em Valmares, amanhecia ao contrário . . . ele expulsava a filha (226)]. His reaction, which abruptly curtails their relationship, is equally harmful to both. Destructive anger on either side may be a necessary stage, but it does not provide a (re)solution.

In *A Costa,* the twenty years that mediated between events and their recollection opened up the possibility of the "thesis" of the short story being deconstructed by an extended commentary, which functioned as its "antithesis." But the novel fell short of providing a "synthesis." In the case of *O Vale,* the twenty years that elapse between the protagonist's childhood idolization of Walter and its antithesis, outright rejection, are followed by an unspecified number of years culminating in Walter's death. Only then does a final reappraisal of her father's ambiguous legacy take place and a synthesis can begin to emerge, signaling a new dawn. The arrival of Walter's unconventional will, that is, the legacy of his soldier's blanket to his niece/daughter and, equally important perhaps, the message scribbled on the package which conveys a belated sense of urgency, constitute not only a peace offering but also indicate his desperate wish to be heard and forgiven by his daughter. Significantly, the lines are scribbled in Spanish, throwing into complete disarray the notion of the purity of the Portuguese language, which is tantamount to acknowledging the collapse of Salazar's imperialist project. Furthermore, the location of the message itself—on the outside, as an adden-dum—inscribes the desire to bypass existing conventions in order to imple-ment a new, alternative, yet visible line of communication between father and daughter.[28]

The ghostly resurfacing of the blanket, putting a different complexion on the father-daughter ties, prompts a fresh reappraisal of the past. It gives the nameless daughter the chance to spend the night going over her past once more in order be released from it, as if condensing the ten months (or is it a life-time?) of the bereavement process into a single night. Thus, when in the last page of the novel she is ready to bury the blanket, this parting scene becomes highly symbolic. The protagonist becomes in essence able to take active responsibility for laying to rest the ghosts of the past, thereby reaching some sort of closure. This owning of responsibility explains why the act of burial can, in an extraordinary role reversal, come to be described as a poten-tial renewal or birth process, complete with the pain of labor.

> With every blow she cries out as if she were giving birth to a child. She places the folded blanket in the hole, pleased with herself and with Walter. Who is whose father? Who is our mother? Perhaps, at that moment, Walter Dias has become her son. (232)

> [Grita a cada cavadela como se lhe nascesse um filho. Coloca lá dentro a manta dobrada, contente consigo mesmo e com Walter. Quem é pai de quem? Quem é a nossa mãe? Acaso, nesta hora, Walter Dias não passará a ser seu filho?] (240)

At the point at which she becomes figuratively Walter's mother, a transfor-mation occurs: she can forgive Walter in effect by claiming him posthu-mously as a lost son. The blanket becomes the missing piece of a puzzle, which reveals him afresh in the splendid innocence of childhood: "It was as if from inside the life of a man there had emerged a very stubborn part offer-ing a childish declaration of innocence" (229) [era como se dentro da vida dum homem aparecesse uma parte renitente a fazer uma prova de criança, eu diria mesmo a inocência da criança (237)].

In retrospect, Walter becomes perhaps best understood as a lost child, who sought to run away from stultifying conformism to patriarchal rigidity em-bodied in the figure of his own father, Francisco Dias. The latter's dictatorial and uncompromising stance pervades the narrative and recalls the castrating authority of Oliveira Salazar himself.[29] With the benefit of hindsight, what emerges is the extent to which Walter, the youngest son in a large family, orphaned at a young age, was shaped by his own deprivation of motherly love, compounded by being in many ways disowned by his father. Although we never find out the exact date or circumstances of his mother's death, the memory of her existence is disseminated in the text, but only comes through indirectly in objects which belonged to her and which he appropriates. Yet, throughout the novel, her trace remains indelibly inscribed in his very name, since his middle name, the feminine Glória, echoes that of his deceased mother (Joaquina Glória).

Once this alternative matrilineal genealogy becomes apparent, one more detail stands out and further unsettles the hegemony of patrilinear anteced-ents. For it is surely not entirely a coincidence that the last earthly meeting between Walter and his illegitimate daughter takes place in Argentina, por-trayed by Jorge as a land where at the time countless mothers were to be found literally clamoring for their lost or dead sons, thus prefiguring the metamorphosis of Walter during the burial scene: "On certain days the Plaza de Mayo was still full of women wearing white headscarves, demanding the return of the disappeared. The fact was that their children had been obliter-ated" (205) [Havia dias em que à Praça de Maio continuavam a acorrer ban-dos de mulheres de lenços na cabeça, reclamando os desaparecidos. Constava que os filhos delas tinham sido aniquilados para sempre (214)].

On a collective level, the misguided globe-trotting journey which, in a burlesque parody of the Discoveries, took the adult Walter from Goa in Asia through Africa and finally dissolved in South America, where Brazil is curi-ously bypassed, having been displaced and contaminated by the Spanish-speaking dictatorial Argentina of the early eighties, reveals the full extent of the collective folly of Portuguese nationalistic discourses. The Portuguese empire, as Fernando Pessoa had so eloquently put it in his celebrated "Portu-guese Sea" [Mar Português (60)], came at a heavy cost indeed.

> For us to cross you, how many mothers cried,
> How many sons' prayers went unanswered!
> How many brides-to-be remained
> Unwed, for you to be ours, O sea!

> [Por te cruzarmos, quantas mães choraram
> Quantos filhos em vão rezaram!
> Quantas noivas ficaram por casar
> Para que fosses nosso, ó mar!]

While Pessoa could conceive of the plight of mothers and brides waiting in vain for their menfolk, yet still go on to confidently proclaim in the second stanza that

Was it worthwhile? All is worthwhile,
So long as the soul is not small

[Tudo vale a pena
Quando a alma não é pequena]

he glosses over the sorrow of daughters. By contrast, Jorge specifically re-
trieves the untold grief of the emotionally scarred daughter, who in order to
free herself from the pernicious side effects of the imperial dream, must bury
her father's symbolic legacy, his soldier's blanket and start afresh.[31]

Despite the protagonist's ability to come to terms with Walter's ambiguous legacy, and in the process truly let go of the past, one point still remains
decidedly unclear in the closing lines of the novel, which significantly bring
the story right up to the narrative present time. Will her relationships with
both her surrogate father-figure Custódio and her biological mother, Maria
Ema, henceforth develop in new directions? As Custódio comes to meet his
"daughter" outside, the mother remains indoors. The official father-figure is
conspicuously endowed with the authority to act in the latter's name: "they
approach . . . on behalf of himself and of Maria Ema too" (232) [vem por
ele próprio e por Maria Ema (241)]. The symbolism of Custódio's invitation
to re-enter the up-till-then stultifying house is deeply ambiguous: "For heav-
en's sake, don't just stand there, it's much too early to be up, go back inside"
(232) [Pelo amor de Deus, não fiquem aí parados, ainda é tão cedo, vão
entrando (241)].[33] It can be read as positive, since it is inclusive, as it extends
to her current boyfriend, who appears to live under their roof. But it could
be equally interpreted as negative, for conceivably Custódio may stubbornly
want her to go back inside the prisonlike house (ironically about to be turned
into a museum) to ensure that some semblance of the evermore crumbling
patriarchal order is restored at all costs.

It follows, then, that the narrative should end in this hiatus and remain
open-ended. As *O Vale da Paixão* comes to an end, the protagonist stands at
crossroads in her personal history. We cannot know for sure whether the
narrator will choose to re-enter the house with her official father Custódio
after completion of the mock burial rite in which he partakes uninvited.
Even if she does, we do not know on exactly what terms. Custódio, the significantly lame father, is in one sense only half of the equation, just as Walter
had been. The daughter's silenced bond with her mother is arguably the
other side of the coin, and the story of that intensely complex and fraught
relationship remains yet to be articulated.

Several twists to the plot, however, suggest a new dawn. Against a background of collective historical change (all the Dias sons except for Custódio,

emigrate; Francisco has died), the notion of family, sedimented over time, is shown to be subject to change and in flux. Furthermore, Jorge stages a protagonist who, as part of her ongoing postrevolutionary trajectory, begins to reclaim lost sons and (potentially at least) silent mothers and grandmothers. This individual story, as Lígia Silva incisively postulates, can also be profitably read on a broader allegorical level, whereby the protagonist may be interpreted as a symbolic representation not only of Portuguese women but also of Portuguese women writers: in this respect, it is telling that the protagonist, despite the coming of age evoked in her symbolic motherhood, is still left on the limits of social intelligibility. She remains, for the time being, outside the house of fiction, the manmade literary canon. This may account for her ongoing namelessness. Yet, as relationship dynamics are shown to be susceptible to historical change, what comes across is the possibility of writing a different future. In other words, the chronicle of women-writers' turbulent relationship with the existing canon will continue to unfold into the new millennium.

REVISING THE SCRIPT: *A Maçon*

In her prose-fiction, especially in *A Costa* and *O Vale*, Jorge seeks to exorcize the ghost of patriarchal discourses, repeatedly portraying familiar yet "unhomely" family contexts where women are often excessively silenced. Simultaneously, however, she endeavors to recover at all costs the life-stories and trajectories of those left without a voice. *O Vale* displayed a subliminal awareness of the need to reclaim silent mothers and grandmothers.[34] But it is in her first play, The Woman Freemason [*A Maçon*], a project whose composition spanned nearly a decade precisely either side of *A Costa* and *O Vale*, that Jorge explicitly reclaims, for the first time, a highly significant, historical grandmother: Adelaide Cabete (1867–1935). The play demonstrates how Cabete's virtual suppression from the nation's cultural memory can in fact be overturned through a series of conscious acts of "re-vision."

Due credit has to be given to Jorge for her boldness in revisiting recent Portuguese history for the stage from a female-centered perspective, all the more so given the relative scarcity of plays about famous Portuguese female forerunners.[35] Admittedly, in the first instance, Jorge's choice of Adelaide Cabete was to some extent circumstantial: the play was originally conceived around 1988–89 as a script for a television program, which was never produced.[36] Nevertheless, after the TV series failed to materialize, Jorge remained sufficiently fascinated by her life story to carry on and complete the script, reworking it for the stage.

Adelaide Cabete was undoubtedly one of the leading figures of Portuguese feminism during the first two decades of the twentieth century. Born into a humble rural background in the Alentejo, she went on to become a doctor (she was only the third woman in Portugal to gain a degree in medicine). Her intellectual trajectory was supported by her enlightened husband, who held progressive Republican convictions. During the early days of their courtship, one of his first gifts to her was a grammar book. In keeping with this, in the play Manuel Cabete is described as follows: "he knew there was far greater sensuality in intelligence that in a slim waist" [sabia que existe muito mais sensualidade na inteligência do que numa cinturinha estreita' (16)].

Like her contemporary Ana de Castro Osório, who penned the first Portuguese feminist manifesto, *Às Mulheres Portuguesas* (To Portuguese Women) in 1905, Cabete became an influential republican and a free-mason. Together, Cabete and Castro Osório co-founded in 1909 the League of Republican Women [Liga das Mulheres Republicanas]. Both women are said to have sewn with their own fair hands the new flag which went up to symbolize the change of regime and celebrate the proclamation of the Republic on October 5, 1910, a fact mentioned twice in the course of the play. What is ironically not recalled in connection with this is that Cabete's sewing credentials were of course impeccable, since she was after all a gynecologist.

The title *A Maçon* confirms the prevailing image of Adelaide Cabete as an emancipated woman who fought for the vote in the context of Republican masonary. The new Republican government, however, rejected educationally restricted women's suffrage in 1912, although the Republic did bring other major improvements in women's status, notably divorce laws, which were among the most progressive in Europe. But despite the failure to secure voting rights for women, over which the League of Republican Women divided, Adelaide Cabete's feminist conciousness-raising efforts remained unrivalled for nearly two decades.

As one of the pioneers in first-wave Portuguese feminism, her greatest legacy was as a founding member of, and participant in, several platforms which furthered women's rights. For instance, she went on to create the National Council of Portuguese Women [Conselho Nacional das Mulheres Portuguesas (CNMP)] in 1914. This leading association, as João Esteves stresses, was "the most important and longest lasting women's organization in the first half of the twentieth century in Portugal, and it was the only one that lasted beyond the [World War I] Armistice, and managed to survive uninterrupted until 1947, when the Salazarist authorities forced it to close."[37] Cabete remained its figurehead until her death in 1935.

Adelaide Cabete, by all accounts a gifted orator, participated in International Feminist Congresses, in 1923 in Rome and in 1925 in Washington, as president of the CNMP. At a national level, she was also involved in the organization of the Congressos Feministas e de Educação in 1924 and 1928, respectively, and participated in the conferences organized in 1924 and 1929 by the Liga Portuguesa Abolicionista, an association which aimed to combat and abolish the "slavery" of prostitution. Its leader was her nephew/ adoptive son, the lawyer Arnaldo Brasão. Brasão, who for many years acted as a kind of private secretary, traveled with her abroad. He was one of her most loyal followers, being for instance instrumental in the creation of the first mixed masonic lodge or "loja" in Portugal in 1923, called "Humanity" [Humanidade], which consisted of nine women and himself. In other words, together, aunt and nephew were influential in the shaping of the masonic establishment itself.[38] In the play, where these facts are evoked early on by way of educating the audience, he remains by Cabete's side throughout as her most important and perhaps only interlocutor.

Far from constituting a straightforward eulogy of Cabete's inspirational achievements as a woman ahead of her time, the main interest of Jorge's 1997 play lies in the fact that we see her at a time of adversity, faced with the temptation to give up. The play shows Cabete as she leaves Portugal with Arnaldo, in a ship bound for Angola, in 1929. Thus the woman that the audience sees on stage at a turning point in her life is a mature woman, aged sixty-two at the time. As she relives the most significant moments of her life, against the backdrop of a changing political landscape, in a Portugal where a military dictatorship had been in place since 1926 and where Salazar was rapidly rising to prominence, the sea voyage affords her ample opportunity to revisit the ideals to which she had devoted her life, and assess their impact and value. In other words, she is traveling not merely in a physical sense, but also experiencing a turbulent inner journey. It is against this backdrop that she has to deal with an epidemic on board, which affects passengers traveling in third class, but not those traveling in first class. The latter remain oblivious to the plight of the former and are intent on carrying on with plans for a party, ostensibly to celebrate Adelaide's birthday.

The callous indifference of first-class passengers proves increasingly tempting for Adelaide. After the first death, that of a child, in sharp contrast to her nephew's vocal indignation, Adelaide voices mere despondency. She now feels that all the changes achieved during a lifetime dedicated to bettering society are tantamount to mere lip-service: "I asked, I demanded. And what happened, Arnaldo? Nothing. Just enough to sound well-meaning, the most perverse way of saying that one does not want to actually do anything" [pedi, reivindiquei. E no que resultou, Arnaldo? Nada. Fez-se apenas o necessário para se falar um boa vontade, a forma mais perversa de se dizer que não se deseja fazer nada (109)]. When Arnaldo urges her to at least carry on writing, she replies, "I am not writing anymore. . . . I think all those who are on their way to Africa to be slaves, and to enslave others, yet more subjugated, are performing a loathsome tragedy. . . . I love their faces too much to help them" [Eu não escrevo mais. . . . Acho que todos aqueles que vão a caminho de África para serem escravos, e escravizarem outros, ainda mais escravos, cumprem uma tragédia detestável . . . Amo demais os seus rostos para os assistir (109–10)]. At this point, she appears to have completely lost faith in masonry as an instrument for democratic social change. Only when she performs the funerary oration for the deceased child does a glimpse of hope begin to emerge as she evokes a transmutation that might transform death into a new beginning.

The tensions between aunt and nephew culminate in a scene where Arnaldo's frustration over his aunt's perceived betrayal of their former ideals becomes such that, in desperation, he tries to kill her with a knife (her own scalpel) in a bid to preserve the memory of her remarkable achievements untainted for posterity. But she fights him off. In her mind, the moment of transfiguration that she intermittently visualizes in a dreamlike trance looms near, to coincide with the voyage through an invisible equatorial line. The momentous crossing of a mysterious threshold does indeed pave the way for aunt and nephew to move toward reconciliation and renewed understanding.

In an extraordinary climatic scene, by way of recognition that "normal" points of reference have undergone irrevocable change, Arnaldo asks Adelaide not to refer to him by his name any longer: "Aunt, I am excited. Do not call me Arnaldo" [Tia estou emocionado. Não me chame Arnaldo]. At first, she calls him by all the masonic names she can think of: Spartacus, Brother [Irmão], passenger [passageiro]. But he considers these inadequate too and pleads, "Call me something in a straight line" [Chame-me alguma coisa em linha recta]. She then refers to him by kinship labels: "nephew" [sobrinho], "son" [filho], "adoptive son" [filho adoptivo] and moreover "only son" [filho único]. However, he does not deem these to be suitable either. Instead he begs her to call him "Daughter, call me daughter" [Filha, chame-me filha], in a truly inspired yet profoundly subversive moment, where biological sexual categories are transcended, and forcefully adds, "Your daughter . . . Legitimate daughter of your mind, raised and loved by you" [Sua filha. . . . Filha legítima do seu espírito, por si criada e querida (127)].

At this point, they become once more united in a dissident life-project, confirming their passage onto a different plane, which appears to be outside time altogether. Significantly, their newfound togetherness enables Adelaide to dictate to him what is, to all intents and purposes, her testament, insofar as it constitutes the last words she utters in the play.

Write, write, write while we are still fugitives at large, and not yet deported and we can still write. Write quickly, in secret, on tiny scraps of paper that you can stuff into the pockets of other passengers without anyone seeing, that you can put into dishes and under glasses . . . Write that in Portugal, not a single word of subversion has yet been spoken.

[Escreve, escreve, escreve enquanto vamos foragidos, ainda não deportados, e ainda podemos escrever. Escreve depressa, às escondidas, em papéis minúsculos que metas nas algibeiras dos passageiros sem ninguém ver, que ponhas dentro dos pratos, debaixo dos copos . . . Escreve que em Portugal, ainda não foi dita uma palavra subversiva]. (128)

Adelaide's rebellious stance is tantamount to a radical and final dissociation from all those who surround them on the ship, not only on an intellectual level, but also in physical terms. Thus, as silence descends, Arnaldo remains by his aunt's side, allowing himself, alongside her, to be covered by a white sheet which Leonor, his would-be lover/wife, brings, and which metaphorically functions as a shroud. In a climatic moment, nephew and aunt's symbolic death is consequently enacted.

According to Elisabeth Bronfen, "As the outsider *per se,* Woman can also come to stand for the complete negation of the ruling norm, for the element which disrupts the bonds of normal conventions. . . . Over her dead body, cultural norms are reconfirmed or secured, . . . because a sacrifice of the dangerous woman reestablishes an order that was momentarily suspended due to her presence."[38]

On one level, over Adelaide's dead body, the ruling order and norm are undoubtedly reestablished. This fact is vividly brought home to the audience in an epilogue which brings events up to the present. Leonor, the only person who still recalls Adelaide and Arnaldo, is at pains to deny, perhaps in vain, that she has been at all affected by their unsettling memory. She airily informs the audience that she would subsequently marry well and lead a conventional existence under the Salazar regime, producing ideologically sound offspring: "in the end, I married honorably and well. I had several children and I took them all to Church and the Portuguese [Fascist] Youth Movement" [Afinal, casei bem e honrada. Tive vários filhos e a todos levei à Igreja e à Mocidade Portuguesa (129)]. The various members of the Establishment are also shown to live on, yet cannot recall the freemason and her nephew properly. This collective erasure of memory seems to indicate that, on the surface at least, as Bronfen argues, "Over her dead body, cultural norms are reconfirmed."

Nevertheless, this blanking out of the disruptive force of Adelaide may not have been as successful as the string of dismissive closing remarks may lead us to believe. For although there are no biological heirs to Cabete, all the more so since her only living relative, her nephew, has allowed himself to be buried alive with her, her intellectual legacy does in fact indirectly survive. Indeed, the last words of the play are uttered by the Captain of the Ship, who tells the audience that he still remembers Arnaldo clearly because, "he stuck an rude note on my cabin door that said—My aunt spoke true when she said not a single word of subversion had yet been written" [colocou, na porta do meu camarote, um papel insultuoso que dizia assim—Bem diz a minha tia que ainda não foi escrita uma palavra subversiva (132)]. As such, Adelaide's dissident message about the need for subversion, stealthily relayed by Arnaldo, continues to hover in the air, insofar as it effectively constitutes the parting words of the play. It is of course wonderfully ironic that Cabete's words should be pinned on the outside of the door, implying exclusion, yet on display for all to see. Therefore, in the mind of the audience, the status quo, while seemingly reinstated, remains destabilized, not least through the adverb "ainda," suggesting that in time disruption may yet (re)-occur.[39]

Arguably, Lídia Jorge is fully conscious of the need for subversive utterances, on more than one count. For, if we stop to think, what is truly extraordinary about the climax of this play is surely that Adelaide does not die alone. In fact, her demise is forcefully reiterated through the aberrant death of her nephew, doubly excessive insofar as it entails the death of her only (biologically male) next of kin and her (ideologically female) double too. This departure, from both factual historical truth and from the likely horizon of expectations of the audience, has far-reaching consequences. Adelaide Cabete did in fact arrive safely in Angola where she continued to practice as a doctor until her return to Portugal in 1934, only to die the following year, in 1935. In his famous novel *O Ano da Morte de Ricardo Reis* [The Year of the Death of Ricardo Reis], Saramago allowed Pessoa's heteronym to live on beyond his creator's demise in 1935. By contrast, Jorge portrayed the premature death of Cabete, ahead of the year 1935. It is possible, of course, that by staging her fictional premature death, Jorge is hinting at her "symbolic death" and oblivion from standard history textbooks as a result of Estado Novo ideology. But this explanation does not account for Arnaldo's simultaneous demise.

Arnaldo who, out of misplaced concern for posterity, nearly succumbed to the temptation of committing the crime of matricide, in the end does not fulfill his socially prescribed position of male guardian of his aunt's reputation, at first uncritically accepted. Moreover he then shockingly opts to be buried with her. His suicidal gesture is on one level the logical outcome of his transgressive ideological bid to be considered her "legitimate daughter." In effect, by envisaging himself as a subversive (albeit, we might note, legitimate) "daughter," this dissident female-gendered position necessarily entails his becoming, like Cabete, and like all other defiant women before them, silenced for refusing to obey the laws of the ruling order. In short, to all intents and purposes, his radical gesture of surrendering his position of male privilege automatically leads to an excessive and self-defeating choice of death over life. In stark contrast to his female opposite number, Leonor, he fails to marry and to reproduce, and by extension to reproduce the patriarchal model, from which he had voluntarily removed himself.

To put it differently, one might argue that Arnaldo becomes akin to a modern-day reincarnation of Antigone. According to Butler, in her analysis of the Antigone myth, death "provides a perspective on the symbolic constraints under which liveability is established." She then adds, "the question becomes: Does it also provide a critical perspective by which the terms of liveability might be rewritten, or indeed, written for the first time?" (55). On the eve of the twenty-first century, by offering (whether consciously or not) a provocative postmodern rewriting of the Antigone myth, Jorge appears to be considering the possibility of articulating alternative terms for liveability.

The death of Arnaldo, then, as a double of Adelaide, is the one that may shock the audience into imagining new "terms of liveability . . . rewritten, or indeed, written for the first time." In the play, Leonor and the ideology of the Estado Novo ostensibly survive, but we, the audience of the 1990s, know that the Estado Novo's premises were severely flawed. With the benefit of historical hindsight, we know that the partying first-class passengers were in fact traveling aboard a sinking Titanic-like ship which, after a questionable colonial experience and a protracted bloody colonial war, was unavoidably doomed to collude with the forces of historical change, namely the 25 April Revolution. By parodically rewriting history a posteriori, Jorge is not only engaging in the act of looking back, she is also creatively laying the foundations to imagine a different future.

CONCLUSION

On one level, the play recovers a pioneer feminist foremother and, as such, constitutes a valuable attempt to recover a historically suppressed matrilineal lineage. Arnaldo's plea to be considered a legitimate daughter, however, is perhaps best understood as part of a broader ongoing reflection on gender and genealogy. Arnaldo's transgendering serves to illustrate, with a postmodern twist, that identity and gender roles are not fixed, despite society's attempts to regulate roles and images. Indeed, we may even ask ourselves which "female freemason" does the "Maçon" in the title actually refer to: Adelaide Cabete or Arnaldo Brasão?

On the eve of the twenty-first century, then, by staging not one but two dissident freemasons, Jorge is urging us to rethink notions of gender, variously sedimented over time yet always susceptible to re-vision. As such, in her works, the need for re-vision is, time and time again, presented as an act of survival, certainly on an individual level, but ultimately, and perhaps just as importantly, on a collective one, too.

Conclusion

The arms and the men of lofty fame [. . .]
I shall sing throughout the globe
As long as art and genius inspire me.

[As armas e os barões assinalados (. . .)
Cantando espalharei por toda a parte
Se a tanto me ajudar o engenho e a arte.]
—Luís de Camões, *Os Lusíadas*

On or about December 1910 human character changed.
—Virginia Woolf, "Mr Bennett and Mrs Brown"

To draw out the monstrous dew
From the inner nights.

[Trazer para fora o monstruoso orvalho
Das noites interiores.]
—Sophia de Mello Breyner Andresen, "Sibilas"

As BATTERSBY OBSERVED, "SINCE THE WOMAN ARTIST DOES NOT STAND IN the same relation to tradition as the male, her face can only emerge clearly by playing two separate games. She has to be positioned in two different, but overlapping patterns: the matrilineal and patrilineal lines of influence and response."[1] Taking our cue from this remark, what our study has attempted to map out in the context of twentieth-century Portuguese literature is: firstly, how women have responded to the historical gendering of literary creativity and operated within a predominantly male-dominated literary canon and, secondly, how they have adjusted their strategies over the course of one century, to allow for shifting political, social, and cultural landscapes.

In the first quarter of the twentieth century, it was all but impossible for a gifted writer such as Florbela Espanca drawing on an apparently nonexistent genealogy of female predecessors. Yet, as Leitão de Barros' 1924 study convincingly demonstrates, there was a vast history of women writing across the centuries for which archaeological recuperation was (and still is) urgently required.[2] One possible missing link was, for instance, Ana Plácido and her partly epistolary novel *Herança de Lágrimas* (1871).[3]

Although a patrilinear evolutionary model undoubtedly structures national literary history in Portugal almost to this day, in general neither Portuguese women writers nor critics have sought to replace this with a matrilinear feminist counterhistory. This is partly a rejection of maternalist sexual essentialism and its complicity with fascist politics, but it is also a consequence of the extreme loss of cultural memory imposed on women, insofar as the New State dictatorship actively suppressed the Republican feminist movements and histories of the early twentieth century.

It is striking, nonetheless that after Florbela's death and early canonization, many subsequent women writers in Portugal felt the need to engage with her, albeit sometimes grudgingly. To mention only the writers covered here, Irene Lisboa did so conspicuously, both in her poetry and at the beginning of her diary. Agustina Bessa Luís attempts to uncover the woman behind the myth in her *biografia romanceada* in 1979. Natália Correia shows her ongoing fascination with this cult poet in several poems as well as in her preface to the *Diário do Último Ano,* where she pays tribute to her predecessor, enshrining her as a goddess. More recently, in the early 1990s, Hélia Correia, admittedly under pressure from Natália Correia, reworked the Florbela myth for the stage. Florbela Espanca turned out, then, to be a fertile source of inspiration, even when partially disowned by her successors.

Of the writers analyzed in this volume, only Lídia Jorge no longer finds it necessary to think back through this early twentieth-century foremother. Tellingly, Jorge felt nonetheless compelled to recover for the stage another female predecessor of the same period, the feminist Republican Adelaide Cabete, in her 1997 play, thereby continuing to place cultural memory, gender, and representation at the forefront of her work.

As the twentieth century gradually unfolded, much as the Three Marias had imagined it in their collaborative *Novas Cartas Portuguesas,* women developed multiple, horizontal as well as vertical, lines of communication and response. Nonetheless, while it is possible to uncover a female genealogy which bypasses man-made lines of influence and legacy, it is simultaneously important, as Battersby implies in the aforementioned quotation, to consider how women position themselves in response to a predominantly male canon. This is all the more true in the context of Portuguese culture where, in the absence of a strong female literary tradition, women's need to identify other genealogies or traditions of writing has often translated itself by virtue of necessity into "intersextuality," that is, as Abranches notes, either into closer "underground interpellations of the alien, masculine word, or into a more intimate dialogue with other [foreign] literary traditions."[4]

As our study suggests, Portuguese women writers not infrequently inter-pellate a range of canonical or "consagrados" writers from earlier centuries (for instance Luís de Camões, Camilo Castelo Branco, Antero de Quental, António Nobre). They also engage with classical tradition, especially Sopho-cles but also Homer, and with foreign writers and intellectuals, male and female alike (Flaubert, Nietzsche, Mann, the English female Gothic tradi-tion, for example). Last but not least, they maintain an ongoing dialogue with contemporary Portuguese artists and men of letters.

Moreover, all the writers we have considered here show themselves to be in extensive dialogue in their aesthetic projects with male creativity and male artists, whether real or, after the revolution, increasingly fictional. Both Hélia Correia and Lídia Jorge feature in their novels invented male writers, such as Álvaro Roiz or the unnamed writer of "The Locusts," in order to decon-struct male authority and concepts of genius. Lídia Jorge not only repeatedly questions clear-cut genealogies and paternally authorized fictions, but also challenges the wisdom attributed to canonical texts, as evidenced in her ir-reverent misquoting of some of Fernando Pessoa's most celebrated poems.

Our choice of half a dozen representative writers, who have helped to shape Portuguese letters over the course of one century, has further implica-tions if we consider them not only diachronically but also synchronically as three pairs. Florbela Espanca and Irene Lisboa, Agustina Bessa Luís and Na-tália Correia, and Hélia Correia and Lídia Jorge represent three distinct gen-erations: the possibility of a limited Modernist opening; the Dictatorship; and finally the postrevolutionary period, respectively. Nevertheless, the cru-cial point that emerges from a close textual analysis of their oeuvre is the extent to which women, who are in some cases exact contemporaries of each other, follow very distinct trajectories and make different strategic choices, be it in terms of style, genre, or themes. It is therefore overly simplistic to see them as a homogeneous group. As Edfeldt points out, treating women writers as a stable and atemporal category apart is precisely one of the ma-noeuvres which has led to women's exclusion from the canon.[5]

As Edfelt further notes, not being able to connect women writers to im-portant classifying categories such as the movements and generations which conventionally structure literary histories and failing to provide sociopolitical and literary contextualization of their work results in ongoing marginaliza-tion.[6] Since established literary movements are notoriously difficult for women to fit into, female writers usually fare better in terms of representa-tion in dictionaries than in literary histories, as she perceptively notes. While the exclusion of women writing before the 1950s was particularly extreme (during the Republic and the early years of the New State Espanca and Lis-boa struggled to publish and be recognized as poets and writers at all), there is still surprisingly little visible change in the hegemonic gendering of literary historiographical discourse, even after this date: it seems that, almost to this day, exceptional women writers can only be "canonized" at the rate of one, or two at a pinch, per generation.

Yet another move mentioned by Edfelt, which confines female writers to the margins, is the failure to flesh out more fully their own literary histories and genealogies. This is why, as Adrienne Rich lucidly argued, the act of looking back becomes akin to an act of survival.[7] Revisiting the past is a necessary stage in moving forward, even if it is not a straightforward enterprise: indeed, the majority of the women we have chosen for this study foreground the theme of mourning and melancholia. Hélia Correia and Lídia Jorge both pen plays in which women die: nonetheless, the use of double time and space in the structure of Hélia Correia's plays allows both the dead Antigone and Florbela Espanca to comment on the actions of their living selves, from the retrospective positions of death. Lídia Jorge's strategy is to deconstruct the fatality of death on stage through excessive iteration and doubling. By contrast, in the postrevolutionary novels of both these authors, women generally emerge alive as survivors, even if they may have been psychologically scarred.

Portuguese women writers, then, mark their dissent not only through explicit acts of recuperation, appropriation, and transgression, but also through deconstructive strategies ranging from excessive conformity through to irony. As such, they graphically reinscribe in their work Antigone's impossible dilemma as a specific mode of resistance in order to put a question mark over the asymmetries of gendered constructions in Western culture, not least that of woman as muse and man as creative genius.

Where the lack of access to neglected female forebears was clearly a material problem for women writers at the beginning of the century and under Salazarism, from the 1970s onwards their continued absence within Portuguese literary tradition functions rather as a self-perpetuating mythology of female cultural memory loss. This can be offset, as Edfeldt proposes, by combining the strategic study of women writers on their own terms with a critique of normatively masculine literary historiography.[8] This two-pronged approach is one we have endeavored to adopt in this study since, as Battersby eloquently put it, "women are not just outside cultural traditions. They structure the spaces that lie between the bold lines picked out by previous generations of art critics and literary critics."[9]

We are naturally aware that the omissions in our own selections here may themselves conspire to structure the way in which the spaces that currently lie in-between become perceived in future. Judith Teixeira, Sophia de Mello Breyner Andresen, Maria Judite de Carvalho, Maria Velho da Costa, Maria

Gabriela Llansol and Ana Luísa Amaral, for instance, and to name but a few, spring to mind as equally rewarding choices, warranting closer study. Accordingly, we hope that the writers we have chosen to analyze here stand not as reinstituted canonical norms, but rather as a thought-provoking cross-sample, aimed at opening the entire question of canonicity, cultural memory, and literary tradition to the interrogation of gender politics. Read in conjunction, all of them certainly afford particular, historical insights into the complex gender politics of achieving institutional acceptance and validation in the national canon at different points in the twentieth century. Globally they, alongside the many others who remain outside the scope of the present work, and the many who remain to be retrieved for feminist scholarship, foreground the ongoing urgency of the gender question in modern Portuguese culture. If our study prompts fresh enquiries into the work of other women writers, both past and present, then our labors will have been amply rewarded.

Notes

INTRODUCTION

1. Virgínia Ferreira, "Engendering Portugal: Social Change, State Politics and Women's Mobilization," in *Modern Portugal,* ed. António Costa Pinto (Palo Alto: The Society for the Promotion of Science and Scholarship, 1998), 162.

2. Chatarina Edfeldt, *Uma história na História. Representações da Autoria Feminina na História da Literatura Portuguesa do Século XX* (Montijo: Câmara Municipal de Montijo, 2006), 182–83.

3. In their work on gender and cultural memory, John Neubauer and Helga Geyer-Ryan have commented that "even if we agree that remembering is not biologically determined, we can assume that memory is influenced by the particular social, cultural, and historical conditions in which individuals find themselves. And since men and women generally assume different social and cultural roles, their way of remembering should also differ." John Neubauer and Helga Geyer-Ryan, "Introduction—Gender, Memory, Literature," in *Gendered Memories. Volume 4 of the Proceedings of the XVth Congress of the International Comparative Literature Association. "Literature as Cultural Memory." Leiden, 16–22 August 1997,* ed. John Neubauer and Helga Geyer-Ryan (Amsterdam: Rodopi, 2000), 6.

4. Maria Isabel Barreno, Maria Teresa Horta and Maria Velho da Costa, *Novas Cartas Portuguesas* (Lisbon: Dom Quixote, 1998). All subsequent references to this work are to this edition and are cited parenthetically within the text. Maria Isabel Barreno, Maria Teresa Horta and Maria Velho da Costa, *New Portuguese Letters,* trans. Helen R. Lane and Faith Gillespie (London: Readers International, 1994). All subsequent references to the English translation of *Novas Cartas Portuguesas* are to this edition, unless otherwise stated, and are cited parenthetically within the text.

5. Mariana Alcoforado, "Lettres Portugaises," in *Cartas Portuguesas,* Edição Bilingue, ed. and trans. Eugénio de Andrade (Lisbon: Assírio e Alvim, 1993 [1669]).

6. For an excellent, thorough-going account of the mythologies that grew up around Mariana Alcoforado, and the different national, linguistic, and gender investments that have determined the academic histories, and literary revisions of *Lettres Portugaises* in France, Portugal, and elsewhere, see Anna Klobucka, *The Portuguese Nun: Formation of a National Myth* (Lewisburg: Bucknell University Press, 2000).

7. See Edfeldt, *Uma história na História,* 207.

8. Ana Paula Ferreira, "Discursos femininos, teoria crítica feminista: para uma resposta que não é" *Discursos. Estudos de Língua e Cultura Portuguesa* 5 (1993): 16.

9. Ferreira, ed. *A Urgência de Contar* (Lisbon: Caminho, 2000), 17.

10. For articles, edited volumes, and books which engage with modern and contemporary Portuguese women's writing as a critical conceptual category, not merely via monographic studies of individual writers, see Isabel Allegro de Magalhães, *O Tempo das Mulheres: a dimensão temporal na escrita feminina contemporânea: ficção portuguesa* (Lisbon: Imprensa Nacional-

Casa da Moeda, 1987); Darlene Sadlier, *The Question of How: Women Writers and the New Portuguese Literature* (New York: Greenwood Press, 1989); Elfriede Engelmayer and Renate Hess, *Die Schwestern der Mariana Alcoforado: Portugiesische Schriftstellerinnen der Gegenwart* (Berlin: edition tranvía, 1993); Ferreira, "Discursos femininos"; Anna Klobucka, "De autores e autoras," *Discursos. Estudos de Língua e Cultura Portuguesa* 5 (1993); Paulo de Medeiros, "O som dos búzios: feminismo, pós-modernismo, simulação," *Discursos. Estudos de Língua e Cultura Portuguesa* 5 (1993); Isabel Allegro de Magalhães, *O Sexo dos Textos e outras leituras* (Lisbon: Caminho, 1995); Hilary Owen, "'Um quarto que seja seu': The Quest for Camões' Sister," *Portuguese Studies* 11 (1995); Cláudia Pazos Alonso and Glória Fernandes, *Women, Literature and Culture in the Portuguese-speaking World* (Lewiston, NY ; Edwin Mellen Press, 1996); Ana Paula Ferreira, "Reengendering History. Women's Fictions of the Portuguese Revolution," in *After the Revolution: Twenty Years of Portuguese Literature, 1974–1994,* ed. Helena Kaufman and Anna Klobucka (Lewisburg: Bucknell University Press, 1997); Maria Irene Ramalho de Sousa Santos and Ana Luísa Amaral, "Sobre a 'Escrita Feminina'," *Oficina do CES* 90 (April 1997); Graça Abranches, "Unlearning in order to speak: politics, writings and poetics of Portuguese women of the twentieth century," University of Manchester. Spanish and Portuguese Studies Department Seminar (23 April 1998); Maria Irene Ramalho de Sousa Santos, "Re-inventing Orpheus: Women and Poetry Today," *Portuguese Studies* 14 (1998); Mónica Rector, *Mulher: objecto e sujeito da literatura portuguesa* (Oporto: Edições Universidade Fernando Pessoa, 1999); Ana Paula Ferreira, "A 'literatura feminina' nos anos quarenta: uma história de exclusão," in *A Urgência de Contar,* ed. Ana Paula Ferreira (Lisbon: Caminho, 2000); Hilary Owen, *Portuguese Women's Writing, 1972 to 1986: Reincarnations of a Revolution* (Lewiston, NY: Edwin Mellen Press, 2000); Maria Graciete Besse, *Percursos no feminino,* (Lisbon: Ulmeiro, 2001); Ana Gabriela Macedo, "Os Estudos Feministas Revisitados: Finalmente Visíveis," in *Floresta encantada: novos caminhos da literatura comparada,* ed. Helena Buescu, João Ferreira Duarte, and Manuel Gusmão (Lisbon: Dom Quixote, 2001); Cláudia Pazos Alonso, "Disrupted Genealogies: the Illegitimate Daughter in Portuguese Literature," in *Women's Writing in Western Europe. Gender, Generation, and Legacy,* ed. Adalgisa Giorgio and Julia Waters (Cambridge: Cambridge Scholars Press, 2007).

11. On the Americanization of feminist theory discussed in Portugal, see Graça Abranches, "'On What Terms Shall We Join the Procession of Educated Men?' Teaching Feminist Studies at the University of Coimbra," *Oficina do CES* 12 (July 1998), 17–18.

12. See Claire Buck, ed. *Bloomsbury Guide to Women's Literature* (London: Bloomsbury Publishing 1992); Antoinette Fouque, Mireille Calle-Gruber, and Béatrice Didier, eds., *Le dictionnaire des femmes créatrices* (Paris: Éditions des Femmes, forthcoming); Anna Klobucka, *O Formato Mulher: A emergência da autoria feminina na poesia portuguesa* (Coimbra: Angelus Novus, 2009).

13. See Ana Gabriela Macedo, ed. *Género, Identidade e Desejo. Antologia crítica do feminismo contemporâneo* (Lisbon: Cotovia, 2002); Ana Gabriela Macedo and Ana Luísa Amaral, eds., *Dicionário da crítica feminista* (Oporto: Edições Afrontamento, 2005).

14. See Magalhães, *O Tempo das Mulheres* and *O Sexo dos Textos.*

15. Sousa Santos and Amaral, "Sobre a 'Escrita Feminina'," 2. See also the special volume of the Universidade Aberta journal *Discursos,* dedicated to "discursos femininos" in 1993. Here a series of international scholars of Portuguese bring poststructuralist feminisms to bear on gender issues in Portuguese literature. For a useful discussion of the foundational 1980s debates in the USA between Nancy Miller and Peggy Kamuf regarding the political urgency versus the impossibility of empirically sexing the author behind the signature, see Klobucka, "De autores e autoras."

16. The "escrita feminina" idea, conceived as "sexing the text" male or female, is notable, not least, for its sheer longevity in Portuguese approaches to feminism, as exemplified by Maria Teresa Horta in her reviews for *Mulheres* magazine throughout the 1980s, but also in public questions and discussions twenty years on, in the context of literature sessions at the Congresso Feminista organized by UMAR (União de Mulheres Alternativa e Resposta) June 26–28, 2008.

17. Sousa Santos, "Re-inventing Orpheus," 126.

18. As a good example of this, Anna Klobucka progressively and playfully exposes the always already male-sexed positions of Eduardo Prado Coelho's "feminine" textualities, in his dissemination of structuralism and Barthesian mythologies in Portuguese literature and critical theory, in order to demonstrate that "the gaze of the theoretical subject can only be figured as masculine, no matter how much it hides, *à la Freud*, behind supposedly feminine spectacles." See Anna Klobucka, "Teoricamente Phalando: Algumas observações sobre a sexualidade do discurso crítico em Portugal," *Colóquio/Letras* 125/126 (1992): 171.

19. On the importance of sex, race, and class power differentials in claiming the social authority to exploit tactics such as gender parody and dragging, see Anne McClintock, *Imperial Leather. Race, Gender and Sexuality in the Colonial Conquest* (New York: Routledge, 1995), 68–69.

20. Andrew Elfenbein, *Romantic Genius: The Prehistory of a Homosexual Role* (New York: Columbia University Press, 1999), 5.

21. Christine Battersby, *Gender and Genius. Towards a Feminist Aesthetics* (London: The Women's Press, 1989), 23.

22. Ibid., 6.

23. Ibid., 3; 8.

24. Ibid., 3.

25. Elfenbein, *Romantic Genius,* 5; 31–32. For a good case made against the classic example of this "feminizing" tendency in the Portuguese literary critical tradition in the poetry of António Nobre, see António Ladeira, "António Nobre. 'A Nossa Maior Poetisa'?," Unpublished paper given at the American Portuguese Studies Association Conference, Yale University, 2008. As Anna Klobucka has also implied in the conclusion to her essay on Adília Lopes, instating Florbela Espanca as the "greatess *poetess* of Portuguese literature," to claim António Nobre as Portugal's most feminine poet, is hardly politically innocent or helpful. See Anna Klobucka, "Spanking Florbela: Adília Lopes and a Genealogy of Feminist Parody in Portuguese Poetry," *Portuguese Studies* 19 (2003): 204.

26. Elfenbein, *Romantic Genius,* 32.

27. Battersby, *Gender and Genius,* 10.

28. Michel Foucault, "Nietzsche, Genealogy, History," in *Language, Counter-Memory, Practice. Selected Essays and Interviews* ed. Donald F. Bouchard, trans. Donald F. Bouchard and Sherry Simon (Oxford: Basil Blackwell, 1977), 148. In this respect, our study is also indebted to the work of Ana Paula Ferreira whose Foucauldian readings of feminine subjection and resistance in Portuguese literary culture have proved particularly effective in disclosing the historical operations of gendered power in the Estado Novo. See Ana Paula Ferreira, "Home Bound: The Construct of Femininity in the Estado Novo," *Portuguese Studies* 12 (1996); Ferreira, ed. *Urgência.*

29. Edfeldt, *Uma história na História.*

30. Ibid., 205.

31. The roots of Portuguese national canonicity lay in Romanticism as Chatarina Edfeldt points out, "literary historiography, as a discipline and a historical genre, is a product of Ro-

manticism and, throughout the Positivist era, it was understood as a project designed to construct and define national identity." See ibid., 23.

32. Klobucka, *The Portuguese Nun,* 75. An important corollary of this, from the perspective of gender and canon-building history, concerns the discourse of threat to Portuguese patriotic identity that emerged in the latter half of the nineteenth century with the rise of emancipated female images in English literature, and the influence of British protofeminism in Portugal, as Graça Abranches observes in her 2001 essay "Homens, Mulheres e Mestras Inglesas." Here Abranches traces Portuguese antifeminist discourses of anglophobic misogyny and gender panic, dating back to nineteenth-century Romantic and Realist fiction, and resurfacing with particular force in patriotic Portuguese reactions to Republican suffragette identities at the beginning of the twentieth century. In this context, Republican feminists themselves affirmed their "feminismo verdadeiro" as patriotically Portuguese in opposition to the masculine, denatured "feminismo falso" of the British suffragette foreigner. As a kind of putative counternarrative to the rise of a Portuguese national literary canonicity, Abranches sets out to explore the specific history of the "antifeminist" idea revealed in the repeated, symptomatic, Portuguese trope of the fair-haired English schoolmistress or governess, who became a Portuguese "space for the crystallization of anxieties of national identity." See Graça Abranches, "Homens, mulheres e mestras inglesas," in *Entre ser e estar: raízes, percursos e discursos da identidade,* ed. Maria Irene Ramalho and António Sousa Ribeiro (Oporto: Afrontamento Edições, 2001), 256.

33. See Carlos Reis, *O Conhecimento da Literatura. Introdução aos Estudos Literários* (Coimbra: Livraria Almedina, 1995), 73; 384–85. For a fuller, earlier discussion of this see also, Edfeldt, *Uma história na História,* 70.

34. Vítor Manuel de Aguiar e Silva, *Teoria da Literatura,* 8th ed. (Coimbra: Almedina, 2007), 429.

35. McClintock, *Imperial Leather,* 38–39.

36. Silva, *Teoria da Literatura,* 264–65.

37. Ibid., 264.

38. Anna Klobucka describes this process effectively, in the Portuguese modernist and structuralist context, as she writes, "the 'waxen figure' of the Eternal Feminine, instead of coming to life under the desiring gaze of the Pygmalions gathered around her, actually melts acquiring a fluidity that is totally beyond all structure: her place is the 'no-place of woman,' considered as the factor that destabilizes all places. Therefore, the 'woman question', formulated in these terms, simply stabilizes the transfer of symbolic power from the old economy of male domination to the drama of controlled self-abandon in which masculine desire is realized in the modern context." See Klobucka, "Teoricamente Phalando," 172–73.

39. On the phenomenon of "extraordinárias" see also Edfeldt, *Uma história na História;* Ferreira, ed. *Urgência.*

40. On women acting as cultural boundary markers in constructions of the nation, see Nira Yuval-Davis, *Gender and Nation* (London: Sage Publications, 1997), 61.

41. Edfeldt, *Uma história na História,* 163–64.

42. Fernando Pinto do Amaral, *100 Livros Portugueses do Século XX: 100 Portuguese Books of the 20th Century* (Lisbon: Camões Institute 2002).

43. Ibid., 10.

44. Ibid., 146–47.

45. Harold Bloom, *Genius. A Mosaic of One Hundred Exemplary Creative Minds* (London: Fourth Estate, 2002).

46. Ibid., 11.

47. Ibid., 513. Challenged about his views in the Portuguese newpaper, *Público,* Bloom makes his opposing "limit case" by complaining "they are going to speak well of terrible poems because they are written by Cape Verdean lesbians." See Bloom, "Só Falta Começarem a Partir-me os Vidros das Janelas. Interview by Luís Miguel Queirós," *Público,* May 26, 2001.

48. See for example, Elaine Showalter, *A Literature of their Own. British Women Novelists from Brontë to Lessing* (London: Virago Press, 1982); Barbara Godard, ed. *Gynocritics/Gynocritiques: Feminist Approaches to Canadian and Québec Women's Writing* (Toronto: ECW Press, 1987); Ellen Moers, *Literary Women* (London: The Women's Press, 1986).

49. The existence of Portuguese women writers from the first half of the twentieth century, needing new editions and critical attention is highlighted by, among others, Cláudia Pazos Alonso, *Imagens do Eu na Poesia de Florbela Espanca* (Lisbon: Imprensa Nacional Casa da Moeda, 1997); Ferreira, ed. *Urgência;* Edfeldt, *Uma história na História.*

50. On the closing of the CNMP in 1947, following their Exhibition of Books Written by Women [Exposicão de Livros Escritos por Mulheres], see Vanda Gorjão, *Mulheres em Tempos Sombrios. Oposição feminina ao Estado Novo* (Lisbon: Imprensa de Ciências Sociais, 2002), 102–3. See also Maria Antónia Fiadeira, *Maria Lamas. Biografia* (Lisbon: Quetzal Editores, 2003).

51. On the treatment of Republican patriotic constructions of womanhood, coopted and transformed by New State official gender politics, see Gorjão, *Mulheres em Tempos Sombrios.* See also Ana Paula Ferreira, "Nationalism and Feminism at the Turn of the Nineteenth Century: Constructing the 'Other' (Woman) of Portugal," *Santa Barbara Portuguese Studies* III (1996).

52. Sophocles, *The Three Theban Plays: Antigone, Oedipus the King, Oedipus at Colonus,* ed. Bernard Knox, trans. Robert Fagles (New York: Penguin, 1984). Sophocles's Antigone has long served as the classic figuration of extreme, sacrificial loyalty to the bonds of kinship, in the face of political pragmatism in the foundation of the state. Antigone publicly opposes Creon, the newly crowned King of Thebes, when he decrees that noone shall give the honor of burial to Antigone's brother Polynices, who has died in combat leading the Argosian army against his brother Eteocles. Both brothers are killed and the throne falls to Jocasta's brother Creon. Antigone defies both king and state to bury her brother, citing the ancient unwritten laws of the gods as her justification. She is punished by being walled up alive but subsequently commits suicide, going childless to her grave, and thus fulfilling the curse laid upon the incestuously begotten children of Oedipus and Jocasta. Her suicide is followed by the death of Creon's son, Haemon, whom Antigone had intended to marry. Haemon's death in turn leads Creon's wife, Eurydice, to commit suicide. As the end of a lineage, living out the curse on Oedipus's children, Antigone becomes, in a conventional reading of the tragedy, a martyred heroine who refuses to subordinate loyalty to family and kin to the absolute law of the state.

53. George Steiner, *Antigones* (New Haven: Yale University Press, 1996), 18. On Steiner, Oedipus and Antigone, see also Cecilia Sjöholm, *The Antigone Complex: Ethics and the Invention of Feminine Desire* (Stanford, CA: Stanford University Press, 2004); Judith Butler, *Antigone's Claim: Kinship between Life and Death* (New York: Columbia University Press, 2000), 57.

54. Isabel Capeloa Gil, "Espectros Literários. *Perdição* de Hélia Correia," in *Furor. Ensaios sobre a obra dramática de Hélia Correia,* ed. Maria de Fátima Sousa e Silva (Coimbra: Imprensa da Universidade de Coimbra, 2006), 70.

55. Butler, *Antigone's Claim,* 22.

56. The three essays by Luce Irigaray which discuss Antigone directly and inform Butler's analytical responses are: Luce Irigaray, "The Eternal Irony of the Community," in *Speculum*

NOTES 215

of the Other Woman, trans. Gillian C. Gill (Ithaca: Cornell University Press, 1985); "The Female Gender," in *Sexes and Genealogies,* trans. Gillian C. Gill, (New York: Columbia University Press, 1993); "An Ethics of Sexual Difference," in *An Ethics of Sexual Difference,* trans. Carolyn Burke and Gillian C. Gill (London: Athlone, 1993). Also relevant to our own and to Butler's discussion of Irigaray's Antigone is, "The Universal as Mediation," in *Sexes and Genealogies,* trans. Gillian C. Gill, (New York: Columbia University Press, 1993). Luisa Muraro provides a particularly useful analysis of the different twists and turns taken by Irigaray's varying positions on Antigone, with her defense of mother-daughter genealogies predominating in "Speculum" and "Ethics of Sexual Difference," only to be challenged in "The Female Gender" where Antigone is seen as belonging to the world of men and ultimately serving male state interests. See Luisa Muraro, "Female Genealogies," in *Engaging with Irigaray,* ed. Carolyne Burke, Naomi Schor, and Margaret Whitford (New York: Columbia University Press, 1994), 327–29.

57. Sjöholm, *The Antigone Complex,* 112.

58. Irigaray, "Universal as Mediation," 134–35.

59. Irigaray, "Eternal Irony," 217; 19.

60. Sjöholm, *The Antigone Complex,* 113.

61. Christine Battersby, *The Phenomenal Woman: Feminist Metaphysics and the Patterns of Identity* (Oxford: Polity, 1998), 124.

62. Butler, *Antigone's Claim,* 1.

63. Ibid., 11.

64. Ibid., 66.

65. Battersby, *Phenomenal Woman,* 121–22. In her critique of Butler, Claire Colebrook claims that the work of Judith Butler actually "intensifies [the] matter/representation dichotomy, despite the fact that her work is ostensibly a critique of the sex/gender distinction." See Claire Colebrook, "From Radical Representations to Corporeal Becomings: The Feminist Philosophy of Lloyd, Grosz, and Gatens," *Hypatia. A Journal of Feminist Philosophy* 15, no. 2 (2000): 78. For Colebrook, Butler's focus on the body, as being bound up with discourse and representation, privileges epistemological questions about corporeality over necessary ontological ones, so that how the body is known becomes more important that how the body is.

66. Battersby, *Phenomenal Woman,* 121.

67. Butler, *Antigone's Claim,* 76.

68. Sjöholm, *The Antigone Complex,* 111.

69. On the process of psychoanalytical transference in *Novas Cartas,* see Linda S. Kauffman, *Discourses of Desire: Gender, Genre, and Epistolary Fictions* (Ithaca: Cornell University Press, 1986).

70. See Friedrich Engels, *The Origin of the Family, Private Property and the State* (Harmondsworth: Penguin, 1985 [1884]).

71. Irigaray, "Eternal Irony," 225.

72. For a fuller discussion of this, see Owen, *Reincarnations of a Revolution.*

73. Muraro, "Female Genealogies," 323–24.

74. Maria Alzira Seixo, "Quatro Razões Para Reler *Novas Cartas Portuguesas,*" in *Outros Erros: Ensaios de Literatura,* ed. Maria Alzira Seixo (Oporto: Asa, 2001), 187. Following from Seixo, Anna Klobucka focuses on the *Novas Cartas'* Schlegelian ability both to "prophesy that past" that is buried in history and to open fertile re-readings of women's literature in the present and future. For Klobucka, this enables, by analogy, a strategically "anachronistic" reworking of gynocritical feminist perspectives, made to function synchronically. See Klobucka, *O Formato Mulher,* 13.

75. It is worth observing in this context that even the ostensibly stable textual grounding of the five "original" *Lettres Portugaises* as the source text for *Novas Cartas* is deceptive. As Patricia Odber de Baubeta has shown, scholarly divergences regarding the existence of the nun and the gendering of the letters' author, find themselves mirrored in the decisions that different editors and translators into English have made as to the correct sequence of the five letters. These reorderings in turn considerably alter the trajectory of passion and female subject assertion that the original five letters present. For an insightful and painstaking account of the different English translations, see Patricia Odber de Baubeta, "Travels (and Travails) of a Portuguese Nun," in *Estudos Anglo-Portugueses. Livro de Homenagem a Maria Leonor Buescu*, ed. Carlos Ceia, Isabel Lousada, and Maria João da Rocha Afonso (Lisbon: Edições Colibri / Faculdade de Ciências Sociais e Humanas, Universidade Nova de Lisboa, 2004). It is worth noting that even Donald Ericson, whose 1941 English translation is the one reproduced in UK and US editions of *New Portuguese Letters* has published another 1986 version, ordering the letters differently.

76. Ana Luísa Amaral, "Desconstruindo identidades: ler *Novas Cartas Portuguesas* à luz da teoria *queer*," *Cadernos de Literatura Comparada, Corpo e Identidades* 3/4 (2001): 82. Amaral draws productively here on founding queer theory texts by Kosovsky Sedgwick, de Lauretis and Butler among others.

77. An important and productive corollary of our argument for reading antihistoricist countergenealogy in *Novas Cartas*, is of course the radical deconstruction and dispersal of the feminine subject as humanist agent of positivist history, pointing as Maria Irene Ramalho astutely argues, in the direction of nonessential transidentity and interidentity. For her excellent reading of *Novas Cartas* as rewriting the sexuality of tradition, see Maria Irene Ramalho, "A sogra de Rute ou intersexualidades," in *Globalização. Fatalidade ou Utopia?*, ed. Boaventura de Sousa Santos (Oporto: Afrontamento, 2001).

78. See *Mulheres contra Homens?* (Lisbon: Dom Quixote, 1971), 95. At least one of the Three Marias must have been familiar with this anthology. The quotation from the American feminist, Ti-Grace Atkinson which is reproduced in *Novas Cartas*, "Text of a Declaration of Honor or an Interrogation, Written by a Woman Named Joana" is drawn verbatim and in its entirety from Ingrid Carlander's essay in *Mulheres Contra Homens?* in which Atkinson is, in fact, paraphrased from an interview with Carlander, not directly quoted. Familiarity with this anthology of essays demonstrates that the Three Marias were aware of Anglo-American, French, and other European feminist discourses circulating during the Primavera Marcelista. For the Three Marias's citing of Atkinson, see Barreno, Horta, and Costa, *New Portuguese Letters*, 261; *Novas Cartas Portuguesas*, 262.

79. Klobucka similarly refers to the Three Marias's relegating the poet Florbela Espanca to "the ambiguous space of the hallway" in the three writers' symbolic "household" representation of their genealogical affinities. See Klobucka, "Spanking Florbela: Adília Lopes and a Genealogy of Feminist Parody in Portuguese Poetry," 193. She draws on the brief reference to her in *Novas Cartas* and on Luciana Stegagno Picchio's "Le Nipoti di Marianna" to read Florbela as an "absent mother or repudiated matrix" of female literary genealogy, notable precisely for her absence. See also the introduction to Engelmayer and Hess, *Schwestern.*

80. Luciana Stegagno-Picchio, "Le nipoti de Marianna. Note sulla letteratura femminile in Portogallo," in *Gli abbracci feriti: poetesse portoghese di oggi*, ed. Adelina Aletti (Milano: Feltrini, 1980).

81. Foucault, "Nietzsche, Genealogy, History," 148.

82. Ibid., 143–45. "Nietzsche, Genealogy, History" was first published the year before *Novas Cartas* in 1971 in *Hommage à Jean Hyppolite.*

83. Ibid., 160.

84. Marianne Hirsch and Valerie Smith, "Feminism and Cultural Memory: An Introduction," *Signs. Gender and Cultural Memory* 28, no. 1 (2002): 2.

85. As the Marias explain in the authors' afterword printed in the English edition, "the book is the written record of a much broader, common, lived experience of creating a sisterhood through conflict, shared fun and sorrow, complicity and competition." See Barreno, Horta, and Costa, *New Portuguese Letters,* 399–400.

86. Chantal Mouffe, *The Return of the Political* (London: Verso, 1993), 78. See also Seixo, "Quatro Razões." It is this powerful interpellation of the always multiple feminist reader in process that accounts for the various public readings, performances, and plays that have been generated by the text of *Novas Cartas*. Both Portuguese and international feminist groups have periodically revived *Novas Cartas,* whether it was in print at the time or not, via theatrical performance and/or readings. This was the case at the time of the solidarity campaign in 1972–73, where performances were arranged on Broadway, in Paris, and in London. On the Broadway event, see Robin Morgan, "International Feminism. A Call for Support of the Three Marias," in *Going too Far. The Personal Chronicle of a Feminist,* ed. Robin Morgan, (New York: Vintage Books, 1978), 205. It was also revived as a series of readings in the late 1990s at London's Little Garden, at Covent Garden, to commemorate twenty five years of the solidarity campaign, and it was reproduced as a performance of dramatized readings called *Marianas,* adapted by Gisela Cañamero, in Lisbon at Espaço Karnart, June 21, 2008 in the context of the Congresso Feminista 2008 organized in Lisbon by UMAR (União de Mulheres Alternativa e Resposta) June 26–28.

87. Abranches, "Unlearning," 2.

88. See Helder Macedo, "Teresa and Fátima and Isabel," *Times Literary Supplement,* December 12, 1975. Macedo's review, although it represented a very important recontextualization at the time for the Anglophone reader, also exemplifies this national versus international dichotomy particularly clearly, viewing the book's feminist status as a largely external, international phenomenon. On one level, this also indexes the very public quarrel which divided the Three Marias after the Revolution, and was conducted through letter writing in the press. This dispute centered on an acute polarization between the increasingly national cause of the Portuguese 25 April Revolution and party communism, espoused at that time by Velho da Costa, and the ongoing dialogue with international feminism favored by Barreno and Horta. See Loretta Porto Slover, "The Three Marias: Literary Portrayals of the Situation of Women in Portugal" (Ph.D. diss., University of Harvard, 1977).

89. We would like to draw attention here to an important project on *Novas Cartas Portuguesas,* being organized by Ana Luísa Amaral at the Universidade do Porto to produce a new edition of the book and also a Portuguese Reader's Guide to *Novas Cartas Portuguesas* drawing together relevant critical works from all different languages.

90. Foucault, "Nietzsche, Genealogy, History," 139–40.

91. Susan Wolstenholme, *Gothic (Re)Visions: Writing Women as Readers* (Albany: State University of New York Press, 1993), xiv.

CHAPTER 1. FLORBELA ESPANCA

1.Teresa Leitão de Barros, *Escritoras de Portugal,* 2 vols (Lisbon: s.ed, 1924), vol. 1, 22–23. All translations into English in this chapter are our own unless otherwise stated. Portuguese spelling has been modernized.

2. Indeed, in volume 2 of *Escritoras de Portugal,* she devoted nearly a whole page to Espanca, situating her, as other critics tended to at the time, in the context of contemporary female poetic production. See ibid., 341–42.

3. Florbela Espanca, *Poemas de Florbela Espanca* (São Paulo: Martins Fontes, 1996), 180. All subsequent references are cited parenthetically in the text, and are to this carefully prepared edition by Maria Lúcia Dal Farra unless otherwise indicated. A selection of Florbela's sonnets in English translations by Richard Zenith has been provided in the appendix to chapter 1. These are: "Vaidade," "Castelã da Tristeza," "A Minha Dor," Renúncia," "Da Minha Janela," "Exaltação," "Charneca em Flor," "Se tu viesses ver-me," "Sou Eu!" and "Deixai entrar a Morte." All other English translations in this chapter are our own.

4. Espanca was born on December 8, 1894 in the provincial town of Vila Viçosa. Together with her younger brother Apeles, she was raised by her father and his childless wife.

5. For futher details see the preface to Maria Lúcia Dal Farra, *Trocando Olhares* (Lisbon: Imprensa Nacional Casa da Moeda, 1995).

6. Florbela Espanca, "Charneca em Flor," *Europa* 3 (1925): 31.

7. Her father was an amateur photographer, a most unusual activity in provincial Portugal at the turn of the century. This fact undoubtedly contributed to making her conscious of the male gaze at an early age. See Rui Guedes, *Fotobiografia* (Lisbon: Dom Quixote, 1985).

8. These include one further compilation of poetry entitled *Reliquiae,* and the volume of short stories *As Máscaras do Destino.* A second volume of short stories, *O Dominó Preto* and a diary, the latter written in the last year of her life, only appeared in 1982 and 1981, respectively. See Florbela Espanca, *As Máscaras do Destino* (Oporto: Editora Marânus, 1931); "Reliquiae," in *Charneca em Flor,* 2nd ed. (Coimbra: Livraria Gonçalves, 1931); *O Dominó Preto* (Amadora: Livraria Bertrand, 1982); *Diário do Último Ano, seguido de um poema sem título.* Amadora: Livraria Bertrand, 1981.

9. See Virginia Woolf, *A Room of One's Own* (London: Penguin Classics, 2000).

10. This line featured in the first edition of Nobre's collection *Só* (Alone) but was subsequently revised and dropped from later editions. See António Nobre, *Só* (Oporto: Livraria Civilização Editora, 1983), 19, n1.

11. See Rui Guedes, *Acerca de Florbela* (Lisbon: Dom Quixote, 1986), 48.

12. Translator's note: The word "martírio" here is a pun on the words for passion flower and martyrdom.

13. Christine Battersby, *Gender and Genius. Towards a Feminist Aesthetics* (London: The Women's Press, 1989), 152.

14. The intertextual dialogue between the two poets is documented in Maria Lúcia Dal Farra, "A Interlocução de Florbela Espanca com a Poética de Américo Durão," *Colóquio/ Letras* 132–33 (1994).

15. See Florbela Espanca, *Obras Completas,* 6 vols., vol. 2 (Lisbon: Dom Quixote, 1985–86), 72–73.

16. Nobre, *Só,* 19.

17. The persona of a Poetisa recurs, however, in the short story "À margem dum soneto." See Florbela Espanca, *Obras Completas,* 6 vols., vol. 3 (Lisbon: Dom Quixote, 1985–86), 85–92.

18. Antero de Quental, *Poesias de Antero de Quental,* ed. Maria Madalena Gonçalves (Lisbon: Editorial Comunicação, 1981), 127. See also José Rodrigues de Paiva, ed. *Estudos sobre Florbela Espanca* (Recife: Associação de Estudos Portugueses Jordão Emerenciano, 1995).

19. Luís de Camões, *Os Lusíadas* (Oporto: Porto Editora, 1980), 337.

20. Quental, *Poesias de Antero de Quental,* 132.

21. Nicole Loraux, *Les mères en deuil* (Paris: Seuil, 1990).

22. Nobre, *Só*, 20.

23. We may wish to contrast Espanca's negative use of the image of "extreme unction" with that of her contemporary Sá-Carneiro, who was able to recast this moment as a new beginning in his opening poem "Partida" from the collection *Dispersão:* "And in an extreme unction of a broadened soul, to travel other senses, other lives" [E numa extrema-unção de alma ampliada, viajar outros sentidos, outras vidas]. See Mário de Sá Carneiro, *Obra Poética de Mário de Sá Carneiro* (Lisbon: Presença, 1985), 57.

24. Luís de Camões, *Lírica Completa* ed. Maria de Lurdes Saraiva, 3 vols. (Lisbon: Imprensa Nacional-Casa da Moeda, 1980–81), vol. 3, 61.

25. Espanca was fully aware of the scorn that would fall upon a woman who was sexually active outside marriage. Indeed, she was to experience it first hand in her own life: when she left her second husband António Guimarães to live with Mário Lage, her father and brother severed all contact with her. Contact was only resumed two years later, when she officialized her liaison through marriage.

26. Judith Butler, *Antigone's Claim: Kinship between Life and Death* (New York: Columbia University Press, 2000), 55.

27. Edgar Allan Poe, "The Philosophy of Composition," in *Essays and Reviews* (New York: Literary Classics of the United States, 1984 [1846]), 19.

28. For further details, see Cláudia Pazos Alonso, "*Tanto poeta em verso me cantou:* The Role of Florbela Espanca's University Colleagues in her Poetic Development," *Portuguese Studies* 11 (1995).

29. João Boto de Carvalho, *Sol Poente* (Lisbon: n.p., 1919).

30. An alternative version featured in the proofs but discarded, possibly by her editor, reads rather more aggressively: "In revolt, tragic, gloomy / Like the infernal gallop of the wind" [Revoltada, trágica, sombria / Como galopes infernais de vento]. See Espanca, *Obras Completas* vol. 2, 150.

31. "Exaltação' was a last-minute addition. For further details see Anna Klobucka, *O Formato Mulher,* (Coimbra: Angelus Novo, 2009), p.132.

32. For further details see chapter 1 of Cláudia Pazos Alonso, *Imagens do Eu na Poesia de Florbela Espanca* (Lisbon: Imprensa Nacional Casa da Moeda, 1997).

33. Espanca. *Obras Completas* (Lisbon: Dom Quixote, 1985–86), vol. VI 69–70.

34. The version of this sonnet published in *Europa* in 1925 still uses "Soror Saudade" in quotations marks.

35. Judith Teixeira, *Decadência* (Lisbon: n.p., 1923). For further details see Fernando Cabral Martins, ed. *Dicionário de Fernando Pessoa e do Modernismo Português* (Lisbon: Caminho, 2008). See also Cláudia Pazos Alonso, "Modernist Differences: Judith Teixeira and Florbela Espanca" in *Portuguese Modernisms. Multiple Perspectives on Literature and the Visual Arts,* edited by Steffen Dix and Jerónimo Pizarro (Oxford: Legenda, forthcoming)

36. Isabel Allegro de Magalhães, "Florbela Espanca e a Subversão de Alguns *Topoi,*" in *A Planície e o Abismo: Actas do Congresso sobre Florbela Espanca realizado na Universidade de Évora,* ed. Óscar Lopes et al, (Lisbon: Vega, 1997), 223.

37. Fernando Pessoa, *Poesias* (Lisbon: Ática, 1980), 56.

38. For a more detailed discussion of this theme, see Maria da Conceição Lopes da Silva, "The Sexual Being in *Charneca em Flor,*" *Portuguese Studies* 20 (2004).

39. Preface to Florbela Espanca, *Diário do Último Ano, seguido de um poema sem título* (Amadora: Livraria Bertrand, 1981).

40. See also the posthumous "Slave" [Escrava (283)] whose title and theme suggest an

intertextual dialogue with Camões's well-known piece "Aquela Cativa" in Camões, *Lírica Completa* vol. 1, 246–47.

41. Jorge de Sena, *Florbela Espanca ou a Expressão do Feminino na Poesia Portuguesa* (Oporto: Biblioteca Fenianos, 1947).

42. Jean Chevalier and Alain Gheerbrant, *Dictionnaire des symboles*, 2nd ed. (Paris: Robert Laffont, 1982).

43. This is a line from "Amor é fogo que arde sem se ver" by Luís de Camões, *Sonetos* (Lisbon: Europa-América, 1990), 56.

44. Ibid.

45. Florbela Espanca, *Obras Completas*, 6 vols., vol. 6 (Lisbon: Dom Quixote, 1985–86), 195–6.

46. Fernando Pessoa and António Botto, eds., *Antologia de Poemas Portugueses Modernos* (Coimbra: Editorial Nobel, 1944).

47. It would be equally worthwhile to consider the possible intertextual dialogue between Sonnet VII and Pessoa's sonnet "Abdicação." See Pessoa, *Poesias*, 217. While it is impossible to determine whether Espanca knew the latter, one cannot help noticing that the line "the shadow of a calm twilight" [A sombra calma dum entardecer] seems to mirror Pessoa's closing line "to return to the calm Night / like a landscape when the day is dying" [regressar à Noite calma/ Como a paisagem ao morrer do dia]. Crucially, however, Espanca's sonnet does not articulate sense of abdication as textualized by Pessoa, but rather female empowerment "over his dead body" so to speak, that is to say, over the dead body of canonical male texts.

48. See Espanca, *Reliquiae*. This collection brings together several scattered sonnets found at the time of her death, but Espanca had no say over its publication or indeed the ordering of the individual poems.

49. Anthony Soares, "Was Florbela's Death Fatal? A Study of Death in the Works of Florbela Espanca," in *Women, Literature and Culture in the Portuguese-Speaking World*, ed. Cláudia Pazos Alonso (Lampeter: Edwin Mellen Press, 1996), 62.

50. Elisabeth Bronfen, *Over her Dead Body. Death, Femininity and the Aesthetic.* (Manchester: Manchester University Press, 1992), 142.

51. See Butler, *Antigone's Claim*, 55.

Chapter 2. Irene Lisboa

1. Ana Paula Ferreira, "A 'literatura feminina' nos anos quarenta: uma história de exclusão" in *A Urgência de Contar*, ed. by Ana Paula Ferreira (Lisbon: Caminho, 2000).

2. For a fuller analysis of this issue, see Chatarina Edfeldt, *Uma história na História. Representações da autoria feminina na História da Literatura Portuguesa do século XX* (Montijo: Câmara Municipal de Montijo, 2006).

3. This correspondence, which remains mostly unpublished, is available in the National Library in Lisbon. See Cartas de José Régio a Irene Lisboa, E24/136–172, Cartas de João Gaspar Simões a Irene Lisboa, E24/184–218.

4. Paula Morão, *Irene Lisboa. Vida e Escrita* (Lisbon: Editorial Presença, 1989).

5. Morão's Editorial Presença editions of the works of Irene Lisboa are those used throughout this chapter with the exception of "Um dito" originally published in Irene Lisboa, *Esta Cidade!*, vol. 4 (Lisbon: Editorial Presença, 1995 [1942]). Reference to this short story in this chapter is to "Um Dito," in *A Urgência de Contar*, ed. Ana Paula Ferreira (Lisbon:

Caminho, 2000). All subsequent references to this work are cited parenthetically within the text.

6. Her early publications were signed Irene Lisboa or I.L. The use of a male pseudonym, after her return from abroad, may have been an attempt to give greater authority to her controversial ideas on education.

7. Irene Lisboa, *Um dia e outro dia . . ., diário de uma mulher e Outono havias de vir (latente triste)* vol. 1 (Lisbon: Editorial Presença, 1991 [1936] [1937]); *Solidão—Notas do punho de uma mulher* 4th ed., vol. 2 (Lisbon: Editorial Presença, 1992 [1939]). All subsequent references to these works are cited parenthetically within the text. All translations into English in this chapter are our own with the exception of the poem "Irony" translated by Richard Zenith in the appendix to Chapter 2.

8. Lisboa, *Um dia,* 283.

9. Lisboa, *Começa uma vida* vol. 3 (Lisbon: Editorial Presença, 1992 [1940]). All subsequent references to this work are cited parenthetically within the text.

10. Lisboa, *Apontamentos,* vol. 8 (Lisbon: Editorial Presença, 1998 [1943]).

11. This image may constitute an oblique intertextual dialogue with Florbela Espanca's sonnet "Tarde no mar" [Afternoon by the Seaside], from *Charneca em flor* (1931), where the middle two verses gruesomely describe the sun as a murderer of virginal white walls: "And on the white houses which it sets ablaze, the sun, / Draws the blood-stained hands of a murderer!" [E o sol, nas casas brancas que incendeia, / Desenha mãos sangrentas de assassino! (217)].

12. Espanca also engaged in an intertextual gendered dialogue with Verlaine in her sonnet "Mistério" [Mystery], 219.

13. Christine Battersby, *Gender and Genius. Towards a Feminist Aesthetics* (London: The Women's Press, 1989), 3.

14. When this poem was subsequently published in *Seara Nova,* the line length was modified in order to make it look more like a conventional poem in terms of layout. See Irene Lisboa, *Folhas Soltas da Seara Nova—1929/1955,* ed. by Paula Morão (Lisbon: Imprensa Nacional/Casa de Moeda, 1986), 134.

15. Battersby, *Gender and Genius,* 3.

16. It may be pertinent to note, however, that halfway through *Solidão* she described the kind of prose texts that she had in mind as "even looser and freer than verse" [ainda mais soltos e mais livres que versos (84)].

17. "I am the proud one, the dissatisfied, the one that / everyone and everything wounds / Ah, but without having anything flower-like" [Sou a orgulhosa, a descontente, aquela a quem / tudo e todos ferem. / Ai, mas sem nada ter de flor]." Lisboa, *Um dia,* 329.

18. Pessoa himself famously impersonated an illiterate girl in the "Carta da Corcunda para o Serralheiro." See Fernando Pessoa, *Prosa Íntima e de Autoconhecimento* (Lisbon: Assírio & Alvim, 2007).

19. For further details, see Ana Paula Ferreira, "Home Bound: The Construct of Femininity in the Estado Novo," *Portuguese Studies* 12 (1996).

20. Although she continued to collaborate in *Seara Nova* sporadically, mainly with writings on education, it is perhaps not a coincidence that she seemed unable to find a publisher for another decade, until 1955.

21. Irene Lisboa, *Voltar atrás para quê?,* vol. 4 (Lisbon: Editorial Presença, 1994 [1956]). All subsequent references to this work are cited parenthetically within the text.

22. The novella was first serialized in the pages of *O Diabo* between January and July 1939. All future references to the work are to this 1992 Presença edition and are cited parenthetically within the text.

23. Ellen W Sapega, *Consensus and Debate in Salazar's Portugal. Visual and Literary Negotiations of the National Text, 1933–1948* (University Park: The Pennsylvania State University Press, 2008).

24. His success is very succinctly evoked by the narrator, who empathizes with her ailing godmother, now deprived of her own wealth. Tellingly, however, the traumatic repercussions for the two daughters are only touched upon in one laconic sentence at the end of the paragraph: "And naturally we were not legitimized, since this no longer mattered to my father" [E nós não fomos naturalmente perfilhadas, porque já não era isso que interessava ao meu pai (79)].

25. In so doing, her account shares many parallels with Vergílio Ferreira's *Manhã Submersa* published the year before, in 1954. He too chose a fictional alter ego in order to recount the trauma of his oppressive formative years in a seminary. See Vergílio Ferreira, *Manhã Submersa* (Amadora: Bertrand, 1980 [1954]).

26. Throughout the text, Esperança remains very explicitly referred to only as a mistress, even though Irene's father had married her.

27. See also the chapter on Irene Lisboa in Sapega, *Consensus and Debate.*

28. Irene Lisboa, *Solidão II* (Lisbon: Portugália, s.d, 1966), 248.

Chapter 3. Agustina Bessa Luís

1. The "parallel text" that developed around *A Sibila* was Bessa Luis's own foundational success in the masculine field of literary fiction. In this sense, we may discern a playful semi-identification between Agustina Bessa Luís and her main character in *A Sibila,* Joaquina Augusta, whose name she partly shares. Indeed the association of Bessa Luís and her sybil became deeply rooted in the national literary imaginary with the writer being commonly characterized as a "sybil," including by feminist critics, for many years to come. See, for example, Maria Teresa Horta, "A Sibila de Agustina Bessa Luís," *Mulheres* 49 (1982). All English translations in this chapter are our own unless otherwise stated.

2. António José Saraiva and Óscar Lopes, *História da Literatura Portuguesa,* 1st ed. (Oporto: Porto Editora, 1954).

3 Saraiva and Lopes, *História da Literatura Portuguesa,* 2nd ed. (Oporto: Porto Editora, 1956).

4. Saraiva and Lopes, *História da Literatura Portuguesa,* 3rd ed., (Oporto: Porto Editora 1965).

5. Saraiva and Lopes, *História,* 1st ed., 872–73.

6. Saraiva and Lopes, *História,* 2nd ed., 948.

7. Ibid., 944.

8. Saraiva and Lopes, *História,* 3rd ed., 1076.

9. Ibid., 1075.

10. As Edfeldt notes, Saraiva and Lopes, in later editions of the *História da Literatura Portuguesa,* establish a clear "break in the genealogy of this [women's] literature" in the 1950s, which seems effectively to enshrine the emergence of Bessa Luís and others of her generation as the officialized "new beginning" of women's prose writing of quality in Portugal, downplaying the importance and literary value of the Republican feminist generation who had preceded them. See Chatarina Edfeldt, *Uma história na História. Representações da autoria feminina na História da Literatura Portuguesa do século XX* (Montijo: Câmara Municipal de Montijo, 2006), 83–84. This foundational status has also been taken up and reinforced by

women's and feminist scholarship, engaging at various levels, as we will see, with the problems Bessa Luís presents for any straightforward feminist recuperation. See for example: Horta, "A Sibila de Agustina Bessa Luís."; Isabel Allegro de Magalhães, *O Tempo das Mulheres: a dimensão temporal na escrita feminina contemporânea: ficção portuguesa* (Lisbon: Imprensa Nacional-Casa da Moeda, 1987); Isabel Allegro de Magalhães, *O Sexo dos Textos e outras leituras* (Lisbon: Caminho, 1995); Laura Fernanda Bulger, *A Sibila. Uma Superação Inconclusa* (Lisbon: Guimarães Editores, 1990); *As Máscaras da Memória. Estudos em torno da obra de Agustina* (Lisbon: Guimarães Editores, 1998); Hilary Owen, "Uma Inconclusão Superadora: A Machereyan Feminist Reading of *A Sibila* by Agustina Bessa Luís" *Bulletin of Hispanic Studies, Liverpool* 75 (1998); Catherine Dumas, *Estética e Personagens nos romances de Agustina Bessa Luís: espelhismos* (Oporto: Campo das Letras, 2002).

11. Agustina Bessa Luís, "A mãe de um rio," in *A Brusca* (Lisbon: Editorial Verbo, 1971). "A mãe de um rio" was also filmed by Bessa Luís's long-time cinema collaborator Manoel de Oliveira as part of the film *Inquietude*, in 1998. See Sérgio C. Andrade, *Ao Correr do Tempo. Duas Décadas com Manoel de Oliveira* (Lisbon: Portugália Editora, 2008), 92.

12. Agustina Bessa Luís, *A Sibila*, 12th ed. (Lisbon: Guimarães Editores, n.d.). All subsequent references to this work are cited parenthetically within the text. Augustina Bessa Luís, *Vale Abraão* (Lisbon: Guimarães Editores, 1991). All subsequent references to this work are cited parenthetically within the text.

13. Silvina Rodrigues Lopes, *Exercícios de Aproximação* (Lisbon: Edições Vendaval, 2003), 119.

14. In this respect, we propose, in gender terms, something like Renato Rosaldo's famous definition of imperial nostalgia whereby, "agents of colonialism . . . often display nostalgia for the colonized culture as it was traditionally (that is when they first encountered it). The peculiarity of their yearning, of course, is that agents of colonialism long for the very forms of life they intentionally altered or destroyed." See Renato Rosaldo, "Imperialist Nostalgia," *Representations* 26 (1989): 107–8.

15. Battersby, *Gender and Genius,* 3.

16. Isabel Pires de Lima, "Agustina, a Conservadora Subversiva," *MeaLibra. Revista de Cultura* 21 (2007).

17. Agustina Bessa Luís, *Fanny Owen* (Lisbon: Guimarães & Ca. Editores, 1979).

18. The following all refer to this at different levels: Bulger, *Superação;* Magalhães, *O Tempo das Mulheres;* Dumas, *Estética e Personagens.*

19. Dumas, *Estética e Personagens,* 69–70.

20. On Bessa Luís's aphoristic and moralizing narrative voice, see also ibid; Bulger, *Superação.*

21. Eduardo Lourenço, "Agustina Bessa Luís ou o Neo-Romantismo," *Colóquio/Letras* 26 (1963): 51. For an insightful account of the continuities linking Bessa Luís's new romanticism with nineteenth-century Portuguese and other European romantic precedents, and analyzing her postmodernist strategies in this context, see also Álvaro Manuel Machado, *Do Romantismo aos Romantismos em Portugal. Ensaios de tipologia comparativista* (Lisbon: Presença, 1996), 149–74.

22. Lourenço, "Agustina Bessa Luís ou o Neo-Romantismo." The tracing of the national canon-building impulse to nineteenth-century Romanticism is of course long-established, as Edfeldt points out: "Literary historiography, as a discipline and an historical genre, is a product of Romanticism and, throughout the Positivist era, it was understood as a project designed to construct and define national identity." See Edfeldt, *Uma história na História,* 23.

23. The Marxist-Feminist Literature Collective, "Women's Writing. *Jane Eyre, Villette,*

Shirley and *Aurora Leigh,"* in *Marxist Literary Theory,* ed. Terry Eagleton and Drew Milne (Oxford: Blackwell, 1996), 344.

24. Bulger, *Superação,* 136.

25. See Magalhães, *O Tempo das Mulheres,* 217.

26. The metaphor of Abraham as the founding biblical patriarch par excellence is, of course, even more central to *Vale Abraão.* On the importance of the Abraham reference in this latter novel, see Carolyn Kendrick, "Refuting the Myth of Motherhood in Portuguese Literature. A Study of Agustina Bessa Luís' *Vale Abraão," Rocky Mountain Review of Language and Literature* 57, no. 2 (2003).

27. For Friedrich Nietzsche, Prometheus represents true power and creativity. See Friedrich Nietzsche, *The Birth of Tragedy* ed. and trans. Douglas Smith (Oxford: Oxford University Press, 2000).

28. In this respect Bessa Luís's views seem to predict those she expressed in more overtly social terms in her contribution in 1968 to *Sobre a Condição da Mulher Portuguesa,* a series of essays by different male and female writers of that period on the state of Portuguese womanhood. Here Bessa Luís expresses a strong belief in rigidly differentiated and complementary gender roles. Her response to the growing fear of 1960's women's sexual liberation and economic independence through work outside the household is twofold. On the one hand she declares it to be nothing new, in relation to the social latitude afforded women, including single mothers, sustaining the family in the female-headed rural households of high-emigration regions. At the same time, in urban environments, coupled with 1960s technological advance and consumerism, women's emancipation is treated as a symptom of modernity running amok, the bad influence of Northern Europe, and a threat to social order, with women responsible for the crisis and degeneration in respect of masculine identity. See Isabel da Nóbrega, Isabel Martins, Augusto Abelaira, Sérgio Ferreira Ribeiro, Natália Nunes, Agustina Bessa Luís, Maria da Conceição H. Gouveia, *Sobre a Condição da Mulher Portuguesa* (Lisbon: Editorial Estampa, 1968), 83.

29. Where *A Sibila* does pose a more challenging alternative for the feminist reader is in the gaps and inconsistencies that emerge from the textual dialogue it establishes between the different aesthetic conventions of Realism, Romanticism, and Gothicism upon which it draws, and the ideologies these represent. For a more detailed development of this argument, see Owen, "Inconclusão Superadora," 203. Here Owen draws on Pierre Macherey to suggest that *A Sibila*'s gaps and disjunctures between narrative modes reveal the novel's irreconcilable ideological inconsistencies and clashes, particularly concerning sexual identity and gendered power relations. Following Bulger's lead on the textual lacuna of Quina's sexuality, Owen claims that *A Sibila*'s interrogative deployment of specific Gothic images and tropes can be explored for signs of the absence and repression of Quina's sexuality at the heart of the novel.

30. Óscar Lopes, *Os Sinais e os Sentidos. Literatura Portuguesa do Século XX* (Lisbon: Caminho, 1986), 156.

31. Agustina Bessa Luís, *Florbela Espanca* (Lisbon: Guimarães, 1984 [1979]). All subsequent references are to this 1984 edition and are cited parenthetically within the text.

32. As Dumas writes of Bessa Luís, the topic of Florbela "was imposed on her." See Catherine Dumas, "Florbela Visitada por Agustina: a mulher poeta e os mitos," in *A Planície e o Abismo. Actas do Congresso sobre Florbela Espanca realizado na Universidade de Évora, de 7 a 9 de Dezembro de 1994,* ed. Óscar Lopes, et al. (Lisbon: Vega, 1997), 196.

33. Battersby, *Gender and Genius,* 70.

34. Dumas, "Florbela Visitada por Agustina: a mulher poeta e os mitos," 204.

35. Agustina Bessa Luís, *Camilo: Génio e Figura* (Cruz Quebrada: Casa das Letras, 2008).

36. Elizabeth A. Fay, *A Feminist Introduction to Romanticism* (Oxford: Blackwell, 1998), 4.

37. Ibid., 6.

38. See Andrade, *Ao Correr do Tempo*, 92.

39. See Bessa Luís, *Camilo: Génio e Figura;* Maria Amélia Campos, *Ana, a Lúcida. Biografia de Ana Plácido, a mulher fatal de Camilo* (Lisbon: Parceria A. M. Pereira, 2008); Manuel Tavares Teles, *Camilo e Ana Plácido* (Oporto: Caixotim, 2008).

40. For the various historical sources on the events in this novel, see Magalhães, *O Sexo dos Textos*, 125.

41. See Maria de Fátima Marinho, *O Romance Histórico em Portugal* (Oporto: Campo das Letras, 1999), 174.

42. Magalhães, *O Sexo dos Textos*, 136. For further discussion of Camilo's relations with Fanny Owen and José Augusto Pinto de Magalhães, see David Gibson Frier, *Visions of the Self in the Novels of Camilo Castelo Branco (1850–1870)* (Lewiston: Edwin Mellen Press, 1996), 129. For specific discussion of Bessa Luís's treatment of the Camilo original, see also Magalhães, *O Tempo das Mulheres*, 228–55; Bulger, *Máscaras da Memória*, 9–28; Marinho, *Romance Histórico*, 174; Magalhães, *O Sexo dos Textos*, 123–36.

43. J. Costa Gomes is an interesting example of local protest in Oporto against Bessa Luís's readings of the Camilo and Fanny story in this novel. Challenging the "incoherences" of the "illustrious woman writer," he objects as follows to her depiction of one particular scene: "It is from this very place that the writer Agustina Bessa Luís in her recent book FANNY OWEN, tells us that, on entering the house, Maria Owen caught sight of Camilo sitting on the church steps. Good grief! You would need the eyes of a lynx to recognize a seated figure at that distance. So I would rather doubt the visibility of the location. And as there are buildings also blocking the view, I would remain very dubious." See J. Costa Gomes, *A Tragédia Romântica de Fanny Owen* (Oporto: Associação Cultural "Amigos de Gaia," 1980), 7–9.

44. On the gendered definition of mastery itself as central to feminist rereadings of Romanticism studies, see Fay, to *Feminist Introduction Romanticism*, 13.

45. We have drawn, for this account, on the literary historical research of Frier and Magalhães. See Frier, *Visions of the Self in the Novels of Camilo Castelo Branco (1850–1870)*, 129–31. See also Magalhães, *O Sexo dos Textos*, 125–26.

46. Mário de Sá-Carneiro, *A Confissão de Lúcio* (Mem Martins: Edições Europa-América 1989).

47. We rely substantially here on Fernando Arenas's ground-breaking reading of Mário de Sá-Carneiro's modernist classic, *A Confissão de Lúcio*, in terms of sexual ambivalence and coded homoerotics. Referring to it as a work in which "homosexual desire is simultaneously present throughout the whole of the novel, and nowhere" (159), Arenas argues that the prism of homophobia which distorts same-sex desire between the two men, "reveals a misogynistic logic which makes 'the woman' indispensable—as in the love triangle Lúcio-Marta-Ricardo—at the same time as she is manipulated, negotiated and finally, ontologically eliminated" (165). See Fernando Arenas, "Onde existir?: a (im)possibilidade excessiva do desejo homoerótico na ficção de Mário de Sá-Carneiro," *Metamorfoses* 6 (2005).

48. Laura Bulger has also noted the desire that links the two male characters in *Fanny Owen*. See Bulger, *Máscaras da Memória*, 18.

49. Andrew Elfenbein, *Romantic Genius: The Prehistory of a Homosexual Role* (New York: Columbia University Press, 1999), 14.

50. Elfenbein has pointed out in respect of Oscar Wilde's famous declaration of genius: "without ever mentioning sex between men or women, eighteenth-century treatises on genius

set in motion an image that would play a large role in defining the homosexual's supposed character. For example, when asked by a customs officer what he had to declare, Wilde did not mention his homosexuality but purportedly answered, 'I have nothing to declare except my genius'." See ibid., 6.

51. Jacques Lacan, "The function and field of speech and language in psychoanalysis," in *Écrits. A Selection* trans. Alan Sheridan (London: Routledge, 1977), 104.

52. We define fetish here in classic Freudian psychoanalytical terms whereby "what is substituted for the sexual object is some part of the body (such as the foot or hair) which is in general very inappropriate for sexual purposes, or some inanimate object which bears an assignable relation to the person whom it replaces and preferably to that person's sexuality (e.g. a piece of clothing or underlinen)." (249) See Sigmund Freud, "Three Essays on the Theory of Sexuality," in *The Freud Reader*, ed. Peter Gay (London: Vintage, 1995), 249. Jan Campbell has also usefully defined fetishism more broadly in the racial and postcolonial context as the "substitution and the desire for some kind of original wholeness, ambivalently dealing with the threat of division through difference, race and culture." See also Jan Campbell, *Arguing with the Phallus: Feminist, Queer and Postcolonial Theory. A Psychoanalytic Contribution* (London: Zed Books, 2000), 195.

53. Elisabeth Bronfen, *Over her Dead Body, Femininity and the Aesthetic* (Manchester: Manchester University Press, 1992), 97.

54. Ibid.

55. See Magalhães for different renditions of it in *O Sexo dos Textos,* 135.

56. Mary S. Gossy, *The Untold Story. Women and Theory in Golden Age Texts* (Ann Arbor: University of Michigan Press, 1989), 49.

57. Gossy, writing about hymen-mending in the famous Spanish early modern theater text, *La Celestina,* takes issue here with Jacques Derrida's famous equation in *Dissemination* of the hymen with the "entre" or undecidable "between" of the text. Refuting Derrida directly, she remarks "metaphorically a hymen in a vagina 'carries all the force of the operation' of phallic analysis in a way that the alternatives Derrida suggests [marriage or crime or identity or difference] do not. Both meanings of hymen—marriage and virginity—are constructs controlled by patriarchy that objectify woman." See Ibid., 47–48. See also Mary S. Gossy, *Empire on the Verge of a Nervous Breakdown* (Liverpool: Liverpool University Press, 2009), 24–36.

58. See Andrade, *Ao Correr do Tempo,* 93.

59. Ibid., 82. Andrade is citing here from an interview with Oliveira in the Portuguese newspaper *Público,* January 6, 1992, given at the time the film was released.

60. Teresa Ribeiro da Silva e Régis Salado, drawing on Gérard Genette and other narratological sources, has written an excellent and particularly detailed close analysis of the multilayered interactions between Flaubertian hypotext and Bessa Luís's hypertext, tracking what she terms the "bovaremes" discernible in *Vale Abraão.* See Teresa Ribeiro da Silva e Régis Salado, "Portrait de l'auteur en lecteur: *Madame Bovary* au miroir de *Vale Abraão,*" *Intercâmbio. Núcleo de Estudos Franceses da Universidade do Porto* (1991), 85–86.

61. Bronfen, *Dead Body,* 157.

62. On the Abraham references in this work and the suppression of matrilinear culture, see Kendrick, "Myth of Motherhood."

63. The classic French Feminist theoretical perspective on this lack of a female cultural symbolic is that taken by Luce Irigaray. See, for example, Luce Irigaray, "An Ethics of Sexual Difference," in *An Ethics of Sexual Difference,* trans. Carolyn Burke and Gillian C. Gill (London: Athlone, 1993).

64. On the paradigmatic underpinnings and commonalities of European realist tradition,

see Bill Overton, *The Novel of Female Adultery. Love and Gender in Continental European Fiction, 1830–1900* (Houndmills and New York: MacMillan and St. Martin's 1996).

65. It is tempting to see here a comically inverted self-citation, perhaps, of that other famous rural "aunt" in Bessa Luís's fiction, the sybil, Joaquina Augusta. The name also, of course, evokes the first name of Agustina Bessa Luís herself.

66. Bronfen, *Dead Body* 159.

67. See Overton, *Novel of Female Adultery*, 3,8.

68. Bronfen, *Dead Body*, 195.

69. Catherine Dumas has produced a detailed and enlightening discussion of the use of water imagery as it relates to language and semiotics, throughout the works of Agustina Bessa Luís, but particularly in *A Sibila*. See Dumas, *Estética e Personagens*, 86–105.

70. Bronfen, *Dead Body*, 161.

71. Ibid., 160.

72. On androgyny and performance see Bulger, *Máscaras da Memória*, 47–55.

73. Salado, "Portrait de l'auteur en lecteur," 97.

74. Judith Butler, *Bodies that Matter. On the Discursive Limits of "Sex"* (London: Routledge, 1993), 98–99.

75. Ibid., 108.

76. Ibid., 102.

77. Maria Semblano has been seen by both Kendrick and Bulger in humanistic terms as the example of what Ema fails to achieve, a sense of female identity, and fulfillment through intellectual companionship with Carlos Paiva. However, it is noteworthy that this relationship collapses following Ema's death, as Carlos also dies two years later, recalling his fictional source, Charles Bovary, and also expressing his fidelity to the image left to posterity by Ema. See Bulger, *Máscaras da Memória;* Kendrick, "Myth of Motherhood."

CHAPTER 4. NATÁLIA CORREIA

1. Natália Correia, *A Pécora*, 2nd ed. (Lisbon: O Jornal, 1990); *A Madona* (Lisbon: Editorial Notícias, 2000); *O Armistício* (Lisbon: Dom Quixote, 1985); *O Progresso de Édipo. Poema Dramático* (Lisbon: N.p., 1957). All subsequent references to these works are cited parenthetically within the text. All translations into English in this chapter are our own unless otherwise stated.

2. Fernando Pinto do Amaral, *100 Livros Portugueses do Século XX: 100 Portuguese Books of the 20th Century* (Lisbon: Camões, 2002), 29.

3. Natália Correia, ed. *O surrealismo na poesia portuguesa* (Lisbon: Frenesi, 2002).

4. From the observations in Edfeldt's study, it would seem that Correia is most frequently remembered in Portuguese literary histories and anthologies for the influential role she played in the Portuguese surrealist movement, rather than for her polemical writings on sex and gender. See Chatarina Edfeldt, *Uma história na História. Representações da autoria feminina na História da Literatura Portuguesa do século XX* (Montijo: Câmara Municipal de Montijo, 2006), 100.

5. Natália Correia, ed. *Antologia de Poesia Portuguesa Erótica e Satírica (dos Cancioneiros Medievais à Actualidade)* (Lisbon: Fernando Ribeiro de Mello/Afrodite, n.d.). See also *Antologia Poética*, ed. Fernando Pinto do Amaral (Lisbon: Dom Quixote, 2002), 32.

6. Natália Correia, *O Encoberto* (Lisbon: Fernando Ribeiro de Mello Afrodite, 1977 [1969]).

7. *D. João e Julieta* (Lisbon: Sociedade Portuguesa de Autores/Dom Quixote, 1999).

8. See Duarte Vidal, *O Processo das Três Marias. Defesa de Maria Isabel Barreno* (Lisbon: Editorial Futura, 1974).

9. For an insightful discussion of Natália Correia's prochoice stance on abortion, see Fernando Rebelo, "A discussão do aborto na voz de Natália Correia," in *Natália Correia, 10 anos depois* . . . ed. Secção Francesa de D.E.P.E.R. (Oporto: Faculdade de Letras da Universidade do Porto, 2003). For the João Morgado poem, see Correia, *Antologia Poética,* 194.

10. See the biographical section of Correia, *Antologia Poética.* Excellent biographical and photographic material on Correia is also available in Ana Paula Costa, *Natália Correia. Fotobiografia* (Lisbon: Dom Quixote, 2005).

11. Luís Adriano Carlos, "A Mátria e o Mal," in *Natália Correia, 10 anos depois* . . . ed. Secção Francesa de D.E.P.E.R. (Oporto: Faculdade de Letras da Universidade do Porto, 2003).

12. See Ania Loomba, *Colonialism/Postcolonialism* (London: Routledge, 1998), 215–18. Loomba notes that, "as mothers to the nation, women are granted limited agency" (218).

13. Madalena Braz Teixeira, "As diferentes faces de Eva," in *Mátria de Natália Correia,* ed. Madalena Braz Teixeira (Lisbon: Museu Nacional de Traje, 2000), 11.

14. This is also the image portrayed in Teresa Tomé's Azorean documentary, *Natália Correia. A Senhora da Rosa.*

15. Correia, *Antologia Poética,* 247. All subsequent references to *Sonetos Românticos* are to this 2002 *Antologia Poética* edition and are cited parenthetically within the text.

16. Natália Correia, *Não Percas a Rosa. Diário e algo mais (25 de abril de 1974–20 de dezembro de 1975)* (Lisbon: Dom Quixote, 1978); Paulo de Medeiros, "The Diary and Portuguese Women Writers," *Portuguese Studies* 14 (1998): 236.

17. Medeiros, "The Diary," 236.

18. In the various journalistic essays collected in *Breve História da Mulher e outros Escritos,* Correia reveals considerable ambivalence about women's emancipation through the ages. She recognizes the role played by enlightenment humanist and positivist philosophies in women's liberation, and the educational and suffragette achievements of the first wave. However, she harshly criticizes women's subsequent assimilation in the work-place and public life to male social values writing, "there is no doubt that feminism, conceived as a caricature of male privilege, was a betrayal of woman. A betrayal involuntarily committed by the champions of feminism who gave her doctrinal and legal access to a markedly masculine culture, in which women's production would always be considered inferior." See Natália Correia, *Breve História da Mulher e Outros Escritos* (Lisbon: Parceria A. M. Pereira, 2003), 146.

19. As Graça Abranches notes, the "true" versus "false" feminist debates of the early twentieth century revealed "a sense of how urgent the 'de-foreignerization' of feminism was, resulting largely from the importance of the association, in the public imagination, between feminist ideals, and representations of women who were asexual, masculine and denatured—in short, English." See Graça Abranches, "Homens, mulheres e mestras inglesas," in *Entre ser e estar: raízes, percursos e discursos da identidade,* ed. Maria Irene Ramalho and António Sousa Ribeiro (Oporto: Afrontamento Edições, 2001), 282.

20. Correia, *Breve História,* 179–80.

21. See ibid., 157–63. This was originally published as "O Manifesto S.C.U.M" in *A Capital, suplemento Literatura e Arte,* Lisbon, April 15, 1970.

22. Texts such as Solanas' *Manifesto,* translated into Portuguese from French and Italian, appeared in the feminist anthology, *Mulheres contra Homens?* (Lisbon: Dom Quixote, 1971). Correia must have had access to Solanas earlier than this, however, since her piece was first published in 1970.

23. Correia, *Breve História*, 15.

24. Antónia de Sousa, Bruno da Ponte, Dórdio Guimarães, and Edite Soeiro, ed. *Entrevistas a Natália Correia* (Lisbon: Parceria A. M. Pereira, 2004), 65. "A Missão da Mulher é Assombrar," in *Entrevistas*, 65. Originally published in the *Diário de Notícias* supplement *Domingo*. On Correia's sexuality see Almeida, *Homossexuais*, 120.

25. Natália Correia, ed. *A Mulher. Antologia Poética* (Lisbon: Artemágica, 2005).

26. For more recent, post-Irigaray, thinking on the Greek construction of the somatic as feminine, and the recuperation of symbolic female figures from the Classics, see Adriana Cavarero, *In Spite of Plato. A Feminist Rewriting of Ancient Philosophy*, trans. Serena Anderlini-D'Onofrio and Áine O'Healey (Cambridge: Polity Press, 1995). Correia consistently takes issue with the gendered split of mind and body in both Cartesian and Christian dualism. In the preface to the poetry anthology *A Mulher*, "The Metamorphoses of Venus," she remarks that Christianity made women "merely carnal, the recipient of those forces of seduction that keep virility enslaved to its most base instincts." See Correia, ed. *Mulher*, 14; see also *Breve História*, 148.

27. Carlos, "Mátria e o Mal," 26.

28. Robert Briffault, *The Mothers. The Matriarchal Theory of Social Origins,* ed. Gordon Rattray Taylor (New York: Grosset and Dunlap, 1963).

29. In 1949, the feminist philosopher Simone de Beauvoir was also clear in dismissing the "Golden Age of the Mother" as proposed by Bachofen. De Beauvoir writes, "in truth, that Golden Age of Woman is only a myth. To say that woman was the *Other* is to say that there did not exist between the sexes a reciprocal relation: Earth, Mother, Goddess—she was no fellow creature in man's eyes; it was *beyond* the human realm that her power was affirmed, and she was therefore *outside* of that realm. Society has always been male; political power has always been in the hands of men." See Simone de Beauvoir, *The Second Sex,* trans. H. M. Parshley (Harmondsworth: Penguin, 1984), 102. Nonetheless, the theories of Briffault enjoyed a certain revival among 1960s and 1970s feminists opposing Simone de Beauvoir. See Ann Taylor Allen, "Feminism, Social Science, and the Meanings of Modernity: The Debate on the Origin of the Family in Europe and the United States, 1860–1914," *The American Historical Review* 104, no. 4 (1999): 1111–12.

30. Allen, "Feminism," 1087.

31. Ibid., 1101.

32. See António P. B. F. Dinis, "Friedrich Nietzsche e Natália Correia: dois espíritos livres," *Actas do VI Encontro Luso-Alemão* (2002); José Augusto Mourão, "A sedução do múltiplo. Natália Correia: Literatura e Paganismo," *Colóquio/Letras* 104/105 (1988).

33. Natália Correia, *Onde Está o Menino Jesus?* (Lisbon: Rolim, 1987).

34. Friedrich Nietzsche, *The Birth of Tragedy,* ed. and trans. Douglas Smith (Oxford: Oxford University Press, 2000).

35. See introduction by Douglas Smith, Ibid.

36. Ibid., 59–60.

37. Ibid., 60.

38. See, for example, Christine Battersby, *Gender and Genius. Towards a Feminist Aesthetics* (London: The Women's Press, 1989); Keith Ansell-Pearson, "Nietzsche, Woman and Political Theory," in *Nietzsche, Feminism and Political Theory,* ed. Paul Patton (London: Routledge, 1993).

39. Battersby, *Gender and Genius,* 122.

40. Ibid., 123.

41. Natália Correia, *Uma Estátua para Herodes* (Lisbon: Arcádia, 1974).

42. Friedrich Nietzsche, *Thus Spoke Zarathustra. A Book for Everyone and No One,* trans. R. J. Hollingdale (London: Penguin, 2003), 92.

43. Correia, *Uma Estátua,* 123. It is curious here that Correia felt the need to actually inform her reader that she makes this inversion deliberately. It is possible that she did not trust her reader to know the original Nietzsche well enough to recognize the inversion, or alternatively that she did not trust her reader to believe that her own witty inversion was deliberate and not merely an (all too feminine?) ignorance of the original on her part.

44. Ibid., 108. See also, Dinis, "Friedrich Nietzsche e Natália Correia," 174.

45. Nietzsche, *Zarathustra,* 91.

46. Friedrich Nietzsche, *Beyond Good and Evil,* trans. Walter Kaufmann (New York: Vintage, 1966 [1886]), 89.

47. Correia, *Uma Estátua,* 109.

48. See Luce Irigaray, "The Female Gender," in *Sexes and Genealogies,* trans. Gillian C. Gill (New York: Columbia University Press, 1993), 111.

49. See Luisa Muraro, "Female Genealogies," in *Engaging with Irigaray,* ed. Carolyne Burke, Naomi Schor, and Margaret Whitford (New York: Columbia University Press, 1994), 329.

50. Her first two plays *Dois Reis e um Sono* and *Sucubina e a Teoria do Chapéu* were collaborations with Manuel de Lima.

51. By recasting not the drama of a noble Antigone, but that of an assertive Jocasta, Correia once again has resonances with Robert Briffault's *The Mothers,* in a passage where he questions the absolutism of the incest taboo. See Briffault, *The Mothers,* 59–63.

52. In terms of the Freudian Oedipus complex, the return to wholeness corresponds to the nostalgic infant world of primary narcissism, the mother/child bond, or in anthropological terms, the brief reign of the matriarchate, brought to an end by the paternal intervention of the incest taboo, the threat of castration, and the historical victory of patriarchy. See Sigmund Freud, "Totem and Taboo," in *The Freud Reader,* ed. Peter Gay (London: Vintage, 1995); Rosalind Coward, *Patriarchal Precedents. Sexuality and Social Relations* (London: Routledge and Kegan Paul, 1983).

53. Nietzsche, *The Birth of Tragedy,* 55.

54. Ibid., 54–55.

55. This statement functions in the manner of a prologue although there is no explicit stage instruction as to what it actually is, nor to who should perform it or how. This raises a question as to whether *O Progresso de Édipo* was ever staged or indeed was intended to be. It was self-published in 1957 by Correia in a "dramatic poem" format, familiar from fifteenth century satirical Vicentine verse drama in Portugal. Maria Eugénia Vasques refers to Correia's *Édipo* as Vicentine, but does not identify any staging of it in her exhaustive catalogue of women's drama productions in twentieth-century Portugal. Eugénia Vasques, *Mulheres que Escreveram Teatro no Século XX em Portugal* (Lisbon: Edições Colibri, 2001), 121.

56. Nietzsche, *The Birth of Tragedy,* 53.

57. In her surrealist reading of the play, Maria Fátima de Marinho suggests that Jocasta is virilized by the fact that she takes up the blinding sword, ultimately liberating both of the main characters from their moralistic dramatic history, insofar as Jocasta's usual death and Oedipus's childhood fantasy fears are defeated. See Maria de Fátima Marinho, *Um Poço Sem Fundo. Novas Reflexões sobre Literatura e História* (Oporto: Campo das Letras, 2005), 182–83.

58. See Correia, *Breve História,* 161–63.

59. See Sousa, ed. *Entrevistas a Natália Correia,* 42–44. For further biographical and contextual information about *A Madona,* see Regina Louro, *Mulheres do Século XX. 101 Livros*

(Lisbon: Câmara Municipal de Lisboa. Departamento Cultural, 2001), 52. See also Costa, *Natália Correia. Fotobiografia,* 122. Costa's book reproduces the dedication to Correia's friend Branca Miranda Rodrigues that names her as the original "Madonna" of the title, although there are also strong autobiographical elements that link the text to Correia herself.

60. Regina Louro has read *A Madona* as a "work of autobiographical transfiguration (childhood on the Island of São Miguel, journeying through Europe, Bacchic fury grounded in spirituality). *A Madona* is a portrait of the great writer, woman and public persona that was Natália." See Louro, *Mulheres do Século XX. 101 Livros,* 152.

61. António Quadros, "Uma peregrinação-iniciação matrista. *A Madona,* de Natália Correia, uma proposta de hermenêutica" in *Estruturas Simbólicas do Imaginário na Literatura Portuguesa* (Lisbon: Átrio, 1992), 177.

62. Her maternalist mission here recalls Nietzsche's motivation for *The Birth of Tragedy,* reviving a mythic and mystical German Romantic culture, as a means of driving out the excessive, rationalism of the French Enlightenment and late nineteenth-century decadence. Nietzsche, *The Birth of Tragedy* xiv.

63. Quadros, "Uma peregrinação," 176.

64. See Correia's views in interview in the 1980s on the nuclear age, and her work on telluric regeneration underlying her long poem "Mátria." Sousa, ed. *Entrevistas a Natália Correia,* 59–60.

65. Correia, *Breve História,* 146.

66. Carlos, "Mátria e o Mal," 27.

67. It should be noted here that Portugal had been a member of NATO since 1949. Correia's homeland, the Azorean archipelago, was also home to American nuclear airbases. It would probably, therefore, have been the Portuguese territory most obviously at risk from nuclear attack in a super-power conflict.

68. Louro, *Mulheres do Século XX. 101 Livros,* 52.

69. Nietzsche, *The Birth of Tragedy,* 144.

70. On the Osiris intertexts in the novel, see Quadros, "Uma peregrinação."

71. References to mythical sources in our reading of *A Madona* are drawn primarily from James George Frazer, *The Golden Bough. A Study in Magic and Religion* (London: Macmillan, 1954). On the dilaceration of Pentheus, see 378–79. On the fertility myths based on the scattering of Osiris, see 362–68.

72. See Andrew Elfenbein, *Romantic Genius: The Prehistory of a Homosexual Role* (New York: Columbia University Press, 1999), 205–6.

73. Judith Butler, *Bodies that Matter. On the Discursive Limits of "Sex"* (London: Routledge, 1993), 104.

74. Muraro, "Female Genealogies," 321.

75. Vasques, *Mulheres que Escreveram Teatro,* 149. The play was apprehended by the PIDE state police in 1966. See Sousa, ed. *Entrevistas a Natália Correia,* 67.

76. Elin Diamond, *Unmaking Mimesis. Essays on Feminism and Theatre* (London: Routledge, 1997), 47.

77. Ibid., 50.

78. See ibid., 52.

79. Ibid.

80. Ibid., 53.

81. Clara Crabbé Rocha, "Florbela Espanca. *Diário do Último Ano," Colóquio/Letras* 69 (1982).

82. Correia, *Antologia Poética,* 229. All subsequent references to Correia's poems about

Florbela Espanca are to this edition and are cited parenthetically within the text. The English translations are by Richard Zenith, and are provided in full in the appendix to chapter 4.

83. On the poetess construction in the work of Espanca, see Anna Klobucka, "On ne naît pas poétesse: a aprendizagem literária de Florbela Espanca," *Luso-Brazilian Review* 29 (1992). See also the discussion on "poetisas" in Cláudia Pazos Alonso, *Imagens do Eu na Poesia de Florbela Espanca* (Lisbon: Imprensa Nacional Casa da Moeda, 1997).

84. Correia, *Breve História.*

85. Muraro, "Female Genealogies," 326. Luce Irigaray, "The Universal as Mediation," in *Sexes and Genealogies,* trans. Gillian C. Gill (New York: Columbia University Press, 1993).

CHAPTER 5. HÉLIA CORREIA

1. Hélia Correia is no family relation to Natália Correia, although they both share this very common Portuguese surname. Where Hélia needs to be distinguished from Natália, first names will be used. Otherwise surnames will continue to be the normal form of reference. All English translations are our own.

2. Hélia Correia's earlier works in particular were clearly influenced to some degree by French Feminist thought, and were viewed by Maria Teresa Horta as the epitome of "escrita feminina," usually taken in this instance to be an unmediated reflection of female maternal biology, unique to the woman writer. This perspective is evident in a number of Horta's reviews, where she characteristically describes Correia's works as "visceral," "matricial," "primordial," and "uterino." See, for example, Maria Teresa Horta, "*Montedemo* de Hélia Correia," *Mulheres,* December 1983; "*Villa Celeste* de Hélia Correia," *Mulheres,* June 1985. In her review of O *Número dos Vivos* in 1982, Horta preempts Correia's anticipated objections stating "que me perdoe **Hélia Correia** tão certa de não haver uma escrita feminina, se eu lhe disse que O *Número dos Vivos* só poderia ser escrito por uma mulher" (Bold in the original). See "O *Número dos Vivos* de Hélia Correia," *Mulheres,* May 1982, 12.

3. Miguel Real, "Realismo Simbólico," *Jornal de Letras, Artes e Ideias* (2006): 25.

4. Hélia Correia has amusingly described Natália Correia's injunction to write a play on Florbela, as a matter of prevailing upon her to do it. See Ana Raquel Fernandes, "Interview with Hélia Correia," *Anglo-Saxonica. Revista do Centro de Estudos Anglísticos da Universidade de Lisboa* 25 (2007): 265.

5. Darlene Sadlier's work on Hélia Correia in the 1980s was the first to note this important link with the Gothic. See Darlene Sadlier, *The Question of How: Women Writers and the New Portuguese Literature* (New York: Greenwood Press, 1989).

6. This is a central theme in her interview with Ana Raquel Fernandes, where she remarks that "since I was very small my Gothic tastes have always been British." Fernandes, "Interview with Hélia Correia," 264.

7. Susanne Becker, *Gothic Forms of Feminine Fictions* (Manchester: Manchester University Press, 1999), 55.

8. Hélia Correia, "The Golden Impossibility" Unpublished lecture at New Brunswick, Rutgers University, 1998.

9. Ibid., 7.

10. Written rather later than the heyday of Victorian Gothicism, *Wuthering Heights* is, of course, conventionally regarded as sitting on the border between Gothicism and Realism. Regarding this mix of Gothic and domestic Realist elements, Punter and Byron write, "Brontë is seen to appropriate the Gothic in order to represent and investigate women's fears

about a restrictive and some times threatening domestic space." They further identify Gothicism in her use of specters, the uncanny, and confinement in spaces set against the freedom of savage nature. See David Punter and Glennis Byron, *The Gothic* (Malden, MA: Blackwell Publishing, 2004), 212. Ellen Moers, in her work on the English female-authored Gothic, claims that *Wuthering Heights* is a novel "which we also place uneasily in the Gothic tradition." Ellen Moers, *Literary Women* (London: The Women's Press, 1986), 99.

11. Correia, "Golden," 7.

12. Hélia Correia, *Contos* (Lisbon: Relógio d'Água, 2008), 110. The English version of the story was written with linguistic input and revision from Patricia Odber de Baubeta.

13. ———, *A Casa Eterna* (Lisbon: Dom Quixote, 1991). All subsequent references to this work are cited parenthetically within the text.

14. As Magalhães notes, "a proximity between the two is readily noticeable. For example, in their passion for words and the way they both use the 'real' to construct their fiction." Isabel Allegro de Magalhães, *O Sexo dos Textos e outras leituras* (Lisbon: Caminho, 1995), 97.

15. Elisabeth Bronfen, *Over her Dead Body. Death, Femininity and the Aesthetic* (Manchester: Manchester University Press, 1992). 163

16. On the process of self-textualization through identification with the dead figures, and dead letters of western culture in *Madame Bovary,* also discussed in chapter 3, see ibid., 162–63.

17. Susan Wolstenholme, *Gothic (Re)Visions: Writing Women as Readers* (Albany: State University of New York Press, 1993), 27.

18. Becker, *Gothic Forms,* 50.

19. Ibid., 26–27;67–70.

20. As Becker notes, "in this early feminist fiction, gothic 'excess' marks the form with its multiple female stories and with the gothic emotions of horror and fear, only to heighten its realism." See ibid., 32.

21. In this respect, *A Casa Eterna* picks up and continues an important theme in Correia's earlier fiction, most notably, *Montedemo* and *O Número dos Vivos,* in which madness and escape textualize the polarized Gothic options traditionally offered to the repressed or imprisoned women characters. See Urbano Tavares Rodrigues, "Loucura e fuga nas narrativas de Hélia Correia," *O Diário,* January 26, 1986; Hilary Owen, *Portuguese Women's Writing, 1972 to 1986: Reincarnations of a Revolution* (Lewiston, NY: Edwin Mellen Press, 2000); "Fairies and Witches in Hélia Correia," in *Women, Literature and Culture in the Portuguese-Speaking World,* ed. Cláudia Pazos Alonso, with assistance by Glória Fernandes (Lewiston: Edwin Mellen Press, 1996); Kathryn Bishop-Sanchez, "Taking the Father's Place: Neo-Bovarism and Female Sexuality in Hélia Correia's *O Número dos Vivos,*" *Bulletin of Spanish Studies* 82, no. 6 (2005); Sadlier, *The Question of How.*

22. Julia Kristeva, *Powers of Horror. An Essay on Abjection* trans. Leon S. Roudiez (New York: Colombia University Press, 1982). Kristeva is a key reference for Correia, particularly her definition of the abject in *Powers of Horror.* In *A Casa Eterna,* a particularly clear example is Filomena's embedded life story which concerns the transgression of socially accepted borders and limits. Filomena was conceived out of wedlock when her mother, "a Caréua," was impregnated by the village undertaker, whom no-one else would touch, because he conducted his sexual liaisons in the room next to his coffins and corpses. His *de facto* social expulsion from the community and his deflowering of a Caréua are evoked in terms of a boundary zone, a violation of appropriate sex and death divisions, described as "plague and sin together in the same bed, their moans and convulsions ringing out from the wooden floor that separated the bedroom from the huge workshop where the coffins were piled up" [a peste e o pecado

juntos na mesma cama, soltando os seus gemidos e as suas contorções por cima do sobrado que separava o quarto da imensa oficina onde se amontoavam os caixões (63)].

23. In *Powers of Horror*, Julia Kristeva defines the role played by the "abject" (as opposed to the "object") in the formation of the subject as it separates from the Mother, and from union with the semiotic, presymbolic space she represents. Kristeva's theory of abjection (literally casting out or throwing away), derived from anthropology and psychoanalysis, refers to the formation of social identity, meaning, and culture, through these necessary processes of separation from the Mother, and also in social rituals, through expelling impure physical fluids, bodily matter, and social practices such as incest, that must be expelled for the social subject to be consolidated as social. Yet, at the same time, this unclean matter cannot ever be fully externalized; it cannot be permanently cast out.

24. Magalhães has observed, in tones highly reminiscent of those used to describe Agustina Bessa Luís's *A Sibila*, four decades earlier, that *A Casa Eterna* "becomes a denunciation of . . . human decadence (through the decadence of provincial life)." See Magalhães, *O Sexo dos Textos*, 101. However, taking the critique of decadence as a space of Gothic parody and excess, it is also possible to read it in more specifically gendered subversive terms.

25. Kristeva, *Powers of Horror*, 77.

26. Fernando Venâncio interestingly criticizes *A Casa Eterna* precisely for its excess of matrilinearity, demonstrated not only by the sheer density of female figures in the novel, but by the fact that the reader is required to understand these female relationships genealogically. Venâncio states "and throughout the book, there are the women, the innumerable females in the life of a rather inscrutable male. . . There are a great many of these women, and one might perhaps wish there were fewer. The genealogical abilities of the reader are sorely tried when, on pp. 83–84, for example, no fewer than six women appear requiring one to locate them within the family tree, as well as outside it. No one's concentration is up to that." See Fernando Venâncio, "Recensão Crítica a *A Casa Eterna* de Hélia Correia," *Colóquio/Letras* 123/124 (1992): 385.

27. Wolstenholme, *Gothic (Re)Visions*, 31.

28. Magalhães notes on this point, in respect of the novel's title, " 'the eternal home' seems to be that space of infancy to which one always returns, the landscape/placenta which it is hard to really leave behind, so that the novel traces the psychoanalytical journey of the poet . . . in his inevitable return to his origins, in the primordial quest for the root, the matrix, the mother." Magalhães, *O Sexo dos Textos*, 101.

29. See Magalhães, *O Sexo des Textos*, 102. This powerfully echoes Kristeva's famous account of subject formation in which the Lacanian imaginary is replaced by a "semiotic chora," a disruptive maternal space prior to and outside of all symbolization in the representational language of the father, but operating through music, sounds, rhythms, pulsions, and particularly poetry, to provide movements of transgression and jouissance that traverse symbolic representation and emerge as art and literature. See Julia Kristeva, "Stabat Mater," in *The Kristeva Reader*, ed. Toril Moi (Oxford: Basil Blackwell, 1986). See also the chapter on Hélia Correia's *Montedemo* in Owen, *Reincarnations of a Revolution*.

30. See Becker, *Gothic Forms*, 48. Becker is drawing here on Macherey, Lacan, and Catherine Belsey, *Critical Practice* (London: Methuen 1980).

31. For a close reading of this Ecclesiastical reference in the novel, see Magalhães, *O Sexo dos Textos*, 100.

32. As Becker observes, the Gothic genre itself has been frequently historically feminized as Other, and marginalized as excessive, hysterical, and not really literature in relation to the establishment dominated by realism. Becker, *Gothic Forms*, 23.

33. The title of *Perdição. Exercício sobre Antígona,* also evokes the classic romantic novel by Camilo Castelo Branco, *Amor de Perdição.*

34. See *Furor. Ensaios sobre a obra dramática de Hélia Correia,* ed. Maria de Fátima Sousa e Silva (Coimbra: Imprensa da Universidade de Coimbra, 2006), 63. In this edited volume, the three articles by Maria de Fátima Sousa e Silva, Carmen Leal Soares e Isabel Capeloa Gil produce stimulating readings of *Perdição* in which its gender implications are very much to the fore.

35. *Perdição. Exercício Sobre Antígona* was first staged by "A Comuna" in 1993 and *Florbela* by "Maizum" in 1991. See Eugénia Vasques, *Mulheres que Escreveram Teatro no Século XX em Portugal* (Lisbon: Edições Colibri, 2001), 159.

36. Hélia Correia, *Perdição. Exercício sobre Antígona. Florbela. Teatro* (Lisbon: Dom Quixote, 1991). All subsequent references to these two works are cited parenthetically within the text.

37. See Hélia Correia, *"Perdição—exercício sobre Antígona.* Uma composição acidental" Unpublished paper given at Coimbra, Faculdade de Letras—Universidade de Coimbra, n.d. This was an academic paper delivered at Coimbra University and dedicated "to my teachers on the postgraduate classical theatre course at Coimbra Arts Faculty." It is an unpublished text and we thank Hélia Correia for making it available to us. In it, Correia writes, "my Antigone is, in fact, shamefully present-day. She has become alienated from the whole world around her, and all she aspires to is her fifteen minutes of fame."

38. In referring to Hélia Correia's rewriting of the Antigone myth, we retain the Portuguese versions of the classical names that she has given them (e.g. Antígona, Eurídice, etc.) in order to distinguish them from the names of the corresponding characters in the English translation that we use to refer to Sophocles's original.

39. Judith Butler, *Antigone's Claim: Kinship between Life and Death* (New York: Columbia University Press, 2000), 76.

40. Ibid., 55.

41. It is tempting here to read also a subtextual rejection of the bacchic myth recuperations that proved so central to the construction of the female writing subject in Natália Correia's work.

42. See Andrew Elfenbein, *Romantic Genius: The Prehistory of a Homosexual Role* (New York: Columbia University Press, 1999), 13–14.

43. Gil, "Espectros Literários," 67.

44. Ibid., 72.

45. Ibid., 74–75.

46. Ibid., 76.

47. Butler, *Antigone's Claim,* 22

48. Butler's essay on Antigone, exploring the normalizing of sexuality through kinship ties, and reviewing the "convergence of social prohibition and melancholia," notes that the public prohibition against certain rituals, such as the mourning of lost homosexual relations, leaves the mourner trapped in the endless, repetitive cycle of a socially-instituted melancholia. See ibid., 80.

49. Sigmund Freud, "Mourning and Melancholia," in *On Metapsychology. The Theory of Psychoanalysis,* ed. Angela Richards, *The Penguin Freud Library,* trans. James Strachey (Harmondsworth: Penguin, 1991), 255.

50. Ibid., 268.

51. Christine Battersby, *Gender and Genius. Towards a Feminist Aesthetics* (London: The Women's Press, 1989), 70.

52. Florbela's suicidal depression, like Antigone's was, as noted in the introduction, historically interpreted in terms of extreme mourning for the dead brother, Apeles, whose untimely death in a plane crash triggered her barbiturate dependency. Following the third of her three disastrous marriages, to her doctor Mário Lage, Florbela finally took an overdose on her birthday in 1930, having prophesied in her diary that this was her intent. See Florbela Espanca, *Diário do Último Ano, seguido de um poema sem título* (Amadora: Livraria Bertrand, 1981), 95. See also Cláudia Pazos Alonso, *Imagens do Eu na Poesia de Florbela Espanca* (Lisbon: Imprensa Nacional Casa da Moeda, 1997).

53. Jorge de Sena, *Florbela Espanca ou a Expressão do Feminino na Poesia Portuguesa* (Oporto: Biblioteca Fenianos, 1947).

54. See Maria Teresa Horta's introduction to Natália Correia, *Breve História da Mulher e Outros Escritos* (Lisbon: Parceria A. M. Pereira, 2003).

Chapter 6. Lídia Jorge

1. Adrienne Rich, "When We Dead Awaken: Writing as Re-vision," in *On Lies, Secrets and Silence* (London: Virago, 1980), 35.

2. Stephanie D'Orey, "Interview with Lídia Jorge," *Portuguese Literary and Cultural Studies* 2 (1999): 157.

3. Maria Augusta Silva, "A escrita não pode deixar a alma sentada," *Diário de Notícias* (October 2, 2002).

4. Lídia Jorge, *Notícia da Cidade Silvestre* (Mem Martins: Publicações Europa-América, 1984); *A Costa dos Murmúrios* (Lisbon: Dom Quixote, 1988); *O Vale da Paixão* (Lisbon: Dom Quixote, 1998). All subsequent references to these three works are to these editions and are cited parenthetically within the text. All English translations for *O Vale da Paixão* are cited from Jorge, *The Migrant Painter of Birds*, trans. by Margaret Jull Costa (New York: Harcourt, Inc., 1998). All English translations from *A Costa dos Murmúrios* are cited from Jorge, *The Murmuring Coast*, trans. by Natália Costa and Ronald W. Sousa (Minneapolis: University of Minnesota Press, 1995). All other English translations in this chapter are our own.

5. Lídia Jorge, *A Maçon* (Lisbon: Sociedade Portuguesa de Autores/Publicações Dom Quixote, 1997).

6. João Gaspar Simões, "Os prodígios de Lídia Jorge," *Diário de Notícias* (January 24, 1985): 31.

7. Regina Louro, "Lídia Jorge: Este 3° livro é o primeiro," *Jornal de Letras, Artes e Ideias* (December 18–24, 1984): 2.

8. There may be an autobiographical element here, as Jorge herself was by then a divorced mother of two.

9. In Portugal, abortion was illegal until 1984, when a limited liberalization occurred. Jorge depicts in gruesome detail not one, but two backstreet abortions undergone by Anabela and Júlia, respectively.

10. See chapter on Lídia Jorge in Hilary Owen, "[W]rites of passage: Portuguese women's narrative after the Three Marias." Ph.D. diss., University of Nottingham, 1992.

11. Stephanie D'Orey, 173.

12. Fernando's angelic androgyny is arguably difficult to reconcile with the traditional paradigm of "masculinity," but this goes precisely toward showing how difficult it is to deconstruct century-old stereotypes. In the closing scene, the breakdown of his car, the ultimate

NOTES

symbol of virility, succinctly encodes his failure to conform to old models of masculinity, yet provides a timely contrast with the earlier car which nearly killed her.

13. Ana Paula Ferreira, "Lídia Jorge's *A Costa dos Murmúrios:* History and the Postmodern She-Wolf," *Revista Hispánica Moderna* 45 (1992).

14. Rui de Azevedo Teixeira, *A Guerra Colonial e o Romance Português* (Lisbon: Editorial Notícias, 1998); Margarida Calafate Ribeiro, *Uma História de Regressos: Império, Guerra Colonial e Pós-Colonialismo na Literatura Portuguesa* (Lisbon: Afrontamento, 2004).

15. Several scholars have developed productive lines of enquiry in directions which avoid tying *A Costa* into the "war novel" paradigm. See Paulo de Medeiros, "'Memória Infinita,'" *Portuguese Literary and Cultural Studies* 2 (1999); Hilary Owen, "Back to Nietzsche: The Making of an Intellectual/Woman. Lídia Jorge's *A Costa dos Murmúrios,*" *Portuguese Literary and Cultural Studies* 2 (1999); Lígia Maria Pereira da Silva, "Novels of Lídia Jorge (1984–1998): Saying Other/wise—Testimony and Alterity." Ph.D. diss., University of Manchester, 2003.

16. Furthermore, the tale starts with a framing of the newlyweds as they kiss, but immediately draws attention to the constructed nature of the event itself by introducing a photographer who makes the couple adopt several poses while he searches for the best angle to capture them on camera.

17. The clearest example of this is the euphemisms used in connection with colonial war, such as "because they are not in a time of complete peace" [porque não se estava em tempo de paz completa (11)].

18. Maria Irene Ramalho de Sousa Santos, "Bondoso Cais: *A Costa dos Murmúrios* de Lídia Jorge," *Colóquio/Letras* 107 (1989).

19. Fernando Pessoa, *Mensagem* (Lisbon: Assírio & Alvim, 2004), 51, 60.

20. Pessoa, *Poesias,* 234.

21. In that connection, Luís Alex's inability to perform sexually on return from the front (and thus procreate) is all the more significant given the contrast with his sexual power in the short story. It functions as an indication of his imminent demise and, on a collective scale, of the unsustainability of the political status quo and intractable fissures within the Salazarist national family project.

22. For a discussion of this point, see Ana Paula Ferreira, "Precisa-se de pai para *Natio* de escrita ou, a Paixão segundo Lídia Jorge," *Mealibra* 9 (2001).

23. Silva, "Novels of Lídia Jorge."

24. In this context, we may wish to note that Francisco has six sons and only one daughter, Adelina, who is in fact a mere mouthpiece of her father.

25. Paulo de Medeiros, "Casas assombradas," in *Fantasmas e fantasias imperiais no imaginário português contemporâneo,* ed. Margarida Calafate Ribeiro and Ana Paula Ferreira (Oporto: Campo das Letras, 2003).

26. Lídia Jorge, "Três passagens rente ao Índico," *Camões. Revista,* no. 1 (1998).

27. If, on the one hand, Dalila seems to take on the role of the missing father, on the other, however, he becomes impotent and is increasingly described as "uma senhora," partly fulfilling her need for the motherly love she never fully experienced. Furthermore, as Lígia Silva points out, his gradual descent into alcohol becomes a metaphor for the slow disintegration of the virile Dictatorship. See chapter on *Vale da Paixão* in Silva, "Novels of Lídia Jorge."

28. Her name is spelt out on the package, twice described as an "invólucro," but readers are still not privy to it: "her name and his were on it" (estava desenhado o nome dela e o dele mesmo).

29. For a fuller discussion of this, see Ferreira, "Precisa-se de pai."

30. The English translations from *Mensagem* are our own.

31. The draft title of the novel "Facing the Soldier's Blanket" [Diante da Manta de Soldado] indicated the necessity of overcoming the paternal imperial legacy.

32. Tellingly, his invitation mirrors in reverse almost word for word her father's invitation, several decades earlier in 1963, for her to get into his car and leave with him: "Get in, please, for God's sake. Don't stay here any longer!" (135) [entra, peço-te, pelo amor de Deus, que entres. Não fiques aqui mais (143)]. This suggestion was significantly not taken up at the time.

33. In this connection, we should note that her first novel, *O Dia dos Prodígios* [The Day of Wonders], is dedicated to her grandmother.

34. See Eugénia Vasques, *Mulheres que Escreveram Teatro no Século XX em Portugal* (Lisbon: Edições Colibri, 2001).

35. See Maria João Martins, "'A Maçon no D. Maria II—Uma mulher livre," interview with Lídia Jorge," *Jornal de Letras, Artes e Ideias* (April 9–15, 1997): 29.

36. João Esteves, "Conselho Nacional das Mulheres Portuguesas," *Faces de Eva. Estudos sobre a Mulher* 15 (2006).

37. Brasão published several pamphlets supporting and furthering feminist causes in which he raised pressing social issues such as child prostitution and society's intolerance toward single mothers.

38. Elisabeth Bronfen, *Over her Dead Body. Death, Femininity and the Aesthetic.* (Manchester: Manchester University Press, 1992), 181.

39. Cabete's original statement was about the need to "say" a subversive word, but it has now been recast as "writing" a subversive word.

CONCLUSION

1. Christine Battersby, *Gender and Genius. Towards a Feminist Aesthetics* (London: The Women's Press, 1989), 152.

2. Teresa Leitão de Barros, *Escritoras de Portugal,* 2 vols (Lisbon: s.ed, 1924).

3. Ana Plácido (under the pseudonym Lopo de Sousa), *Herança de Lágrimas,* Guimarães: Vimaranense Editora, 1871. Instead, Florbela Espanca read the 1910 novel *Doida de Amor* by the minor writer Antero de Figueiredo, most probably identifying herself with the predicament of the female protagonist. For further details see Cláudia Pazos-Alonso, *Imagens do Eu na Poesia de Florbela Espanca* (Lisbon: Imprensa Nacional Casa da Moeda, 1997), 61.

4. Graça Abranches, "Unlearning in order to speak: politics, writings and poetics of Portuguese women of the twentieth century" (University of Manchester. Spanish and Portuguese Studies Department Seminar, April 23, 1998), 2.

5. Chatarina Edfeldt, *Uma história na História. Representações da autoria feminina na História da Literatura Portuguesa do século XX* (Montijo: Câmara Municipal de Montijo, 2006), 73–108.

6. Ibid., 133–44.

7. Adrienne Rich, "When We Dead Awaken: Writing as Re-vision," in *On Lies, Secrets and Silence* (London: Virago, 1980), 35.

8. Edfeldt, *Uma história na História,* 207–8.

9. Battersby, *Gender and Genius,* 152.

Bibliography

Manuscript Sources

Cartas de José Régio a Irene Lisboa, E24/136–172, Biblioteca Nacional.

Cartas de João Gaspar Simões a Irene Lisboa, E24/184–218, Biblioteca Nacional.

Other Sources

Abranches, Graça. "Homens, mulheres e mestras inglesas." In *Entre ser e estar: raízes, percursos e discursos da identidade,* edited by Maria Irene Ramalho and António Sousa Ribeiro. Oporto: Afrontamento Edições, 2001.

———. "'On What Terms Shall We Join the Procession of Educated Men?' Teaching Feminist Studies at the University of Coimbra." *Oficina do CES* 125, July 1998.

———. "Unlearning in order to speak: politics, writings and poetics of Portuguese women of the twentieth century." Unpublished lecture. University of Manchester. Spanish and Portuguese Studies Department Seminar, April 23, 1998.

Alcoforado, Mariana. "Lettres Portugaises." In *Cartas Portuguesas,* 57–101. Lisbon: Assírio e Alvim, 1993 [1669].

Allen, Ann Taylor. "Feminism, Social Science, and the Meanings of Modernity: The Debate on the Origin of the Family in Europe and the United States, 1860–1914." *The American Historical Review* 104, no. 4 (1999): 1085–113.

Almeida, São José. *Homossexuais no Estado Novo.* Oporto: Sextante Editora, 2010.

Amaral, Ana Luísa. "Desconstruindo identidades: ler *Novas Cartas Portuguesas* à luz da teoria *queer.*" *Cadernos de Literatura Comparada, Corpo e Identidades* 3/4 (2001): 77–91.

———. "Excesses: The Poetry of Florbela Espanca and Irene Lisboa," *Cadernos de Literatura Comparada,* 8/9, (2003).

Amaral, Fernando Pinto do. *100 Livros Portugueses do Século XX: 100 Portuguese Books of the 20th Century.* Lisbon: Camões, 2002.

Andrade, Sérgio C. *Ao Correr do Tempo. Duas Décadas com Manoel de Oliveira.* Lisbon: Portugália Editora, 2008.

Andresen, Sophia de Mello Breyner. *Obra Poética.* 3 vols. Lisbon: Caminho, 1995–96.

Ansell-Pearson, Keith. "Nietzsche, Woman and Political Theory." In *Nietzsche, Feminism and Political Theory,* edited by Paul Patton, 27–48. London: Routledge, 1993.

Arenas, Fernando. "Onde existir?: a (im)possibilidade excessiva do desejo homoerótico na ficção de Mário de Sá-Carneiro" *Metamorfoses* 6 (2005): 159–68.

Barreno, Maria Isabel, Maria Teresa Horta, and Maria Velho da Costa. *New Portuguese Letters*. London: Readers International, 1994.

———. *Novas Cartas Portuguesas*. Lisbon: Publicações Dom Quixote, 1998.

Barros, Teresa Leitão de. *Escritoras de Portugal*, 2 vols. Lisbon: s.ed, 1924.

Battersby, Christine. *Gender and Genius. Towards a Feminist Aesthetics*. London: The Women's Press, 1989.

———. *The Phenomenal Woman: Feminist Metaphysics and the Patterns of Identity*. Oxford: Polity, 1998.

Beauvoir, Simone de. *The Second Sex*. Translated by H. M. Parshley. Harmondsworth: Penguin, 1984.

Becker, Susanne. *Gothic Forms of Feminine Fictions*. Manchester: Manchester University Press, 1999.

Belsey, Catherine. *Critical Practice*. London: Methuen 1980.

Bessa Luís, Agustina. *Camilo: Génio e Figura*. Cruz Quebrada: Casa das Letras, 2008.

———. *Fanny Owen*. Lisbon: Guimarães & Ca. Editores, 1979.

———. *Florbela Espanca*. Lisbon: Guimarães, 1984 [1979].

———. "A mãe de um rio." In *A Brusca*, 103–17. Lisbon: Editorial Verbo, 1971.

———. *A Sibila*. 12th ed. Lisbon: Guimarães Editores, n.d.

———. *Vale Abraão*. Lisbon: Guimarães Editores, 1991.

Besse, Maria Graciete. *Percursos no feminino*. Lisbon: Ulmeiro, 2001.

Bishop-Sanchez, Kathryn. "Taking the Father's Place: Neo-Bovarism and Female Sexuality in Hélia Correia's *O Número dos Vivos*" *Bulletin of Spanish Studies* 82 no. 6 (2005): 793–813.

Bloom, Harold. *Genius. A Mosaic of One Hundred Exemplary Creative Minds*. London: Fourth Estate, 2002.

———. "Só Falta Começarem a Partir-me os Vidros das Janelas. Interview by Luís Miguel Queirós." *Público,* May 26, 2001.

Briffault, Robert. *The Mothers. The Matriarchal Theory of Social Origins*. Edited by Gordon Rattray Taylor. New York: Grosset and Dunlap, 1963.

Bronfen, Elisabeth. *Over her Dead Body. Death, Femininity and the Aesthetic*. Manchester: Manchester University Press, 1992.

Buck, Claire, ed. *Bloomsbury Guide to Women's Literature*. London: Bloomsbury Publishing, 1992.

Bulger, Laura Fernanda. *As Máscaras da Memória. Estudos em torno da obra de Agustina*. Lisbon: Guimarães Editores, 1998.

———. *A Sibila. Uma Superação Inconclusa*. Lisbon: Guimarães Editores, 1990.

Butler, Judith. *Antigone's Claim: Kinship between Life and Death*. New York: Columbia University Press, 2000.

———. *Bodies that Matter. On the Discursive Limits of "Sex."* London: Routledge, 1993.

Camões, Luís de. *Lírica Completa*. Edited by Maria de Lurdes Saraiva. 3 vols. Lisbon: Imprensa Nacional-Casa da Moeda, 1980–81.

———. *Os Lusíadas*. Oporto: Porto Editora, 1980.

———. *Sonetos*. Lisbon: Europa-América, 1990.

Campbell, Jan. *Arguing with the Phallus: Feminist, Queer and Postcolonial Theory. A Psychoanalytic Contribution*. London: Zed Books, 2000.

Campos, Maria Amélia. *Ana, a Lúcida. Biografia de Ana Plácido, a mulher fatal de Camilo.* Lisbon: Parceria A. M. Pereira, 2008.

Carlos, Luís Adriano. "A Mátria e o Mal." In *Natália Correia, 10 anos depois . . .* edited by Secção Francesa de D.E.P.E.R., 23–30. Oporto: Faculdade de Letras da Universidade do Porto, 2003.

Carvalho, João Boto de. *Sol Poente.* Lisbon: n.p., 1919.

Cavarero, Adriana. *In Spite of Plato. A Feminist Rewriting of Ancient Philosophy.* Translated by Serena Anderlini-D'Onofrio and Áine O'Healey. Cambridge: Polity Press, 1995.

Chevalier, Jean, and Alain Gheerbrant. *Dictionnaire des symboles,* 2nd ed. Paris: Robert Laffont, 1982.

Cixous, Hélène. "The Laugh of the Medusa." In *New French Feminisms,* edited by Elaine Marks and Isabelle de Courtivron, 245–64. Brighton: The Harvester Press, 1981.

Clemente, Alice R. entry on Irene Lisboa in *Dictionary of Literary Biography. Portuguese Writers,* edited by Monica Rector and Fred M. Clark. Detroit: Gale, 2004.

Colebrook, Claire. "From Radical Representations to Corporeal Becomings: The Feminist Philosophy of Lloyd, Grosz, and Gatens." *Hypatia. A Journal of Feminist Philosophy* 15, no. 2 (2000): 76–93.

Collective, The Marxist-Feminist Literature. "Women's Writing. *Jane Eyre, Villette, Shirley* and *Aurora Leigh.*" In *Marxist Literary Theory,* edited by Terry Eagleton and Drew Milne, 328–50. Oxford: Blackwell, 1996.

Correia, Hélia. *A Casa Eterna.* Lisbon: Dom Quixote, 1991.

———. *Contos.* Lisbon: Relógio d'Água, 2008.

———. "The Golden Impossibility." Unpublished lecture given at New Brunswick, Rutgers University, 1998.

———. *"Perdição—exercício sobre Antígona.* Uma composição acidental." Coimbra: Faculdade de Letras-Universidade de Coimbra, n.d.

———. *Perdição. Exercício sobre Antígona. Florbela. Teatro.* Lisbon: Dom Quixote, 1991.

Correia, Natália. *Breve História da Mulher e Outros Escritos.* Edited by Zetho Cunha Gonçalves and introduction by Maria Teresa Horta. Lisbon: Parceria A. M. Pereira, 2003.

———. *D. João e Julieta.* Lisbon: Sociedade Portuguesa de Autores/Dom Quixote, 1999.

———. *A Madona.* Lisbon: Editorial Notícias, 2000

———, ed. *A Mulher. Antologia Poética.* Lisbon: Artemágica, 2005.

———. *Não Percas a Rosa. Diário e algo mais (25 de abril de 1974–20 de dezembro de 1975).* Lisbon: Dom Quixote, 1978.

———. *O Armistício.* Lisbon: Dom Quixote, 1985.

———. *Onde Está o menino Jesus?.* Lisbon: Rolim, 1987.

———. *O Progresso de Édipo. Poema Dramático.* Lisbon: N.P., 1957.

———. ed. *O surrealismo na poesia portuguesa.* Lisbon: Frenesi, 2002.

———. *Uma Estátua para Herodes.* Lisbon: Arcádia, 1974.

———. *Antologia de Poesia Portuguesa Erótica e Satírica (dos Cancioneiros Medievais à Actualidade).* Lisbon: Fernando Ribeiro de Mello/Afrodite, n.d.

———. *Antologia Poética.* Edited by Fernando Pinto do Amaral. Lisbon: Dom Quixote, 2002.

———. *O Encoberto.* Lisbon: Fernando Ribeiro de Mello Edições Afrodite, 1977 [1969].

———. *A Pécora*. 2nd ed. Lisbon: O Jornal, 1990.

Costa, Ana Paula. *Natália Correia. Fotobiografia*. Lisbon: Dom Quixote, 2005.

Coward, Rosalind. *Patriarchal Precedents. Sexuality and Social Relations*. London: Routledge and Kegan Paul, 1983.

D'Orey, Stephanie. "Interview with Lídia Jorge." *Portuguese Literary and Cultural Studies* 2 (1999): 167–74.

Dal Farra, Maria Lúcia. "A Interlocução de Florbela Espanca com a Poética de Américo Durão." *Colóquio/Letras* 132–33 (1994): 99–110.

———. *Trocando Olhares*. Lisbon: Imprensa Nacional Casa da Moeda, 1995.

Diamond, Elin. *Unmaking Mimesis. Essays on Feminism and Theatre*. London: Routledge, 1997.

Dinis, António P. B. F. "Friedrich Nietzsche e Natália Correia: dois espíritos livres." *Actas do VI Encontro Luso-Alemão* (2002): 169–85.

Dumas, Catherine. *Estética e Personagens nos romances de Agustina Bessa Luís: espelhismos* Oporto: Campo das Letras, 2002.

———. "Florbela Visitada por Agustina: a mulher poeta e os mitos." In *A Planície e o Abismo. Actas do Congresso sobre Florbela Espanca realizado na Universidade de Évora, de 7 a 9 de Dezembro de 1994*, edited by Óscar Lopes, Fernando J. B. Martinho, António Cândido Franco, Paula Mourão and Helena Carvalhão Buescu e Outros, 195–204. Lisbon: Vega, 1997.

Edfeldt, Chatarina. *Uma história na História. Representações da autoria feminina na História da Literatura Portuguesa do século XX*. Montijo: Câmara Municipal de Montijo, 2006.

Elfenbein, Andrew. *Romantic Genius: The Prehistory of a Homosexual Role*. New York: Columbia University Press, 1999.

Eliot, T. S. "Tradition and the Individual Talent." In *The Sacred Wood*. London: Faber and Faber, 1997 [1919].

Engelmayer, Elfriede, and Renate Hess. *Die Schwestern der Mariana Alcoforado: portugiesische Schriftstellerinnen der Gegenwart*. Berlin: edition tranvía, 1993.

Engels, Friedrich. *The Origin of the Family, Private Property and the State*. Harmondsworth: Penguin, 1985 [1884].

Espanca, Florbela. *As Máscaras do Destino*. Oporto: Editora Marânus, 1931.

———. "Charneca em Flor." In *Europa* 3, (1925): 31.

———. *Diário do Último Ano, seguido de um poema sem título*. Amadora: Livraria Bertrand, 1981.

———. *O Dominó Preto*. Lisbon: Livraria Bertrand, 1982.

———. *Obras Completas*. 6 vols. Lisbon: Dom Quixote, 1985–86.

———. *Poemas de Florbela Espanca*. São Paulo: Martins Fontes, 1996.

———. *Reliquiae*. In *Charneca em Flor*. 2nd ed. Coimbra: Livraria Gonçalves, 1931.

Esteves, João. "Conselho Nacional das Mulheres Portuguesas." *Faces de Eva. Estudos sobre a Mulher* 15 (2006).

Fay, Elizabeth A. *A Feminist Introduction to Romanticism*. Oxford: Blackwell, 1998.

Fernandes, Ana Raquel. "Interview with Hélia Correia." *Anglo-Saxonica. Revista do Centro de Estudos Anglísticos da Universidade de Lisboa* 25 (2007): 259–74.

Ferreira, Ana Paula. "Discursos femininos, teoria crítica feminista: para uma resposta que não é." *Discursos. Estudos de Língua e Cultura Portuguesa* 5 (1993): 13–27.

———. "Home Bound: The Construct of Femininity in the Estado Novo." *Portuguese Studies* 12 (1996): 133–44.

———. "Lídia Jorge's *A Costa dos Murmúrios:* History and the Postmodern She-Wolf." *Revista Hispánica Moderna* 45 (1992): 268–78.

———. "A 'literatura feminina' nos anos quarenta: uma história de exclusão." In *A Urgência de Contar,* edited by Ana Paula Ferreira, 13–53. Lisbon: Caminho, 2000.

———. "Nationalism and Feminism at the Turn of the Nineteenth Century: Constructing the 'Other' (Woman) of Portugal." *Santa Barbara Portuguese Studies* 3 (1996): 123–40.

———, ed. *Para Um Leitor Ignorado: Ensaios Sobre O Vale da Paixão e Outras Ficções de Lídia Jorge.* Lisbon: Texto Editora, 2009.

———. "Precisa-se de pai para *Natio* de escrita ou, a Paixão segundo Lídia Jorge." *Mealibra* 9 (2001): 27–36.

———. "Reengendering History. Women's Fictions of the Portuguese Revolution." In *After the Revolution: Twenty Years of Portuguese Literature, 1974–1994,* edited by Helena Kaufman and Anna Klobucka, 219–42. Lewisburg: Bucknell University Press, 1997.

———, ed. *A Urgência de Contar.* Lisbon: Caminho, 2000.

Ferreira, Vergílio. *Manhã Submersa.* Amadora: Bertrand, 1980 [1954].

Ferreira, Virgínia. "Engendering Portugal: Social Change, State Politics and Women's Mobilization." In *Modern Portugal,* edited by António Costa Pinto, 162–88. Palo Alto: The Society for the Promotion of Science and Scholarship, 1998.

Fiadeira, Maria Antónia. *Maria Lamas. Biografia.* Lisbon: Quetzal Editores, 2003.

Flax, Jane. "Re-Membering the Selves. Is the Repressed Gendered?" *Michigan Quarterly Review* 26, no. 1 (1987): 92–110.

Foucault, Michel. "Nietzsche, Genealogy, History." In *Language, Counter-Memory, Practice. Selected Essays and Interviews,* edited by Donald F. Bouchard, 139–64. Oxford: Basil Blackwell, 1977.

Fouque, Antoinette, Mireille Calle-Gruber, and Béatrice Didier, eds. *Le dictionnaire des femmes créatrices.* Paris: Éditions des Femmes, forthcoming.

Frazer, James George. *The Golden Bough. A Study in Magic and Religion.* London: Macmillan, 1954.

Freud, Sigmund. "Mourning and Melancholia." In *On Metapsychology. The Theory of Psychoanalysis,* edited by Angela Richards, 245–68. Harmondsworth: Penguin, 1991.

———. "Three Essays on the Theory of Sexuality." In *The Freud Reader,* edited by Peter Gay, 239–93. London: Vintage, 1995.

———. "Totem and Taboo." In *The Freud Reader,* edited by Peter Gay, 481–513. London: Vintage, 1995.

Frier, David Gibson. *Visions of the Self in the Novels of Camilo Castelo Branco (1850–1870).* Hispanic Literature. Lewiston: Edwin Mellen Press, 1996.

Gil, Isabel Capeloa. "Espectros Literários. *Perdição* de Hélia Correia." In *Furor. Ensaios sobre a obra dramática de Hélia Correia,* edited by Maria de Fátima Sousa e Silva, 61–76. Coimbra: Imprensa da Universidade de Coimbra, 2006.

Godard, Barbara, ed. *Gynocritics/Gynocritiques: Feminist Approaches to Canadian and Québec Women's Writing.* Toronto: ECW Press, 1987.

Gomes, J. Costa. *A Tragédia Romântica de Fanny Owen*. Oporto: Associação Cultural "Amigos de Gaia," 1980.

Gorjão, Vanda. *Mulheres em Tempos Sombrios. Oposição feminina ao Estado Novo*. Estudos e Investigações, 24 Lisbon: Imprensa de Ciências Sociais, 2002.

Gossy, Mary S. *Empire on the Verge of a Nervous Breakdown*. Liverpool: Liverpool University Press, 2009.

———. *The Untold Story. Women and Theory in Golden Age Texts*. Ann Arbor: University of Michigan Press, 1989.

Guedes, Rui. *Acerca de Florbela*. Lisbon: Dom Quixote, 1986.

———. *Fotobiografia*. Lisbon: Dom Quixote, 1985.

Hirsch, Marianne, and Valerie Smith. "Feminism and Cultural Memory: An Introduction." *Signs. Gender and Cultural Memory* 28, no. 1 (2002): 1–19.

Horta, Maria Teresa. *"Montedemo* de Hélia Correia." *Mulheres* (December 1983): 77.

———. *"O Número dos Vivos* de Hélia Correia." *Mulheres* (May 1982): 12

———. *"A Sibila* de Agustina Bessa Luís." *Mulheres* 49 (1982): 71.

———. *"Villa Celeste* de Hélia Correia." *Mulheres* (June 1985): 68–69.

Irigaray, Luce. "The Eternal Irony of the Community." In *Speculum of the Other Woman*, 214–26. Ithaca: Cornell University Press, 1985.

———. "An Ethics of Sexual Difference." In *An Ethics of Sexual Difference*, 116–29. London: Athlone, 1993.

———. "The Female Gender." In *Sexes and Genealogies*, 105–23. New York: Columbia University Press, 1993.

———. "The Universal as Mediation." In *Sexes and Genealogies*, 125–49. New York: Columbia University Press, 1993.

Jordão, Ana Paula, *Echoes of Transidentity. The transmission and construction of identity in two novels by Lídia Jorge*, Ph.D. diss. University of Utrecht, 2001.

Jorge, Lídia. *A Costa dos Murmúrios*. Lisbon: Dom Quixote, 1988.

———. *A Maçon*. Lisbon: Sociedade Portuguesa de Autores/Publicações Dom Quixote, 1997.

———. *The Migrant Painter of Birds*. Translated by Margaret Jull Costa. New York: Harcourt, Inc., 1998.

———. *The Murmuring Coast*. Translated by Natália Costa and Ronald W. Sousa. Minneapolis: University of Minnesota Press, 1995.

———. *Notícia da Cidade Silvestre*. Mem Martins: Publicações Europa-América, 1984.

———. *O Vale da Paixão*. Lisbon: Dom Quixote, 1998.

———. "Três passagens rente ao Índico." *Camões. Revista* no. 1 (1998): 92–99.

Kauffman, Linda S. *Discourses of Desire: Gender, Genre, and Epistolary Fictions*. Ithaca: Cornell University Press, 1986.

Kendrick, Carolyn. "Refuting the Myth of Motherhood in Portuguese Literature. A Study of Agustina Bessa Luís' *Vale Abraão*." *Rocky Mountain Review of Language and Literature* 57, no. 2 (2003): 43–56.

Klobucka, Anna. "De autores e autoras." *Discursos. Estudos de Língua e Cultura Portuguesa* 5 (1993): 49–65.

———. *O Formato Mulher: A emergência da autoria feminina na poesia portuguesa.* Coimbra: Angelus Novus, 2009.

———. "On ne naît pas poétesse: a aprendizagem literária de Florbela Espanca." *Luso-Brazilian Review* 29 (1992): 51–61.

———. *The Portuguese Nun: Formation of a National Myth.* Lewisburg: Bucknell University Press, 2000.

———. "Spanking Florbela: Adília Lopes and a Genealogy of Feminist Parody in Portuguese Poetry" *Portuguese Studies* 19 (2003): 190–204.

———. "Teoricamente Phalando: Algumas observações sobre a sexualidade do discurso crítico em Portugal." *Colóquio/Letras* 125/126 (1992): 169–76.

Kristeva, Julia. *Powers of Horror. An Essay on Abjection.* Translated by Leon S. Roudiez. New York: Columbia University Press, 1982.

———. "Stabat Mater." In *The Kristeva Reader,* edited by Toril Moi, 160–86. Oxford: Basil Blackwell, 1986.

Lacan, Jacques. "The function and field of speech and language in psychoanalysis." In *Écrits. A Selection,* 30–113. London: Routledge, 1977.

Ladeira, António. "António Nobre. 'A Nossa Maior Poetisa'?" Unpublished paper given at the American Portuguese Studies Association Conference, Yale University, 2008.

Lima, Isabel Pires de. "Agustina, a Conservadora Subversiva." *MeaLibra. Revista de Cultura* 21 (2007): 28–29.

Lisboa, Irene. *Obras de Irene Lisboa;* edited by Paula Morão, 10 vols *Apontamentos.* vol. 8. Lisbon: Editorial Presença, 1998 [1943].

———. *Obras de Irene Lisboa;* edited by Paula Morão, 10 vols *Começa uma Vida.* vol. 3. Lisbon: Editorial Presença, 1992 [1940].

———. *Obras de Irene Lisboa;* edited by Paula Morão, 10 vols *Esta Cidade!* vol. 5. Lisbon: Editorial Presença, 1995 [1942].

———. *Folhas Soltas da Seara Nova—1929/1955.* Edited by Paula Morão. Lisbon: Imprensa Nacional/Casa de Moeda, 1986.

———. *Obras de Irene Lisboa;* edited by Paula Morão, 10 vols *Solidão—Notas do punho de uma mulher.* 4th edition ed. vol. 2. Lisbon: Editorial Presença, 1992 [1939].

———. *Solidão II.* Lisbon: Portugália, n.d, 1966.

———. *Obras de Irene Lisboa;* edited by Paula Morão, 10 vols *Um dia e outro dia . . . Outono havias de vir* vol. 1. Lisbon: Editorial Presença, 1991 [1936] [1937].

———. "Um Dito." In *A Urgência de Contar,* edited by Ana Paula Ferreira. Lisbon: Caminho, 2000.

———. *Obras de Irene Lisboa;* edited by Paula Morão, 10 vols *Voltar atrás para quê?* vol. 4. Lisbon: Editorial Presença, 1994 [1956].

Loomba, Ania. *Colonialism/Postcolonialism.* London: Routledge, 1998.

Lopes, Óscar. *Os Sinais e os Sentidos. Literatura Portuguesa do Século XX.* Lisbon: Caminho, 1986.

Lopes, Silvina Rodrigues. *Exercícios de Aproximação.* Lisbon: Edições Vendaval, 2003.

Loraux, Nicole. *Les mères en deuil.* Paris: Seuil, 1990.

Lourenço, Eduardo. "Agustina Bessa Luís ou o Neo-Romantismo." *Colóquio/Letras* 26 (1963): 49–52.

Louro, Regina. "Lídia Jorge: Este 3 o livro é o primeiro." *Jornal de Letras, Artes e Ideias* (December 18–24, 1984): 2–3.

———. *Mulheres do Século XX. 101 Livros.* Lisbon: Câmara Municipal de Lisboa. Departamento Cultural 2001.

Macedo, Ana Gabriela, ed. *Género, Identidade e Desejo. Antologia crítica do feminismo contemporâneo.* Lisbon: Cotovia, 2002.

———. "Os Estudos Feministas Revisitados: Finalmente Visíveis." In *Floresta encantada: novos caminhos da literatura comparada,* edited by Helena Buescu, João Ferreira Duarte, and Manuel Gusmão, 271–87. Lisbon: Dom Quixote, 2001.

Macedo, Ana Gabriela, and Ana Luísa Amaral, eds. *Dicionário da crítica feminista.* Oporto: Edições Afrontamento, 2005.

Macedo, Helder. "Teresa and Fátima and Isabel." *Times Literary Supplement* (December 12, 1975): 1484.

Machado, Álvaro Manuel. *Do Romantismo aos Romantismos em Portugal. Ensaios de tipologia comparativista.* Lisbon: Presença, 1996.

Magalhães, Isabel Allegro de. "Florbela Espanca e a Subversão de Alguns *Topoi.*" In *A Planície e o Abismo: Actas do Congresso sobre Florbela Espanca realizado na Universidade de Évora,* edited by Óscar Lopes et al. Lisbon: Vega, 1997.

———. *O Sexo dos Textos e outras leituras.* Lisbon: Caminho, 1995.

———. *O Tempo das Mulheres: a dimensão temporal na escrita feminina contemporânea: ficção portuguesa.* Lisbon: Imprensa Nacional-Casa da Moeda, 1987.

Marinho, Maria de Fátima. *O Romance Histórico em Portugal.* Oporto: Campo das Letras, 1999.

———. *Um Poço Sem Fundo. Novas Reflexões sobre Literatura e História.* Oporto: Campo das Letras, 2005.

Martins, Fernando Cabral, ed. *Dicionário de Fernando Pessoa e do Modernismo Português.* Lisbon: Caminho, 2008.

Martins, Maria João. "'A Maçon no D. Maria II—Uma mulher livre', interview with Lídia Jorge." *Jornal de Letras, Artes e Ideias* (April 9–15, 1997): 29.

McClintock, Anne. *Imperial Leather. Race, Gender and Sexuality in the Colonial Conquest.* New York: Routledge, 1995.

Medeiros, Paulo de. "Casas assombradas." In *Fantasmas e fantasias imperiais no imaginário português contemporâneo,* edited by Margarida Calafate Ribeiro and Ana Paula Ferreira, 127–49. Oporto: Campo das Letras, 2003.

———. "The Diary and Portuguese Women Writers." *Portuguese Studies* 14 (1998): 227–41.

———. "'Memória Infinita'." *Portuguese Literary and Cultural Studies* 2 (1999): 61–78.

———. "O som dos búzios: feminismo, pós-modernismo, simulação." *Discursos. Estudos de Língua e Cultura Portuguesa* 5 (1993): 29–47.

Menéres, Clara. "O Veludo, o Útero e a Rosa." In *Mátria de Natália Correia,* edited by Madalena Braz Teixeira, 25–26. Lisbon: Museu Nacional de Traje, 2000.

Moers, Ellen. *Literary Women.* London: The Women's Press, 1986.

Morão, Paula. *Irene Lisboa. Vida e Escrita.* Lisbon: Editorial Presença, 1989.

Morgan, Robin. "International Feminism. A Call for Support of the Three Marias." In *Going too Far. The Personal Chronicle of a Feminist,* edited by Robin Morgan. New York: Vintage Books, 1978.

Mouffe, Chantal. *The Return of the Political.* London: Verso, 1993.

Mourão, José Augusto. "A sedução do múltiplo. Natália Correia: Literatura e Paganismo." *Colóquio/Letras* 104/105 (1988): 85–92.

Mulheres contra Homens? Lisbon: Dom Quixote, 1971.

Muraro, Luisa. "Female Genealogies." In *Engaging with Irigaray,* edited by Carolyne Burke, Naomi Schor, and Margaret Whitford, 317–33. New York: Columbia University Press, 1994.

Neubauer, John, and Helga Geyer-Ryan. "Introduction—Gender, Memory, Literature." In *Gendered Memories. Volume 4 of the Proceedings of the xvth Congress of the International Comparative Literature Association. "Literature as Cultural Memory." Leiden, 16–22 August 1997,* edited by John Neubauer and Helga Geyer-Ryan, 5–8. Amsterdam: Rodopi, 2000.

Nietzsche, Friedrich. *Beyond Good and Evil.* Translated by Walter Kaufmann. New York: Vintage, 1966 [1886].

———. *The Birth of Tragedy.* Translated and edited by Douglas Smith. Oxford: Oxford University Press, 2000.

———. *Thus Spoke Zarathustra. A Book for Everyone and No One.* Translated by R. J. Hollingdale. London: Penguin, 2003.

Nobre, António. *Só.* Oporto: Livraria Civilização Editora, 1983.

Nóbrega, Isabel da, Isabel Martins, Augusto Abelaira, Sérgio Ferreira Ribeiro, Natália Nunes, Agustina Bessa Luís, Maria da Conceição H. Gouveia. *Sobre a Condição da Mulher Portuguesa.* Lisbon: Editorial Estampa, 1968.

Overton, Bill. *The Novel of Female Adultery. Love and Gender in Continental European Fiction, 1830–1900.* Houndmills and New York: MacMillan and St. Martin's, 1996.

Owen, Hilary. "Back to Nietzsche: The Making of an Intellectual/Woman. Lídia Jorge's *A Costa dos Murmúrios.*" *Portuguese Literary and Cultural Studies* 2, (1999): 79–98.

———. "Fairies and Witches in Hélia Correia." In *Women, Literature and Culture in the Portuguese-Speaking World,* edited by Cláudia Pazos Alonso, with assistance by Glória Fernandes, 85–103. Lewiston: Edwin Mellen Press, 1996.

———. *Portuguese Women's Writing, 1972 to 1986: Reincarnations of a Revolution.* Lewiston, NY: Edwin Mellen Press, 2000.

———. "*Um quarto que seja seu* The Quest for Camões' Sister." *Portuguese Studies* 11 (1995): 179–91.

———. "Uma Inconclusão Superadora: A Machereyan Feminist Reading of *A Sibila* by Agustina Bessa Luís" *Bulletin of Hispanic Studies, Liverpool* 75 (1998): 201–12.

———. "[W]rites of passage: Portuguese women's narrative after the Three Marias." Ph.D. diss., University of Nottingham, 1992.

Paiva, José Rodrigues de, ed. *Estudos sobre Florbela Espanca.* Recife: Associação de Estudos Portugueses Jordão Emerenciano, 1995.

Pazos Alonso, Cláudia. "Disrupted Genealogies: the Illegitimate Daughter in Portuguese Literature." In *Women's Writing in Western Europe. Gender, Generation, and Legacy,* edited by Adalgisa Giorgio and Julia Waters, 234–47. Cambridge: Cambridge Scholars Press, 2007.

———. *Imagens do Eu na Poesia de Florbela Espanca.* Lisbon: Imprensa Nacional. Casa da Moeda, 1997.

————, "Modernist Differences: Judith Teixeira and Florbela Espanca." In *Portuguese Modernisms. Multiple Perspectives on Literature and the Visual Arts,* edited by Steffen Dix and Jerónimo Pizarro (Oxford: Legenda, forthcoming).

————. "'Que a minha ironia calada e quase séria fosse o meu baluarte': Re-Thinking Gender and Genius in Selected Works by Irene Lisboa." *Bulletin of Hispanic Studies, Liverpool,* 84 (2007): 609–23.

————. "*Tanto poeta em verso me cantou:* The Role of Florbela Espanca's University Colleagues in her Poetic Development." *Portuguese Studies* 11 (1995): 168–78.

Pazos Alonso, Cláudia, with assistance by Glória Fernandes. *Women, Literature and Culture in the Portuguese-speaking World.* Lewiston, NY; Lampeter: Edwin Mellen Press, 1996.

Pereira, José Carlos Seabra. "De Rastros, Com Asas." In *Florbela Espanca. Obras Completas.* 6 vols. vol. 2. Lisbon: Dom Quixote, 1985–86.

Pessoa, Fernando. *Mensagem.* Lisbon: Assírio & Alvim, 2004.

————. *Poesias.* Lisbon: Ática, 1980.

————. *Prosa Íntima e de Autoconhecimento.* Lisbon: Assírio & Alvim, 2007.

Pessoa, Fernando, and António Botto, eds. *Antologia de Poemas Portugueses Modernos.* Coimbra: Editorial Nobel, 1944.

Plácido, Ana Augusta, *Herança de Lágrimas.* Vila Nova de Famalicão: Lello&Irmão-Câmara Municipal de Vila Nova de Famalicão, 1995.

Plath, Sylvia. *Ariel.* London: Faber and Faber, 1965.

Poe, Edgar Allan. "The Philosophy of Composition." In *Essays and Reviews.* New York: Literary Classics of the United States, 1984 [1846].

Punter, David, and Glennis Byron. *The Gothic.* Malden, MA: Blackwell Publishing, 2004.

Quadros, António. "Uma peregrinação–iniciação matrista. *A Madona,* de Natália Correia, uma proposta de hermenêutica" In *Estruturas Simbólicas do Imaginário na Literatura Portuguesa,* 173–79. Lisbon: Átrio, 1992.

Quental, Antero de. *Poesias de Antero de Quental.* Edited by Maria Madalena Gonçalves. Lisbon: Editorial Comunicação, 1981.

Ramalho, Maria Irene. "A sogra de Rute ou intersexualidades." In *Globalização. Fatalidade ou Utopia?,* edited by Boaventura de Sousa Santos, 525–55. Oporto: Afrontamento, 2001.

Real, Miguel. "Realismo Simbólico." *Jornal de Letras, Artes e Ideias* (2006): 25.

Rebelo, Fernando. "A discussão do aborto na voz de Natália Correia." In *Natália Correia, 10 anos depois . . .* edited by Secção Francesa de D.E.P.E.R., 53–58. Oporto: Faculdade de Letras da Universidade do Porto, 2003.

Rector, Mónica. *Mulher: objeto e sujeito da literatura portuguesa.* Oporto: Edições Universidade Fernando Pessoa, 1999.

Régio, José. *Poemas de Deus e do Diabo.* 4th ed. Lisbon: Portugália, 1925.

Reis, Carlos. *O Conhecimento da Literatura. Introdução aos Estudos Literários.* Coimbra: Livraria Almedina, 1995.

Ribeiro, Margarida Calafate. *Uma História de Regressos: Império, Guerra Colonial e Pós-Colonialismo na Literatura Portuguesa.* Lisbon: Afrontamento, 2004.

Rich, Adrienne. "When We Dead Awaken: Writing as Re-vision." In *On Lies, Secrets and Silence.* London: Virago, 1980.

Rocha, Clara Crabbé. "Florbela Espanca. *Diário do Último Ano*." *Colóquio/Letras* 69 (1982): 79–80.

Rodrigues, Urbano Tavares. "Loucura e fuga nas narrativas de Hélia Correia." *O Diário* (January 26, 1986): 4.

Rosaldo, Renato. "Imperialist Nostalgia." *Representations* 26 (1989): 107–22.

Sá-Carneiro, Mário de. *A Confissão de Lúcio*. Mem Martins: Edições Europa-América 1989.

———. *Obra Poética de Mário de Sá-Carneiro*. Lisbon: Presença, 1985.

Sadlier, Darlene. *The Question of How: Women Writers and the New Portuguese Literature*. New York: Greenwood Press, 1989.

Salado, Teresa Ribeiro da Silva e Régis. "Portrait de l'auteur en lecteur: *Madame Bovary* au miroir de *Vale Abraão*." *Intercâmbio. Núcleo de Estudos Franceses da Universidade do Porto* (1991): 84–122.

Sapega, Ellen W. *Consensus and Debate in Salazar's Portugal. Visual and Literary Negotiations of the National Text, 1933–1948*. University Park: The Pennsylvania State University Press, 2008.

Saraiva, António José, and Óscar Lopes. *História da Literatura Portuguesa*. 1st ed. Oporto: Porto Editora, 1954.

———. *História da Literatura Portuguesa*. 2nd ed. Oporto: Porto Editora, 1956.

———. *História da Literatura Portuguesa*. 3rd ed. Oporto: Porto Editora 1965.

Seixo, Maria Alzira. "Quatro Razões Para Reler *Novas Cartas Portuguesas*." In *Outros Erros: Ensaios de Literatura*, edited by Maria Alzira Seixo, 179–87. Oporto: Asa, 2001.

Sena, Jorge de. *Florbela Espanca ou a Expressão do Feminino na Poesia Portuguesa*. Oporto: Biblioteca Fenianos, 1947.

Showalter, Elaine. *A Literature of their Own. British Women Novelists from Brontë to Lessing*. London: Virago Press, 1982.

Silva, Lígia Maria Pereira da. "Novels of Lídia Jorge (1984–1998): Saying Other/wise— Testimony and Alterity." Ph.D. diss., University of Manchester, 2003.

Silva, Maria Augusta. "A escrita não pode deixar a alma sentada." *Diário de Notícias* (October 2, 2002).

Silva, Maria da Conceição Lopes da. "The Sexual Being in *Charneca em Flor*." *Portuguese Studies* 20 (2004): 123–33.

Silva, Vítor Manuel de Aguiar e. *Teoria da Literatura*. 8th ed. Coimbra: Almedina, 2007.

Simões, João Gaspar. "Os prodígios de Lídia Jorge." *Diário de Notícias* (January 24, 1985): 31.

Sjöholm, Cecilia. *The Antigone Complex: Ethics and the Invention of Feminine Desire*. Stanford, CA: Stanford University Press, 2004.

Slover, Loretta Porto. "The Three Marias: Literary Portrayals of the Situation of Women in Portugal." Ph.D. diss., University of Harvard, 1977.

Soares Junqueira, Renata. *Florbela Espanca. Uma estética da teatralidade*. São Paulo: Editora UNESP, 2003.

Soares, Anthony. "Was Florbela's Death Fatal? A Study of Death in the Works of Florbela Espanca." In *Women, Literature and Culture in the Portuguese-Speaking World*, edited by Cláudia Pazos Alonso, 53–63. Lampeter: Edwin Mellen Press, 1996.

Sophocles. *The Three Theban Plays: Antigone, Oedipus the King, Oedipus at Colonus.* Translated by Robert Fagles. Edited by Bernard Knox. New York: Penguin, 1984.

Sousa, Antónia de, Bruno da Ponte, Dórdio Guimarães and Edite Soeiro, ed. *Entrevistas a Natália Correia.* Lisbon: Parceria A. M. Pereira, 2004.

Sousa Santos, Maria Irene Ramalho de. "Bondoso Cais: *A Costa dos Murmúrios* de Lídia Jorge." *Colóquio/Letras* 107 (1989): 64–67.

———. "Re-inventing Orpheus: Women and Poetry Today." *Portuguese Studies* 14 (1998): 122–37.

Sousa Santos, Maria Irene Ramalho de, and Ana Luísa Amaral. "Sobre a 'Escrita Feminina'." *Oficina do CES* 90, April 1997.

Stegagno-Picchio, Luciana. "Le nipoti de Marianna. Note sulla letteratura femminile in Portogallo" In *Gli abbracci feriti: poetesse portoghese di oggi* edited by Adelina Aletti, 5–11. Milano: Feltrini, 1980.

Steiner, George. *Antigones.* New Haven: Yale University Press, 1996.

Teixeira, Judith. *Decadência.* Lisbon: n.p., 1923.

Teixeira, Madalena Braz. "As diferentes faces de Eva." In *Mátria de Natália Correia,* edited by Madalena Braz Teixeira, 7–11. Lisbon: Museu Nacional de Traje, 2000.

Teixeira, Rui de Azevedo. *A Guerra Colonial e o Romance Português.* Lisbon: Editorial Notícias, 1998.

Teles, Manuel Tavares. *Camilo e Ana Plácido.* Oporto: Caixotim, 2008.

Vasques, Eugénia. *Mulheres que Escreveram Teatro no Século XX em Portugal.* Lisbon: Edições Colibri, 2001.

Venâncio, Fernando. "Recensão Crítica a *A Casa Eterna* de Hélia Correia." *Colóquio/Letras* 123–124, (1992): 385–86.

Vidal, Duarte. *O Processo das Três Marias. Defesa de Maria Isabel Barreno.* Lisbon: Editorial Futura, 1974.

Warner, Marina. *Alone of All Her Sex. The myth and cult of the Virgin Mary.* London: Picador, 1990.

Williams, Claire "Mind the Generation Gap! Portuguese Women's Narratives In the Second Half of the 20th-Century." In *Women's Writing in Western Europe. Gender Generation, and Legacy,* edited by Adalgisa Giorgio and Julia Waters, 294–309. Cambridge: Cambridge Scholars Press, 2007.

Wolstenholme, Susan. *Gothic (Re)Visions: Writing Women as Readers.* Albany: State University of New York Press, 1993.

Woolf, Virginia. "Mr Bennett and Mrs Brown." London: Leonard and Virginia Woolf, 1928.

———. *A Room of One's Own.* London: Penguin Classics, 2000.

Yuval-Davis, Nira. *Gender and Nation.* London: Sage Publications, 1997.

FILMOGRAPHY

Natália Correia—A Senhora da Rosa (Teresa Tomé, 1999)

Index